St. Thomas Aquinas
ON POLITICS AND ETHICS

NORTON CRITICAL EDITIONS IN THE
HISTORY OF IDEAS

AQUINAS • ST. THOMAS AQUINAS ON POLITICS AND ETHICS
translated and edited by Paul E. Sigmund

DARWIN • DARWIN
selected and edited by Philip Appleman (Third Edition)

ERASMUS • THE PRAISE OF FOLLY AND OTHER WRITINGS
translated and edited by Robert M. Adams

HERODOTUS • THE HISTORIES
translated by Walter Blanco, edited by Walter Blanco and Jennifer Tolbert Roberts

HOBBES • LEVIATHAN
edited by Richard E. Flathman and David Johnston

LOCKE • THE SELECTED POLITICAL WRITINGS OF JOHN LOCKE
edited by Paul E. Sigmund

MACHIAVELLI • THE PRINCE
translated and edited by Robert M. Adams (Second Edition)

MALTHUS • AN ESSAY ON THE PRINCIPLE OF POPULATION
edited by Philip Appleman (Second Edition)

MARX • THE COMMUNIST MANIFESTO
edited by Frederic L. Bender

MILL • MILL
edited by Alan Ryan

MORE • UTOPIA
translated and edited by Robert M. Adams (Second Edition)

NEWMAN • APOLOGIA PRO VITA SUA
edited by David J. DeLaura (Second Edition)

NEWTON • NEWTON
selected and edited by I. Bernard Cohen and Richard S. Westfall

ROUSSEAU • ROUSSEAU'S POLITICAL WRITINGS
translated by Julia Conaway Bondanella, edited by Alan Ritter

ST. PAUL • THE WRITINGS OF ST. PAUL
edited by Wayne A. Meeks and John T. Fitzgerald (Second Edition)

THOREAU • WALDEN AND RESISTANCE TO CIVIL GOVERNMENT
edited by William Rossi (Second Edition)

THUCYDIDES • THE PELOPONNESIAN WAR
translated by Walter Blanco, edited by Walter Blanco and Jennifer Tolbert Roberts

WATSON • THE DOUBLE HELIX: A PERSONAL ACCOUNT OF THE DISCOVERY OF
THE STRUCTURE OF DNA
edited by Gunther S. Stent

WOLLSTONECRAFT • A VINDICATION OF THE RIGHTS OF WOMAN
edited by Carol H. Poston (Second Edition)

FOR A COMPLETE LIST OF NORTON CRITICAL EDITIONS, VISIT
www.norton.com/college/English/nce_home.htm

A NORTON CRITICAL EDITION

St. Thomas Aquinas
ON POLITICS AND ETHICS

A NEW TRANSLATION
BACKGROUNDS
INTERPRETATIONS

Translated and Edited by

PAUL E. SIGMUND

PRINCETON UNIVERSITY

W · W · NORTON & COMPANY · *New York* · *London*

The Editor: PAUL E. SIGMUND was professor of politics at Princeton University. He was the author of numerous books, including *The Ideologies of the Developing Nations*, *Natural Law in Political Thought*, *The Overthrow of Allende and the Politics of Chile*, and *Liberation Theology at the Crossroads*. He previously taught at Harvard.

This title is printed on permanent paper containing 30 percent post-consumer waste recycled fiber.

The text of this book is composed in Electra, with display type set in Bernhard Modern. Composition by Vail-Ballou. Manufacturing by The Maple-Vail Book Group. Book design by Antonina Krass.

Library of Congress Cataloging-in-Publication Data

Thomas, Aquinas, Saint, 1225?–1274.
St. Thomas Aquinas on politics and ethics. (A Norton critical edition)
    Bibliography: p. 249
Partial contents: The Summa against the gentiles, On kingship, or,
    The governance of rulers—The Summa of theology.
1. Theology.   2. Christian ethics.   3. Kings and
    rulers.   4. Thomas, Aquinas, Saint, 1225?–1274.
I. Sigmund, Paul E.   II. Title.
BX890.T62E6   1987b   230'.2   87-12196

ISBN 0-393-95243-6

W. W. Norton & Company, Inc., 500 Fifth Avenue, New York, N.Y. 10110
        www.wwnorton.com

W. W. Norton & Company Ltd., Castle House, 75/76 Wells Street,
        London W1T 3QT

2 ● 3 ● 4 ● 5 ● 6 ● 7 ● 8 ● 9 ● 0

Contents

Introduction   xiii
Note on Translation   xxviii

Selections from the Work of St. Thomas Aquinas   1

*The Summa against the Gentiles (Summa contra Gentiles,
1259–1264)*   3

BOOK I

3. The Two Ways of Knowing the Truth about God.   3
4. Truths about God that are Known by Reason are also
   Properly Made Available to Man by Faith.   4
7. The Truths Based on Reason Are Not Contrary to the
   Truth of the Christian Faith.   4
8. The Relationship between the Human Reason and the
   Primary Truth of Faith.   5

BOOK II

68. How an Intellectual Substance Can Be the Formative
    Principle of the Body.   5

BOOK III

2. Everything that Acts Acts for an End.   6
3. Everything that Acts Acts for a Good.   6
25. The End of Every Intellectual Substance Is to Know
    God.   6
27. Human Happiness Does Not Consist in Bodily
    Pleasures.   7
32. Happiness Does Not Consist in the Goods of the Body.   7
37. Man's Ultimate Happiness Consists in the
    Contemplation of God.   8
48. Man's Ultimate Happiness Is Not in this Life.   8
51. How God May Be Seen in His Essence.   8
53. A Created Intellect Needs the Influence of (Divine)
    Light in Order to See God in His Essence.   9
63. In that Final Happiness Every Human Desire Will Be
    Fulfilled.   9

64. God Governs the Universe by His Providence. 10
81. Order among Men and in Relation to Other
  Things. 10

BOOK IV

54. It Was Fitting for God to Become Man. 11
76. On the Rank of Bishop and (the Pope) Who Is Highest
  in That Rank. 12

*On Kingship or The Governance of Rulers (De Regimine
Principum, 1265–1267)* 14

1. Men in Society Must Be under Rulers. 14
2. Is It Better for a Group to Be under One Ruler or
  Many? 17
3. Just Rule by One Person Is the Best Form of
  Government; Its Opposite Is the Worst. 18
4. The Kinds of Government in Rome, and How the
  Republic Sometimes Prospered under Popular Rule. 20
5. Tyranny is More Likely to Develop from the Rule of
  the Many than of One Person. Therefore Monarchy Is
  Preferable. 21
6. The Rule of One Man Is Best. How to Limit the
  Possibility of Tyranny. Tyranny Is to Be Tolerated to
  Avoid Greater Evils. 22
12. The Duties of a King. The Likeness of the King in His
  Kingdom to the Soul in the Body and to God in the
  Universe. 25
14. The King Should Follow the Example of God's Rule.
  The Similarity between Government and Piloting a
  Ship. A Comparison of the Rule of Priests and Kings. 26
15. To Gain the Ultimate End, the King Should Direct
  His Subjects to a Life of Virtue as Well as to
  Intermediate Ends. What is Needed for the Good
  Life. 28

The Summa of Theology (Summa Theologiae, 1266–1273) 30

I PART I (1266–1268)

Qu. 2. The Existence of God 30
  a. 3. Does God Exist? 30
Qu. 12. How We Know God 32
  a. 12. Can We Know God in this Life by Natural
    Reason? 32
  a. 13. Do We Know God Better through Grace than
    through Natural Reason? 33
Qu. 20. On God's Love 33
  a. 2. Does God Love All Things? 33
Qu. 75. The Essence of the Soul 33
  a. 2. Is the Soul Self-Subsistent? 33
  a. 5. Is the Soul Composed of Matter and Form? 34

a.	6.	Is the Human Soul Corruptible?	35
Qu.	79.	The Powers of the Intellect	35
a.	12.	Is *Synderesis* a Special Power?	35
Qu.	85.	The Manner and Order of Understanding	36
a.	1.	Does Our Intellect Know Bodily and Material Things through Abstraction from Sense Images?	36
a.	2.	Are the Intelligible Types *(Species)* Abstracted from Sensory Images Known by the Intellect?	36
Qu.	92.	The Creation of Woman	37
a.	1.	Should Woman Have Been Made in the Original Creation?	37
Qu.	96.	Dominion among Men in the State of Innocence	38
a.	3.	Would All Men Have Been Equal in the State of Innocence?	38
a.	4.	Would One Man Have Been Lord over Another in the State of Innocence?	39
Qu.	98.	The Preservation of the Race *(Species)*	40
a.	2.	In the State of Innocence Would Procreation Have Taken Place through Sexual Intercourse?	40
Qu.	108.	The Hierarchies and Orders of the Angels	41
a.	2.	Are there Several Orders in Each Hierarchy of the Angels	41

I–II THE FIRST PART OF PART II (1269–1270)   42

Qu.	3.	What is Happiness *(Beatitudo)?*	42
a.	8.	Does the Happiness of Man Consist in the Vision of the Divine Essence?	42
Qu.	5.	The Attainment of Happiness	42
a.	3.	Can Anyone Be Happy in this Life?	42
Qu.	21.	The Consequences of Human Acts	42
a.	4.	Are Good and Evil Human Acts Meritorious or Lacking in Merit in Relation to God?	42
Qu.	62.	The Theological Virtues	43
a.	3.	Is it Right to Call Faith, Hope, and Charity the Theological Virtues?	43
Qu.	81.	The Cause of Sin in Man	43
a.	1.	Was the First Sin of our First Parent Passed on to His Descendants as Original Sin?	43

THE TREATISE ON LAW (Qu. 90–97)   44

Qu.	90.	The Essence of Law	44
a.	1.	Is Law a Matter of Reason?	44
a.	2.	Is Law Always Directed toward the Common Good?	44
a.	3.	Can Any Person Make Law?	44
a.	4.	Is Promulgation Necessary for a Law?	46
Qu.	91.	The Kinds of Law	46
a.	1.	Is There an Eternal Law?	46
a.	2.	Is There a Natural Law?	46

a.	3.	Is There Human Law?	46
a.	4.	Was There a Need for Divine Law?	46
Qu.	92.	The Effects of Law	47
a.	1.	Is an Effect of the Law to Make Men Good?	47
Qu.	93.	The Eternal Law	48
a.	1.	Does the Eternal Law Exist in the Highest Reason of God?	48
a.	3.	Is All Law Derived from the Eternal Law?	48
Qu.	94.	The Natural Law	48
a.	2.	Does the Natural Law Contain One Precept or Many?	48
a.	4.	Is the Natural Law the Same for All Men?	50
a.	5.	Can the Natural Law Be Changed?	51
Qu.	95.	Human Law	52
a.	1.	Was it Useful for Man to Make Human Laws?	52
a.	2.	Are All Human Laws Derived from the Natural Law?	53
a.	4.	What Are the Divisions of Human Law?	53
Qu.	96.	The Power of Human Law	54
a.	2.	Should Law Repress All Vices?	54
a.	4.	Does Human Law Oblige in Conscience?	55
a.	5.	Is Everyone Subject to the Law?	55
a.	6.	May Someone Subject to the Law Act Contrary to the Letter of the Law?	55
Qu.	97.	Change in the Law	56
a.	1.	Should Human Laws Ever Be Changed?	56
a.	2.	Should Human Law Be Changed Whenever an Improvement Is Possible?	57
a.	3.	Can Custom Obtain the Force of Law?	57
a.	4.	Can Rulers Grant Dispensations from Human Law?	58
Qu.	100.	The Moral Precepts of the Old Law	58
a.	1.	Do All the Precepts of Morality Belong to the Natural Law?	58
Qu.	105.	The Reason for the Judicial Precepts	58
a.	1.	Did the Old Law Contain Useful Provisions on Government?	58
Qu.	109.	The Grace of God—the External Foundation of Human Acts	59
a.	2.	Can Man Will or Do Anything Good without Grace?	59

II–II THE SECOND PART OF PART II (1271–1272)

Qu.	10.	Unbelief	61
a.	8.	Are Unbelievers to be Forced to Accept the Faith?	61
a.	9.	May One Associate with Unbelievers?	61

a. 10. May Unbelievers Exercise Government or
        Dominion over the Faithful?   62
a. 11. Are the Rites of Unbelievers to be Tolerated?   62
a. 12. Are the Children of Jews and Other Unbelievers
        to be Baptized against the Will of Their Parents? 63
Qu. 11. Heresy   63
a.   3. May Heretics Be Tolerated?   63
Qu. 12. Apostasy   64
a.   2. Are Subjects Obliged to Obey a Ruler Who
        Apostasizes from the Faith?   64
Qu. 40. War   64
a.   1. Is Warfare Always Sinful?   64
Qu. 42. Sedition against Peace   65
a.   2. Is Sedition Always a Mortal Sin?   65
Qu. 57. Justice   66
a.   2. Is it Correct to Divide Law (*Jus*) into Natural
        Law and Positive Law?   66
a.   3. Is the Law of Nations (*Jus Gentium*) the Same
        as the Natural Law?   67
a.   4. Should Paternal Law and Property Law Be
        Specifically Distinguished?   68
Qu. 60. Judicial Decisions   69
a.   6. Are Judicial Decisions Made by Usurpers
        Invalid?   69
Qu. 64. Homicide   69
a.   3. Can a Private Person Kill a Criminal?   69
a.   5. Is Suicide Permissible?   70
a.   7. Is It Permissible to Kill in Self-Defense?   70
a.   8. Is Someone Who Kills a Man by Accident
        Guilty of Murder?   71
Qu. 66. Theft and Robbery   71
a.   1. Is the Possession of External Goods Natural to
        Man?   71
a.   2. Is Private Property Legitimate?   72
a.   7. Is Stealing Allowed in a Case of Necessity?   72
Qu. 69. Self-Defense   73
a.   4. Is it Permissible for Someone Who Has Been
        Condemned to Death to Defend Himself?   73
Qu. 77. Fraud   73
a.   4. Is It Legitimate to Sell Something for More than
        its Cost?   73
Qu. 78. The Sin of Usury   74
a.   1. Is It Sinful to Charge Interest (Usury) for
        Lending Money?   74
Qu. 104. Obedience   75
a.   1. Is One Man Obliged to Obey Another?   75

a. 5. Are Subjects Obliged to Do Everything that
Their Superiors Command? 75
a. 6. Are Christians Obliged to Obey Secular
Authorities? 76
Qu. 110. Lying 76
a. 3. Is Every Lie a Sin? 76
Qu. 150. Drunkenness 77
a. 2. Is Drunkenness a Mortal Sin? 77
Qu. 152. Virginity 77
a. 2. Is Virginity Lawful? 77
Qu. 154. The Types of Lechery 78
a. 2. Is Ordinary Fornication a Grave Sin? 78
a. 4. May Caresses and Kisses be Mortally Sinful? 79
a. 8. Is Adultery a Specific Kind of Lechery? 79
a. 11. Is Unnatural Vice a Kind of Lechery? 79
a. 12. Is Unnatural Vice the Worst Sin of all the Types
of Lechery? 80
III PART III (1272–1273)
Qu. 8. The Grace of Christ as Head of the Church 81
a. 3. Is Christ the Head of All Mankind? 81
SUPPLEMENT (POSTHUMOUS COMPILATION, 1274 ff.)
Qu. 52. Slavery as an Impediment 82
a. 1. Is Slavery an Impediment to Marriage? 82

Backgrounds and Sources 85

Aristotle
• Physics 87
Bk. II, ch. 1 [Nature and the Natural] 87
Bk. II, ch. 3 [The Four Causes] 88
• On the Soul 89
Bk. II, ch. 1 [The Soul and the Body] 89
• Metaphysics 90
Bk. XII, ch. 5 [The Unmoved Mover] 90
• Nicomachean Ethics 91
Bk. I, ch. 7 [Happiness as the Life of Virtue in accord
with Reason] 91
Bk. II, ch. 6 [Virtue as the Mean between Extremes] 92
Bk. V, ch. 7 [Natural Justice] 93
Bk. X, ch. 7 [Contemplation as Perfect Happiness] 94
• Politics 94
Bk. I, ch. 1–2 [Man Is by Nature a Political Animal] 94
ch. 3–6 [Natural Slavery] 97
ch. 8–10 [Interest-Taking is against Nature] 99
Bk. II, ch. 5 [The Natural Basis of Property] 100
Bk. III, ch. 11 [The Collective Wisdom of the Many] 101
St. Augustine
• The City of God 103

Bk. IV, ch. 4 [Kingdoms as Large-Scale Robberies]   103
Bk. XIV, ch. 28 [The Two Cities]   103
Bk. XIX, ch. 6 [Judges Condemn the Innocent]   104
        ch. 13 [Peace as the Tranquillity of Order]   104
        ch. 15 [Slavery as Punishment for Sin]   105
        ch. 20 [True Wisdom]   106
Bk. XXI, ch. 16 [Sinful Man and Grace]   106
Dionysius the Areopagite
 • The Celestial Hierarchy   108
  Chapter III [Hierarchy Leads to God]   108
  Chapter X [Hierarchies of Angels and Men]   109
 • The Ecclesiastical Hierarchy   109
  Chapter I [Definition of Hierarchy]   109
  Chapter V [Hierarchy in the Church]   110

Interpretations   113

THE INGREDIENTS OF THE THOMISTIC SYNTHESIS   115
St. Thomas and Aristotle   115
  Walter Ullmann • The New Orientation   115
  Harry Jaffa • Thomism and Aristotelianism   120
St. Thomas and Platonism   124
  Fernand van Steenberghen • Thomism as a New Philosophy   124
  Etienne Gilson • The Christian Philosophy of St. Thomas
  Aquinas   126
St. Thomas and Augustinian Christianity   131
  Frederick Copleston, S.J. • Aquinas and Augustine   131
  THOMISM AND POLITICS   136
Aquinas as Medieval Conservative   136
  Katherine Archibald • The Concept of Social Hierarchy in the
  Writings of St. Thomas Aquinas   136
The Transmission of Thomism   142
  Paul Oskar Kristeller • The Thomist Tradition   142
*Thomism and Early Modern Political Thought—England and
Spain*   145
  Richard Hooker • The Laws of Ecclesiastical Polity—Book I
  Laws in General   145
  Francisco Suarez, S.J. • Political Authority and Community
  Consent   148
Thomism in Papal Social Thought, 1888–1963   152
  Leo XIII • Human Liberty (1888)   152
  Leo XIII • Rerum Novarum—The Condition of Labor
  (1891)   155
  Pius XI • Quadragesimo Anno—Reconstructing the Social
  Order (1931)   162
  John XXIII • Mater et Magistra—Christianity and Social
  Progress (1961)   165
  John XXIII • Pacem in Terris—Peace on Earth (1963)   168

Neo-Thomism and Christian Democracy in Europe and Latin America   172

    Jacques Maritain • The Rights of Man; Church and State   172

    Jaime Castillo • Natural Law and Communitarianism   176

    Julio Silva Solar • St. Thomas and Property—A View From the Christian Left in Chile   178

    Paul E. Sigmund • Thomistic Natural Law and Social Theory   180

        THOMISTIC NATURAL LAW   189

    John Finnis • Nature, Reason, and God in Aquinas   189

    Mortimer Adler and Bill Moyers • A Dialogue on the Nature of Goodness   193

    Jacques Maritain • Natural Law   204

    Kai Nielsen • An Examination of the Thomistic Theory of Natural Moral Law   211

    Vernon J. Bourke • Natural Law, Thomism—and Professor Nielsen   217

    Reinhold Niebuhr • Christian Faith and Natural Law   222

        CONTEMPORARY PROBLEMS IN THOMISTIC ETHICS   226

The Just War and Self-Defense   226

    Paul Ramsey • War and the Christian Conscience   226

Contraception   229

    John T. Noonan, Jr. • Aquinas on Contraception   229

    Pius XI • Casti Connubii—Christian Marriage (1930)   233

    Germain Grisez • A New Formulation of a Natural Law Argument against Contraception   234

    Louis Dupré • A Thomistic Argument against the Ban on Contraception   241

Abortion   245

    John T. Noonan, Jr. • Aquinas on Abortion   245

Selected Bibliography   249

Introduction

St. Thomas Aquinas (1225–1274) was the most important and influential philosopher of the Middle Ages. His *Summa Theologiae* (the correct title of the work usually called the *Summa Theologica*) is regarded as the most comprehensive treatment of the relation of philosophy and theology. In the area of ethics and politics, his influence is still felt. Contemporary theories of the just war, discussions of sexual ethics including abortion and contraception, arguments about property rights, and theories of natural law frequently refer to his writings. Political figures as diverse as Martin Luther King, Jr. and the apologists for the 1973 coup in Chile have cited his works in defense of their actions. Yet many students of intellectual history, ethics, political thought or religion have never read his writings. Courses in these areas often skip the medieval period entirely or resort to secondary sources that do not provide direct contact with his thought. [1] Many translations of his works, particularly in the areas of ethics and politics, are inadequate or misleading (see discussion below on Translations). The technical terminology of scholastic philosophy [2] may appear difficult or abstruse—although this is much less true of ethics and politics than in areas such as metaphysics. Yet behind the sometimes awkward scholastic format, Aquinas's thought is, on the whole, lucid, logical and accessible. This edition is aimed at increasing that accessibility by careful selection and comprehensible translations of the ethical and political writings of one of the towering figures of Western thought.

Besides the continuing relevance of its substantive content, there are also important historical reasons for studying St. Thomas's political and ethical works. While it would be a mistake to take his writings as typical of all of medieval thought—no single writer could be regarded as typical of what was a wide-ranging and disparate group of thinkers—his attempt to integrate the various strains of medieval thought into a comprehensive system conveys a better understanding of medieval intellectual life than does the work of any other philosopher of the period. His natural law theory, for example, combines elements drawn from Platonism, Aristotle, Roman law, Stoicism, the Christian Fathers (especially Augustine), feudal theory, and the contemporary political practice of the Holy Roman Empire and the Italian city-state. It forms an important element in *The Higher Law Background of the American Constitution* about which Edward S. Corwin wrote (Ithaca, NY: Cor-

---

1. A survey of teachers of political theory quoted one of its respondents who listed "having to teach medieval thinkers" as one of the most disagreeable aspects of his profession. The survey indicated that all respondents assigned Plato's *Republic*, most used Aristotle's *Politics*, four assigned parts of St. Augustine's *City of God*, but none used Aquinas.

See Steven Brzezinski and Sami Hajjar, *Teaching Political Theory: Preliminary Findings* (Laramie; WY: University of Wyoming, mimeographed), 7.
2. The scholastic method of philosophical inquiry was developed by the "schoolmen," the teachers in the medieval schools of philosophy—hence its name.

nell University Press, 1955)—and it contributed to the transformation of the traditional, customary, and localized social order of the earlier Middle Ages into the centralized, legalistic, and rationalistic politics of the modern world.

The Setting

In the century before Aquinas wrote, the intellectual life of the West had suddenly come alive. Philosophical speculation and argument developed rapidly, stimulated by the teaching and writing of Peter Abelard in Paris. John of Salisbury's *Policraticus* was evidence of the revival of political theory. Gratian's canon law collection (1139) provided the texts for the use by canon lawyers in the service of the papal centralization and the legal analysis of religious institutions. The twelfth-century revival of the study of Roman law at Bologna helped to give the emergent states of Western Europe a legal foundation, and produced a legal profession which supported the claims of kings and emperors. In England a "common law" had been forged by the king's justices in eyre (circuit judges) and a central treasury and administrative records created. At the time that Aquinas was writing, the papacy was promoting administrative and legal centralization of the church through direct legislation in Councils or by papal decrees that regularized its teaching and institutional structure. The first representative institutions were beginning to meet in inchoate form (the English Parliament dates its foundation from 1265), developing out of the king's feudal court *(Curia Regis)*. In the church, legal analyses of the structure of the monastic orders and of cathedral chapters were producing theories of representation and consent which were to form the basis for more general theories that could be applied to the whole church by later writers. Drawing on the typology of Ernst Kantorowicz *(The King's Two Bodies*, Princeton, NJ: Princeton University Press, 1957) one might say that "law-centered kingship" had replaced the "Christ-centered kingship" of the earlier Middle Ages, and the foundations were being laid for the "polity-centered kingship" of the succeeding centuries. Aquinas's theories reflected and developed these themes.

Life

Thomas Aquinas was born in 1224 or 1225 in the castle of Roccasecca near Aquino, north of Naples, to a family that belonged to the lesser nobility of the area. The castle was located in the northwestern province of the Kingdom of Sicily, not far from the southern boundary of the Papal States.[3] When Thomas was five he was placed in the Benedictine monastery of Monte Cassino for elementary and religious schooling. He remained there until 1238 when he entered the *studium generale*—later university—at Naples, which had been founded by Emperor Frederick II in 1224. There he became acquainted with the representatives of a dynamic new monastic order, the Dominicans who had been founded in Toulouse in 1216 in order to combat the Albigensian heresy.[4] The Dominicans had opened houses of study at

---

3. This summary is based principally on James A. Weisheipl, *Friar Thomas d'Aquino, His Life and Work* (Garden City, NY: Doubleday, 1974).
4. The Albigensians (From Albi in south-central France) or Cathari ("pure ones") lived ascetic lives and believed in the opposition of corrupt matter

and pure spirit. They denounced the worldliness of the church, and were the object of a crusade, declared by Pope Innocent III. The Inquisition was established to root out the remnants of Albigensianism.

the emerging universities of Western Europe to pursue philosophy and theology, while at the same time continuing to carry out their original aim of
evangelization through preaching (O.P.—Order of Preachers). In the universities they devoted particular attention to the newly-translated works of
Aristotle which were seen by some as a threat to the Catholic faith. In 1244,
Thomas decided to join the Dominican order, but his family, which had
hoped that he might join the local Benedictine order and someday become
abbot of Monte Cassino, opposed his decision and his brothers imprisoned
him by force in one of the family castles. After being detained by the family
at Roccasecca for a year, he was permitted to leave and went to Paris to
begin his Dominican novitiate, studying with the German Dominican theologian, Albert the Great, who was lecturing in the Dominican chair of
theology "for foreigners" and working on the scientific works of Aristotle.
When Albert established a *studium generale* in Cologne in 1248, Thomas
went to Cologne to study with him.[5] Aquinas's biographer, William of Tocco,
states that his fellow-Dominicans in Cologne called him "the dumb ox"—
referring to his physique and his laconic character (not his lack of intelligence) and possibly also to his lack of German—but that when Albert heard
him in disputation he said, "the bellowing of that ox will be heard throughout the world." In 1252 on the recommendation of Albert he returned to
the University of Paris to study for the degree of master (i.e., professor) in
theology. His program included lecturing under the direction of a master as
a "Bachelor of the Sentences" on the standard theology textbook, the *Sententiae* (Opinions) of Peter Lombard, and engaging in public disputations
on theological topics. Over the next four years he prepared his *Commentary
on the Sentences* which was completed in 1256, at which time he was admitted as a master to the faculty of theology and granted a license to teach by
the Chancellor of the University.

For the next three years he lectured, principally on the Gospel of St.
Matthew, engaged in frequent public disputations on theological topics, and
began the first of his Summae, the *Summa contra Gentiles* (Summary against
the Gentiles) which was intended to help Dominican missionaries in their
efforts to convert Moslems and Jews in Spain and North Africa. He continued to write the work after his return to the Dominican house at Naples in
1259, from which he was assigned to the Dominican priory at the papal
court at Orvieto, Italy, in 1261. He remained at Orvieto for four years,
completing the *Summa contra Gentiles* in 1264, and writing a number of
other works. In 1265, he opened a new house of studies in Rome, where he
seems to have begun his only strictly political work, the unfinished *On Kingship* or *The Governance of Princes (De Regimine Principum)* for the young
king of Cyprus. In 1266 he began what was to be his most important work,
the *Summa Theologiae* or Summary of Theology, which was initially intended
as a systematic introduction to theology for Dominican novices—possibly
because of his dissatisfaction with existing manuals of seminary instruction.[6]

---

5. Albert lectured on Aristotle's *Ethics* and Aquinas's notes and questions on his lectures have sur-
vived (Weisheipl, p. 46). A manuscript in the
Naples library in Aquinas's handwriting of Albert's
lectures on *The Divine Names* by Pseudo-Dionysius indicates that at this time he also studied the
Christian Neo-Platonism of Dionysius the Areopagite, a fifth-century monk accorded almost

scriptural respect in the Middle Ages because he
was mistakenly believed to be the convert of St.
Paul, mentioned in the Acts of the Apostles 17:34,
in the first century A.D.
6. See Leonard B. Boyle, O.P., *The Setting of the
Summa Theologiae of St. Thomas* (Toronto: Pontifical Institute of Medieval Studies, 1982).

In the next two years he completed the First Part (S.T.I.), which deals with God's existence and attributes, and the relation of creatures to Him, writing the last section in 1267–68 at Viterbo where the pope was residing. Here, if not earlier, he worked with the Flemish Dominican, William of Moerbeke, who had been engaged in preparing more accurate translations of Aristotle's works than those that had been made available to the West from Arabic, by way of the Moslem-controlled parts of Spain.

In 1269 Thomas returned as a professor to the University of Paris. In the next three years he composed both parts of Part II of the *Summa*,[7] a monumental effort which involved writing and dictating to as many as three or four secretaries at a time, even, it was said, continuing to dictate in his sleep. (It was here, sitting at a banquet next to King Louis IX, that he is supposed to have fallen into a trance, struck the table, and shouted "That settles the Manicheans" and called for his secretary to dictate an answer to the Manichean heresy[8] before he realized where he was.) He also engaged in refutation of the Parisian followers of the Moslem philosopher, Averroes, arguing from Aristotle against the Averroist beliefs in the eternity of the world, the mortality of the soul, and the existence of a separable intellect that is common to all men.

He wrote many other works in this period, among them twelve commentaries on the works of Aristotle, including the *Ethics* and the *Politics*. In 1272 he returned to Naples, working on Part III (S.T., III) of the *Summa Theologiae* on Christ and redemption until December 6, 1273 when he suddenly announced that he could not write any more since "All that I have written seems like straw to me." From accounts of difficulties that he had in speaking and walking thereafter, his modern biographers conjecture that he may have had a stroke, or at least a breakdown occasioned by overwork, but earlier writers attributed the change to a mystical experience of the inadequacy of the human mind to express the divine. In February 1274 he left Naples to attend the Council of Lyons, but on the way struck his head on a tree across the road and died of the ensuing complications on March 7, 1274. During his life he had written over a hundred works including a *Summa Theologiae* consisting of 512 questions, 2,669 articles, and 10,000 objections and replies.

The Intellectual Challenge

The principal contribution of Aquinas was to develop a systematic philosophical and theological response to the challenge posed to medieval Christianity by the rediscovery of the whole of Aristotle's philosophy which, except for his works on logic, had been unavailable to the West until the thirteenth century. Earlier medieval thought had relied for its view of the world upon the Bible, St. Augustine, Plato, and the Neo-Platonist writers such as Proclus and Pseudo-Dionysius. The intellectual revival which began in the twelfth century looked to Plato as its principal philosophical inspiration, despite the fact that only his *Phaedo*, *Meno*, and part of the *Timaeus* were available in Latin. The works of Plato and his followers, along with Aristotle's writings

---

7. The first part of Part II of the *Summa Theologiae* (S.T., I–II) discusses happiness, virtue, sin, law, and grace, while the second part (S.T., II–II) analyzes specific moral questions.

8. Manicheanism, developed in Persia in the third century, held that the two principles of good and of evil, represented respectively by the soul and the body were in eternal conflict in the world.

on logic, formed the basis for the philosophical teachings of the masters in the cathedral schools who laid the groundwork for the "scholastic" philosophical method, which achieved currency in the arts and theological faculties of the emerging universities in the thirteenth century. The scholastics developed a standardized logical method of treating philosophical questions which attempted to resolve logical contradictions and disputed philosophical and theological problems through oral and written disputations. [9]

In theology the basic text was the Bible itself, along with the standard commentary (ordinary gloss) upon it, supplemented by Peter Lombard's twelfth-century selection of the opinions (*sententiae* or sentences) of the Fathers of the Church. (A formal *Commentary on the Sentences* was a requirement for the Master's degree in theology.)

Legal studies also developed rapidly. Those who specialized in church law (the canon lawyers) used Gratian's *Concordance of Discordant Canons* or *Decretum* to organize and integrate conflicting quasi-legal statements by the Fathers of the Church and earlier councils and popes. Gratian was supplemented in the thirteenth century by several collections of decrees *(decretals)* by recent popes. On the side of the newly emerging temporal powers the civil lawyers worked from the legislation and commentaries in the collection of Roman law *(Corpus Juris Civilis)* published by the Emperor Justinian in the sixth century and revived as the basis of legal study and practice. Both the canonists (*canon*—a rule) and the civilians (*civilis*—pertaining to the city—*civitas*—of Rome) used the canon and Roman law texts to argue the respective claims of popes and emperors or kings in the numerous disputes between the spiritual and temporal powers that followed the revival of papal power and the centralization of royal and imperial authority in the eleventh century. Rival claimants either exalted papal power or glorified the kings and emperors as God's earthly representatives (minister of God, even vicar of Christ) in order to extend papal, royal or imperial claims to taxation, legal jurisdiction, or the loyalties of their subjects. Their writings discussed many of the basic problems of political theory, including the origin of political obligation, the best form of government, the nature of law, and the limits of political obligation, especially with reference to religious questions.

By the thirteenth century the specialized schools of law, theology, or liberal arts (often associated with cathedrals) had given way to a more diversified institution, first called a *studium generale* (school of general studies) and then a *universitas studiorum* (guild or corporate body of studies) with faculties of liberal arts, theology, law, etc. Aquinas studied liberal arts at Naples, and from his writings we know that he was also familiar with some of the

---

9. The scholastic method as developed in the oral disputations and reflected in the writings of the scholastic philosophers involved a series of steps. At the beginning of the disputation the master would announce the "Article" or subject to be debated, which was itself a subdivision of a broader "Question" being discussed. This was followed by a number of objections which were put forward by the audience, to which preliminary responses were made by "bachelors" (in present-day terms, teaching assistants) who were working with the master (professor), possibly also referring to authorities who held views contrary to the objections. The next day the master would give his response ("I answer that") to the basic issue or issues posed and would follow this with formal replies to each of the initial objections. The disputation was sometimes taken down by a secretary and later edited by the master for publication. The oral disputation thus gave rise to the formal structure used by the scholastics to analyze philosophical and theological problems—a statement of an issue, alternative opinions or objections, contrary quotations from recognized authorities, the author's response to the problem, followed by answers to each of the initial objections. For examples of the scholastic form, see the selections from the *Summa Theologiae*, I, qu. 2, a. 3 on the existence of God (below, pp. 30–32) and I–II, qu. 90, a. 3 on legislation (below, pp. 44–45).

texts of Roman and canon law. His principal area of study, teaching, and writing, however, was theology.

Before Aquinas's arrival in Paris both the arts and theology faculties had faced an intellectual challenge to which they had reacted in an ambiguous fashion. Beginning around the year 1200 the scientific and metaphysical works of Aristotle had become available in Latin translations from Arabic, often with commentaries by Moslem philosophers. The Christian world was thus suddenly presented with a fully-integrated system of thought that was persuasive in its rational structure, uninfluenced by religious themes, and in some of its doctrines directly antithetical to Christian revelation. Aristotle described a world in which matter and motion were eternally derived by inflexible necessity from the potentiality of "prime matter" by a "First Mover" whose essential characteristic is the uncaused self-activity of reason (pure act). Man was described by Aristotle as a composite of bodily *matter* and a rational soul that was its *form*. Moslem commentators had interpreted Aristotle in ways that made his writings seem even more threatening—arguing for the existence of a single "world-soul" in which individual souls participate, thereby denying personal immortality and rewards and punishments after death, and reaffirming Aristotle's theories of the eternity and necessity of the world, which contradicted the Christian belief in the creation of the world by God.

The diocese of Paris responded to the Aristotelian threat by banning "the reading of books of Aristotle on natural philosophy and commentaries upon them" (1210)—a ban that was formally applied to the faculty of arts of the university in 1215.[1] The prohibition was reaffirmed by Pope Gregory IX in 1231, although it was only to be applied to the works "until they are examined and purged of all suspicion of error." The writings of the Moslem commentator on Aristotle, Averroes, began to be translated and quoted in the 1230s and Aristotle's *Metaphysics* and *Nicomachean Ethics* soon thereafter. By the time that Aquinas's mentor, Albert the Great, began to lecture in Paris the ban was no longer observed by the theology faculty, and by 1255 the arts faculty made a knowledge of all of the works of Aristotle a formal requirement.

The original ban seems to have been initiated by the more conservative theological faculty in an effort to restrain the masters in the arts faculty who were showing an inordinate enthusiasm for the novel ideas contained in the new scientific and metaphysical writings. That the fears of the theologians were not unjustified was demonstrated by the action of the bishop of Paris in 1277 specifically condemning a set of 219 propositions drawn from the teaching of the Latin "Averroists"—professors at Paris who propagated the doctrines of Averroes.[2]

An alternative approach to the new knowledge, however, was to develop a synthesis of Aristotelian philosophy and the Christian faith—rejecting the elements that contradicted Christianity but using Aristotle's analytic tools in

1. For the texts of the prohibitions and a history of thirteenth-century Aristotelianism, see Fernand van Steenberghen, *Aristotle in the West* (Louvain: E. Nauwelaerts, 1955).

2. The condemnation included several propositions drawn from Aquinas. They were specifically revoked in 1325 after his canonization. A translation of the text of the condemnation appears in

R. Lerner and M. Mahdi, eds., *Medieval Political Philosophy, A Source Book* (Ithaca, NY: Cornell University Press, 1972), 335–355. In 1270 Aquinas wrote *On the Unity of the Intellect* refuting the Averroists. In *On the Eternity of the World* written in the same year, he argued that one can neither prove nor disprove by reason that the world had a beginning.

a way that demonstrated that there was no fundamental incompatibility between his philosophy and the Christian faith. Albert the Great seems to have begun to work out such a synthesis when Thomas studied with him. This quest became the central focus of Aquinas's philosophical and theological efforts.

Aristotle and Christianity

The problem of the relationship of Aristotelianism and Christianity reflected at least two broader problems that Christianity had always been compelled to consider. The first was the Christian's conflicting attitudes to "the world" which according to the Christian faith had both been created by a beneficent God and corrupted by man's sin. If the Christian emphasized the world as part of the divine plan, he or she would take a much more positive attitude towards it than if the emphasis was placed on the corruption resulting from sin. Both attitudes had been present in the history of Christianity—and continue to be represented among modern Christians. Aquinas, while not ignoring the reality of sin, tended towards the first position, considering creation as the working out of the purposes of God in ways that demonstrate his love for man and his desire that humans achieve happiness—but arguing that man can only find true happiness and complete fulfillment in the vision of God after death.

A second and related problem suggested by the apparent conflict between Aristotle's writings and Christianity was the relationship between faith and reason. Again it was possible to take either of two attitudes—to insist on the compatibility of the two approaches to truth, the one through reason and the other through faith, with both intended by God to assist man in knowing his divine plan—or to denigrate the capacities of the human reason, to emphasize man's sinful tendency to use his reason for self-deception and pride, and to urge him rather to rely on Christian revelation as contained in the Bible and the teaching of the church as the only safe way to true knowledge. In contrast to some of his predecessors—for example, St. Augustine (354–431), who stressed the weakness and fallibility of human reason—St. Thomas, while recognizing the limits of man's reason and the weakness of his will, believed that the two approaches to truth are not incompatible— that as he says, "Grace does not destroy nature, but completes it." Natural reason can only go so far, but as far as it goes it can help us to know God and his creation. The truths of faith and those of reason are not contradictory.

This belief in the possibility of a harmony between man's eternal destiny and his life in this world, between what he knows by faith and what his reason tells him, and between the actions that are the result of divine grace and those prompted by his nature pervades Aquinas's philosophy—especially his writings in the areas of politics and ethics. It leads him to explore and develop a central intuition that is common both to Aristotelianism and Christianity—that of the fundamental rationality and purposiveness of nature and human nature. In Aristotle this intuition is expressed in his doctrine of final causation or teleology—the claim that "nature does nothing in vain" which both Aristotle and Thomas use to argue for an order and purpose in nature and man that can be determined by the study of their structure and development. A similar conclusion is drawn from the Christian doctrine of divine providence, God's purposive and beneficent activity in support of his creation, which appears to coincide with the Aristotelian insight. As Aquinas argues in the Treatise on Law in the *Summa Theologiae* (I–II, qu. 91), once we grant that the world is governed by divine providence, "it is evident that the whole community of the universe is governed by divine reason." The divine purposes are accessible to some degree to rational creatures "who are under divine providence in a more excellent way" because they possess reason which they can use to perceive the goals or purposes that are proper to them, both because of the intention of nature and of God.

In describing the Thomistic synthesis as combining Aristotle and Christianity, it is important not to ignore another component, the contribution of Neo-Platonism, as contained principally in the writings of St. Augustine and Pseudo-Dionysius. In the Christianized version of later Platonism all of creation is the result of God's love as expressed through the emanation of his creative power, operating on the basis of the ideas in the divine mind through the various levels or hierarchies of created things. Man is lower than the angels, but differs from animals in the possession of reason and free will, capacities of the human soul which transcend the limits of matter and are never completely fulfilled until he sees God. God has made man for himself, and after the fall sent his Son to redeem him and to make it possible for him to receive the free gift of divine grace which will enable him to enjoy the direct vision of God which gives him complete happiness *(beatitude)*. There is a "Great Chain of Being" from God through the angels to man and beneath him to animals, plants, and all created beings. [3]

The Platonic doctrine of Ideas or Forms formed one pole of the debate among the scholastic philosophers between the Platonist realists who argued for the real existence of universal Ideas or Forms, apart from individual things, and the nominalists who believed that universals were simply names *(nomina)* given to similar characteristics in collections of individual things. Here Aristotle was useful to Aquinas and others who followed him in developing the doctrine of moderate realism—that universals existed but only as perceived in things through the intellect's power of abstraction. The intellect could know being in its essential aspects—what made something what it was—but this did not imply a separate world of Ideas, except in the mind of God.

It is important to note that the Aristotelian belief in the possibility of true knowledge based on the action of the intellect upon sense experience meant that in the area of theory (speculative reason) it was possible to know some truths with certainty and to argue, for example, that the human experience of limitation and dependence (contingency) can lead the philosopher to reason to the existence of an unlimited and independent (necessary) being— God. On the other hand, Aristotle also emphasized the more uncertain character of practical judgments. Here the virtue of prudence would come into play, circumstances would alter cases, and experience was important in making prudential judgments about the appropriate conduct of individuals or society.

---

3. The classic treatment of the history of this idea is Arthur O. Lovejoy, *The Great Chain of Being* (Cambridge, MA: Harvard University Press, 1936).

The Thomistic Synthesis
in Ethics and Politics

What did all this mean for ethical and political thought? It meant that Aquinas was able to use Aristotle to develop a kind of Christian rationalism in approaching ethical and political questions. Where moral theology was earlier seen as the working out of the implications of the moral commands explicit or implicit in Scripture, it now could use Aristotle's teleological method to approach fundamental ethical questions in a less authoritarian and deductive manner. Similarly in politics Aristotle's writings could be used to justify the autonomy of the temporal authority against the overriding claims of a Church increasingly intent on employing the recently developed centralized system of canon law and church courts to translate its moral superiority into a claim of legal jurisdiction over many areas that earlier had been considered part of the temporal order (e.g., peace treaties, widows and orphans, taxation, feudal relationships sealed by oaths, etc.).

The selections below illustrate the way that Aquinas used Aristotelian teleology to develop an integrated theory of ethics, law, and government. The famous Treatise on Law in the *Summa Theologiae* (I–II, qu. 90–97) is an example. The fourfold structure of the Eternal Law (God's plan for the universe), Natural Law (Man's participation in the eternal law by the use of his reason), Human Law (the application to specific societies of natural law by way of "conclusions" and "determinations"), and Divine Law (divine revelation in the Old and New Testaments which guides and extends the human understanding of legal and moral principles) draws on and synthesizes neo-Platonic ideas of hierarchy and participation, Roman law conceptions of legislation, feudal beliefs in the community origin of law and government, and the Stoic vision of a rational and moral order in the universe. But what ties it all together is a fundamental belief in the ability of the human mind to understand the purposive order of nature intended by God. Thus for Aquinas the natural law deals with the fulfillment of "natural inclinations" towards self-preservation, food, sex and family life, knowledge, and worship—divinely-implanted human needs and potentialities that provide the subject matter of natural law. Not all inclinations, of course, are "natural" but only those that form a rational set of purposes of nature in man. They are related to natural law not by rational deduction but by derivation from a conception of an integrated and socially responsible human personality oriented towards the fulfillment of potentialities intended by a beneficent and purposive God. [4]

This Christianized Aristotelian rationalism in ethics contrasts with the earlier Augustinian pessimism about the capacities of the human reason to know the good and of the will to do it. It came at a time when the Church had a particular need for a methodology to deal with concrete ethical problems because of the spread of the practice of auricular confession. In 1215 the Second Lateran Council made annual confession to a priest a religious duty for all Christians and their confessors needed guidance in the imposition of penance and the spiritual direction of the penitent. Thus the latter

---

4. For examples of the argument from natural purposes see the selections on theft (p. 71), suicide (p. 70), usury (p. 74), lying (p. 76), fornication, adultery, and homosexuality (pp. 78–80).

section of Part II of the *Summa Theologiae* uses appeals to nature and the natural law to deal with moral questions of concern to clergy and laity alike, such as the degrees of seriousness of sexual sins and the classification of different types of drunkenness.

Political life is also based on human nature, an expression of natural human sociability and different talents. Sin has led to the need for coercion in government—and here Thomas agrees with Augustine—but it does not, as some medieval writers influenced by Augustine had argued, require all government to seek legitimation by the church. [5] "Infidel," (i.e. Moslem) rulers have a right to rule which is derived from natural law, and "divine law based on grace does not abolish human law based on reason" (see selection, p. 62), although the church may nullify that right for compelling religious reasons. Jewish parents have a right, based on nature, to educate their children in the Jewish faith, although when the children become mature they have a right—again by nature—to decide on religious matters for themselves.

It is less clear where the argument from purpose or goal leads Aquinas when he discusses the relation of the spiritual and temporal powers. Aquinas argues in *On Kingship* (ch. XIV) for a hierarchy of ends with the one whose special responsibility is man's eternal salvation directing the one who is only concerned with his earthly happiness, so that "kings should be subject to priests." In the *Summa Theologiae*, however (S.T., II–II, 9v. 60, a. 2) he seems to argue that the ruler is responsible for the common good of civil society and governs as the representative of the community so that the only justification for clerical intervention is a direct threat to the salvation of souls.

A similar ambiguity is to be found in Aquinas's treatment of property. He follows Aristotle in considering it as having both individual and social aspects. To resolve the tension between Aristotle's view of property as natural to man and the attitude of the Fathers of the Church who saw it as a consequence of the Fall, Aquinas gives property a special status as something "added" to the natural law for human convenience—that is now necessary because of human selfishness. [6]

Aquinas's view of society, too, combines organic and individualistic elements. On the one hand, every person has an individual soul and an eternal destiny and "man is not ordered to the political community in all that he is and has * * * [but] to God" while on the other, "the whole is greater than its parts" and man can only find his fulfillment and happiness in organized society. As in the political philosophy of his mentor, Aristotle (*Politics*, Bk. I), the principles of social organization are based on human nature, and society is ordered in a hierarchy of social groupings beginning with the household, then the local community, then higher "natural" associations, culminating in the state that has within it all it needs for human fulfillment. [7] As in Aristotle, in the household there is also a similar order with the husband naturally superior to the wife, and the two of them cooperating

---

5. For examples of "political Augustinianism" see the letter of Pope Gregory VII to Bishop Hermann of Metz (1081) translated in Brian Tierney, *The Crisis of Church and State 1050–1300* (Englewood Cliffs, NJ: Prentice Hall, 1964), 66–73 and the selections from Giles of Rome (1246–1316) in R. W. and A. J. Carlyle, *A History of Medieval*

Political Theory in the West, vol. 5 (Edinburgh and London: William Blackwood, 1950), 402–409.
6. See selection below, p. 72.
7. On the "organic" and "corporatist" elements in medieval thought see Ewart Lewis, *Medieval Political Ideas*, vol. 1 (New York: Alfred Knopf, 1954), ch. 4.

in the procreation and education of children with the assistance of servants and/or slaves. However, the slaves have a family and personal life that are not subject (as Aristotle's slaves were) to the decisions of their master.

In his prescriptions for government Aquinas again takes an intermediate position. He characterizes monarchy as the best form of government because it gives unified direction to the community but he recommends that it also benefit from the virtue of the aristocracy and the democratic participation of the people. Furthermore, he is acutely conscious of the need for limits on the monarch to prevent him from abusing his power in tyrannical fashion. Those limits include the customary and statutory law of the community, the historical claims of the people in many cases to select and/or depose their ruler, the moral and spiritual guidance of the church, and above all, the ruler's own awareness of his responsibilities to God. Thomas discusses the subjects' right to resist their ruler, but he does not refer to representative institutions since parliamentary bodies were only beginning to emerge at the time he was writing, while conciliar theories of church government were not formulated until the fourteenth century.

The concept of inherent structural limits is, in a sense, a key to an understanding of Aquinas's approach. It enables him to develop a theory that maintains a middle position between faith and reason, rationalism and empiricism, individualism and collectivism, and authority and participation. If medieval political thought can be described as involving two principal traditions—a populist tradition "ascending" from the community and a theocratic monarchist tradition "descending" from God, Aquinas can be seen as representing both. [8] This explains both the variety of interpretations that have been given to this thought over the centuries and its continuing appeal.

The Influence of Aquinas
on Later Political Thought

Aquinas's initial influence was exercised through his own Dominican order. Although he was canonized in 1323 and recognized as an eminent theologian, it was not until the sixteenth century that the *Summa* replaced Peter Lombard's *Commentary on the Sentences* as the standard text for instruction in theology. [9] At the Council of Trent which was first convened in 1545 to combat the Protestant reformers his *Summa Theologiae* lay open on the altar beside the Scriptures, and in 1567 he was proclaimed "Angelic Doctor" by Pope Pius V.

The diffusion of Thomism in the early modern period was aided by the institutional need of the Roman Catholic church for a philosophical basis for its response to Protestant attacks, and Aquinas's thought seemed to the defenders of the church the most persuasive and systematic statement of the medieval theological and philosophical tradition. It was developed and modernized by Jesuit and Dominican writers in Spain and Italy such as Fran-

8. See selection below (pp. 115–119) from Walter Ullmann, *History of Political Thought in the Middle Ages* (Baltimore, MD: Penguin Books, 1965). A similar typology is used in Paul E. Sigmund, *Nicholas of Cusa and Medieval Political Thought* (Cambridge, MA: Harvard University Press, 1963).

9. Dante puts Aquinas in heaven along with Bon-

aventure and Peter Lombard but does not accord him a special position (*Paradiso*, Cantos 1–11, 13). Dante's political theory is Aristotelian, but differs in many respects from that of Aquinas. See the argument of Etienne Gilson, *Dante and Philosophy* (New York: Harper and Row, 1963), ch. 3.

cisco Suarez, Juan de Mariana, and Robert Bellarmine, and through them exercised an influence on Grotius and the emerging theories of international law.[1] A similar need in the Anglican church also led Richard Hooker to make use of Thomism in his response to Puritan theological and political doctrines, *The Laws of Ecclesiastical Polity* (1594 ff.). John Locke (1632–1704) was familiar with Bellarmine's writings, and quoted "the judicious Hooker" frequently, but his one direct reference to Aquinas in the early *Essays on the Law of Nature* seems to have been taken from Hooker rather than directly from the *Summa*.

In the nineteenth century the Catholic church drew on Aquinas's political thought to respond to the challenges of industrialism, liberalism, and socialism. Leo XIII was elected pope in 1878, after the long reign of Pius IX had culminated in the seizure of the Papal States in 1870 by the Italian nationalists, the formal definition of the doctrine of papal infallibility by the First Vatican Council in 1871, and anti-clerical agitation in France after the Franco-Prussian War. Leo began his pontificate by formally endorsing the study of Thomism in Catholic educational institutions in his encyclical, *Aeterni Patris* (1879) and drew heavily on Aquinas's thought in a number of subsequent encyclicals designed to provide an approach to contemporary political and philosophical problems based on the Catholic intellectual tradition. The most important of those encyclicals, *Rerum Novarum*, published in 1891, outlined a social order based on widespread distribution of property, the organization of trade unions, and the guarantee of a living wage to the worker. The Catholic political parties and trade unions that had emerged in many European countries used the encyclicals and Thomist categories of thought to develop a "communitarian" or "personalist" alternative both to socialism and to free-enterprise capitalism that claimed to provide for both the individual and social aspects of private property. In these organizations, as well as in seminaries, universities, and secondary schools run by the church, Thomism provided the structure through which political and ethical questions were articulated and analyzed.

In the twentieth century the neo-Thomist movement in philosophy and the Christian Democratic parties in European and Latin American politics developed and reformulated aspects of Thomist social thought, abandoning the conservatism of its original formulation in favor of liberal theories of democracy and human rights that claimed Aquinas as their inspiration. The most important philosopher in this movement was Jacques Maritain (1891–1965),[2] but Yves Simon, Heinrich Rommen, and Josef Fuchs also wrote on the subject and the Christian Democratic parties in Germany, France, Italy, and Chile produced Thomist-influenced theoretical publications for their followers. In the United States beginning in the 1930s Mortimer Adler and Robert Hutchins at the University of Chicago interested a whole generation of American students in Thomism, and the books published by the University of Chicago Press in the Walgreen Foundation series gave wide circulation to Thomistic ideas. The post-World War II revival of interest in natural law in Europe connected with the search for a philosophical basis for human rights, and in the case of Germany with a basis for appeals against unjust

---

1. See James Brown Scott, *The Spanish Origin of International Law* (Oxford: Oxford University Press, 1934); Bernice Hamilton, *Spanish Political Thought in the Sixteenth Century* (Oxford: Clarendon Press, 1963).

2. On the development of Maritain's political thought see Paul E. Sigmund, "Maritain on Politics," in Deal Hudson and Matthew Mancini, eds., *Understanding Maritain* (Macon, GA: Mercer University Press, 1987).

laws such as those adopted by the Nazis, also aroused interest in the Thomist formulation of a higher legal standard.

Following the Second Vatican Council (1962–1965) Thomism virtually ceased to be the official philosophy of Catholicism and papal documents no longer cited Aquinas, preferring to go directly to Scripture and the early Fathers. In Europe and Latin America the Christian Democratic parties adopted a vocabulary similar to that of their secular counterparts and only rarely referred to Maritain and Aquinas. One significant exception appeared in Peru between 1968 and 1975 where a reformist military regime borrowed concepts and even economic analyses from Catholic-influenced theories of worker participation and worker ownership that could trace their genealogy to Thomist doctrines of the social function of property. [3]

While the direct influence of Thomism, particularly as mediated by Catholicism, has diminished, his religiously-based but rationally grounded philosophy of man and society has a continuing appeal. His writings on philosophy, ethics, and politics are now viewed not as *the* answer to all the problems of the contemporary world, but as a particularly brilliant and influential approach to understanding God, man, and the world that permits us to rank Aquinas with Plato, Aristotle, Hobbes, Locke, Marx, and Freud among the thinkers who have enabled us to see the world differently because of what they wrote.

Evaluation

Who was Thomas Aquinas and why was he important? First, he was a committed Christian who was attracted to the religious life from an early age, working in a dynamic new religious order with branches in many parts of Western Europe. Second, he was an academician in the forefront of the intellectual life of his day teaching, debating, writing, and making use of the scholastic method which had been developed in the nascent universities of Western Europe to engage in the logical analysis and resolution of philosophical and theological problems in defense of Catholic orthodoxy. Third, he was an Aristotelian who devoted most of his life to studying and understanding the newly available works of the Greek philosopher and relating them to the truths of Christianity in the belief that reason and faith were not contradictory, but merely two different ways through which God had made it possible for man to know truth. Aristotle gave him concepts such as matter and form, act and potentiality, substance and accident, and above all a belief in final causality—teleology or purposiveness in nature—which he used to organize and systematize the intellectual inheritance of Christian Europe in a rationally defensible way. A fourth element in his thinking which is not usually noted is the influence on Aquinas of Neo-Platonism—through Proclus, Augustine, and Pseudo-Dionysius—with its vision of a hierarchical and ordered world beginning with God and proceeding through various degrees or levels of being as emanations of God's overflowing being (in Christian formulations, God's love). Man is a unique part of this "Great Chain of

3. See Peter T. Knight, "New Forms of Economic Organization in Peru: Toward Workers' Self-Management," in Abraham Lowenthal, ed., *The Peruvian Experiment* (Princeton, NJ: Princeton University Press, 1975), ch. 9. See also Alfred Stepan, *The State and Society: Peru in Comparative Perspective* (Princeton, NJ: Princeton University Press, 1978), ch. 1 on the "organic statist" approach to government, which was transmitted to Latin America through St. Thomas and the papal encyclicals.

Being" because he links earth and heaven, and possesses a soul which receives a special aid, grace, from God, enabling it to transcend its natural capacity so as to achieve the direct vision of God after death required for complete happiness.

As applied in Aquinas's political and ethical thought, these elements result in a vision of an objective and purposive order of justice in the universe in which reasons and purposes can be found for what we observe in the external world, in society, and in man. The teleological outlook of Aristotle is used to fashion a rational philosophical basis for the Christian belief in a purposive and loving Creator. Their combination leads Aquinas to look for an order and harmony in human society, politics, and ethics that is free of contradiction, although not of tension. There is no place in Aquinas's thought for Niebuhr's "impossible ethic" or Machiavelli's opposition of personal ethics and a political ethic of survival. Protestant Christians are critical of the excessive rationalism of Thomistic ethics, and its refusal to recognize that there are contradictions between a rationalistic teleological ethics and certain aspects of the message of Christ (e.g., sacrificial love, martyrdom, rejection of wealth and worldly possessions, and "turning the other cheek"). Radicals are suspicious of Aquinas's emphasis on the "natural" character of a social order which they insist is subject to human control and conditioned by economic structures. [4] At least until the changes in Thomism introduced by twentieth-century neo-Thomists in favor of democracy, freedom, pluralism, and human rights, liberals were suspicious of its clericalism, implicit authoritarianism, sexism, and a hierarchical outlook that seemed to prefer order to freedom. [5] Recognizing that many aspects of Aquinas's ethical and political views that are not accepted today (e.g., his preference for monarchy, his qualified acceptance of slavery, the prohibition of taking interest, his attitudes towards Jews, the defense of the burning of heretics, his belief in the natural inferiority of women) were historically conditioned or the result of an uncritical acceptance of Aristotle, the modern reader can still share Aquinas's central belief that man should use his intellect critically to resolve human problems of individual and social conduct. In addition, as a number of contemporary philosophers and political theorists have recognized, Aquinas shares with his mentor, Aristotle, a belief in the human capacity to identify goals, values, and purposes ("teleology") in the structure and functioning of the human person that can provide the basis of a theory of ethics that responds to the argument of the eighteenth-century philosopher, David Hume, that values cannot be derived from the facts of human existence. [6]

Aquinas may be too optimistic about the possibility of certain knowledge in ethics and politics, giving less attention than he should to historical conditions and the limits of human reason. [7] Nevertheless his thinking contin-

4. For one instance, however, in which Aquinas has been interpreted in a radical quasi-Marxist direction, see the selection by Julio Silva Solar (pp. 178–180).

5. On the reinterpretation of Aquinas as a liberal, see the selection by the editor (pp. 180–188).

6. Cf. John Wild, *Plato's Modern Enemies and the Theory of Natural Law* (Chicago: University of Chicago Press, 1953); Alan Donagan, *The Theory of Morality* (Chicago: University of Chicago Press, 1977), 59–63; John Rawls, *A Theory of Justice*

(Cambridge, MA: Harvard University Press, 1971), ch. 7; Paul E. Sigmund, *Natural Law in Political Thought* (Cambridge, MA: Winthrop Publishers, 1971; reprint, Lanham, MD: University Press of America, 1980), conclusion; John Finnis, *Natural Law and Natural Rights* (New York: Oxford University Press, 1980); Alisdair McIntyre, *After Virtue* (Notre Dame, IN: University of Notre Dame Press, 2nd ed., 1984), chs. 12, 13, 16, 18.

7. Note, however, that as an Aristotelian, Aquinas did not believe that it was possible to achieve

ues to offer a model for the possibilities as well as the limitations of the application of reason to human affairs—not in its narrowly empirical or logical meaning as in much of contemporary philosophy, but in the broader sense of sustained argument based on evidence and clear statement of one's assumptions and the conclusions derived from them. His Christian belief in the providence of God and his Aristotelian doctrine of teleology combine to convince him that life has meaning, and that that meaning is, at least in part, available to the human reason. This basic assumption is an important element in the continuing attraction of what his followers like to call the perennial philosophy *(philosophia perennis)*.

Paul E. Sigmund
Princeton, N.J.

the same certainty in the practical application of the principles of ethics and politics as in logic or metaphysics, and as a Christian he was aware of the finite character of human reason, particularly in relation to God.

Note on Translation

With the exception of a nineteenth century collection of translations of parts of the ethical sections of the *Summa Theologiae* by Joseph Rickaby S.J., *Aquinas Ethicus* (London: Burnes, Oates, 1896) there is no translation of the sections of Aquinas's work devoted to specific ethical questions, although there are many editions of the section of the *Summa* devoted to law (I–II, qu. 90–97) that includes a discussion of natural law which has considerable relevance for ethics. In the area of political thought, there are two collections available in English, but there are difficulties with both. Dino Bigongiari, ed., *The Political Ideas of St. Thomas Aquinas* (New York: Hafner, 1953) includes the questions on law and *On Kingship* as well as a few questions from the Second Part of Part II (II–II) of the *Summa Theologiae*, but it uses the antiquated English Dominicans' translation (London: Burnes, Oates and Washburn, 22 vols., 1912–36) which includes such prize mistranslations as an article entitled "Whether the Right of Nations is the Same as the Natural Right" (S.T., II–II, qu. 57, a. 3) which is unintelligible to any but those who know the meaning of the Latin word, *jus* ("right" as a system of law). Bigongiari's selections give the questions from the *Summa* in full and this gives a good sense of the scholastic method of argument, but their length and complexity may deter introductory students who try to find their way through them.

A. P. D'Entreves, *Aquinas, Selected Political Writings* (Oxford: Blackwells, 1948) goes to the other extreme. It takes Aquinas out of the scholastic form entirely, excerpting only his responses, totally out of their context. For some reason the selections from Aquinas's works appear out of chronological order with the early *Commentary on the Sentences* (1256) appearing last. In addition, the translations are excessively free, distorting the meaning in many cases in a way that makes Aquinas much less "medieval" than he in fact was. Thus, for example, the emphasis on order in the statement at the beginning of *De Regimine Principum* "In all things that are ordered to some end" *(In omnibus quae ad finem aliquem ordinantur)*, becomes a liberal democratic "Whenever a certain end has been decided upon" (p. 3), and in the discussion of law in the *Summa Theologiae* (I–II, qu. 90, a. 2) the Latin says, "Since every part is ordered to a whole as the imperfect to the perfect" *(Cum omnis pars ordinetur ad totum sicut imperfectum ad perfectum)*, but the translation reads, "Since every part bears the same relation to its whole as the imperfect to the perfect" (p. 111).

The new translation which I have undertaken in these selections attempts to combine the advantages of Bigongiari and D'Entreves, without their disadvantages. Some selections are left in the scholastic form while others are taken only from Aquinas's responses. The excerpts are as readable as possible while remaining close to the literal sense of the Latin except when doing so renders Aquinas's meaning obscure. I have also included selections on topics such as the existence of God, the immortality of soul, divine providence, the incarnation, nature and grace, and human psychology which are not included in any of the above collections but are useful in understanding the context of Aquinas's ethical and political thought. While his ethics and politics are separable from his theology and cosmology, the latter provide the framework and assumptions behind his theories in these areas.

The selections that follow are taken from the *Summa contra Gentiles, On Kingship (De Regimine Principum)*, and the *Summa Theologiae*. Footnotes also quote politically significant passages from the early *Commentary on the Sentences of Peter Lombard* and *The Government of the Jews*. I have not included excerpts from Aquinas's commentaries on Aristotle's *Ethics* and *Politics* since I believe that they do not add much to the interpretations of Aristotle included in the selections that I have translated. Occasionally I have used different translations for the same Latin word. This is especially the case with *multitudo* for which "multitude" is inadequate. *Beatitudo* is usually translated as "happiness," but sometimes as "beatitude." *Civitas* is sometimes translated as "city" but more often the later term, "state," seems more appropriate. In these and other doubtful cases I have usually included the Latin original in parentheses. The footnotes identify Aquinas's sources, give biographical or other descriptions where necessary, and refer to other places where Aquinas's theory varies from that presented in a given text. The Latin text of the Leonine edition has usually been used for the *Summa Theologiae*, the 1924 Turin edition for the *De Regimine Principum*, and the 1948 New York reissue of the 1855 Parma edition for the *Summa contra Gentiles*.

Paul E. Sigmund

SELECTIONS FROM
THE WORK OF
ST. THOMAS AQUINAS

THE SUMMA AGAINST THE GENTILES
(SUMMA CONTRA GENTILES, 1259–1264)†

Book 1

Chapter 3

The Two Ways of Knowing the Truth about God.

There are two ways of knowing what we hold to be true about God. There are some truths about God that exceed the capacity of human reason—for example the fact that God is three and one. There are also some truths that natural reason can attain, such as that God exists, that he is one, and other truths of this kind. These are truths about God that have been conclusively proved by philosophers making use of their natural reason.

It is evident that there are some things to be known about God that completely exceed the capacity of human reason. Since all the knowledge that a person has about a thing is based on his understanding of its substance (according to the Philosopher [Aristotle] the basis for any argument is "what a thing is"),[1] the way the substance of a thing is understood must determine what is known about it. Thus if the human intellect comprehends the substance of, say, a stone or a triangle, no intelligible aspect of that thing is beyond the capacity of the human reason. However this is not the case for us with God. The human intellect can not achieve the understanding of God's substance by means of its natural capacity because in this life all knowledge that is in our intellects originates in the senses. Hence things that are not perceived by the senses cannot be grasped by the human intellect except in so far as knowledge of them is gathered from the senses. But the objects of the senses cannot lead the human intellect to the point that in them it can see the divine substance as it is, for they are effects that are not equal in power to their cause. However our intellect is led from the objects of the senses to the knowledge of the existence of God—as well as to other attributes of the First Principle.[2] Therefore there are some things that can be known

---

† Those interested only in Aquinas's politics and ethics may prefer to omit the *Summa contra Gentiles* and to begin with the *Summa Theologiae*, I, qu. 92. The *Summa* or summary defense of Catholicism against the "gentiles," principally the Moslems, was originally entitled *On the Truth of the Catholic Faith against the Gentiles*. It was written in Paris and Italy as an aid to Dominican missionaries working among the Moslems and Jews in Spain and North Africa.

1. Aristotle, *Posterior Analytics*, II, 3. For medieval philosophy, *substantia* is the underlying reality that distinguishes a thing from others and gives it independent existence.

2. First Principle—God as the Foundation of all creation. For Aquinas's argument that reason can lead us to the knowledge of the existence of God, see *Summa Theologiae*, I, qu. 2, a. 3 (p. 30).

about God that are available to human reason, but there are others that totally exceed its power.

Chapter 4

Truths about God that are Known by Reason are also Properly Made Available to Man by Faith.

If it were left solely to reason to seek the truth about God, few men would possess a knowledge of God. There are three reasons why most men are prevented from carrying out the diligent inquiry that leads to the discovery of truth. Some are prevented from doing so because of their physical disinclination—as a result of which many men by nature are not disposed to learning. And so however earnest they are, they cannot attain the highest level of human knowledge which consists in knowing God. Others are prevented from doing so by the pressures of family life. Some men must devote themselves to managing temporal affairs and thus are not able to spend time in leisurely contemplative inquiry, so as to reach the highest point of human inquiry—the knowledge of God. Laziness prevents others. To know what reason can investigate concerning God requires that one already have a knowledge of many things, since almost all of philosophy is directed towards the knowledge of God. This is why we learn metaphysics, which is concerned with the divine, last among the subjects in the field of philosophy. The study of truth requires a considerable effort—which is why few are willing to undertake it out of love of knowledge—despite the fact that God has implanted a natural appetite for such knowledge in the minds of men.

Chapter 7

Truths Based on Reason Are Not Contrary to the Truth of the Christian Faith.

Although the truth of the Christian faith exceeds the capacity of human reason, truths that reason is fitted by nature to know cannot be contrary to the truth of faith. The things that reason is fitted by nature to know are clearly most true, and it would be impossible to think of them as false.[3] It is also wrong to think that something that is held by faith could be false since it is clearly confirmed by God. Since we know by definition that what is false is contrary to the truth, it is impossible for the principles that reason knows by nature to be contrary to the truth of faith.

*   *   *

We conclude therefore that any arguments made against the doctrines of faith are incorrectly derived from the self-evident first principles of

---

3. Nature, for Aquinas, is purposive and man's intellect is directed by nature to the knowledge of truth.

nature. Such conclusions do not have the force of proofs, but are either doubtful opinions or sophistries, and so it is possible to answer them.

Chapter 8

The Relationship between the Human Reason and the Primary Truth of Faith.

There is a further point to be considered. The objects of the senses on which human reason bases its knowledge retain some traces of likeness to God, since they exist and are good. This resemblance is inadequate because it is completely insufficient to manifest the substance of God. Effects possess a resemblance to causes in their own particular way because everything that acts does so in ways like itself, but effects do not always exhibit a perfect likeness to their cause. Now human reason is related to the knowledge of the truth of faith—which can only be known fully by those who see the divine substance—in such a way that reason can attain likenesses of it that are true but not sufficient to comprehend the truth conclusively or as known in itself. Yet it is useful for the human mind to exercise its powers of reasoning, however weak, in this way provided that there is no presumption that it can comprehend or demonstrate [the substance of the divine]. For it is most pleasing to be able to see some aspect of the loftiest things, however weak and inadequate our consideration of them may be.

Book II

Chapter 68

How an Intellectual Substance Can Be the Formative Principle of the Body.

In this way a wonderful linkage of things can be seen, for the lowest member of a higher classification *(genus)* is always found just above the highest member of a lower classification. For example, the lowest members of the class of animals are only a little above plant life, such as oysters that are immobile, and possess only the sense of touch, and are attached to the ground. Thus Dionysius says, "Divine wisdom has linked the lowest examples *(fines)* of higher beings to the first examples *(principia)* of those below them."[4] This is true of the human body in the classification *(genus)* of bodies. It is an equal composite of two classifications. It touches the lowest level of the next higher *genus* because the human soul is the lowest in the series of intellectual substances, as we can tell from the way in which it acquires knowledge. Therefore the

---

4. Dionysius, *Divine Names*, VII. On the influence on the middle ages exercised by the writings of Pseudo-Dionysius, a fifth century Christian neo-Platonist writer who was erroneously believed by medieval writers to be Dionysius the Areopagite, a disciple of St. Paul, see Paul E. Sigmund, *Nicholas of Cusa and Medieval Political Thought* (Cambridge, Mass.: Harvard University Press), ch. 3.

intellectual soul is at the borderline or limit of things corporeal and incorporeal since it is an incorporeal substance that acts as the formative principle *(forma)* of the body.

Book III

Chapter 2

Everything that Acts Acts for an End.[5]

When something clearly acts for an end we say that the end is that toward which the movement of the thing that acts tends; when it is reached, we say that the end has been reached, and if it fails to reach it, we say that it has failed to reach its intended end. We see this in the case of a doctor who aims at health or a runner who runs towards a finish line. It does not matter whether the thing tending towards an end is endowed with consciousness or not. A target is both the end of the archer, and the end of an arrow's flight. When things act for an end the thing beyond which they seek nothing further is said to be their last end. Thus a doctor's action goes as far as health and once that is achieved he seeks nothing further. And in the action of everything that acts there is a point beyond which the actor does not seek anything further. Otherwise actions would go on forever—which is impossible.

Chapter 3

Everything that Acts Acts for a Good.

An intellectual agent acts for an end that it has chosen for itself, while things in nature that act for ends do not decide on their ends, for they do not know the meaning of an end but are moved to ends chosen for them by someone else. When someone uses his intellect to act, he always chooses an end that he thinks is good because the object of his intellect only moves him when it appears to be a good—and good is the object of the will. Everything in nature moves and acts for an end that is a good since the end of something acting in nature is the result of a natural appetite. Therefore everything that acts acts for a good.

Chapter 25

The End of Every Intellectual Substance is to Know God.

For everything that acts and moves in an ordered way, the purpose *(finis*—end) of the first actor and mover should be the final purpose of all, just as the goal *(finis)* of the commander of an army is the goal of

5. Aquinas's doctrine of ends or purposes in nature and man is central to the structure of his politics and ethics. Like the universe as a whole, man and society possess inherent structures that indicate their purpose and value.

all the soldiers under his command. Now the purpose of the intellect is what moves all the parts of man; the intellect moves the appetites by proposing their objects to them. The intellectual appetite or will moves the sense appetites of spirit and passion. We do not obey the passions unless the will commands, and the sense appetite, once the will consents, moves the body. Therefore the end (goal, purpose) of the intellect is the end of all human actions. The end and good of the intellect is truth. Therefore the ultimate end of the whole man and of all his actions and desires is to know the first truth; namely, God.

Furthermore, there is a natural desire in all men to know the causes of what they see. Because men wondered about the underlying causes of what they saw, they first began to philosophize, and when they found the cause they were satisfied. Human inquiry does not cease until it comes to the first cause and we think that we have full knowledge when we know the first cause. Therefore man desires by nature to know the first cause as his ultimate end. But the first cause of everything is God. Therefore man's ultimate end is to know God.

Chapter 27

Human Happiness Does Not Consist in Bodily Pleasures.

In the order of nature, pleasure is the result of a function and not the reverse. Therefore if a function is not the ultimate end, the pleasure that results from it cannot be the ultimate end, or accompany the ultimate end. Now it is clear that the functions that are followed by the (bodily) pleasures mentioned above are not man's ultimate end but are directed at certain specific ends—for instance eating at the preservation of the body, and sexual intercourse at the procreation of children. Therefore these joys are not the ultimate end, nor do they accompany the ultimate end. Therefore (ultimate) happiness is not located in such pleasures.

Chapter 32

Happiness Does Not Consist in the Goods of the Body.

The soul is better than the body—which needs the soul to live and to possess these goods. Therefore a good of the soul, such as understanding and the like is better than a good of the body. Therefore the good of the body is not man's highest good.

Furthermore these (bodily) goods are common to man and to other animals. But happiness is a good proper to man alone. Man's happiness therefore does not consist in the things mentioned above.

Moreover, many animals surpass man in the goods of the body. Some are speedier, some stronger, and so on. If the highest good of man were in these things man would not be the best of the animals—which is obviously false. Therefore human happiness does not consist in the goods of the body.

Chapter 37

Man's Ultimate Happiness Consists in the Contemplation of God.

Man's ultimate happiness consists in the contemplation of truth for this operation is specific to man and is shared with no other animals.[6] Also it is not directed to any other end since the contemplation of truth is sought for its own sake. In addition, in this operation man is united to higher beings (substances) since this is the only human operation that is carried out both by God and by the separate substances *(angels)*. Through this operation too man is united with those higher beings by knowing them in a certain way.

Chapter 48

Man's Ultimate Happiness Is Not in this Life.

Man's ultimate end fulfills his natural appetite in such a way that once he achieves it he desires nothing more. If he is still moved towards something else, he has not reached the end which satisfies him. This cannot happen in this life because the more someone knows the more his desire for knowledge increases. And this occurs by nature.

*   *   *

Everyone agrees that happiness is a kind of perfect good, since it satisfies the appetite. Now a perfect good is one in which there is no admixture of evil. A thing that is perfectly white has no admixture of black. It is not possible for man in this life to be wholly free from evils—not only from those of the body and the flesh such as hunger, thirst, cold and so on, but also those of the spirit. There is no one who is not sometimes upset by disorderly passions, who does not sometimes exceed the virtuous mean either because of excess or deficiency,[7] who is not deceived for one reason or another, or at least is not ignorant of things he would like to know, or doubtful about things of which he would like to be certain. No one therefore is happy in this life.

Chapter 51

How God May Be Seen in His Essence.

Since it is impossible for a natural desire to be frustrated—which would be the case if it were not possible to arrive at the understanding of the divine substance that all minds naturally desire—we must conclude that the substance of God can be seen through the intellect, by both the separate intellectual substances (angels) and our souls. How God can be seen is clear from what has been said. We have proved that the divine

---

6. On the contemplative life as man's highest and happiest pursuit, see Aristotle, *Nicomachean Ethics*, X, 7–8.

7. On the doctrine that virtue lies in the mean or intermediate point between excess and deficiency of a quality, see Aristotle, *Nicomachean Ethics*, II, 6–9.

substance cannot be seen by the intellect through any created thing (*specie*). Hence if God's essence is to be seen it must be seen in itself so that in that vision the divine essence is both the object of our vision and the medium through which we see it.

Chapter 53

A Created Intellect Needs the Influence of (Divine) Light in Order to See God in His Essence.

The divine essence is a higher form than any created intellect.[8] In order for God in his essence to be known by any created intellect as is required for the divine substance to be seen, the created intellect must be elevated by action from on high. * * *

Since we come to the knowledge of intelligible things from the objects of the senses, we transfer the terms we use for sensory knowledge to intellectual knowledge. This is especially true of sight which is the most noble and spiritual of the senses and the one that is most akin to the intellect. Because bodily vision is not possible without light, we call what makes intellectual vision possible "light" as well. * * * Accordingly the action by which a created intellect is elevated to the intellectual vision of the divine substance is appropriately called the light of glory.

Chapter 63

In that Final Happiness Every Human Desire Will Be Fulfilled.

There is a certain desire in man, as an intellectual being, to know truth. Men achieve this by pursuing the contemplative life. This is fulfilled in that vision of the First Truth through which everything that the intellect naturally desires to know becomes known to it.

* * *

Secondly, there is a certain desire in man for a basis on which to order all lesser things. Men achieve this by pursuing the active life in society. This is principally the desire of man to order his whole life according to reason, that is, to live in accordance with virtue, since the end of the action of any virtuous person is the good of virtue itself, just as that of a brave man is to act bravely. This desire will be completely fulfilled when reason is at its fullest strength, illuminated by the divine light so that it cannot depart from what is right.

There is a third desire of man that he shares with animals—to enjoy pleasure. Those men who live lives of voluptuousness achieve this goal but because of lack of moderation they become intemperate and incontinent. But in that ultimate happiness there will be perfect pleasure—a more perfect delight of the senses than that which animals enjoy, since the intellect is higher than the senses. That good in which we will delight

8. The essence of a thing is its ultimate unchanging nature, its defining characteristics.

is greater than any sense good. It is more intimate and continuous as well as more pure because it is not mixed with sadness or worry that it may be disturbed. * * *

Therefore it is clear that through the vision of the divine, intellectual substances attain the true happiness in which all desire is at rest—which is the full sufficiency of all goods that Aristotle says is required for happiness. * * *[9] Nothing is as similar to this perfect ultimate happiness in this life as the life of contemplation of truth, as far as is possible in this life. Therefore philosophers who could not have full knowledge of that ultimate happiness have said that the ultimate happiness of man consists in the contemplation which is possible in this life.[1]

Chapter 64

God Governs the Universe by His Providence.

From what has been said above, it has been sufficiently proved that God is the end of all things. From this we can further conclude that he governs and rules the universe by his providence.

Whenever things are ordered to some end, they are subject to the direction of the one who is principally concerned with that end. Thus all the parts and activities of an army are directed as their ultimate end to the goal of the general, which is victory, and therefore the general commands the whole army. In the same way an art which is concerned with an end controls and lays down rules for an art which is concerned with the means to an end. The art of government directs the military, the military art the cavalry, and navigation shipbuilding. Therefore since all things are ordered to the Divine Goodness as to their end, God who is that Goodness substantially possessed, and known, and loved, must be the one who governs all things.

Chapter 81

Order among Men and in Relation to Other Things.

Relative to other intellectual substances, the human soul is lowest in rank because when it is created it only receives knowledge of the order of divine providence in a general way. The (human) soul must acquire a full knowledge of the individual aspects of that order from the particular ways in which the order of divine providence is expressed. Consequently the human soul needs bodily organs to derive its knowledge from bodily things. But because of the weakness in the light of its intellect it cannot acquire from them a perfect knowledge of the things that concern man without the help of light from higher spirits. For God has directed that lower beings should be perfected by higher spirits. * * * But since man has some share in intellectual light divine providence has decreed that brute animals that have no share in it should be subject to

9. Aristotle, *Nicomachean Ethics*, X, 7.　　　1. Aristotle, *Nicomachean Ethics*, X, 8.

him. * * * Since brute animals, although they lack intellects, have a certain kind of knowledge, by divine providence they are over plants and other things which are without knowledge. * * * Since man possesses an intellect, senses, and bodily powers, divine providence has decreed that these should be ordered to one another in a way that is similar to the order in the universe. The power of the body is subject to the powers of the senses and the intellect, carrying out their commands. The power of the senses is subject to that of the intellect and is limited by its control.

In the same way we find an order among men. Those of superior intellect are the natural rulers while those who are less intelligent but have stronger bodies seem to be made by nature to serve, as Aristotle says in the *Politics*. * * *[2]

Just as in the case of an individual man disorder results if the intellect follows the senses, or if because of an indisposition of the body the senses are drawn by the motion of the body, as occurs in the case of someone with a limp, so in human government disorder results when someone rules not because he excels in intellect but because he has usurped power by physical force or because someone has been given authority to rule because of sensual affection. * * *

It is evident therefore that divine providence imposes order on all things. Thus what the Apostle [Paul] says is true, "Whatever things are are ordained by God."[3]

Book IV

Chapter 54

It was Fitting for God to Become Man.

Since perfect happiness *(beatitudo)* for man consists only in the enjoyment of God, it follows that whoever devotes himself to things that are less worthy than God as his end is prevented from participating in true happiness. Not knowing the true dignity of his nature man can be led astray so that he devotes himself to lesser things than God as his end. Thus it happens that some who consider themselves as possessing (only) the bodily and sentient nature that they share with other animals seek a kind of bestial happiness in bodily things and the pleasures of the flesh. * * * Although in some respects man does resemble the lowest of created things, with respect to the end towards which he is directed there is nothing higher than man but God alone in whom all the perfect happiness of man consists. It was most fitting that God should manifest this dignity of man—that he should find his happiness in the immediate vision of God—by directly assuming the nature of man. Hence we see

---

2. Aristotle, *Politics*, I, 5. For fuller statements in the *Summa Theologiae* of Aquinas's view of slavery which differs in important respects from that of Aristotle, see S.T. I, qu. 96, a.4 (p. 55); S.T., II–II, qu. 57, a.3 (p. 67), and qu. 104, a.5 (p. 75).
3. Romans, 13:1.

that as a result of God having become man a great part of mankind, spurning the pleasures of the flesh and bodily things, has dedicated itself to the worship of God alone.

Furthermore, because the perfect happiness *(beatitudo)* of man consists in a knowledge of God that exceeds the possibilities of any created intellect it was necessary that man should receive a certain foretaste of this kind of knowledge, so as to direct himself towards the fullness of the blessed knowledge that takes place through faith. Now the knowledge that directs man to his final end should be very certain since it is the basis for all his actions that are aimed at achieving his final end. The principles which are known to us by nature are of the greatest certainty. Something is known with the greatest certainty either because it is self-evident—such as the first principles of argument—or because it is derived from things that are self-evident such as conclusions from self-evident principles. However, what is proposed to us from God to be held by faith is not self-evident since it exceeds the capacity of the human intellect. It should therefore be proposed to man by someone to whom it is self-evident. And although it may be self-evident in a certain way to those who see God in his essence, in order to have certain knowledge it was appropriate that we should be directed to the first principle of this knowledge, God, to whom such knowledge is self-evident by nature, who makes it known to all in a way similar to the way we know things with certainty by resolving them into indemonstrable first principles. It was fitting therefore that to achieve absolute certainty man should be instructed in the truth of faith by God himself made man so that man could receive instruction in divine matters in a human way. * * *

Furthermore, we learn from the tradition of the church that the whole human race is infected by sin. We know from the nature of divine justice that sin is not remitted by God without reparation. However no man, however pure, could make reparation for the sin of the whole human race since any pure man would still be worth something less than the whole human race. It was fitting therefore that the human race should be freed from the sin that is common to it by someone who was both a man, as the one who was to make reparation, and something greater than man so that his merit was sufficient to make reparation for the sin of the whole human race. As to beatitude only God is greater than man since the angels, although they are superior to man in the condition of their natures, are not superior in the order of ends since they achieve beatitude in the same way. In order for man to achieve beatitude it was necessary therefore that God should become man to take away the sin of the human race.

Chapter 76

On the Rank of Bishop and (the Pope) Who Is Highest in that Rank.

It is evident, however, that although the people are divided into different dioceses and cities, just as there is one church there also must be one Christian people. Just as the particular people of one church must have one bishop who is head of all the people, so also the whole Christian people must have one who is head of the whole church.

Likewise if the church is to be united, all the faithful must agree on the faith. But there are many questions concerning matters of faith. Because of the difference of opinions, the church would be divided unless it was kept in unity by the decision of one person. Thus one person must be over the whole church in order to keep it united. But it is obvious that Christ never failed to give what is necessary to the church that he loves and for which he sheds his blood. The Lord says of the synagogue, "What more is there that I should have done for my vineyard, and have not done."[4] There is no doubt therefore that it is by Christ's command that one person is over the whole church.

Furthermore no one doubts that the government of the church is ordered in the best way, since this has been done by the one through whom "Kings rule and legislators make just laws."[5] The best government of a society *(multitudo)* is one that is ruled by one person. This is clear from the end of government which is peace. Peaceful unity among his subjects is the end of a ruler, and one ruler, rather than many rulers, is a more proximate cause of unity. It is clear therefore that the government of the church is so arranged that one person is over the whole church. * * *

This then refutes the presumptuous error of those who try to withdraw from obedience and subjection to Peter and do not recognize his successor, the Roman Pontiff, as the pastor of the universal church.

4. Isaiah, 5:4.   5. Proverbs, 8:15.

ON KINGSHIP or
THE GOVERNANCE OF RULERS
(DE REGIMINE PRINCIPUM, 1265–1267)†

Chapter 1

Men in Society Must Be under Rulers.

We must first explain what is meant by the term, king. When a thing is directed towards an end, and it is possible to go one way or another, someone must indicate the best way to proceed toward the end. For example, a ship that moves in different directions with the shifting winds would never reach its destination if it were not guided into port by the skill of its helmsman. Man too has an end towards which all the actions of his life are directed, since all intelligent beings act for an end. Yet the diversity of men's pursuits and activities means that men proceed to their intended objectives in different ways. Therefore man needs someone to direct him towards his end. Now every man is naturally endowed with the light of reason to direct his actions towards his end. If men were intended to live alone as do many animals, there would be no need for anyone to direct him towards his end, since every man would be his own king under God, the highest king, and the light of reason given to him from on high would enable him to act on his own. But man is by nature a political and social animal.[1] Even more than other animals he lives in groups *(multitudine)*. This is demonstrated by the requirements of his nature. Nature has given other animals food, furry covering, teeth, and horns and claws—or at least speed of flight—as means to defend themselves. Man however, is given none of these by nature. Instead he has been given the use of his reason to secure all these things by the work of his hands. But a man cannot secure all these by himself, for a man cannot adequately provide for his life by himself. Therefore it is natural for man to live in association with his fellows.

In addition, nature has instilled in other animals the ability to perceive what is useful or harmful to them. For example, a sheep knows by nature that the wolf is its enemy. Some animals even have the natural ability to know the medicinal herbs and other things necessary to their existence. Man, on the other hand, has a natural knowledge of what is necessary to his life only in a general way, using his reason to move from general principles to the knowledge of particular things that are neces-

---

† In 1265 Aquinas was asked to write a treatise on kingship for the king of Cyprus. He left it unfinished in 1267, probably because of the king's death. It was later completed by Polemy of Lucca, but manuscript evidence indicates that the chapters translated here were written by Aquinas.

1. Aristotle (*Politics*, I, 2) says man is a "political animal" *(zoon politikon)*. Aquinas, following William of Moerbeke's translation, recognizes that in Greek thought the political had a broader meaning than in medieval times, and included society and social life as a whole.

sary for human life. And it is not possible for one man to arrive at the knowledge of all these things through the use of his reason. Thus it is necessary for him to live in society so that one person can help another and different men can employ their reasons in different ways, one in medicine, and others in this or that endeavor. This is most clearly demonstrated by the fact that man uses words to communicate his thoughts fully to others. It is true that other animals express their feelings in a general way. Dogs express their anger by barking and other animals express their feelings in other ways. But man is more able to communicate with others than other gregarious animals such as cranes, ants, or bees. [King] Solomon refers to this when he says "It is better for two to live together than alone, for they have the advantage of mutual company."[2]

Therefore if it is natural for man to live in association with others, there must be some way for them to be governed. For if many men were to live together and each to provide what is convenient for himself, the group (*multitudo*) would break up unless one of them had the responsibility for the good of the group, just as the body of a man or an animal would disintegrate without a single controlling force in the body that aimed at the common good of all the members. As Solomon says, "Where there is no ruler, the people will be dispersed."[3] This is reasonable since the private good and the common good are not the same. Private concerns divide the community, while common concerns unite it. Those differences exist for different reasons. Therefore besides what moves each person to his own private good there must be something that moves everyone to the common good of the many. Therefore in everything that is ordered to a single end, one thing is found that rules the rest. In the physical universe, by the intention of divine providence all the other bodies are ruled by the first or heavenly body, as divine providence directs, and all material bodies are ruled by rational creatures.[4] In each man the soul rules the body and within the soul reason rules over passion and desire. Likewise among the parts of the body there is one ruling part, either the heart or the head that moves all the others. So in every group, there must be something that rules.

When things are ordered to some end, one can proceed in the right way and the wrong way. So the government of a group can be carried out in the right way or the wrong way. Something is done in the right way when it is led to its appropriate end, and in the wrong way when it is led to an inappropriate end. The proper end of a group of free men is different from that of a group of slaves, for a free man determines his own actions while a slave, *qua* slave, is one who belongs to another. If then a group of free men is directed by a ruler to the common good of

---

2. Ecclesiastes, 4:9. Ecclesiastes was attributed to Solomon, King of Israel between 971 and 920 B.C.
3. Proverbs, 11:14. The central chapters of Proverbs are also attributed to King Solomon.
4. According to Aquinas's cosmology the stars and planets are arranged hierarchically in a series of spheres with the heavenly sphere and fixed stars on the outside, giving motion to the rest. All the motions of the universe are subject to rational control of God and the intelligences of the angels. For the origins of this cosmology in Aristotle see his *De Caelo (On the Heavens)* I–II.

the group, his government will be right and just because it is appropriate for free men, but if the government is directed not at the common good of the group but at the private good of the ruler it will be unjust and a perversion. God warns such rulers in the Book of Ezekiel, "Woe to shepherds that feed themselves (because they seek their own benefit). Should not the flocks be fed by the shepherd?"[5] Shepherds must seek the good of their flocks, and rulers, the good of those subject to them.

If a government is under one man who seeks his own benefit and not the good of those subject to him, the ruler is called a tyrant. The word is derived from *tyro*, the Greek word for "strength," because he uses force to oppress the people instead of justice to rule. Hence among the ancients all powerful men were called tyrants. But if an unjust government is exercised not by one but by more than one, if they are few it is called an oligarchy which means "rule by the few." In this case a few rich men oppress the people. Such a government differs only in number from a tyranny. An unjust government exercised by the many is called a democracy, that is, "rule by the people," which occurs when the common people use the force of numbers to oppress the rich. In this case the whole people acts like a tyrant.[6]

We can also classify the types of just government. If the government is carried out by a large number, as when a group of warriors governs a city or province, it is usually called a polity.[7] But if a few virtuous men carry out the administration, a government of this kind is called an aristocracy, that is the best rule, or rule of the best, who for this reason are called the aristocrats. But if a good government is in the hands of one man alone, it is appropriate to call him a king. So the Lord said in [the Book of] Ezekiel, "My servant David will be king all over, and there will be one shepherd over all of them."[8] Thus it is very clear that it is the nature of kingship that there should be one to rule and that he should be a shepherd who seeks the common good of all and not his own benefit.

Since men must live together because they cannot acquire what is needed to live if they remain by themselves, a social group is more perfect if it provides better for the necessities of life. A family in a single household provides adequately for some of the needs of life such as the natural acts of nourishment and the procreation of children, etc. In a single locality you will find self-sufficiency in a given manufacture. But a city which is a perfect community contains whatever is needed for life, and even more so a province because of the need for common defense and mutual aid against enemies. Therefore the right name for someone who rules a perfect community, whether a city or a province, is a king,

---

5. Ezekiel, 34:2.
6. This classification is derived from Aristotle's *Politics*, III, 7–8.
7. This is a garbled reference to Aristotle's assertion (*Politics*, III, 7) that the shared excellence or virtue of a good government by the many is likely to be military, and the franchise will be related to the possession of arms.
8. Ezekiel, 37:24. The reference is to King David who ruled over Israel in the 10th Century B.C. and was believed to be author of the Pslams.

while someone who directs a household is not called a king but the father of a family. Yet there is a certain resemblance to a king in his position so that sometimes kings are called the fathers of their people.

From what we have said it is clear that a king is one who rules over the people of a city or a province for the common good. So Solomon says in [the Book of] Ecclesiastes. "A king commands all the lands subject to him."[9]

Chapter 2

Is it Better for a Group to Be under One Ruler or Many?

Next we must inquire as to whether it is better for a province or a city to be ruled by one person or by many. We will approach this question from the point of view of the purpose of government.

The aim of any ruler should be to promote the welfare of the territory that he has been given to rule. The aim of a helmsman is to preserve his ship from the dangers of the sea and to bring it safely to port. The welfare of any organized group is based on the preservation of its unity in what we call peace. Without peace life in society is no longer beneficial and its divisions make social life burdensome. Thus the most important responsibility of the ruler of a community is to achieve unity in peace. Just as a doctor does not debate whether to cure a sick man under his care there is no reason for a ruler to question whether he should maintain the peace of the community under him. No one should debate about the end of an action but about the appropriate means. Therefore the Apostle [Paul] when he endorses the unity of the faithful says, "Be solicitous to preserve the unity of the spirit in the bond of peace."[1] Thus the more effective a government is in promoting unity in peace, the more useful it will be. We say more useful, because it leads more directly to its end. But it is evident that that which is itself one can promote unity better than that which is a plurality, just as the most effective cause of heat is that which is in itself hot. Therefore government by one person is better than by many.

Furthermore, it is evident that many persons cannot preserve the unity of a group if they generally disagree. Some agreement among them is necessary for them to govern at all. A number of men could not move a ship in one direction unless they worked together in some way. But a number of people are said to be united to the extent that they come closer to unity. It is better therefore for one person to rule than for many to try to achieve unity.

In addition, whatever is in accord with nature is best, for nature always operates for the best. But in nature government is always by one. Among the members of the body, the heart moves all the other parts; among the parts of the soul one power, reason, predominates. Among the bees there is one king bee, and in the whole universe one God is the Maker and

Ruler of all.[2] This is in accord with reason since every plurality derives from unity. Therefore since art imitates nature and a work of art is better to the degree that it resembles what is in nature, it follows that it is best for a human group *(multitudo)* to be ruled by one person.

This is also apparent from experience. Provinces and cities that are not ruled by one person are torn by dissension and disputes without peace so that the words of the Lord spoken through the Prophet [Jeremiah] seem to be fulfilled, "Many shepherds have destroyed my vineyard."[3] On the other hand provinces and cities under a single king enjoy peace, justice flourishes, and they delight in the abundance of wealth. Hence the Lord through his prophets promises the people as a great favor that he will place them under one hand and that there will be "one prince in the midst of them."[4]

Chapter 3

Just Rule by One Person Is the Best Form of Government; Its Opposite Is the Worst.

Just as government by a king is best, so government by a tyrant is the worst. Democracy stands in opposition to polity as indicated above, since both are governments by the many. Oligarchy is opposed to aristocracy, since both are governments by the few. Kingship is the opposite of tyranny since both are governments by one person. We have shown above that kingship is the best form of government. Since that which is opposite to the best is the worst, it follows that tyranny is worst form of government.[5]

In addition a force that is united is more effective than one that is divided. Many persons working together can pull a load that individually they could not pull. Thus just as a force operating for good is better at producing good if it is one, so a force operating for evil is more harmful if it is one rather than divided. The power of an unjust ruler operates to the detriment of the group because he replaces the common good of the group with his own advantage. Similarly in good governments, since a more unified government is a more effective one, monarchy is better than aristocracy, and aristocracy is better than polity, while in bad governments the opposite is the case so that the more unified it is the more harmful it is. Thus tyranny is more harmful than oligarchy and oligarchy is more harmful than democracy.

Furthermore what makes a government unjust is the fact that the private interest of the ruler is pursued in preference to the common good of the society. The further he departs from the common good, the more unjust his government will be. An oligarchy departs from the common good more than a democracy because it seeks the good of the few rather

2. Aquinas probably derived his (inaccurate) knowledge of bees from Aristotle, *History of Animals*, V, 21.
3. Jeremiah, 12:10.

4. Jeremiah, 30:21. However, see the warning of the dangers of monarchy in I Samuel, 8.
5. See Aristotle, *Politics*, III, 7.

than the many. Tyranny departs still more from the common good because it seeks the good of only one person. The greater number comes nearer to the whole than a few, and the few nearer than only one person. Tyranny therefore is the most unjust form of government.

We can see this when we consider the order of divine providence which directs everything in the best way. The good in things results from a single perfect cause, that is, from everything working together for good, while evil results from individual defects. There is no beauty in a body unless all its parts are properly integrated. Ugliness results from one member not fitting in properly. And so ugliness comes in different ways from many different causes while beauty comes in one way from a single perfect cause. In all cases of good and evil God seems to provide that good from one cause will be stronger and evil from many causes will be weaker. It is proper therefore that just government should be exercised by one person so that it can be stronger. But if the government becomes unjust it is better that it be exercised by many, so that it is weaker because of internal divisions. Therefore among unjust governments democratic government is the most tolerable of the unjust forms of government, while tyranny is the worst.

This is also apparent when one considers the evils that result from tyranny. The tyrant despises the common good and seeks his private good and as a result he oppresses his subjects in different ways and which goods will be affected will depend on the various passions to which he is subject. If he is subject to the passion of greed, he steals the property of his subjects. Thus Solomon says "A just king improves the land; a greedy man destroys it."[6] If he is dominated by the passion of anger, he sheds blood for nothing, so that it is said in Ezekiel "The princes among them are like wolves seizing their prey and shedding blood."[7] The wise man advises us to avoid this kind of government when he says "keep away from the man with the power to kill"[8] for he does not kill in pursuit of justice but uses his power to satisfy his willful lust. Thus when the ruler departs from law there is no security and everything is uncertain. No reliance can be placed on the will, not to speak of the lust, of another. He threatens not only the bodies of his subjects but also their spiritual welfare, since those who seek to use rather than to be of use to their subjects oppose any progress by their subjects since they suspect that any excellence among their subjects is a threat to their unjust rule. Tyrants always suspect the good rather than the evil and are always afraid of virtue. They seek to prevent their subjects from becoming virtuous and developing a public spiritedness which would not tolerate their unjust domination. They prevent the bond of friendship from developing among their subjects and the enjoyment of mutual peace since as long as there is mutual distrust no attempt can be made to overthrow their rule. Therefore tyrants sow discord among them, promote dissension, and

6. Proverbs, 29:4.
7. Ezekiel, 22:27.

8. Sirach (Wisdom), 9:13.

prohibit gatherings such as marriage celebrations and feasts and the like
that foster familiarity and mutual trust among men.[9] They try to prevent
their subjects from becoming powerful or rich since, judging their subjects on the basis of their own bad consciences, they suspect that they
will also use their power and wealth to harm them. Thus Job says of the
tyrant, "The sound of terror is always in his ears and even when there is
peace (that is, no one is trying to harm him) he always suspects plots."[1]
Thus it is that because rulers instead of inducing their subjects to be
virtuous are wickedly jealous of their virtue and hinder it as much as
they can, very few virtuous men are found under tyrants. For as Aristotle
says, "Brave men are found where brave men are honored,"[2] and Cicero
says, "What is despised by everyone decays and ceases to grow."[3] It is
natural that men who are brought up in fear should become servile in
spirit and cowardly in the face of any difficult or strenuous endeavor. So
the Apostle [Paul] says "Fathers, do not provoke your children to indig-
nation lest they become discouraged."[4] King Solomon had these evil
effects of tyranny in mind when he said "When the wicked reign it is
the ruination of men"[5] because the wickedness of tyranny leads their
subjects to fall away from the perfection of virtue. He also says "When
the wicked take power, the people weep as if they were being led into
slavery" and "When the wicked rule, men will go into hiding" to avoid
the cruelty of tyrants.[6] This is no wonder since one who does not rule
according to reason but following the lusts of his spirit is no different
from a beast, so that Solomon says "A wicked prince over his poor people is like a roaring lion and a ravenous bear."[7] So men hide from tyrants
as from cruel beasts and there is no difference between being subject to
a tyrant and being ravaged by a wild beast.

Chapter 4

*The Kinds of Government in Rome, and How the Republic Sometimes
Prospered under Popular Rule.*

Because monarchy, defined as the rule of one man, can result in both
the best and worst forms of government, kingship is considered by many
people as odious because it is associated with the evils of tyranny. Sometimes those who desire to be ruled by a king are subjected to the savagery
of tyrants and many rulers who are tyrants disguise themselves as kings.
The Roman Republic is an example of this. The Roman people drove
out their kings because they could not support the burden of their tyrannical rule. They established consuls and other magistrates who began to
rule and govern them since they wished to change from monarchy to
aristocracy. Sallust refers to this when he says, "It is incredible to recall
how rapidly the city of Rome grew in a short time, once it had won its

9. The preceding description is similar to Aristotle's discussion of methods of preserving a tyranny in *Politics*, V, 11.
1. Job, 15:21.
2. Aristotle, *Nicomachean Ethics*, III.

3. Cicero, *Tusculan Disputations*, I, 2, 4.
4. Colossians, 3:21.
5. Proverbs, 28:12.
6. Proverbs, 29:2; 28:28.
7. Proverbs, 28:15.

liberty."[8] It often happens that men who live under a king are reluctant to work for the common good since they think that what they do for the common welfare will not benefit them but someone else who seems to have the common good under his control. But if they do not see one person in control of the community, they all work for the common good as if it were their own rather than belonging to someone else. Thus experience shows that a city that changes its administration every year can sometimes accomplish more than three or four cities ruled by a king, and small services exacted by kings weigh more heavily than heavy burdens imposed by a community of citizens. This was true in the development of the Roman Republic. The common people were conscripted for military service and were paid wages for their military service. When the general treasury was not sufficient to pay those wages, private wealth was put to public use so that even the senators did not keep anything made of gold for themselves except one gold ring and their individual seals of office.[9] However when their continual dissension finally led to civil war, the liberty for which they had worked so hard was snatched from their hands and they came under the power of emperors who never called themselves kings because that title was hated by the Romans.[1] Some of them faithfully served the common good like kings, and by their efforts the Roman commonwealth was increased and preserved. But most of them became tyrants over their subjects and weak and vacillating to their enemies and brought the Roman commonwealth to naught.

A similar process took place among the Jewish people. At first when they were ruled by judges they were devastated by their enemies everywhere, for everyone did what he pleased. But when at their insistence God gave them kings, the kings became wicked and they withdrew from the worship of the one God and finally were led into captivity.[2] Thus there are dangers on both sides. Either because of fear of tyranny the advantages of the best form of government, kingship, are lost, or when they seek those advantages, the government of the king turns into an evil tyranny.

Chapter 5

Tyranny is More Likely to Develop from the Rule of the Many than of One Person. Therefore Monarchy Is Preferable.

If a choice has to be made between two courses of action both of which involve danger, one should choose the course that leads to the lesser evil. A monarchy which changes into a tyranny leads to less evil

---

8. This discussion is based on St. Augustine, *The City of God*, V, 12. Here as elsewhere Aquinas demonstrates the profound influence of Augustine (354–430) upon his thought. Sallust was a Roman historian (86–34 B.C.). Tarquin the Proud, the last Roman king was expelled in 509 B.C., and the executive power was divided between two consuls.
9. St. Augustine, *The City of God*, III, 19.
1. Aquinas is referring to the series of civil wars in

Rome that began with the wars between Marius and Sulla in 86 B.C. and culminated in the victory of Julius Caesar over Pompey and his followers between 49 and 45 B.C. They are discussed in St. Augustine, *The City of God*, III, 30.
2. 1 Samuel, 8 describes the request for a king by the elders of the Jewish people, and God's description of the negative aspects of kingship.

than the corruption of an aristocracy. The dissension that usually results from a government involving many people works against peace which is the most important social good. But a tyrant does not destroy peace but only takes away some of the goods of individual men—unless the tyranny is so excessive that it adversely affects the whole community. Therefore government by one person is preferable to government by many, although there are dangers in both.

In addition, we should avoid the course from which dangers more frequently follow. The greatest dangers to the community more often result from the government of the many than from government by one person. When there are many people in government it is more likely that any one of them will fail to be concerned with the common good than when there is only one. When many people are exercising rule and one of them ceases to be concerned with the common good, there is danger of strife among their subjects because dissension among the rulers leads to general dissension. But if one person is in charge, he will generally be concerned with the common good, or if he diverts his attention from the common good, it does not immediately follow that he will proceed to oppress his subjects and become an extreme tyrant, which is the worst kind of wicked government as we have shown above. So the dangers that arise from government by the many are more to be avoided than those that result from monarchy.

Furthermore, government by the many is not less likely than monarchy to become tyrannical, but more likely to do so. When dissension breaks out in a government by the many it often happens that one person dominates the others and usurps power over the multitude for himself, as can be clearly seen from the record of history. Nearly all governments by the many have ended in tyranny, as is demonstrated in the case of the Roman commonwealth. After it had been ruled by magistrates for a long time, plots, dissension, and civil war arose and it fell under the most cruel tyrants. Whether we look to the past or the present we see that tyranny more often is exercised in lands that were governed by the many rather than in those ruled by one. Thus if (it is argued that) monarchy—the best form of government—is to be avoided mainly because of the danger of tyranny, and tyranny is more likely to result from government by the many, the conclusion is simply that it is better to live under a single monarch than under the government of the many.[3]

Chapter 6

The Rule of One Man Is Best. How to Limit the Possibility of Tyranny. Tyranny Is to Be Tolerated to Avoid Greater Evils.

The rule of one man is preferred as the best form of government, but because it can change into a tyranny—the worst form of government—a particular effort must be made to ensure that the community will have

3. On the debate among the scholastic philosophers over the relative merits of monarchy and republicanism, see Quentin Skinner, *The Foundations of Modern Political Thought,* vol. 1, (Cambridge: Cambridge University Press, 1978), ch. 3.

a king who will not become a tyrant. In the first place those whose duty it is to select the king should elevate someone to that office who is of such a character that it is unlikely that he will become a tyrant. Hence Samuel commends the providence of God in establishing a king when he says, "The Lord has sought for himself a man after his own heart."[4] Then once the king is established the government of the kingdom should be so constituted as to provide no opportunity for him to become a tyrant. His power should be limited so that he can not easily fall into tyranny. We will discuss later how this can be done.[5] Finally we must consider what to do if the king does become a tyrant.

If the tyranny is not extreme, it is better to tolerate a mild tyranny for a time rather than to take action against it that may bring on many dangers that are worse than the tyranny itself. For it may be that those who revolt against the tyrant cannot prevail, and the tyrant then is provoked to become more extreme. If the opposition to the tyrant does prevail, the result is that there are deep divisions in the populace, and the community is divided into rival groups either during the revolt or regarding the structure of the government after the tyrant has been overthrown. Again it sometimes happens that after someone has aided the community to overthrow the tyrant, he uses the power he has acquired to seize control of the tyranny, and out of fear that he may share the fate of his predecessor imposes a worse slavery upon the subjects. It often happens with tyrannies that a subsequent tyrant is worse than his predecessor because he abandons none of the oppressive measures of his predecessor but with intensified malice invents new ones. Thus at a time when everyone in Syracuse wished for the death of Dionysius, an old woman kept praying for his safety and continued survival. When the tyrant found out about this he asked her why she did it. She replied, "When I was a little girl we were ruled by an evil tyrant and I kept praying that he would die. When he was killed his successor was still more oppressive, and I kept wishing for his rule to end. Then we began to have a third ruler who was even worse—you. And so if you are taken from us a worse ruler will take your place."[6]

If the tyranny is so extreme that it is unbearable, some have argued that it is a virtuous act for brave men to run the risk of death in order to kill a tyrant and liberate the community. We have an example of this in the Old Testament where a certain Ehud killed Eglon, the king of Moab, with the dagger on his thigh because he was oppressing the people of God—and was made a judge of the people.[7] But this is not in accord-

4. 1 Samuel, 13:14. Samuel an eleventh-century B.C. Hebrew prophet, anointed Saul as Israel's first king.

5. This discussion never takes place since Aquinas did not complete the treatise. For his ideas on how kingship should be limited, see his discussion of the mixed constitution in the Summa Theologiae, I–II, qu. 105, on p. 58.

6. The source of this story is probably the work of the thirteenth century Dominican historian, Vin-

cent of Beauvais (1190–1264), Speculum Historiale, III, 73. Dionysius was a tyrant who ruled the Greek colony of Syracuse in Sicily in the time of Plato (fourth century B.C.).

7. Judges, 3:15–24. Aquinas may be replying to the argument for tyrannicide made by the medieval political theorist, John of Salisbury (1120–1180), who cites the Old Testament example in his Policraticus (VIII, 20).

ance with Apostolic teaching. Peter teaches us to be subject not only to good and temperate rulers but also to the ill-tempered. "If anyone bears undeserved suffering out of reverence for God, this is (the work of) grace."[8] Thus when the Roman emperors persecuted the Christian faith the great number of people, both nobles and commoners, who were converted to the faith did not resist but patiently suffered death for Christ, as happened in the case of the holy legion of Thebes.[9] In Ehud's case, he must be understood as having killed an enemy king rather than a ruler of the people who was a tyrant. Again in the Old Testament we read that those who killed Joas, the King of Judah, were put to death despite the fact that he was an apostate—but that following the provisions of the law their children were spared.[1] It would be very dangerous for the community and for its rulers if any individual, using his private judgment, could attempt to kill those in government, even when they are tyrants.[2] This is because evil men are more likely to expose themselves to the danger involved (in an assassination attempt) than are good men. Evil men find the rule of kings no less oppressive than that of tyrants since, [King] Solomon says, "A wise king scatters the impious."[3] The more likely consequences of such presumption would therefore be to threaten the community with the loss of its king, rather than to benefit it by getting rid of a tyrant.

It seems that the solution for the evils of tyranny lies not in the private decision of a few but in proceeding through public authority. First of all, if a given community has the right to appoint a ruler it is not unjust for the community to depose the king or restrict his power if he abuses it by becoming a tyrant. The community should not be accused of disloyalty if it desposes a tyrant even if it had previously agreed to obey him forever, since he did not rule the community as the office of king requires and thus he deserved to have his subjects break their agreement. So the Romans who had accepted Tarquin the Proud (as their king) expelled him from the kingdom because of the tyrannous rule that he and his children exercised and replaced him with the lesser power of the consuls. So also Domitian after he had succeeded two mild emperors, Vespasian, his father, and Titus, his brother, was executed by the Roman senate when he ruled tyrannically, and all the wicked actions that he had done to the Romans were properly annulled by senatorial decree.[4] It was as a result of that senatorial decree that Blessed John the Evange-

---

8. I Peter, 2:19.

9. The Theban Legion was a legendary legion of 6600 Christian soldiers under St. Mauritius who were supposed to have been killed by Emperor Maximilian (285–310) for refusing to participate in the persecution of Christians. Historians doubt the authenticity of the legend.

1. II Kings, 14:5–6. Joas was king of Judah, 835–796 B.C.

2. Note that elsewhere Aquinas took different positions on resistence to tyranny. In the *Summa Theologiae*, II–II, qu. 42, a.2 (below, p. 65) he says that the overthrow of tyrants is not sinful. In the *Commentary on the Sentences of Peter Lombard*, II, D.44 qu. 2 (see footnote 8 on p. 65), written when he was a young man, he seems to endorse killing a tyrant who has usurped his office (as distinct from one who has abused his power).

3. Proverbs, 20:26.

4. St. Augustine, *The City of God*, V, 12 and 21. Domitian was Roman emperor from A.D. 81–96 during the last years of the life of St. John, the author of the Fourth Gospel.

list, the beloved disciple of God who had been exiled to the island of Patmos, was brought back to Ephesus.

If on the other hand it is the right of a higher authority to appoint a king over a certain community, then the remedy for the wickedness of the tyrant is to be sought from that authority. Thus when Archelaus began to rule in Judea in place of Herod, his father, and proceeded to imitate his father's wickedness, the Jews complained about him to Caesar Augustus. At first his power was limited by taking away the title of king from him and dividing half of his kingdom between his two brothers. Then when this did not keep him from ruling in a tyrannical fashion, he was exiled by Tiberius Caesar to Lyons, a city in Gaul.[5]

However if no human aid is possible against the tyrant, recourse is to be made to God, the king of all, who is the help of those in tribulation. * * * But for a people to merit such a benefit from God, they must abstain from sin, since God allows the impious to rule as a punishment for sin, as the Lord says in [the Book of] Hosea, "I will give you a king in my wrath"[6] and in [the Book of] Job, "He maketh a man who is a hypocrite to rule because of the sins of the people."[7] Therefore, for the scourge of tyranny to cease, guilt must first be expiated.

Chapter 12

The Duties of a King. The Likeness of the King in His Kingdom to the Soul in the Body and to God in the Universe.

Next we will consider the duty of a king and how he should act. Since art imitates nature and we learn from nature how to act in accordance with reason, it seems best to derive the duties of a king from the examples of government that appear in nature. In nature we find both a universal and a particular form of government. The universal government is the one by which God through his providence governs everything in the universe. The particular rule that is found in man is like God's rule, and therefore he is called a microcosm *(minor mundus)* because the form in which the universe is ruled is also found within him. Just as all created material things and all spiritual powers come under the rule of God, so also the parts of the body and other powers of the soul are ruled by reason, so that reason acts in man in the way that God acts in the world. Moreover since we have shows above, man is by nature a social animal who lives in community, there is a likeness to the divine rule not only in the fact that the individual is directed by his reason, but that the reason of one man directs the group *(multitudo)*, as the special responsibility of the king. Among certain animals that are organized socially, there is (also) a kind of likeness to this form of rule. The bees are said to have kings, not because they are ruled by reason in this way,

---

5. Aquinas's source is the standard commentary *(Glossa Ordinaria)* to the Gospel of Matthew which in turn relies on Josephus's *History of the Jews.*

Archelaus ruled Judea from 4 B.C. to A.D. 6.
6. Hosea, 13:11.
7. Job, 34:30.

but by a natural instinct implanted by the Highest Ruler, the Author of Nature. Therefore the king should recognize that he has a duty to act in his kingdom like the soul in the body and God in the world. If he recognizes this, he will be driven by a zeal for justice when he considers that he has been appointed to exercise judgment over the kingdom in God's place, and he will acquire kindness and mercy when he regards the individuals under his rule as members of his own body. * * *

Chapter 14

The King Should Follow the Example of God's Rule. The Similarity between Government and Piloting a Ship. A Comparison of the Rule of Priests and Kings.

Just as the way to establish a city or a kingdom can be learned from the creation of the world, so its principle of government can be taken from the governance of the world. We must first keep in mind that to govern is to direct what is governed to its appropriate end. A ship is said to be governed when the sailor guides it on its right course safely to port. If a thing is ordered to an end beyond itself, as a ship is to its port, it is the duty of the one who directs it not only to keep it safe but to bring it to the goal which is beyond it. But if something did not have an end beyond itself, the task of the one who directed it would be to keep it unharmed and in good condition. While there is nothing of this kind among created things—only God Himself who is the end of all—things that are ordered to an external goal are cared for in many ways by different people. One man may be responsible for keeping something in good condition, and another for improving it, as in the case of a ship that we have given as an example of government. The carpenter has the responsibility for repairing any damage on the ship while the sailor has the task of guiding the ship to port. The same thing happens in the case of man. The doctor is responsible for keeping a man in good health; the steward for keeping him supplied with the necessities of life; the scholar is responsible for his knowing truth; and the instructor in morals for teaching him to live according to reason. If man were not ordered to some good beyond himself, these attentions would suffice for him.

There is a good that is extraneous to man as long as he lives his mortal life—final happiness *(beatitudo)* in the enjoyment of God which awaits him after death. As the Apostle [Paul] says, "While we are in the body, we are exiled from the Lord."[8] So it is that the Christian for whom that happiness has been bought by the blood of Christ and who has received the gift of the Holy Spirit to attain it, needs further spiritual guidance to direct him to the port of eternal life. This responsibility over the faithful is exercised by the ministers of the Church of Christ.

The same conclusion must be drawn for the end of a whole society or that of an individual man. If the end of man were some good in man

---

8. II Corinthians, 5:6.

himself, then the end of the government of society *(multitudinis)* would also be to secure and preserve that good for society. If that ultimate end of man and society were the life and health of the body, doctors would rule. If the ultimate end were affluence and wealth a steward would be king. If the knowledge of truth were to be attained by the multitude, the king would be a scholar. But it seems that the end of organized society is to live a life of virtue. Men gather together so that they may live well which they could not do if they lived by themselves. The good life is one that is lived in accordance with virtue. Therefore the virtuous life is the end of human society.

An indication of this is the fact that only those who share in the good life are parts of organized society *(multitudinis)*. If men came together simply for the sake of mere existence, animals and slaves would have a part in civil society *(congregationis)*. If they did so in order to acquire riches, all those engaged in trade would belong to one city. But we see that only those who are under the same laws and government for the purpose of living the good life are considered to be members of a society.[9] Now, because the man who lives the life of virtue is destined for a higher end which is, as we have said, the enjoyment of the divine, this must also be the final end of human society. The final end of organized society then is not [merely] to live the life of virtue but through a life of virtue to attain the enjoyment of God. If it were possible to arrive at this end by the power of human nature, it would be the duty of kings to direct men to this end. (We mean by the term, king, the one who has the highest responsibility for human affairs.) Government is of a higher order when it is ordered towards a further end. The one who is responsible for the last end directs those who are responsible for carrying out the things that are ordered to that end. Thus the navigator who is responsible for piloting the ship directs the shipbuilder as to the most suitable type of ship to construct and the citizen who bears arms tells the blacksmith what kind of weapons to make. But man cannot attain the enjoyment of God by human power but only by the power of God as the Apostle [Paul] tells us, "The gift of God is eternal life."[1] Divine, not human rule, will lead to that end. This kind of rule belongs to the king who is both God and man, Our Lord Jesus Christ, who by making men sons of God has led them to the glory of heaven.

This is the government given to him, a rule which will never pass away, by virtue of which he is called both priest and king in the Sacred Scriptures, where [the Prophet] Jeremiah says, "The king shall reign and he shall be wise."[2] From him a royal priesthood derives. What is more, all those who believe in Christ as his members are called priests and kings. So that spiritual and earthly things may be kept distinct, the ministry of this kingdom is entrusted not to earthly kings but to priests, and especially to the Highest Priest, the successor of Peter, the Vicar of Christ,

9. See Aristotle, *Politics*, I, 2, 4, 9; III, 1.   2. Jeremiah, 23:5.
1. Romans, 6:23.

the Roman Pontiff, to whom all kings over Christian peoples should be subject as to Christ himself. For those who are responsible for intermediate ends should be subject to the one who is responsible for the ultimate end, and be directed by his command.[3] Since the pagan priesthood and the whole cult of the gods were for the purpose of acquiring temporal goods to serve the common good of society which was the responsibility of the king, it was proper that the priest should be subject to the pagan kings. Also in the Old Law since the people who espoused the true religion were promised early goods not by demons but by God, we read that in the Old Law priests were subject to kings. But under the New Law there is a higher priesthood that leads men to the joys of heaven, so that under the law of Christ, kings should be subject to priests.

Chapter 15

To Gain the Ultimate End, the King Should Direct His Subjects to a Life of Virtue as Well as to Intermediate Ends. What is Needed for the Good Life.

Just as the good life of men here is directed to the blessed life which we hope for in heaven as its end, so also all the good things that men secure, whether wealth or money or health or skill or learning, are directed to the good of the community as their end. As has been said, the one who is responsible for an ultimate end should rule over those who are in charge of things that are ordered to that end and should direct them by his rule. It is clear from this that just as the king ought to be subject to the dominion and rule of the priestly office, so he should rule over all human offices and direct them by the power of his rule. Whoever is to do something that is ordered to another end should see to it that his work is suited to that end. The swordmaker makes a sword that can be used in battle and the builder makes a house that is suitable for habitation. Therefore since the end of the good life that we live on earth is the happiness *(beatitudo)* of heaven, it is the duty of the king to promote the good life of the community so that it leads to happiness in heaven— so that he should command the things that lead to heavenly bliss and as far as possible forbid their opposite. The way to true bliss as well as the obstacles to achieving it are known from the Divine Law which priests are obliged to teach. * * * A king therefore, being instructed in the Divine Law, should make a special effort to ensure that the society under him lives well. This involves three things—first, he should establish the

---

3. Compare this apparent assertion of the direct subordination of the temporal to the spiritual authority with a passage that appears to support a theory justifying indirect intervention for spiritual reasons ("indirect power in temporals") in *Summa Theologiae*, II–II, qu. 60, a. 6 (below, p. 69). Note also the combination of the two theories in the *Commentary on the Sentences*, D. 44, qu. 2, a. 4 (below, p. 69). See James A. Weisheipl, *Friar Thomas D'Aquino* (New York: Doubleday, 1974),

190–195, for an attempt to harmonize the three passages by arguing that "the jurisdiction of the secular ruler can in no way be at the sufferance of the Pope, and the author of *De Regno*, I, 14 does not teach this." Weisheipl believes Aquinas is only asserting the moral authority of the Church, not its legal right to intervene by, for example, deposing rulers and transferring titles to kingdoms which the adherents of the direct power claimed for the pope.

good life of the community *(multitudine)* under him; second, he should defend it once it is established; and third, once secured he should foster its improvement.

Two things are required for an individual man to lead a good life. The first and most important is to act in accordance with virtue since virtue is what makes one live well. The second—and it is secondary and a means to the first—is a sufficiency of the material goods that are necessary for virtuous action.[4] Nature makes man a unity, but the unity of society which we call peace is achieved through the efforts of the ruler. There are three requirements for the good life of a social group. First, the society must be united in peace. Secondly, the society thus united must be directed towards acting well. Just as a man cannot do anything unless there is unity among the parts of his body, so a number of men who are disunited can not act well because they fight among themselves. A third requirement is that the king work to see that there is a sufficient supply of the necessities required to live well. * * *

4. Cf. Aristotle, *Nicomachean Ethics*, X, 8.

THE SUMMA OF THEOLOGY
(SUMMA THEOLOGIAE, 1266–1273)

I   Part I (1266–1268)

Qu. 2. The Existence of God

3   Does God Exist?
Obj. 1.   It seems that there is no God. For if one of two opposing entities were to exist without limitation the other would be totally destroyed. But the word, God, means something that is infinitely good. Therefore if there were a God, evil would not exist. But we encounter evil in the world. Therefore there is no God.

Obj. 2.   Furthermore what can be explained by a few causes should not be explained by many. But it seems that everything we see in the world can be explained by other causes without assuming that God exists, because natural things are explained by natural causes, while those that are done for a purpose are the products of human reason and will. Therefore there is no need to suppose that God exists.

On the contrary, God says in the Scripture, "I am who am."[1]

I answer that the existence of God can be proved in five ways:
The first and most obvious way is the argument from motion.[2] It is certain and evident to our senses that things are in motion in this world. Everything that moves is moved by something else, for nothing can move unless it has the potentiality of acquiring the perfection of that towards which it moves. To move something is to act, since to move is to make actual what is potential. Now nothing can be changed from a state of potentiality to actuality except by something that itself is in a state of actuality.[3] A fire that is actually hot makes wood that is potentially hot become actually hot, and so moves and changes it. Now it is impossible for the same thing to be both in actuality and in potentiality at the same time and in the same respect—only in different respects. What is actually hot cannot at the same time be potentially hot, although it is potentially cold. Therefore it is impossible for a thing to be both the mover and the thing moved in the same way, or for it to move itself. Therefore everything that moves must be moved by something else. If that by which it is moved also moves, it must itself be moved by something else and that by something else again. But things can not go on forever because then there would be no first mover, and consequently no subsequent mover since intermediate things move only from the motion they receive from

1. Exodus, 3:14.
2. Cf. Aristotle, *Physics*, VIII, 4–5.
3. Cf. Aristotle, Metaphysics, IX, 7–8.

the first mover—just as a staff moves only because it is moved by a hand. Therefore it is necessary to go back to some first mover who is not moved by anyone, and this everyone understands as God.

The second way is from the nature of an efficient cause.[4] In the world of the senses we find that there is a sequence of efficient causes, but we never find something that causes itself, and it is impossible to do because it would precede itself—which is impossible. Now the series of finite causes cannot go on to infinity because in every series of causes the first cause is the cause of the intermediate cause and intermediate causes cause the last cause, whether the intermediate causes are many or only one. However if you take away a cause you also take away its effect. If there is no first cause among the efficient causes, there will be no last or intermediate cause. But if we proceed to infinity in the series of causes there will be no first cause and therefore no final or intermediate effects would exist—which is obviously not true. Thus it is necessary to posit some first efficient cause which all men call God.

The third way is based on what can exist (possibility) and what must exist (necessity). It is the following: We find things in nature that can exist or not exist, since things are found to come into existence (be generated) and to cease to exist (be corrupted) and therefore it is possible for them to exist or not exist. Now it is impossible for such things always to have existed, for if it is possible for something not to exist, at some time it did not exist. Therefore if it is possible for everything not to exist, at one time nothing was in existence. But if this is true then nothing would exist even now, since that which does not exist only begins to exist through something else that is in existence. But if nothing was in existence it was impossible for anything to begin to exist, and so nothing would exist now—which is obviously not true. Everything cannot be [merely] possible but there must be some necessary being in existence. Something is a necessary being either as a result of the action of another or not. However it is impossible to go on to infinity in [the series of] necessary beings that must exist because they are caused by another, as we have already proved above in the case of efficient causes. We must therefore posit a [necessary] being that must exist in itself and does not owe its existence to anything else, but is the reason that other things must be. This all men call God.

The fourth way is based on the gradations that exist in things. We find in the world that some things are more or less true, or good, or noble and so on. The description of "more" or "less" is given to things to the degree that they approach the superlative in various ways. For example a thing is said to be hotter as it approaches more closely what is hottest. Therefore there is something that is the most true, and best, and most noble, and consequently most fully in being, for the things that are the

---

4. Following Aristotle (*Metaphysics*, V, 2) Aquinas has a broader notion of causality than does modern philosophy. A thing's matter, form, and purpose he calls, respectively, its material cause, formal cause, and final cause, while what we call a cause, Thomas calls an "efficient cause."

greatest in truth are the greatest in being, as is said in the *Metaphysics*.[5]
Now the superlative in any classification *(genus)* is the cause of all the
things in that classification. Fire, for example, which is the hottest of all
things is the cause of everything that is hot, as is said in the same book.
Therefore there is something that is the cause of being and goodness and
whatever perfection everything has, and this we call God.

The fifth way is based on the order *(gobernatio)* in the universe. We
see that things that lack consciousness such as bodies in nature function
purposively. This is evident from the fact that they always, or nearly
always, function in the same way so as to achieve what is best. Therefore
it is evident that they achieve their end, not by chance but by design.
But things that do not possess consciousness tend towards an end only
because they are directed by a being that possesses consciousness and
intelligence, in the same way that an arrow must be aimed by an archer.
Therefore there is an intelligent being who directs all things to their
goal, and we say that this is God.

Reply to Obj. 1.   Augustine says, "Since God is the supremely highest good he would not allow evil to exist in his creation unless he were
so all powerful and good that he could even make good out of evil."[6]
Thus it is part of the infinite goodness of God that he permits evils to
exist so that he can bring good from them.

Reply to Obj. 2.   Since nature acts for a given end at the direction
of a higher agent, the things that take place in nature go back to God as
their first cause. Similarly what is done for a purpose must go back to
some higher cause which is not the reason and will of man because these
are changeable and can cease to exist. Everything that is changeable and
perishable must go back to an unchangeable and necessary first cause
that is unchangeable and self-existent *(per se necessarium)*.

Qu. 12. How We Know God

12   Can We Know God in this Life by Natural Reason?

Our natural knowledge begins from the senses. Therefore our natural
knowledge can only extend as far as it can be led by the objects of the
senses. On the basis of sensory objects our intellect can not go so far as
to see the essence of God, because sensory creatures are effects of God
which are not equal in power to their cause. Hence we cannot know the
full power of God on the basis of the objects of the senses and consequently we cannot see his essence. However because they are effects that
are dependent on a cause, we can be led from them to know that God
exists, and to know the characteristics that he must possess as the first
cause of all things that transcends everything caused by him. Hence we
know about his relationship to his creatures that he is the cause of all,

---

5. Aristotle, *Metaphysics*, II, 1.   6. St. Augustine, *Enchiridion*, ch. 11.

and that creatures differ from him in that he is not a part of the things that he has caused, and that they are separate from him not because of any deficiency on his part but because of his transcendence. * * *

13   *Do We Know God Better through Grace than through Natural Reason?*

We have a more perfect knowledge of God through grace than through natural reason. This is true for the following reason: The knowledge we have by natural reason requires two things, images derived from the objects of the senses and the natural light of the intellect which enables us to abstract intelligible concepts from them. In both these operations human knowledge is assisted by the revelation of grace. The natural light of the intellect is strengthened by the infusion of the light of grace, and by the action of God images are sometimes placed in the imaginations of men that better express divine things than those which we naturally receive from the senses. * * * Although by the revelation of grace in this life we do not know what God is and so are joined to him as to one who is not known, we still know him more fully because many of his most excellent works are demonstrated to us, and because through divine grace we attribute to him many things that the natural reason cannot attain— as, for example, that God is three and one.

Qu. 20. On God's Love

2   *Does God Love All Things?*

God loves everything in existence. Everything in existence in so far as it exists is good, because its existence is a kind of good as is any perfection that it has. We have shown above that the will of God is the cause of everything. Therefore for anything to have existence or any other good it must be willed by God. And so God wills good for every existing thing. Hence it is clear that God loves all things that exist, because to love something is nothing else than to will its good.

God does not love in the same way that we do. Our will is not the cause of the goodness of the things we love but is moved by them as by its object, so that the love by which we will something good is not the cause of the good in it, but on the contrary, what is good or true in it, or thought to be so, evokes our love, which is the will that something should keep the good that it has or acquire what it does not have, and we work to this end. The love of God, however, infuses and creates goodness in things.

Qu. 75. The Essence of the Soul

2   *Is the Soul Self-Subsistent?*

The principle of intellectual operation that we call the soul of man is necessarily a kind of incorporeal and subsistent principle. It is evident that man's intellect can know the natures of bodily things. But for something to know things in this way it cannot have any of their nature in its own because what was in it by nature would obstruct the knowledge of the other things, just as we see that the tongue of a man sick with a bitter fever cannot perceive anything sweet since everything seems bitter to him. Thus if the intellectual principle had the nature of any bodily thing in it, it would not be able to know all bodies [as such] since every body has its own specific nature. It is impossible, therefore, for the principle of the intellect to be something bodily.

It is also impossible for it to know through a bodily organ since the specific nature of the bodily organ would prevent it from knowing all bodies. Thus if a certain color were in the pupil of the eye and in a glass container, liquid poured into it would appear to be of that color.

The intellectual principle that is called the mind or the intellect has an operation of its own that the body does not share. Only that which subsists on its own can function by itself. Only what actually exists can function, and something functions by virtue of what it is. Therefore we do not say that heat causes heat, but that what is hot gives heat. We conclude therefore that the human soul which is called intellect or mind is something incorporeal and subsistent.[7]

5 Is the Soul Composed of Matter and Form?

The soul is not material. * * * This may be demonstrated by considering the specific nature of the human soul as intellectual. It is clear that the way in which something is perceived depends on the character of the thing that does the perceiving. Thus something is known in the way that its form is perceived by the knower. But the intellectual soul knows the nature of a thing absolutely. For example, it knows a stone absolutely as a stone, i.e., the form of the stone is in the intellectual soul in an absolute way as to its nature as a form. Therefore the intellectual soul is absolute form, not something composed of matter and form. If the intellectual soul were something composed of matter and form, the forms of things would be perceived by it individually, and so it would only know the individual thing, as is the case with the senses that receive the forms of things in the organs of the body. For matter is the principle that individualizes the forms. Therefore we conclude that the intellectual soul and every intellectual substance that knows forms as such (absolute) is not a composite of matter and form.[8]

---

7. On the development of the ideas of "substance" and "subsistence," see Appendix 2 of volume 11 of the Blackfriar's Latin-English edition of the *Summa Theologiae* (New York: McGraw Hill, 1970).
8. Aquinas derives the doctrine of hylomorphism—that corporeal things are composed of individualizing matter (*hylē*) and universalizing form

(*morphē*) from Aristotle (*Metaphysics*, VII, 3, XII, 3; *Physics*, II, 1). Every corporeal being shares its formal character or innermost sharping principle with others in the same classification but possesses material quantifiable elements which make it a separate individual instance of the more general group.

6   Is the Human Soul Corruptible?

We must say that the human soul which we call the intellectual principle is incorruptible. * * * Whatever has being in itself cannot be generated or corrupted except in itself, while things that are not self-subsistent
such as incidental characteristics (*accidentia*) and forms that are material
are described as coming into existence and passing away through generation and corruption. We proved earlier that the souls of brute animals
cannot survive by themselves while the human soul can do so. Therefore the souls of animals are corrupted when their bodies are corrupted,
but the human soul could not be corrupted unless it were corrupted of
itself. This is completely impossible, not only for the soul but for any
subsistent entity that is made up only of form. For it is clear that what
belongs to something by virtue of what it is, is inseparable from it. Now
being in itself belongs to a form which is in actualization (*actus*). Therefore matter acquires actual existence when it acquires form, and it ceases
to exist when its form is separated from it. Now it is impossible for a
form to be separated from itself and therefore it is impossible for a self-
subsistent form to cease to exist.[9]

* * *

In things that have knowledge, desire follows knowledge. The senses
only know being as it is, here and now, but the intellect knows it absolutely and for all time. Therefore everything that has an intellect naturally desires to exist forever. However a natural desire can not be in vain.
Therefore every intellectual substance is incorruptible.

Qu. 79. The Powers of the Intellect

12   Is Synderesis a Special Power?

Man's reasoning is a kind of movement which begins with the understanding of certain things that are naturally known as immutable principles without investigation. It ends in the intellectual activity by which
we make judgments on the basis of those principles that are naturally
known in themselves concerning what has been discovered by reasoning. Now it is clear that the practical reason engages in reasoning about
practical matters in the same way that the speculative reason does so
about speculative matters. Therefore just as we must be endowed by
nature with speculative principles, we must also be endowed with practical principles. The basic principles of the speculative reason with which
we are endowed by nature are not based on a power but a disposition
(*habitus*) which is called "the understanding of principles," as the Philosopher [Aristotle] explains.[1] Therefore the first principles of the practical reason with which we are naturally endowed are not based on a

9. This is Aquinas's argument for the immortality
of the soul, as an immaterial and intellectual form.
It is based on the soul's capacity to carry out universal activities, especially the knowledge of "being,"
that are not immediately dependent on sense-per-
ception.
1. Aristotle, *Nicomachean Ethics*, VI, 6.

special power but on a special natural disposition which we call *synderesis*.[2] And so synderesis is described as impelling us to good and opposing evil when we proceed to investigation on the basis of principles and make judgments about what we have discovered.

85. The Manner and Order of Understanding

1 Does Our Intellect Know Bodily and Material Things through Abstraction from Sense Images?

There are three grades of cognitive powers. One cognitive power is the act of a bodily organ, for example, of one of the senses. The object of one of the senses is the form that exists in the bodily matter that makes it an individual. Therefore every sensory power can only know particular things. There is another cognitive power that is not the action of a bodily organ and is not connected with bodily material in any way. An example of this is the intellect of the angels, the cognitive power of which is directed to form, apart from matter, as its object. The angels know material things but only in immaterial things—either in themselves or in God. The human intellect, however, is in an intermediate position. It does not act as an organ, but is a power of the soul which is the form of the body, as is clear from what has been said earlier. Therefore it is is able to know the form that exists individually in corporeal matter but not as it exists in that matter. It knows what is in the individual matter, not as it is in that matter, but by abstracting the form from individual matter as it is represented by sensory images. Therefore we must say that our intellect knows material things by abstracting from sensory images and comes to some knowledge of immaterial things by considering material things in this way.[3]

2 Are the Intelligible Types (Species) Abstracted from Sensory Images Known by the Intellect?

The nature that happens to be known or abstracted or intended to be considered as a universal only exists in individual things, but it is understood, abstracted, or universalized in the intellect. We can see the same thing in the case of the senses. With our sight we see the color of an apple apart from its smell. If someone asks where is the color that is seen apart from the smell it is clear that the color that is seen is only in the apple. However it is perceived apart from the smell by the vision which has received the likeness of the color, not of the smell. Similarly we know humanity only through this or that man but in order to understand humanity apart from individual conditions, that is, to abstract it and as

2. "Synderesis" is a technical term used in medieval philosophy to describe the general disposition or capacity to understand the basic principles of morality, as distinct from conscience which guides us in specific cases. It was first used by St. Jerome in the late classical period, while Thomas probably drew it from St. Bonaventure or Albert the Great.

See article by W. R. Inge in the *Encyclopedia of Religion and Ethics*, vol. 12 (New York: Scribner's, 1922), 157. *Habitus* should not be translated as "habit," although it shares with it the notion of stability and permanence.
3. Cf. Aristotle, *On the Soul*, III, 4–7.

a result to intend to universalize it, humanity must be perceived by the intellect as the likeness of the typical nature, not of the individual men.

Qu. 92. The Creation of Woman

1 Should Woman Have Been Made in the Original Creation?

Obj. 1. It seems that women should not have been made in the original creation, for the Philosopher [Aristotle] says that "A woman is a misbegotten man."[4] Nothing misbegotten or defective should have existed in the original creation. Therefore woman should not have been made in the original creation.

Obj. 2. Subjection and inferiority are the result of sin, for it was said to woman after she sinned, "Thou shalt be under the power of man"[5] and [Pope] Gregory says, "Where we have not sinned we are all equal."[6] Now women by nature are of less virtue and dignity than men, for "That which acts is more honorable than that which is acted upon" as Augustine says.[7] Therefore woman should not have been made in the original creation before man's sin. * * *

I answer that it was necessary for woman to be made, as Scripture says, as a "helpmate" to man—not to help him in other work as some have said[8]—since he can get more effective help from another man—but as a helpmate in procreation.

This can be seen more clearly if we look at the pattern of reproduction among living things. Some things have no active reproductive power in themselves but are reproduced by the action of another species, for example, plants and animals that reproduce without seeds as a result of the action of heavenly bodies upon suitable matter. Others have both the active and passive powers of reproduction as in the case of plants that reproduce from seeds. This is because the noblest activity of plants is reproduction so that it is appropriate that the active power to reproduce should be permanently joined to the passive power to do so.

Perfect animals however possess the active power of reproduction in the male sex and the passive power in the female sex. And because animals possess a vital activity that is more noble than that of procreation, towards which their lives are principally directed, the male sex is not permanently joined to the female sex in perfect animals but only at the time of mating—so that we may think of male and female as becoming one in sexual intercourse in the same ways as plants in which the male and female principles are permanently united, although in some one of them predominates and in some the other. Man however is directed

---

4. Aristotle, The Generation of Animals, II, 3. The "sexism" of Aquinas is derived from Aristotle, and is in tension with the sexual egalitarianism of some parts of the New Testament ("In Christ there is neither male nor female").

5. Genesis, 3:16.
6. Gregory, On Pastoral Care, 2, 6. St. Gregory the Great was pope from A.D. 590 to 604.
7. Augustine, On the Words of Genesis, 12, 16.
8. Augustine, On the Words of Genesis, 9, 3.

towards a still nobler vital activity, which is knowledge. Therefore there was a stronger reason for the distinction between the sexes according to which the female is produced separately from the male but they are joined together as one flesh in the work of procreation, so that immediately after woman was formed, it was said "They shall be two in one flesh."[9]

Reply to Obj. 1.   With respect to her particular nature woman is somewhat deficient and misbegotten. For the active power in the male seed tends to produce a perfect male like itself while when a female is produced it is because of a weakness of active power or some material indisposition or some external change such as a moist south wind as appears in *The Generation of Animals.*[1] However with respect to nature in general, a woman is not something misbegotten but intended by nature to be directed to the work of procreation. What is intended by nature in general derives from God who is the universal author of nature. Therefore when he established nature, he produced both male and female.

Reply to Obj. 2.   Subjection is of two kinds. There is that of the slave in which a superior uses someone subject to him for his own benefit, and this kind of subjection is the result of sin. However there is another type of subjection which is that of the household or the citizen in which the superior makes use of his subjects for their benefit or good. This subjection existed before men sinned. For there would have been a lack of proper order in human society if some were not governed by others who were wiser than they. Woman is naturally subject to man in this kind of subjection because by nature man possesses more discernment of the reason. Inequality among men also existed in the state of innocence, as we will explain below.

Qu. 96. *Dominion among Men in the State of Innocence*

3   *Would All Men Have Been Equal in the State of Innocence?*[2]
There would have been some inequality in the original state—at least as to sex since reproduction could not have taken place without the difference between the sexes. Also with respect to age since some would have been born from others and those who were born would have produced children.

There would also have been differences of goodness [justice] and knowledge in the soul, for man would have functioned on the basis of free will, not by necessity. Therefore he could give greater or lesser attention to the development of his moral and intellectual faculties.

---

9. Genesis, 2:24.
1. Aristotle, *The Generation of Animals*, IV, 2.
2. "The state of innocence" refers to the condition of man before the Fall, (i.e., in the Garden of Eden). For other statements on the natural inferiority of women, see S.T., I, qu.98, a.2 (p. 40) and *Supplement*, qu. 52, reply to obj. 2 (p. 82).

Therefore some would have advanced further in goodness or knowledge than others.

There would also have been physical differences. For the human body was not totally exempt from the law of nature so as not to receive more or less useful and helpful things from outside, and it also needed food to sustain life. And so nothing prevents our saying that depending on the climate or the movements of the stars some would have been born more robust in body than others, and taller or more beautiful or of a better constitution. However there would have been no defect or sin either of soul or body in those who had less of these qualities.

4 Would One Man Have Been Lord over Another in the State of Innocence?

Lordship (Dominium) has two meanings. In the first meaning, it is contrasted with slavery and a lord is someone who has another person as his slave. In another sense it is commonly understood in relation to any kind of subjection so that someone who has the office of governing and directing free men can be called a lord (dominus). In the state of innocence one man would not have been lord over another in the first sense, but in the second sense one man could have had dominion over another. The reason for this is that a slave differs from a free man in that a free man acts for himself (literally—is his own cause) as is said in the beginning of the Metaphysics but a slave is ordered to another.[3] Someone is under the dominion of someone else as a slave when the lord controls him for his own benefit. Since everyone seeks his own good and consequently finds it painful to yield to the decisions of another what should be one's own, this kind of dominion could only be a punishment for those subject to it. Therefore in the state of innocence this kind of dominion of one man over another could not have existed.

However someone can have dominion over another person as a free man, when he directs him to his own good or to the good of the community. There are two reasons that this kind of dominion of man over man would have existed in the state of innocence. First, because man is by nature a social animal so that men in the state of innocence would have lived in society. Now people cannot live in society unless someone is in authority to look after the common good, for the many as such seek different objectives, while one person seeks only one. Therefore the Philosopher [Aristotle] says that when many things are directed to one goal we always find one person at the head to direct them.[4] Secondly, because if one man were superior to the others in knowledge and justice it would not have been appropriate for him not to exercise this superiority for the benefit of the others.

---

3. Aristotle, Metaphysics, I, 2.   4. Aristotle, Politics, I, 2.

Qu. 98. The Preservation of the Race (Species)

2   In the State of Innocence Would Procreation Have Taken Place through Sexual Intercourse?

God made mankind male and female before sin, as Genesis says.[5] Now God does nothing in vain. Therefore, even if man had not sinned sexual intercourse would have taken place because this is the purpose of the differentiation between the sexes. * * * What is natural to man was neither taken away nor added to him by sin. It is clear that as to the animal life that man had before he sinned, it is natural for him to reproduce through sexual intercourse, as it is in the case of other perfect animals. This is proved by the natural members that are assigned by nature to this purpose. Therefore we should not say that these natural members would not have been used before man sinned, just as in the case of his other members.

Sexual intercourse as it exists in this present life should be considered from two points of view. First by nature there is a union of the male and female for the purpose of procreation. In every kind of reproduction there is an active and a passive principle. Since in all things in which there is a difference between the sexes, the active principle is in the male and the passive in the female, the order of nature demands that the male and female reproduce by sexual intercourse.

We can also consider it from the point of view of the deformity produced by excessive desire which would not have existed in the state of innocence because the lower powers would have been subordinated to reason. * * * Beasts are without reason. When man engages in sexual intercourse he becomes like a beast because the reason can not moderate the pleasure of sexual intercourse and the heat of desire. In the state of innocence this would have been moderated by reason not because there would have been less sensual pleasure as some say[6]—for the sensual pleasure would have been greater because it would have been purer in its nature and the body more sensitive—but because the force of desire would not have flowed out in such a disordered way in this type of pleasure since it would have been moderated by reason which does not lessen sensual pleasure but prevents desire from holding to the pleasure in an immoderate fashion. * * * Thus a sober man who eats in moderation has no less pleasure than a glutton, but his desire lingers less over this kind of pleasure. * * * Therefore continence would not have been praiseworthy in the state of innocence, but it is praiseworthy in our present state, not because it prevents reproduction but because it eliminates disordered lust. In the state of innocence, however, reproduction would have taken place without lust.

5. Genesis, 1:27; 2:22.
6. St. Bonaventure (1221–1274) Commentary on the Sentences, II, D.20, qu. 3, following Alexander of Hales (1180–1245), Summa Theologica, I–II, n. 496.

Qu. 108. The Hierarchies and Orders of the Angels

2   Are There Several Orders in Each Hierarchy of the Angels?

A hierarchy is a single principality, that is a group that is ordered in a given way under the government of one ruler *(princeps)*. Now a group would not be ordered but confused if there were not different orders within it. The very nature of hierarchy requires that it contain different orders. The different orders are based on different duties and functions, just as in a city there are different orders according to the different functions. One order is made up of those who are judges, another of those who are soldiers, another of those who labor in the fields, and so on. Where there are many orders in the city, they can all be reduced to three, since every group has a beginning, a middle, and an end. And so in every city three orders of men are found—some who are the highest, the nobles, others who are the lowest, the common people, and others in the middle, the respectable *(honorabilis)* people. In the same way we find that in every hierarchy of the angels there are orders that are differentiated according to their various functions and actions and duties. That differentiation can be reduced to three—the highest, the middle, and the lowest. Therefore Dionysius puts three orders in each hierarchy [of the angels]the Seraphim, Cherubim, and Thrones in the first; the Dominations, Virtues, and Powers in the second, the Principalities, Archangels, and Angels in the third.[7]

---

7. Dionysius, *The Celestial Hierarchy*, VI. Aquinas cites Dionysius 143 times in the *Summa Theologiae*.

I–II The First Part of Part II (1269–1270)

Qu. 3. *What Is Happiness* (Beatitudo)?

8 *Does the Happiness of Man Consist in the Vision of the Divine Essence?*
Final perfect happiness *(beatitudo)* can only come from the vision of
the divine essence. To prove this, two points should be considered. First,
man is not perfectly happy as long as something more remains to be
desired or sought. Second, the perfection of any power is related to the
characteristics of its object. But the object of the intellect is being, that
is the essence of a thing, as is stated in *On the Soul*, Book III.[1]

* * *

If the human intellect knows the essences of created effects but does
not know anything more about God than the fact that he exists it has
not yet been fulfilled by attaining the First Cause directly but it continues to have a natural desire to find out more about that Cause. Therefore
it is not perfectly happy. To be perfectly happy the intellect must reach
to the very essence of the First Cause. In this way it will have its fulfillment by being united with God as its object in whom alone the happiness of man consists.

Qu. 5. *The Attainment of Happiness*

3 *Can Anyone Be Happy in this Life?*
Some partial happiness can be achieved in this life, but true perfect
happiness cannot. * * * Full and sufficient happiness excludes every
evil and fulfills every desire. But in this life all evils cannot be excluded,
since there are many evils in this life that cannot be avoided—ignorance
in the intellect, disordered affection on the part of the appetites, and
different kinds of suffering in the body, as Augustine carefully enumerates in Book XIX of *The City of God*.[2] In addition man's desire for the
good cannot be satisfied in this life, for man has a natural desire that his
good be a lasting one. However the goods of the present life are transitory
since life itself is transitory, although by nature we desire and wish it to
last forever—since man naturally shuns death. Therefore it is impossible
to have true happiness in this life.

Qu. 21. *The Consequences of Human Acts*

4 *Are Good and Evil Human Acts Meritorious or Lacking in Merit in
Relation to God?*
Man is not ordered to the political community in all that he is and
has. Therefore not all of his actions are meritorious or lacking in merit

---

1. Aristotle, *On the Soul*, III, 7.   2. St. Augustine, *The City of God*, XIX, 4.

in relation to the political community. All that man is, or can be, or has, is ordered to God. Therefore every human act that is good or bad is meritorious or lacking in merit in relation to God by virtue of the act itself.

62. The Theological Virtues

3   *Is it Right to Call Faith, Hope, and Charity the Theological Virtues?*
The supernatural virtues direct man to supernatural happiness in the same way that his natural inclinations direct him to his natural end. This happens in two ways. First, through the reason or intellect which contains the universal first principles that are known to us by the natural light of the intellect and are the basis from which reason proceeds in both speculative and practical matters. Second, through a right will that tends naturally to the good as defined by reason. Both of these, however, are inadequate to attain supernatural happiness—as is said in 1 Corinthians, "Eye has not seen nor ear heard nor has it entered into the heart of man the things that God has prepared for those who love him."[3] Therefore some supernatural addition to both the intellect and will was necessary to direct him to his supernatural end. First, certain supernatural principles are added to man's intellect which are received by divine light and these are the objects of belief with which *faith* is concerned. Second, the will is directed to its supernatural end—both as to the movement of its intention towards something that is possible to attain—and this pertains to *hope*, and as to a certain spiritual union which transforms the will to that end—and this takes place through *charity*.

Qu. 81. The Cause of Sin in Man

1   *Was the First Sin of Our First Parent Passed on to His Descendants as Original Sin?*
All men born of Adam may be considered as a single man in that they share in the nature which they have received from their first parent—just as the citizens of one community are considered as one body and the whole community as one man. * * * Thus men are derived from Adam like different members of one body. The acts of one part of the body, for example, a hand, do not take place as a result of the volition of that hand but by the volition of the soul which first moves it. Therefore if a hand commits murder the sin is not considered to have been committed by the hand by itself separately from the body, but it is considered to have been committed by it as part of a man who is moved by the first principle of motion of that man. Thus the disorder that exists in this man born of Adam is not the result of the volition of that man but of that of our first parent who through generation moves all those who derive from him, just as the will of the soul moves all the parts of the

3. 1 Corinthians, 2:9.

body to act. Therefore the sin which is passed on in this way from our first parent to his posterity is called *original sin*, while the sin that is the result of [the action of] the soul upon the parts of the body is called *actual sin*. And just as the actual sin that is committed by any part of the body is not the sin of that member except insofar as it is part of the man—which is the reason that it is called human sin—so original sin is not the sin of this person except insofar as this person receives his nature from his first parent.

The Treatise on Law (Qu. 90–97)

Qu. 90. The Essence of Law

1 Is Law a Matter of Reason?

Law is a rule or measure of action by which one is led to action or restrained from acting. The word law (*lex*) is derived from *ligare*, to bind, because it binds one to act. The rule and measure of action is the reason, which is the first principle of human action. * * * Reason has the power to move the will, as explained above, because whenever someone desires an end, reason commands what is to be done to reach it. In order for an act of will that something is to be done to have the character of law, it must be guided by some reason. This is how we should understand the saying [of Roman law] that "the will of the prince has the force of law."[4] Otherwise the will of the prince would be iniquity rather than law. * * *

2 Is Law Always Directed toward the Common Good?

Every part is ordered to the whole as the imperfect is to the perfect. The individual is part of a perfect whole that is the community. Therefore law must concern itself in particular with the happiness of the community. * * *

3 Can Any Person Make Law?

Obj. 1.   The Apostle [Paul] says that "since the gentiles who have no law do by nature the things that are of the law, they are a law for themselves."[5] But this is applied to everyone. Therefore anyone can make a law for himself.

Obj. 2.   Furthermore as the Philosopher [Aristotle] says in the *Ethics*, "The intention of the legislator is to lead men to virtue."[6] But any man can lead another to virtue. Therefore the reason of any man can make law.

---

4. *Digest*, I, iv, 1.
5. Romans, 2:14.

6. Aristotle, *Nicomachean Ethics*, II, 1.

Obj. 3.   As the prince in a state *(civitas)* is the ruler of the state so also the father of a family is the ruler of the household. But the prince can make law for the state. Therefore any father of a family can make law in his household.

On the contrary, the *Decretum* quotes Isidore as saying, "A law is an ordination of the people which is sanctioned by the elders and approved by the people."[7] Therefore not any person can make a law.

I answer that properly speaking, law has as its first and foremost purpose the ordering of the common good. To order something to the common good is the responsibility of the whole people, or of someone who represents the whole people. Therefore making law belongs either to the whole people or to the public personage who has the responsibility for the whole people, since, as in all other cases, direction towards an end is the responsibility of the one to whom the end belongs.

Reply to Obj. 1.   As is stated above, a law is said to be in someone not only because it involves the participation of the one who makes the law but also that of the one to whom the law applies. And in this way everyone can be said to be a law for himself, because he shares in the action of the legislator. Hence Scripture says in the same place, "they show the work of the law written in their hearts."[8]

Reply to Obj. 2.   A private person cannot effectively lead others to virtue. He can only give advice and if that advice is not followed he has no power of compulsion. Law, however, should have the power to lead to virtue as the Philosopher [Aristotle] says.[9] But the power of compulsion belongs to the whole people *(multitudo)* or to the public personage whose duty it is to inflict punishment, as we explain below. Therefore making law belongs only to him. * * *

Reply to Obj. 3.   A man is part of a household, and a household is part of a city *(civitas).*[1] Now a city [state] is a perfect community as is stated in Book I of the *Politics*. Therefore the good of one man is not a final end but is directed toward the common good, and the good of a single household is ordered to the good of the state that is a perfect community. Therefore the head of a family can make some rules or regulations but they do not, properly speaking, have the character of law.

---

7. Gratian, *Decretum*, I, ii, 1 quoting Isidore, *Etymologies*, V, 10. The *Decretum* is the authoritative twelfth century canon law collection by the Italian monk, Gratian, who systematically organized earlier sources in an attempt to harmonize and integrate church law. Isidore of Seville (560–

636) was the last of the Fathers of the church.
8. Romans, 2:15.
9. Aristotle, *Nicomachean Ethics*, X, 9.
1. Note that Aristotle's "city" *(polis)* is more like our "state" than the city of today.

4   Is Promulgation Necessary for a Law?

In order for a law to have the binding force that is proper to legislation, it must be applied to those who are to be ruled by it. It is applied by being made known to them through promulgation. Therefore promulgation is necessary for a law to have binding force. From the foregoing articles we can derive a definition of law. Law is nothing else than an ordination of reason for the common good promulgated by the one who is in charge of the community.

Qu. 91. The Kinds of Law

1   Is There an Eternal Law?

We have stated above that law is nothing else than a certain dictate of practical reason by a ruler who governs some perfect community. Assuming that the world is governed by divine providence as we argued in Part I, it is evident that the whole community of the universe is governed by the divine reason. Therefore the rational governance of everything on the part of God, as the ruler of the universe, has the quality of law. And since the divine reason's conception of things is not subject to time but is eternal, this kind of law must be called the eternal law.

2   Is There a Natural Law?

Since everything that is subject to divine providence is regulated and measured by the eternal law, as we have shown above, it is evident that all things participate in the eternal law in a certain way because it is imprinted upon them through their respective inclinations to their proper actions and ends. Rational creatures are under divine providence in a more excellent way than the others since by providing for themselves and others they share in the action of providence themselves. They participate in eternal reason in that they have a natural inclination to their proper actions and ends. Such participation in the eternal law by rational creatures is called the natural law.

3   Is There Human Law?

The speculative reason proceeds from naturally known indemonstrable principles to the conclusions of the various sciences which are not innate in us but are acquired by the effort of our reason. In the same way human reason must proceed from the precepts of the natural law as from certain common and indemonstrable principles to other more particular dispositions. Those particular dispositions arrived at by reason are called human laws.

4   Was There a Need for Divine Law?

Besides the natural law and human law it was necessary to have the divine law to direct human life.[2] This is for four reasons: First, law

---

2. Note that divine law for Aquinas meant God's direct revelation in Scripture. It is to be distinguished from eternal law, God's rational governance of the universe. Not all medieval writers followed Aquinas's usage.

directs man to actions that are appropriately ordered to his final end. If man were destined to an end which did not exceed the natural capacity of mankind, there would be no need for his reason to direct him in any other way than through the natural law and the humanly enacted law that is derived from it. But because man is destined to the end of eternal bliss *(beatitudo)* which exceeds the capacity of the natural human faculties, as explained above, it was necessary for him to be directed to this end by a divinely revealed law, in addition to the natural and human law. Secondly, because of the uncertainty of human judgment, especially in contingent and particular matters, it happens that different decisions are made about different human acts, so that laws are often divergent and even contradictory. For man to know what he should do and not do without any doubt it was necessary for him to be directed in his actions by a law given by God, for it is certain that such a law cannot err. Thirdly, man can make laws about matters that are capable of being judged. But man cannot make a judgment about internal motivations that are hidden, but only about external actions that are public. To be perfectly virtuous, however, man must be upright in both kinds of action. Therefore since human law could not punish or direct interior actions sufficiently, it was necessary for there to be a divine law. Fourthly, as Augustine says, human law cannot punish or prohibit every evil action, because in trying to eliminate evils it may also do away with many good things and the interest of the common good which is necessary for human society may be adversely affected. [3] Therefore in order for no evil to go unforbidden and unpunished, it was necessary for there to be a divine law which forbids all sin.

* * *

By the natural law human nature participates in the eternal law in proportion to the capacity of human nature. But man needs to be directed to his supernatural end in a higher way. Hence there is an additional law given by God through which man shares more perfectly in the eternal law.

Qu. 92. The Effects of Law

1   Is an Effect of the Law to Make Men Good?

If the intention of the legislator is directed at the true good, i.e., the common good, and regulated according to the principles of divine justice, it follows that the law will make men good absolutely. If however the intention of the legislator is directed not at what is absolutely good but at what is useful or pleasurable for himself or opposed to divine justice, then the law does not make men good absolutely, but only relatively to a particular regime. In this sense good is found even in things

3. St. Augustine, *On Free Choice*, I, 51. For an English translation see St. Augustine, *The Teacher, The Free Choice of the Will, Grace and Free Will*, Robert P. Russell, trans. (Washington: The Catholic University Press, 1968), 80ff.

that are evil in themselves, such as when one speaks of a good robber
because he works in a way that is adapted to his end.

*   *   *

A tyrannical law, since it is not in accordance with reason, is not a
law in the strict sense, but rather a perversion of law. However it has
something of the character of law to the extent that it intends that the
citizens should be good. It only has the character of a law because it is a
dictate of a superior over his subjects and is aimed at their obeying law—
which is a good that is not absolute but only relative to a specific regime.

Qu. 93. The Eternal Law

1   Does the Eternal Law Exist in the Highest Reason of God?

Just as in the mind of every artist there is a plan of what he will create
by his art, so in the mind of every ruler there must already exist a plan
as to what is to be done by those subject to his government. And just as
the plan of the things to be produced by an art is called the art or exemplar of the things to be produced, so the plan of a ruler concerning the
actions of his subjects has the quality of law, provided that the other
conditions for a law that we have mentioned are met. God in his wisdom
is the creator of all things and is related to them in the same way as an
artist is related to his works of art, as we said in Part I. He governs all the
actions and motions that are found in individual creatures, as we also
explained in Part I. Therefore just as the plan of divine wisdom in
accordance with which all things are created by it has the character of
an art, or exemplar, or idea, so the plan of divine wisdom moving all
things to their appropriate ends has the quality of law. Accordingly, the
eternal law is nothing else than the rational plan of divine wisdom considered as directing all actions and movements.

3   Is All Law Derived from the Eternal Law?

Human law has the quality of a law in so far as it is in accordance
with right reason and in this respect it is evident that it is derived from
the eternal law. If it deviates from the right reason it is said to be an
unjust law, and thus does not have the character of a law but rather that
of an act of violence. However even an unjust law to the extent that it
maintains the appearance of law because of the authority of the one who
makes it is derived in this respect from the eternal law.

Qu. 94. The Natural Law

2   Does the Natural Law Contain One Precept or Many?

The precepts of the natural law are related to the practical reason as
the first principles of [logical] demonstration are related to the speculative reason. Both are principles that are self-evident. Something can be
described as self-evident in two ways—either, in itself, or in relation to

us. A proposition is said to be self-evident in itself if its predicate is contained in its subject—although it may happen that someone who does not know the subject will not know that the proposition is self-evident. Thus the proposition, "Man is a rational being" is by its nature self-evident since when we say "man" we are also saying "rational," but for someone who does not know what a man is, this is not a self-evident proposition. Thus Boethius says that certain axioms and propositions are generally known in themselves by everyone.[4] The terms of these propositions are known to everyone—for example, that every whole is greater than its parts or that two things equal to the same thing are equal to each other. But some propositions are only known to the wise who understand the meaning of the terms used in the proposition. For example to someone who knows that an angel is not a body it is self-evident that it is not located in a particular place, but this is not evident to the unlearned for they can not grasp it.

A certain order is to be found in the things that are apprehended by men. The first thing that is apprehended is being, and a knowledge of this is implied in every act of apprehension. Therefore the undemonstrable first principle is that something cannot be affirmed and denied at the same time. This principle is based on the notion of being and non-being. All other principles are based on this, as Book IV of the *Metaphysics* says.[5] Just as being is the first thing that is apprehended absolutely, so also good is the first thing that is apprehended by the practical reason which is directed towards action, since everything that acts does so for an end which possesses the quality of goodness. Therefore the first principle of the practical reason is based on the nature of the good, i.e., "Good is that which all things seek." Hence the first precept of law is that good is to be done and pursued, and evil is to be avoided. All the other precepts of the law of nature are based on this, so that all the things that are to be done or evils to be avoided belong to the precepts of the natural law which the practical reason naturally apprehends as human goods.

*   *   *

Since good has the nature of an end and evil its opposite, all the things to which man has a natural inclination are naturally apprehended by the reason as good and therefore as objects to be pursued, and their opposites as evils to be avoided. Therefore the order of the precepts of the natural law follows the order of our natural inclinations. There is in man, first, an inclination to the good that he shares by nature with all substances, since every substance seeks to preserve itself according to its own nature. Corresponding to this inclination the natural law contains

---

4. Boethius, *De Hebdomadibus*. In 1257 Aquinas wrote a commentary on this short theological work by Boethius, the late classical writer (480–525), who was responsible for transmitting Aristotle's works of logic to the Middle Ages. It is translated in H. F.

Stewart and E. K. Rand, eds., *Boethius, The Theological Tractates* (New York: Putnam's 1918), under the title "Quomodo Substantiae. . . ."
5. Aristotle, *Metaphysics*, IV, 3.

those things that preserve human life and prevent its destruction. Secondly, there is in man an inclination to certain more specific ends in accordance with the nature that he shares with other animals. In accordance with this, the natural law is said to contain "what nature has taught all animals,"[6] such as the union of man and woman, the education of children, etc. Thirdly, there is in man a natural inclination to the good of the rational nature which is his alone. Thus man has a natural inclination to know the truth about God and to live in society. Thus the things that pertain to inclinations of this kind belong to the natural law, such as that man should avoid ignorance, that he should not offend others with whom he must associate, and other related actions.* * *

4. Is the Natural Law the Same for All Men?

Obj. 3.   We have said above that whatever man is inclined to by his nature belongs to the natural law. But different men are naturally inclined to different things—some to a desire for pleasure, others to a desire for honor and other men to other things. Therefore the Natural Law is not the same for all men.

I answer that, as we have just said, all the things to which man is inclined by nature belong to the natural law. One of the things that is proper to man is that he is inclined to act in accordance with reason. Reason proceeds from general principles to particulars, as is stated in Book I of the Physics.[7] However the speculative reason differs from the practical reason in the way that it does this. The speculative reason is concerned with necessary truths which cannot be other than they are, so that truth is found as surely in its particular conclusions as in its general principles. Practical reason, however, works with the contingent things related to human actions. Therefore although there is a certain necessity in its general principles, the further one goes down into specifics the more frequently one encounters exceptions.

* * * And so it is evident that as to the general principles of reason, whether speculative or practical, there is a single standard of truth and right for everyone which is known by everyone. However when it comes to the specific conclusions of the speculative reason, the truth is the same for everyone but it is not equally known by everyone. It is universally true, for instance, that the three angles of a triangle are equal to two right angles but not everyone knows this. When we come to the particular conclusions of the practical reason there is neither the same standard of truth and rightness for everyone nor are these conclusions equally known by everyone. It is right and true for everyone to act in accordance with reason. A particular conclusion that follows from this principle is that loans should be repaid. This is true in most cases, but it can happen in a particular case that it would be harmful and therefore

irrational to repay a loan, for instance if someone wanted to use it to make war on his country. And exceptions become more likely the more we come down to particular cases, for instance, if the loan was to be repaid with a certain guarantee or in a certain way. The more particular conditions are involved, the more exceptions there can be as to whether it is right to repay or not to repay the loan.

Thus we must conclude that as far as its general first principles are concerned the natural law is the same for all, both as a standard of right action and as to the possibility that it can be known. However as to more particular cases which are conclusions, as it were, from its general principles it is the same for everyone in most cases, both as a standard of right action and as known (by all). However in particular instances there can be exceptions both with regard to their rightness because of certain obstacles (just as obstacles can produce exceptional cases among the things that grow and decay in nature) and to their being known. This can happen because the reason of some has been corrupted by passion or bad habits, or because of an evil disposition of nature, as Julius Caesar writes that at one time robbery was not considered wrong among the Germans even though it is expressly contrary to the law of nature.[8] * * *

5   Can the Natural Law Be Changed?

Obj. 2.   The killing of the innocent, adultery, and theft are contrary to the natural law. But we find these things changed by God. God commanded Abraham to kill his innocent son; He commanded the Jews to steal the borrowed vessels of the Egyptians; and He commanded Hosea to take a "wife of fornication."[9] Therefore the natural law can be changed.

Obj. 3.   Isidore [of Seville] says that "the possession of all things in common and universal freedom are part of natural law."[1] However we see that these things have been changed by human laws. Therefore it seems that natural law is changeable.

I answer that the natural law can be changed in two ways. First, something can be added to it. Nothing prevents the natural law from being changed in this way, since both the divine law and human laws have added to the natural law many provisions that are useful to human life. Secondly, the natural law can be understood to have changed by having something taken away from it, so that what was previously in accordance with the natural law ceases to be part of it. In this respect as far as its first principles are concerned, the natural law is altogether unchangeable.

---

8. Julius Caesar, *Gallic Wars*, VI, 23. Julius Caesar (100–44 B.C.) was a Roman military and political leader who was assassinated in 44 B.C.

9. Genesis, 22:2; Exodus, 12:35; Hosea, 1:2. Abraham was the patriarch and legendary Father of the Jewish people whose faith was tested by the command of God to kill his son, Isaac. The Jews took gold and silver vessels belonging to the Egyptians when they left the country under Moses's leadership. Hosea was (metaphorically) commanded to marry a prostitute.

1. Isidore of Seville, *Etymologies*, V, 4, quoted in Gratian, *Decretum*, D. 1, c. 7 [translated in Paul E. Sigmund, *Natural Law in Political Thought* (Cambridge, Mass.: Winthrop Press, 1971), 48].

But as to the secondary precepts which we have said follow as immediate conclusions from the first principles the natural law does not change in the sense that what the natural law contains is always right in the majority of cases. However it can be changed in some particular aspect and in a few cases because some special reasons make its precepts impossible to observe. * * *

Reply to Obj. 2.   Both the guilty and the innocent die natural deaths. Natural death is inflicted by the power of God as a result of original sin, according to I Kings [Samuel], "The Lord killeth and maketh alive."[2] Therefore it is not unjust for God to command that death be inflicted on any man, whether guilty or innocent. In the same way adultery is intercourse with the wife of another man who has been given to him by the divine law that comes from God. Therefore for someone to have intercourse with another woman at the command of God is not adultery or fornication. The same thing is true of theft which is taking something that belongs to someone else. If someone takes something because of the command of God to whom everything belongs he is not taking something against the will of its owner which is what theft is. It is not only in human things that whatever God does is right. In the natural world as well whatever God does is in a certain sense natural.[3]

Reply to Obj. 3.   Something is said to be part of the natural law in two ways. First because there is a natural inclination to it, for example, that one should not harm other persons. Second, if nature does not produce the contrary. Thus we could say that man goes naked by natural law because human invention, not nature, has given him clothes. In this sense "the possession of all things in common and universal freedom" can be said to be part of natural law since neither separate possessions nor slavery resulted from nature, but they were produced by human reason for the benefit of human life. Thus in these cases the law of nature was not changed but added to.

Qu. 95. Human Law

1 Was it Useful for Man to Make Human Laws?

Man possesses a natural aptitude for virtue but he needs a certain discipline to perfect that virtue. The man who can develop such discipline by himself is rare. * * * Parental discipline through moral suasion is sufficient for those young people who are inclined to the life of virtue by natural disposition, or custom, or even more because of the help of God. But since there are some who are dissolute and prone to vice who cannot easily be moved by words alone, these have to be restrained from

2. I Samuel, 2:6.
3. This passage is used by John Giles Milhaven, *Towards a New Catholic Morality* (Garden City: Doubleday Image, 1970), ch. 10, to argue that Aquinas was not as committed to "negative moral absolutes" as is commonly assumed by his interpreters.

doing evil by force and fear so that they will cease to do evil and leave others in peace, and so that after they become habituated in this way they will do voluntarily what they did earlier out of fear—and become virtuous. Now this kind of discipline through fear of punishment is the discipline of law. Therefore laws are adopted to bring about peace and virtue among men. As the Philosopher [Aristotle] says, "Man is the noblest of animals if he is perfect in virtue, but if he departs from law and justice he is the worst."[4] For unlike other animals man possesses the weapons of reason which he can use to satisfy his passions and base instincts.

2 Are All Human Laws Derived from the Natural Law?

Saint Augustine says "A law that is unjust is considered to be no law at all."[5] Thus its quality as a law depends on the extent to which it is just. A thing is said to be just in human affairs when it is right because it follows the rule of reason. Now as we have said, the first rule of reason is the law of nature. Hence every human law that is adopted has the quality of law to the extent that it is derived from natural law. But if it disagrees in some respect from the natural law, it is no longer a law but a corruption of law.[6]

However it should be noted that there are two ways in which something is derived from natural law—first, as a conclusion from its principles, and second, as a specific application of what is expressed in general terms. The first way is like the method of the sciences that derive conclusive proofs from first principles. The second way is like that of the arts in which a specific application is made of a general form. For example an architect must apply the general idea of a house to the shape of this or that house. Thus some precepts are derived from the general principles of the natural law as conclusions; for example "Do not kill" is a conclusion that can be drawn from the principle, "Do not do evil to anyone." Others are arrived at as specific applications. Thus the law of nature says that the evildoer should be punished but the particular penalty is a kind of specific application of the natural law. * * *

Both kinds of derivation are found in human law. The things that are derived in the first way are not only contained in human law because they were adopted as law but because part of their force comes from the natural law. Those arrived at in the second way have their force only from human law.

4 What Are the Divisions of Human Law?

In the first place, as we have explained above, a characteristic of human law is that it is derived from natural law. On this basis human law is

---

4. Aristctle, *Politics*, I, 2.
5. St. Augustine, *On Free Choice*, I, 5.
6. Cf. Martin Luther King, *Letter from a Birmingham Jail* (1963): "I would agree with St. Augustire that 'an unjust law is no law at all.' * * *

An unjust law is a code that is out of harmony with the moral law. To put it in terms of St. Thomas Aquinas, 'An unjust law is a human law that is not rooted in eternal and natural law.' "

divided into the law of nations *(jus gentium)* and the civil law, following
the two ways of deriving human law from natural law that we discussed
above. To the law of nations belong the things that are derived from the
law of nature as conclusions from its principles, for example fairness in
buying and selling and the like without which men could not live in
society—which is a part of the law of nature because man is by nature a
social animal, as is proved in Book I of the *Politics.*[7] The things that are
derived from the law of nature by way of specific application belong to
the civil law according to which each community *(civitas)* decides what
is convenient for itself.

* * * It is a characteristic of law that it is adopted by the ruler of the
civic community as explained above. This means that human laws are
classified on the basis of the different forms of government. One of these,
as the Philosopher [Aristotle] says in Book III of the *Politics*, is a kingdom—which is the name of a state *(civitas)* that is governed by one
man.[8] The legislation that corresponds to this in Roman Law is the
ordinances of princes *(constitutiones principum)*. Another form of government is an aristocracy, that is, rule by the best men or *optimates* and
here we have legislation in the form of replies by legal experts *(responsa
prudentum)* and the decrees of the senate *(senatus consulta)*. Another
form of government is oligarchy—i.e., rule by a few rich and powerful
men, and corresponding to this is the law of the praetors which is also
known as honorary law *(jus honorarium)*. Another form is government
by the people which is called democracy, and corresponding to this is
popular legislation *(plebiscita)*. Another form [of government] is tyranny
which is totally corrupt, and therefore has no law. There is also another
form which is a mixture of these and this is the best form of government,
and the definition of Isidore corresponds to this, "a law is what has been
approved by the elders and the people."[9]

Qu. 96. The Power of Human Law

2 Should Law Repress All Vices?

The power or capacity to act results from a habit or interior disposition. Not everything is possible for both the virtuous man and one who
does not have the habit of virtue, just as the same thing is not possible
for a boy and a full-grown man. Therefore many things are permitted to
children which would be punished or at least criticized in adults. Similarly many things are allowed to men who are not advanced in virtue
that would not be tolerated in a virtuous man.

Human law is framed for the mass of men, the majority of whom are

---

7. Aristotle, *Politics*, I, 1. In ancient and medieval thought "the law of nations" referred to the
common elements in all legal systems, rather than
to its modern meaning as international law. See
the selection on natural law by Jacques Maritain
(pp. 204–211) for his dubious argument, based

partly on this passage, that for Aquinas, once natural law is expressed in propositions ("conclusions") it becomes *jus gentium*.
8. Aristotle, *Politics*, III, 5.
9. Isidore, *Etymologies*, V, 10.

not perfectly virtuous. Therefore human law does not prohibit every vice from which virtuous men abstain, but only the more serious ones from which the majority can abstain, especially those that harm others and which must be prohibited for human society to survive, such as homicide, theft, and the like.

4   Does Human Law Oblige in Conscience?

A law may be unjust in two ways. First if it is contrary to human good in the way we have explained—either in its object, for example when a ruler imposes onerous laws on his subjects which are not for the benefit of the community but for his own cupidity and vainglory—or in its author as when someone makes a law that exceeds the power given to him—or in its form, for example, when burdens are placed on the community in an unequal fashion even if they are aimed at the common good. These are acts of violence rather than laws, for as Augustine said, "A law that is unjust is considered to be no law at all."[1] Therefore laws of this kind do not bind in conscience except to avoid scandal or disorder. In such a case a man should give up his right to disobey—as Matthew's Gospel says, "If someone forces you to go a mile, go with him an extra two; if he takes your coat, give him your cloak as well."[2]

Secondly, a law may be unjust because it is contrary to divine goodness. For example, laws enforcing idolatry or another action that is against divine law. Under no circumstance may such laws be obeyed, for as it says in the Acts [of the Apostles] "We must obey God rather than men."[3]

5   Is Everyone Subject to the Law?

Law has two characteristics. First, it is a rule for human actions, and secondly, it has coercive force. * * * A ruler is said to be above the law in its coercive force since properly speaking no one can coerce himself, and the law derives its coercive force only from the power of the ruler. Thus the ruler is said to be above the law because if he violates it there is no one to impose a sentence of condemnation upon him. * * *[4] In the judgment of God (however) the prince is not above the law in its directive force, but should carry out the law of his own free will and without constraint. In addition the prince is above the law because he can change it, if it is expedient, or dispense from it according to the time and place. * * *

6   May Someone Subject to the Law Act Contrary to the Letter of the Law?

It often happens that the observance of a law may be useful to the community in most cases but very harmful in particular situations. However since the legislator cannot foresee every individual case he makes

---

1. St. Augustine, On Free Choice, I, 5.
2. Matthew, 5:40–41.
3. Acts, 5:29.

4. Aquinas is interpreting the Roman law statement, "the prince is free of the law" (Princeps legibus solutus est), Digest I, ii, 31 (Ulpian).

a law that fits what happens in most cases, since he intends it to be of general benefit. Therefore if a case emerges in which the observance of the law would be harmful to the general good, it should not be observed. For example, in a city under siege a law might be passed that the gates of the city should be kept closed and this would be generally useful for the common welfare. However if there were a case in which the enemy was pursuing citizens on whom the city depended for its safety it would be very harmful for the city not to open its gates. In this case the gates should be opened in violation of the letter of the law in order to protect the common interest as the legislator intended.

However it should be kept in mind that if the observance of the letter of the law does not result in a danger that requires an immediate response it is not up to any individual to decide what is, or is not, useful to the city. This is the sole responsibility of the ruler who has the authority to dispense from the law in cases of this kind. But if there is imminent danger and there is no time to refer the question to a superior, necessity carries with it its own dispensation, because necessity is not subject to law.[5]

Qu. 97. Change in the Law

1   Should Human Laws Ever Be Changed?

Human law is a certain dictate of reason that directs human acts. There can be two reasons to justify changing human law—one, because of the nature of reason, and the other because of those whose actions are regulated by the law. Reason may cause laws to be changed because it seems to be the nature of human reason to progress by stages from the less perfect to the more prefect. Thus we see that in the speculative sciences the teachings of the early philosophers were inadequate, and later their successors improved upon them. The same thing is true in practical affairs. Those who first tried to discover something useful for the human community were not able to take account of everything by themselves and established institutions that were inadequate in many respects. These were then modified by their successors who set up institutions that proved to be less deficient from the point of view of the public interest.

Those whose actions are regulated by the law may cause a law to be changed if the circumstances have changed that make different laws appropriate for different circumstances. Augustine gives an example in *On Free Choice*, "If a people are moderate, serious, and diligently defend the public interest, it is right for the law to provide that the people should elect their magistrates to administer the commonwealth. But if the same people gradually become corrupt and sell their votes and turn over the

5. The medieval discussion of "necessity" has been seen by some writers as the ancestor of modern doctrines of "reason of state." See, Gaines Post, *Studies in Medieval Legal Thought* (Princeton, N.J.: Princeton University Press, 1964), ch. 5.

government to flagrant criminals, then it is right to take away the power of election from those people and let the few decide once again."[6]

2 Should Human Law Be Changed Whenever an Improvement Is Possible?

The mere fact of a change in law itself can be adverse to the public welfare to some degree. This is because custom is very important in the observance of law since things done contrary to general custom, even if they are not important, are considered very serious offenses. Therefore when a law is changed the restraining power of the law is lessened because custom is set aside. Therefore human law should never be changed unless the common welfare is compensated in some way for the harm done in that respect. This happens when either a substantial and obvious benefit derives from a new statute or when there is an urgent necessity because the old law produces manifest injustice or its observance proves very harmful.

3 Can Custom Obtain the Force of Law?

All law proceeds from the reason and will of the legislator—divine and natural law from the rational will of God and human law from the will of man as guided by his reason. The reason and will are manifested in action through words and deeds, for the way one acts shows what he considers to be good. It is clear that human words can change and develop law because they reveal the motives and concepts of the human reason. So also a law can be changed and developed by the repeated actions that comprise custom. In addition something can be established by custom that obtains the force of law because such repeated external actions effectively reveal internal motives of the will and concepts of the reason, since if something is done a number of times it seems to be the result of a deliberate rational decision. In this sense custom has the power of law, it abolishes law, and it acts as the interpreter of law.

* * *

A community within which a custom is introduced may be of two kinds. If it is a free community that can make its own laws the consent of the whole community which is demonstrated by its customary observance is worth more than the authority of the ruler who does not have the power to make law except as the representative of the people. In this case individual persons cannot make law but the whole people can do so. However if the community does not have the right to make its own laws or to abrogate a law made by a superior authority, a custom which becomes established acquires the force of law if it is tolerated by those whose responsibility it is to make law for the community, since in this way they seem to approve what custom has established.

6. St. Augustine, On Free Choice, I, 6.

4 Can Rulers Grant Dispensations from Human Law?

The general precepts of the natural law that are always applicable cannot be the object of a dispensation. However in the case of other precepts that are like conclusions from the general precepts man can sometimes grant a dispensation—for example, that a loan should not be paid back to someone who betrays his country or something similar. However, every man stands in relation to the divine law as does a private person to the public law to which he is subject. Therefore just as no one can grant dispensations from the public law except the one from whom the law derives its authority or his representative, so in the case of the precepts of the divine law which come from God no one can grant dispensations except God or someone whom he specifically designates.

Qu. 100. The Moral Precepts of the Old Law[7]

1 Do All the Precepts of Morality Belong to the Natural Law?

Moral precepts are distinct from ceremonial and judicial precepts because moral precepts by their very nature are concerned with good morals. Since human moral conduct is directed by reason which is the basic principle of human action, those moral actions that are in accord with reason are called good, and those that depart from reason are called evil. Just as every judgment of the speculative reason proceeds from our natural knowledge of first principles, so every judgment of our practical reason proceeds from certain principles that we know by nature, as we have said earlier. From these principles we can proceed to make practical judgments about different things in different ways. Some human actions are so clearly connected with general first principles that we can approve or reject them immediately with very little reflection. There are other cases in which different circumstances must be taken into account in order to make a decision, which not everyone can do with care, but only the wise—just as not everyone can reach the particular conclusions of the sciences, but only the wise. But there are other matters in which man needs the help of divine instruction—i.e., matters of faith.

Qu. 105. The Reason for the Judicial Precepts

1 Did the Old Law Contain Useful Provisions on Government?

Two points should be noted concerning the right ordering of rulers in any city or nation. The first is that all should have a share in the government. In this way peace is preserved among the people and everyone loves and protects the constitution, as is stated in the *Politics*, Book II.[8] The second regards the form of government or constitution. As the Philosopher [Aristotle] tell us in *Politics*, Book III, there are various forms of government.[9] The most outstanding are a kingdom in which one man

---

7. The Old Law—i.e., the legal provisions contained in the Old Testament.
8. Aristotle, *Politics*, II, 1. A better source would

be *Politics* III, 1.
9. Aristotle, *Politics*, III, 5–7.

rules in accordance with virtue, and an aristocracy—that is, government by the best men in which a small number of people rule in accordance with virtue. And so the best constitution for a city or kingdom is one in which one person rules in accordance with virtue, and under him there are others who govern in accordance with virtue, and all have some part in government because they are all eligible to govern and those who govern are chosen by all. This is the best form of polity since it is a judicious combination of kingship—rule by one man, aristocracy—rule by many in accordance with virtue, and democracy—i.e., popular rule in that the rulers can be chosen from the people and the people have the right to choose their rulers.[1]

This was the form of government established by the divine law. Moses and his successors governed the people as sole rulers over all so that there was a kind of kingship. Seventy-two elders were chosen in accordance with their virtue, as Dueteronomy says, "I took out of your tribes wise and noble men and made them rulers" and this was the aristocratic aspect. But it was democratic in that they were elected from all the people, since Exodus says, "Provide wise men from all the people" and also because the people chose them, as Deuteronomy says, "Give me wise men from among you" etc.[2] Therefore it is clear that the constitution that the [Old] Law established was the best.

※　※　※

A kingdom is the best form of government for a people, provided that it does not become corrupt. However because of the great power given to a king, a kingdom can easily degenerate into a tyranny, unless the one who has been given such power is perfect in virtue, because, as the Philosopher [Aristotle] says in *Ethics*, Book IV, "Only the virtuous man acts well in good fortune."[3] Perfect virtue, however is found in few men. The Jews were especially prone to cruelty and avarice—the vices that chiefly incline men to tyranny.[4] Hence at the beginning the Lord did not establish a king with full power over them but appointed a judge and governor to rule them. Later as though in anger he granted their petition for a king, as is clear from what he said to Samuel, "They have not rejected you but me—that I should not reign over them."[5]

Qu. 109. The Grace of God—the External Foundation of Human Acts

2　Can Man Will or Do Anything Good without Grace?

Man's nature can be considered in two ways—first, in its integral state as it was before the sin of our first parent, and secondly, corrupted as it

---

1. Compare this with the arguments for limited monarchy in *On Kingship*, ch. 2 and 6 (pp. 17 and 22).
2. Deuteronomy, 1:15; Exodus, 18:21; Deuteronomy, 1:13.
3. Aristotle, *Nicomachean Ethics*, IV, 3.
4. For other examples of Aquinas's attitude toward the Jews, see S. T., II–II, qu. 10, a. 11 (p. 62) and qu. 78, a. 1 (p. 74).
5. I Samuel, 8:7.

is in us, following the sin of our first parent. Now in both states human nature needs the help of God as the Prime [First] Mover to do or will anything good. However in the state of natural integrity man possessed sufficient virtue for action that by his natural powers he could will and do the good that was proportionate to his nature—that is, the good resulting from acquired virtue. However he could not do the good actions that result from infused virtue which exceeded his nature.[6] However in the state of corrupted nature man is deficient even in what he can do by nature since he cannot perform all good actions of this kind by his natural powers. However since human nature is not so completely corrupted by sin as to be totally lacking in natural goodness, it is possible for him in the state of corrupted nature to do some particular good things by virtue of his nature—for example, build houses, plant vineyards, and the like. Yet he cannot do all the good that is natural to him so as never to fall short in any respect. In the same way a sick man can make some movements on his own but to move with the full motion of a man who is healthy he must be cured with the help of medicine.

Therefore in the state of natural integrity the only reason that man needs the power of grace added to the power of nature is to do or will supernatural good, but in the state of corrupted nature he needs it for two reasons—to be healed [of the effects of sin] and also in order to perform acts of supernatural goodness that are meritorious. In addition man needs divine help in both states to move him to good actions.

6. The theological virtues of faith, hope, and charity are infused by the direct action of divine grace.

Qu. 10. Unbelief

8   Are Unbelievers to be Forced to Accept the Faith?

There are some unbelievers such as the Gentiles[1] and the Hebrews who have never accepted the Christian faith. These should in no way be forced to believe, for faith is a matter of the will. Appropriate force may be used by the faithful to prevent them from interfering with the faith through blasphemy, or evil inducements, or open persecution. This is the reason that Christians often make war on unbelievers, not to force them to believe—since even if they conquered them and made them prisoners they would leave them free as to whether they wished to believe—but to prevent them from interfering with the Christian faith.[2] However there are other unbelievers such as heretics and all apostates who once accepted and professed the faith. These are to be compelled, even by physical force, to carry out what they promised and to hold what they once accepted.

9   May One Associate with Unbelievers?

Believers are forbidden to associate with someone for two reasons—first, to punish the one who is cut off from association with the faithful and secondly, for the protection of those who are forbidden to associate with him. Both reasons can be drawn from the words of the Apostle [Paul], "Do you not know that a little leaven corrupts the whole lump?"[3] And below he adds a reason for having a penalty decided upon by the church when he says, "Do you not judge those who are within the church?"[4]

On the basis of the first reason, the church does not forbid believers to associate with unbelievers who have never accepted the Christian faith—that is, pagans and Jews—for it is the responsibility of the temporal, not the spiritual, judge to judge them if while they are living among Christians they commit some crime and receive earthly punishment from believers. However, the church does forbid as a punishment association with those unbelievers who depart from the faith they have accepted or corrupt the faith such as heretics, or those who completely reject their faith such as apostates. The church imposes a sentence of excommunication on both of them.

As for the second reason, it seems that we should distinguish among the various circumstances as to persons, commerce, and time. If someone is so strong in his faith that it is more likely that the unbelievers will be converted as a result than that believers will turn away from the faith,

---

1. Mainly the Moslems.
2. This is Aquinas's justification for the Crusades.
3. I Corinthians, 5:6.
4. I Corinthians, 5:13.

association with unbelievers who have never accepted the faith such as pagans and Jews should not be forbidden—especially if necessity requires it. However if they are ignorant and weak in faith so that one can fear that their faith may be endangered, they should be forbidden to associate with unbelievers, particularly to have close relationships with them or deal with them without a good reason (necessity).

10 May Unbelievers Exercise Government or Dominion over the Faithful?

I answer this in two ways. First, the establishment of new dominion or government on the part of unbelievers over the faithful can in no way be permitted, for it gives rise to scandal and endangers the faith. Unless they are of great virtue those who are under the jurisdiction of others can easily be moved by those to whom they are subject to follow their commands. Also unbelievers will despise the faith if they get to know the failings of the faithful. Therefore the Apostle [Paul] forbade the faithful to engage in legal disputes before a judge who was an unbeliever.[5] Therefore the church does not permit infidels to acquire dominion over the faithful or to be placed in authority over them in any way. On the other hand we can speak of dominion or government that is already in existence. Here we must consider that dominion and government are matters of human law, while the distinction between believers and unbelievers is a matter of divine law. Now the divine law which is based on grace does not abolish human law which is based on reason. Therefore the mere fact of a difference between believers and unbelievers does not abolish dominion or government by unbelievers over believers. However it is permissible for this right of dominion or government to be taken away by the decision and direction of the church because of the authority it has from God, since unbelievers because of their lack of belief rightly deserve to lose their power over believers who are being transformed into sons of God. However the church does this on some occasions and at other times it refrains from doing so.

11 Are the Rites of Unbelievers to be Tolerated?

Human government is derived from divine government and should imitate it. God, who is omnipotent and supremely good, permits some evils which he could prevent to exist in the universe, because if he did so a greater good might be taken away or worse evils follow. So also in human government it is right for those who are in authority to tolerate some evils so as not to prevent other goods or to avoid some worse evil from occurring. As Augustine says, "Suppress prostitution and the world will be torn apart by lust."[6] Therefore unbelievers although they sin by their rites may be tolerated either because a greater good may come of it or some evil may be avoided. Thus it is good that the Jews observe rites which once prefigured the true faith that we hold because we have a testimony of our faith from our enemies[7] and our belief is represented to us as prefigured. The rites of other unbelievers that have no truth or usefulness in them are not to be tolerated unless to avoid some evil such as the avoidance of the scandal or discord which might arise or interference with the salvation of those who if they are tolerated will gradually be converted to the faith. For this reason the church has even tolerated the rites of heretics and pagans at times when there was a great number of unbelievers.

12   Are the Children of Jews and Other Unbelievers to be Baptized against the Will of Their Parents?

* * * Another reason is that it would be a violation of natural justice. By nature a son belongs to his father. Initially as long as he is in his mother's womb he is not physically separate from his parents. After he leaves the womb, before he has the use of free will he is under the care of his parents as a kind of spiritual womb. As long as he does not have the use of reason, the child does not differ from an irrational animal. * * * Thus it is part of the natural law that a son should be under the care of his father before he has the use of reason. Therefore it is against natural justice for a child to be taken from the care of his parents before he has the use of reason or for something to be decided about him against the will of his parents. However after he begins to have the use of free will he begins to make his own decisions and to provide for himself regarding the things contained in the divine and natural law. At that time he can be induced to accept the faith not by force but by persuasion, and he can consent to the faith and be baptized even against the will of his parents—but not before he has the use of reason.

Qu. 11. Heresy

3   May Heretics Be Tolerated?

* * * Two points should be considered regarding heretics, one concerning the heretics themselves and the other concerning the church. As for the heretics themselves they have committed a sin that deserves not only excommunication by the church but their removal from the world by death. It is a much more serious matter to corrupt the faith that sustains the life of the soul than to counterfeit money which sustains temporal life. If it is just for counterfeiters or other criminals to be executed immediately by secular rulers, it is all the more just for heretics once they are convicted of heresy not only to be excommunicated but to be put to death.

The church, however, is merciful and desires the conversion of those who are in error. Therefore she does not condemn them immediately "but after a first and second admonition" as the Apostle [Paul] teaches.[8]

---

7. Note that in a society based on religious uniformity, those who did not conform were seen as "enemies" and religious toleration was viewed as a threat to the social order.
8. Titus, 3:10.

However if the heretic still remains pertinacious the church, despairing of his conversion, provides for the salvation of others by separating him from the church by the sentence of excommunication and then leaves him to the secular judge to be exterminated from the world by death.[9]

Qu. 12. Apostasy

2 Are Subjects Obliged to Obey a Ruler Who Apostasizes from the Faith?

We have said earlier that unbelief is not incompatible with dominion, because dominion is a matter of the law of nations (jus gentium) which is human law, while the distinction between believers and unbelievers is a matter of the divine law which does not abrogate human law. However if someone commits the sin of unbelief he can be deprived of his right to rule by judicial sentence, just as for other failings. However the church does not have the right to punish unbelief in those who have never accepted the faith—as the Apostle [Paul] says, "What have I to do with judging those who are outside?"[1] However the unbelief of those who have accepted the faith can be punished by a judicial sentence and it is appropriate for them to be punished by losing the right to rule over believers. For this could lead to great corruption of the faith since in accordance with the quotation already cited, the apostate "breeds evil in his depraved heart and sows discord."[2] Therefore as soon as someone falls under a sentence of excommunication for apostasy from the faith, his subjects are ipso facto absolved from his rule and from the oath of fealty by which they were bound to him.

Qu. 40. War

1 Is Warfare Always Sinful?

There are three conditions for a just war. First the ruler under whom the war is to be fought must have authority to do so. A private person does not have the right to make war since he can pursue his rights by appealing to his superior. In addition a private person does not have the right to mobilize (convocare) the people as must be done in war. But since the responsibility for the commonwealth has been entrusted to rulers it is their responsibility to defend the city or kingdom or province subject to them. And just as it is legitimate for them to use the material sword to punish criminals in order to defend it against internal disturbances—as the Apostle [Paul] says in Romans 13, "He does not bear the sword without cause, for he is a minister of God, an avenger in wrath against the evildoer"[3]—so they also have the right to use the sword of war to defend the commonwealth against external enemies. * * *

✲ Secondly, a just cause is required—so that those against whom the

---

9. Aquinas assumes 1) that the heretic has turned away from orthodoxy deliberately and in bad faith, and 2) that heresy is a threat to the social order and a criminal offense.

1. I Corinthians, 5:12.
2. Proverbs, 6:14.
3. Romans, 13:4.

war is waged deserve such a response because of some offense on their part. Augustine says, "Just wars are usually defined as those that avenge injuries, when a nation or a city should be punished for failing to right a wrong done by its citizens, or to return what has been taken away unjustly."[4]

The third condition that is required on the part of those making the war is a right intention, to achieve some good or avoid some evil. St. Augustine says in his book, *On the Words of the Lord*, "For the true followers of God even wars are peaceful if they are waged not out of greed or cruelty but for the sake of peace, to restrain the evildoers and assist the good."[5] Yet it may happen that even if the war is initiated by a legitimate authority and its cause is just, it can become unjust because of evil intentions.[6]

Qu. 42. Sedition against Peace

2 *Is Sedition Always a Mortal Sin?*
Obj. 3.   Those who liberate a society (*multitudo*) from the power of a tyrant are praised. But this can not be done without some dissension in the society when one group tries to keep the tyrant and another tries to overthrow him. Therefore sedition can take place without sin. * * *

I answer that * * * it is manifest that sedition is opposed both to justice and to the common good. Therefore by its nature sedition is a mortal sin and all the more serious because sedition opposes the common good rather than the private good. * * *

Reply to Obj. 3.   Tyrannical government is unjust because it is directed not to the common good but to the private good of the ruler, as is evident in Book III of the *Politics*, and Book VIII of the *Ethics*.[7] Therefore the overthrow of this kind of government does not have the character of sedition—unless perhaps it produces such disorder that the society under the tyrant suffers greater harm from the resulting disturbance than from the tyrant's rule. Rather it is the tyrant who is guilty of sedition because he spreads discord and division among the people under him so as to control them more easily. It is characteristic of a tyranny that it is directed to the personal interest of the ruler and harms the community.[8]

4. Augustine, as quoted in Gratian, *Decretum*, C. 23, qu. 2, c. 2.

5. Augustine, as quoted in Gratian, *Decretum*, C. 23, qu. ., c. 6. See also Augustine, *The City of God*, XIX, 12.

6. See the selection from Paul Ramsey, *War and the Christian Conscience: How Shall Modern War Be Conducted Justly?* (Durham, N.C.: Duke University Press, 1961), for a contemporary analysis that is influenced by this passage, (pages 226–229).

7. Aristotle, *Politics*, III, 5; *Nicomachean Ethics*, VIII, 10.

8. Note that, in *On Kingship*, Aquinas advises leaving tyrants to the judgment of God (p. 25, above). In the *Commentary on the Sentences of Peter Lombard*, written in 1256 as the medieval equivalent of his doctoral dissertation Aquinas takes a different position on the question of obedience to tyrants (II, D.44, qu. 2):

   2 *Are Christians Obliged to Obey Tyrants?*
   Obj. 5.   No one is obliged to obey someone whom it is legitimate and even praiseworthy to kill. But Cicero in his book, *On Duties*, justifies those who killed Julius Cae-

Qu. 57. Justice

2   Is it Correct to Divide Law (Jus) into Natural Law and Positive Law?
Obj. 1.   It would seem that it is not appropriate to divide [all] law
into natural law and positive law, for that which is natural is immutable
and the same for all. Nothing like this is found in human affairs for all
the rules of human law are deficient in some cases and do not apply
everywhere. Therefore there is no such thing as natural law. * * *

On the contrary, the Philosopher [Aristotle] says that "political justice is
partly natural and partly legal"[9]—that is, established by law.

I answer that it should be said that what is right or just is an action
which is appropriate for another person in a relationship of equality.
Something can be appropriate for a person in two ways. The first is based
on the nature of the thing, for instance when a person gives something
in order to get equal value in return. This is called right by natural law
(jus naturale). In the second way, what is appropriate for, or commensurate to, another person is settled by agreement or mutual consent, for
instance when a person declares that he is content to receive a given
amount. This again can take place in two ways—either by private agreement, for example, when a contract is signed between private persons,
or by public agreement, as when a whole people agrees that something
is appropriate or commensurate, or when it is decided by a prince who
rules over a community and represents it. This is called right by positive
law *(jus positivum)*.
   Objection 1 can be answered by arguing that something which is by
nature immutable must be the same everywhere and always. Man's nature
is mutable in that what is natural to him can sometimes be lacking.
Thus it is a matter of natural equality that a loan should be paid back
and if it were the case that human nature were always [morally] upright,
this rule should be observed. But because it sometimes happens that the

---

sar although he was their friend and relative
because he usurped imperial power as a tyrant.
[Cicero, *On Duties (De Officiis)*, 1, 26.]
Therefore no one is obliged to obey a tyrant.

I answer that * * * the Christian is obliged to
obey authority that comes from God but not
that which is not from God. As we have already
said, authority can fail to come from God in
two ways either from the way it was acquired
or from the way it has been used. * * *
Whoever seizes power by violence does not
become a true ruler and lord, and therefore it
is permissible when the possibility exists for
someone to reject that rulership, unless perhaps afterwards he has become a legitimate
ruler because of the consent of his subjects or
the action of a superior authority.
   Authority to rule can be abused in two ways.
First, because what has been commanded by
the ruler is contrary to the purpose of his rule—

for example, if he commands a sinful act
contrary to virtue, since his rule was established to protect and maintain virtue—and in
this case there is an obligation to disobey him
as did the holy martyrs who suffered death
rather than obey the unholy commands of
tyrants. Second [rulers abuse their authority]
because they command things outside their
sphere of authority, as when a master demands
a payment which a slave is not obliged to make
or something similar. In this case the subject
is obliged neither to obey or disobey. * * *
Reply to Obj. 5.   Cicero speaks of a case
in which someone has violently seized power
against the will of his subjects or has forced
them to consent and when there is no recourse
to a superior who can pass judgment on the
invader. In this case someone who kills a tyrant
in order to liberate his country is to be praised
and rewarded. * * *
9. Aristotle, *Nicomachean Ethics*, V, 7.

will of man is corrupted there are cases in which a loan should not be returned for fear that an evil man would misuse it—for instance, if a madman or an enemy of the commonwealth demands the return of his weapons. * * * Human will can make something just by general agreement if it is not in itself contrary to natural justice. This is the area of positive laws. Therefore the Philosopher [Aristotle] says in book V of the *Ethics* that "something is legally just if it makes no difference in principle whether it is one way or another, but becomes right or wrong because it is adopted as a law."[1] However if something is contrary to natural law, it cannot be made just as a result of human volition—for instance, if a law is passed that theft or adultery is permissible. * * * Divine law is the law that is promulgated by God. It is made up partly of things that are just by nature although men do not know this, and partly of things that are just because God has commanded them. Thus the divine law can be divided into two parts like human law, and there are some precepts in the divine law that are commanded because they are good or prohibited because they are evil, and some that are good because they are commanded or evil because they are forbidden.

3   *Is the Law of Nations* (Jus Gentium) *the Same as the Natural Law?*
Obj. 1.   It would seem that the law of nations is the same as the natural law. All men agree only on that which is natural to them. All men agree on the law of nations, for the Jurist says that the law of nations is what all nations observe.[2] Therefore the law of nations is the natural law.

Obj. 2.   Furthermore slavery is natural among men. Some men are natural slaves, as the Philosopher [Aristotle] proves.[3] Now Isidore says that slavery is part of the law of nations.[4] Therefore the law of nations is the natural law.

Obj. 3.   Moreover we have said that [all] law is divided into the natural and the positive law. However the law of nations is not positive law for all the nations have agreed to adopt it by common consent. Therefore the law of nations is the natural law.

On the contrary, Isidore says that law is either natural or civil or the law of nations, so that he distinguishes the law of nations from the natural law.[5]

I answer that, as we have said, natural law or justice is that which is by its nature appropriate or commensurate to another person. This can take place in two ways. First considered simply in itself—for example the

---

1. Aristotle, *Nicomachean Ethics*, V, 7.
2. *Digest*, I, i, 1, 4. The Jurist is Ulpian.
3. Aristotle, *Politics*, I, 2.
4. Isidore of Seville, *Etymologies*, V, 6, as quoted
in Gratian, *Decretum*, D. 1, c. 9.
5. Isidore of Seville, *Etymologies*, V, 4, as quoted
in Gratian, *Decretum*, D. 1, c. 6.

natural relationship of the male to the female is to have children by her, and that of parents to their child is to nourish him. Second, something is related naturally to another not simply in itself but as a consequence of something else. For example in the case of the ownership of property, considered in itself there is no reason why a given field should belong to one person rather than another, but considered in relation to the opportunity it provides for cultivation and peaceful use, there is a certain appropriateness about its being owned by one man and not another, as is made clear by the Philosopher [Aristotle].[6]

Animals as well as men can perceive something as it is in itself. Hence the law that is called natural in the first way is common to us and to all animals. However the law of nations departs in this respect from the natural law, says the Jurist [Ulpian] for the latter [the natural law] is common to all animals while the former [the law of nations] is shared only by men.[7] To consider something by comparing it with its consequences is proper to reason and to do this is natural to man because it is dictated by natural reason. Therefore the jurist Gaius says, "Whatever natural reason has established among men is observed by all nations and is called the law of nations."[8]

Reply to Obj. 1.　　　This clearly answers the first objection.

Reply to Obj. 2.　　　In an absolute sense natural reason does not make this man a slave rather than someone else, but only a kind of resultant utility, since it is useful for a slave to be guided by someone who is wiser, and for the master to receive the slave's help, as the *Politics* says.[9] Therefore the slavery that is contained in the law of nations is natural in the second sense, but not in the first sense.

Reply to Obj. 3.　　　To the third objection we must reply that natural reason dictates the things that are in the law of nations, for instance that a neighbor be treated equitably. They do not need to be adopted as laws but, as stated by the authorities cited above, natural reason itself has established them.

4　Should Paternal Law and Property Law Be Specifically Distinguished?

What is right or just is defined in relation to another. "Another" can be described in two ways. First, it can simply mean a person who is entirely distinct from someone else, as in the case of two men, neither of whom is subject to the other but both of whom are under the same governmental ruler. Between them according to the Philosopher [Aristotle] there is a relationship of unqualified justice.[1] Secondly, someone

6. Aristotle, *Politics*, II, 3.
7. *Digest*, I, i, 1, 1 (Ulpian).
8. *Digest*, I, i, 1, 9. Gaius was a second-century Roman jurist, extracts from whose *Institutes* were

included in the *Digest*.
9. Aristotle, *Politics*, I, 6.
1. Aristotle, *Nicomachean Ethics*, V, 6.

is said to be "another" in relation to someone else not in an unqualified sense but as belonging to him. In this way, a son belongs to a father since in a way he is part of him as the *Ethics* says, and a slave is property of his master because he is his instrument, as the *Politics* says.[2] Accordingly the relationship between a father and a son is not an unqualified one and therefore it is not one of unqualified justice but justice of a special kind called paternal justice. And for the same reason between a master and a slave there is a relationship of proprietary justice. A wife, however, although she is part of her husband, since she is related to him as a part of his body, as the Apostle [Paul] declares,[3] is more distinct from her husband than the child from his father or the slave from his master. For she is involved in a certain social life in marriage. Therefore as the Philosopher [Aristotle] says there is more possibility for justice between them than between father and son, or master and slave, since the husband and wife have an immediate relationship in the domestic community, as is clear in the *Politics*, although the relationship between them is not one of political justice but rather of household justice.[4]

Qu. 60. Judicial Decisions

6   Are Judicial Decisions Made by Usurpers Invalid?

The secular power is subject to the spiritual power as the body is subject to the soul. Therefore the power to judge is not usurped if a spiritual authority enters into temporal affairs in matters in which the secular power is subject to it or which have been given to it by the secular power.[5]

Qu. 64. Homicide

3   Can a Private Person Kill a Criminal?

It is permissible to kill a criminal if this is necessary for the welfare of the whole community. However this right belongs only to the one entrusted with the care of the whole community—just as a doctor may cut off an infected limb, since he has been entrusted with the care of the health of the whole body. The care of the public good has been entrusted to rulers who have public authority and so only they, and not private persons, may kill criminals.

---

2. Aristotle, *Nicomachean Ethics*, VIII, 12; *Politics*, I, 4.

3. Ephesians, 5:28.

4. Aristotle, *Nicomachean Ethics*, V, 6; *Politics*, I, 2–3.

5. This differs both from the views expressed in *On Kingship*, Ch. 14 (see p. 26), and from Aquinas's early *Commentary on the Sentences* (II, D. 44, qu. 2, exp. text.) where he says the following: "Both the spiritual and the secular powers are derived from the power of God. Therefore the secular power is only under the spiritual power to the extent intended by God, that is, in the matters that relate to the salvation of the soul. Therefore in these matters the spiritual power is to be obeyed rather than the temporal. In those matters that pertain to the good of civil society the secular power is to be obeyed rather than the spiritual, in accordance with Matthew, 22, "Render to Caesar the things that are Caesar's"—unless perhaps the spiritual and secular power are joined together as in the Pope who is at the summit of both the spiritual and temporal power, by the intention of him who is both priest and king. * * *"

5 Is Suicide Permissible?

Suicide is totally wrong for three reasons. First, everything naturally loves itself, and therefore it naturally seeks to preserve itself and to resist what would injure it as much as it can. Therefore suicide is contrary to a natural inclination, as well as against the [virtue of] charity in accordance with which one should love oneself. Therefore suicide is always a mortal sin because it is against the natural law and violation of charity. Secondly, every part that exists is part of a whole. Man is part of the community and the fact that he exists affects the community. Therefore if he kills himself he does harm to the community as the Philosopher [Aristotle] makes clear.[6] Thirdly, life is a gift given by God to man and subject to his power as the one who takes away and gives life. Therefore a man who takes his own life sins against God, just as someone who kills a slave injures his master or someone who acts by an authority that has not been given to him commits a sin. God alone has authority over life and death.

*   *   *

A woman may not kill herself to avoid being raped for she may not commit the greatest crime against herself she can commit, suicide, in order to prevent another person from committing a lesser crime—since a woman who is forcibly raped commits no crime if she does not consent. * * * Also no one is allowed to kill himself for fear of consenting to sin because "evil may not be done that good may come of it,"[7] or to avoid an evil, especially those that are less serious and not certain.

7 Is It Permissible to Kill in Self-Defense?

One act may have two effects only one of which is intended and the other outside of our intention.[8] Moral acts are classified on the basis of what is intended, not of what happens outside of our intention since that is incidental to it, as explained above. The action of defending oneself may produce two effects—one, saving one's own life, and the other, killing the attacker. Now an action of this kind intended to save one's own life can not be characterized as illicit since it is natural for anyone to maintain himself in existence if he can. An act that is prompted by a good intention can become illicit if it is not proportionate to the end intended. This is why it is not allowed to use more force than necessary to defend one's life. However if moderation is used in repelling violence this is justified self-defense, for according to the [canon] law, "It is legitimate to meet force with force if it is an act of innocent self-defense and

6. Aristotle, *Nicomachean Ethics*, V, 11.
7. Romans, 3:8.
8. This is the classic statement of "the principle of double effect," which became very important in Christian ethics, especially in the areas of war and abortion. Thus for example, contemporary Christian ethicists have argued that bombing of military targets in a just war is morally permissible despite the fact that innocent non-combatants will be killed as an "indirect" or "secondary" effect. A similar argument is used concerning operations to remove an ectopic pregnancy. For discussion, see Paul Ramsey, *War and the Christian Conscience* (Durham, N.C.: Duke University Press, 1961), 39–59, and excerpted on pp. 226–229).

exercises restraint."[9] It is not required for salvation that a man not carry out actions of <u>proportionate self-defense in order to avoid killing</u> another person, for a man is more obliged to provide for his own life than for that of another. However because killing is only allowed by action of public authority for the common good, it is not lawful for someone who is acting in self-defense to intend to kill another man—except for those who in the exercise of public authority justify the act of self-defense as related to the public good. This is the case with a soldier fighting against the enemy or an officer of the law combatting robbers—although these too commit a sin if they are motivated by private animosity. * * *

8   *Is Someone Who Kills a Man by Accident Guilty of Murder?*
Obj. 2.   Exodus 21 says, "If anyone should strike a pregnant woman and produce an abortion, if death follows, let a life be taken for a life." But this can happen without intent to kill. Therefore killing by accident is punishable as murder. * * *

I answer that * * * Sin is a voluntary action, so that something that occurs by accident is not sinful * * * but if someone performs an unlawful act or even a lawful action without due care, he will not escape the penalty for murder if a person dies because of his action.

Reply to Obj. 2.   Someone who strikes a pregnant woman performs an unlawful act. Therefore if it results in the death of the woman or of an animated fetus, he will not escape the crime of murder, especially if death follows as the immediate result of the blow.[1]

Qu. 66. Theft and Robbery

1   *Is the Possession of External Goods Natural to Man?*
   We can look at external goods in two ways. From the point of view of their nature they are not subject to any human power but only to that of God whom all things instantly obey. On the other hand they can be considered from the point of view of their use, and in this respect man has a natural property right *(dominium)* over external things since he has a reason and a will that can make use of external things for his benefit. These seem to be made for him since imperfect things are for the sake of the more perfect. For this reason the Philosopher [Aristotle] proves that the possession of external things is natural to man.[2] This natural dominion over the rest of creation which man has because of his reason

9. *Decretals*, V, 12, 18. The Decretals were a collection of papal laws and decrees issued by Pope Gregory IX in 1234. It continued as part of the basic law of the Roman Catholic Church until 1917.

1. Note that the destruction of the fetus is only considered murder after ensoulment or animation—considered by medieval writers, following classical biological theories, to occur after 40 days in the case of the male embryo, and 80 days in the case of the female. Earlier abortions were considered as sinful, but not equivalent to murder. See discussion in John Noonan "Aquinas on Abortion," selection below (pp. 245–248).

2. Aristotle, *Politics*, II, 5.

which makes him the image of God was manifested in the very creation of man in Genesis where it says, "Let us make man in our image and likeness and he shall rule over the fish of the sea" etc.[3]

2 Is Private Property Legitimate?

Man has two capacities in regard to external things. First, he has the power to care for and dispose of them. To do this it is legitimate for a man to possess private property; indeed it is necessary for human life for three reasons. First, everyone is more concerned to take care of something that belongs only to him than of something that belongs to everyone or to many people, since in the case of common property he avoids effort by leaving its care to others, as occurs when one has a large number of servants. Secondly, human affairs are more efficiently organized if the proper care of each thing is an individual responsibility. There would only be confusion if everyone took care of everything in a disorganized fashion. Third, peace is better preserved among men if each one is content with his property. So we see that quarrels frequently arise among those who hold a thing in common and undivided.[4]

Man is also capable of making use of external things. In regard to this a man should not possess external things as his alone but for the community, so that he is ready to share them with others in cases of necessity. Thus the Apostle Paul says in I Timothy, "Command the rich of this world to be ready to share and to give."[5]

* * * Community of goods is said to be part of the natural law not because the natural law decrees that all things are to be possessed in common and nothing held privately, but because the distribution of property is not a matter of natural law but of human agreement which pertains to the positive law, as we have said. Therefore private property is not against natural law but it has been added to natural law by the inventiveness of human reason.[6]

7 Is Stealing Allowed in a Case of Necessity?

In cases of necessity everything is common property and thus it is not a sin for someone to take the property of another that has become common property through necessity. * * * Human law cannot violate natural or divine law. The natural order established by Divine Providence is such that lower ranking things are meant to supply the necessities of men. Therefore the division and appropriation of property by human law does not prevent its being used for the needs of man. Thus the things that anyone has in superabundance ought to be used to support the poor. * * * However since the needy are many and they cannot all be supplied from the same source, the decision is left to each individual as to how

3. Genesis, 1:26. On Judaeo-Christian attitudes towards the mastery of nature, see Lynn T. White Jr., *Machina ex Deo: Essays in the Dynamism of Western Culture* (Cambridge, Mass.: MIT Press, 1968) ch. 3.

4. Cf. Aristotle, *Politics*, II, 5.
5. I Timothy, 6:17-18.
6. For an interpretation of this passage to support socialism in Latin America, see the selection of Julio Silva Solar (pp. 178-180).

to manage his property so as to supply the requirements of those in need. But if there is an urgent and clear need, so urgent and clear that it is evident that an immediate response must be made on the basis of what is available, such as when a person is in imminent danger and cannot be helped in any other way—then a person may legitimately supply his need from the property of someone else, whether openly or secretly. Strictly speaking such a case is not theft or robbery.[7]

Qu. 69. Self-Defense

4   Is It Permissible for Someone Who Has Been Condemned to Death to Defend Himself?
A man may be condemned to death in two ways. First the death sentence may be just and in this case it is not permissible for someone to defend himself—indeed, the judge can use force on him if he resists. His action would be a case of unjust war and without doubt would be sinful. On the other hand he may be condemned unjustifiably. Such a decision is like an act of violent robbery as Ezekiel says, "The princes in their midst are like wolves seizing their prey and shedding blood."[8] Therefore just as we are allowed to resist robbers, it is also permissible in such a case to resist evil rulers—except to avoid a serious disturbance that is feared as likely to result.

Qu. 77. Fraud

4   Is It Legitimate to Sell Something for More than its Cost?
As Aristotle says there are two kinds of business exchanges.[9] One is natural and necessary. It consists in the exchange of one commodity for another, or of a commodity for the money to buy what is needed for life. This kind of exchange is not strictly that of tradesmen but more of heads of families or governments who have to provide what is needed for life by households or political communities (cities). The other kind of exchange of money for money, or money for goods, is not concerned with the needs of life but with making money, and this is the exchange in which tradesmen engage. According to Aristotle[1] the first kind of exchange is praiseworthy because it serves natural needs but the second is rightly condemned since in itself it is motivated by greed for money which has no limit but tends to increase to infinity. It follows that trade in itself has a certain quality of baseness since it does not of its own nature involve an honorable or necessary end.

Profit which is the purpose of trade, while it does not in itself involve something honorable or necessary, also does not of its nature imply something vicious or contrary to virtue. Nothing prevents profit from

---

7. See John Locke, *First Treatise of Civil Government*, ch. 4, sec. 42, for a reiteration of this view by a political philosopher who is often described as a defender of absolute property rights.

8. Ezekiel, 22:27.
9. Aristotle, *Politics*, I, 9.
1. Aristotle, *Politics*, I, 10.

being directed to a necessary or even honorable goal, so that trade is thereby made licit. For example someone may seek to secure a moderate profit through trade to maintain his household or to support the poor or he may also engage in trade for the public welfare to provide his country with the necessities of life and seek profit not as his goal but as a recompense for his labor.

Qu. 78. The Sin of Usury

1   Is It Sinful to Charge Interest (Usury) for Lending Money?

To receive interest (usury) for lending money is unjust in itself for something is sold that does not exist, and this obviously results in an inequality which is contrary to justice. To understand this one must realize that there are some things that are consumed when they are used. We consume wine when we use it to drink, and wheat when we use it as food. In such cases the use of the thing should not be considered separately from the thing itself so that when someone is given the use of the thing, he is given the thing itself. Therefore in these cases ownership is transferred in the case of a loan. If someone wants to sell wine and to sell the use of wine, he sells the same thing twice or sells what does not exist—a clear sin against justice. For the same reason it is unjust to require two payments for a loan of wine or wheat, one on the return of an equal amount of the thing and a second as the price for using it. We call this usury.

There are other things that are not consumed when they are used, such as the use of a house which is inhabited and not destroyed. In such cases both the use and the thing can be lent, for instance someone can give the ownership of a house to someone else but keep the use of the house for a certain period for oneself. Therefore it is legitimate for a man to receive a payment for the use of a house and in addition to ask that the house that has been provided be returned, as happens in the rental and leasing of houses.

However according to the Philosopher [Aristotle] money was devised to facilitate exchange, so that the proper and principal use of money is its use or expenditure when exchanges are carried out.[2] Therefore it is wrong in itself to receive a payment for the use of a loan of money— which is called usury. And just as a man is obliged to make restitution of other things that he has acquired unjustly, he also must do so with money that he has obtained from usury. * * *

The Jews were forbidden to take interest "from their brothers," i.e. from other Jews. We should understand this to mean that to receive interest from any man is intrinsically evil, since we ought to consider all men as our neighbors and brothers. * * * They were allowed to take interest from foreigners not because it was right but in order to avoid a greater

2. Aristotle, Nicomachean Ethics, V, 5; Politics, I, 3.

evil, that of taking interest from Jews, God's chosen people, because of the avarice to which they were inclined.[3]
* * * Human laws leave some sins unpunished because of the imperfection of men who would lack many things that are useful to them if all sins were strictly prohibited by the application of legal penalties. Therefore human law allows usury not because it considers it just but to avoid interference with the useful activities of many people.[4]

Qu. 104. Obedience

1   Is One Man Obliged to Obey Another?

The actions of things in nature proceed from natural forces, while human actions proceed from the human will. In nature higher beings necessarily move lower ones to act by virtue of a natural superiority which is given them by God. So also in human affairs it is necessary for superiors to move inferiors through volitional acts by virtue of an authority which is established by God. To move the reason and the will means to command. Therefore just as in the order of nature established by God lower elements in nature must be subject to higher ones, so in human affairs inferiors are bound to obey their superiors according to the order contained in the natural and divine law.

5   Are Subjects Obliged to Do Everything that Their Superiors Command?

There are two ways in which it can happen that a subject is not obliged to obey every command of his superior. First, if it is contrary to the command of a higher power. * * * Secondly, a subject is not obliged to obey his superior if he commands something over which he has no authority. As Seneca says, "It is wrong to think that slavery applies to the whole person. The better part is unaffected by it, for the lower bodily elements are subject to a master but the mind is free."[5] Therefore in matters that relate to the internal movements of the will a man is not obliged to obey man, but God alone. One man is obliged to obey another

3. See Deuteronomy, 23:19–20, which allows the taking of interest from foreigners. Some scholars believe that what was permitted was the taking of security for repayment. Aquinas's attitude towards the Jews and its policy consequences are stated in *The Government of the Jews (De Regimine Judaeorum)* written in 1270–71 to the Duchess of Brabant. In reply to the Duchess's question whether she could tax the Jews, Aquinas advised her not to impose forced loans upon them as had been the practice, despite the fact that "the Jews are culpable and were destined to eternal slavery so that territorial rulers can take their property for their own — although they must leave them what is necessary to sustain life." However heavier legal fines could be imposed on Jews or any other usurer "since the money taken from them does not belong to them." At the end of the letter he reminded the Duchess that a general council (Fourth Lateran Council,

1215) had decreed that "Jews of both sexes in every Christian land should always be distinguished from other people by a special dress." Aquinas's attitude towards the Jews was typical of medieval Christianity. For details see James Parkes, *The Jew in the Medieval Community* (New York: Herman Press, 1976).
4. On the development of medieval theological and legal attitudes towards usury see John T. Noonan, *The Scholastic Analysis of Usury* (Cambridge, Mass.: Harvard University Press, 1957). Later writers began to develop exceptions to the absolute prohibition on the taking of interest.
5. Seneca, *De Beneficiis*, III, 20. Seneca (A.D. 4–64) was a Roman Stoic philosopher whose views on the sinfulness of human nature and the superiority of an earlier Golden Age were seen as anticipations of Christian doctrines.

in outward bodily actions, but in matters relating to human nature, for example, those relating to bodily sustenance and the procreation of offspring, a man is bound to obey God alone, not another man, because by nature all men are equal. Therefore slaves are not obliged to obey their masters, nor children their parents, in contracting marriages or deciding to remain a virgin or the like. However, in matters that relate to the ordering of human actions and affairs a subject is obliged to obey his superior in the area in which he is his superior—a soldier, for example, should obey the commander of an army in matters that relate to war, a slave his master in what pertains to his work as a slave, a son his father in what pertains to preparation for life and the management of the household, and so on with other matters.

6   Are Christians Obliged to Obey Secular Authorities?

The order of justice is not abolished but rather confirmed by faith in Jesus Christ. The order of justice requires that inferiors obey their superiors, for otherwise stability (*status*) could not be maintained in human affairs. Therefore the Christian faith does not exempt the faithful from obeying secular rulers. * * * The subjection of one man to another pertains to the body, not to the soul which remains free. Now in this life on earth we are freed by the grace of Christ from defects of the soul but not from those of the body, as is clear when the Apostle [Paul] says that he serves the law of God with his mind but the law of sin with the flesh.[6] Therefore those who are made sons of God by grace have been freed from the spiritual slavery of sin but not from the bodily subjection which binds them to serve their earthly masters.

Qu. 110. Lying

3   Is Every Lie a Sin?

Obj. 4.   A lesser evil should be chosen to avoid a greater evil. A doctor, for example, amputates a limb to prevent the whole body from becoming infected. Now there is less harm in producing an untrue idea in someone's mind than for someone to murder or be murdered. Therefore it is permissible to lie to prevent someone from killing or being killed.

I answer that there is no way that something that is evil in itself can become good or permissible. For something to be good it is required that all its elements be right, for good is a single whole, while evil is the result of individual defects, as Dionysius says.[7] A lie is evil in itself. It is an action involving improper material elements. Words are natural signs of thoughts and therefore it is both unnatural and improper for someone to signify in words what he does not have in his mind. * * *

---

6. Romans, 7:25.   7. Dionysius, *On the Divine Names*, IV, 30.

Reply to Obj. 4. A lie has the quality of sinfulness not only because it injures others but because it is disordered in itself. Now it is not permissible to employ something that is forbidden because it is disordered, in order to prevent harm or loss to others—just as it is forbidden for a man to steal in order to give alms—except in cases of necessity when everything becomes common property. Therefore it is not permissible for anyone to tell a lie in order to save someone from a danger. One may however prudently conceal the truth by some dissimulation, as Augustine says.[8]

Qu. 150. *Drunkenness*

2 *Is Drunkenness a Mortal Sin?*

We have pointed out that what is wrong with drunkenness is the disordered use of wine, and an excessive desire for it. * * * This may happen in three ways. First, if someone does not know that his drinking is excessive and intoxicating, then there is no sin. Second, if someone realizes that his drinking is excessive but does not think that the drink will make him drunk, then his drunkenness may be a venial sin.[9] Third, if someone is well aware that his drinking is excessive and intoxicating and still would rather get drunk than stop drinking he commits the sin of drunkenness (is properly called a drunkard) because the moral character of an action depends not on what happens by accident and unintentionally but on what is intended in itself. Thus drunkenness (of this kind) is a mortal sin because through it a man willingly and knowingly deprives himself of the use of reason which enables him to act virtuously and avoid sin—and so he commits a mortal sin by putting himself in danger of sin.

Qu. 152. *Virginity*

2 *Is Virginity Lawful?*

Vice in human acts is that which is against right reason. Right reason requires that one should make use of the means to an end in the measure that is appropriate to the end. According to the *Ethics* there are three kinds of good for man.[1] The first consists in the external goods or wealth, the second consists in the health of the body, and the third in the goods of the soul among which the life of contemplation is of higher value than the active life, as the Philosopher [Aristotle] proves in the *Ethics* and the Lord says in the Gospel of Luke, "Mary has chosen the better part."[2] External goods are ordered to those of the body and those of the

8. Augustine, *Against Lying*, ch. 10, available in Roy J. Deferrari, ed., *St. Augustine, Treatises on Various Subjects* (New York: The Fathers of the Church, 1952), 125ff.

9. In Catholic moral theology venial sins are less serious offenses which if unforgiven must be expiated in purgatory. A mortal sin is an offense that is so serious and willful that it causes the soul to be cut off completely from the grace of God and to deserve damnation.

1. Aristotle, *Nicomachean Ethics*, I, 8.

2. Aristotle, *Nicomachean Ethics*, X, 7–8; Luke, 10:43.

body to those of the soul, and those of the active life are ordered to the contemplative life. It is appropriate to right reason to use external goods in the measure that suits the body, and so on with the others. Therefore if anyone for the good health of his body or also for the contemplation of truth gives up material possessions that it would otherwise be good for him to have, this is not a vice but according to right reason. Similarly if someone abstains from bodily pleasures in order to devote oneself more freely to the contemplation of truth,this is in harmony with right reason. Therefore holy virginity abstains from all sexual pleasure in order to be more free for the contemplation of the divine. The Apostle[Paul] says, "The unmarried woman who is a virgin thinks of the things of the Lord so that she may be holy in body and spirit. The woman who is married thinks of things of the world and how to please her husband."[3] We conclude that virginity is not a vice but worthy of praise.

*   *   *

The command of the natural law given to man regarding eating must be fulfilled by every person,otherwise the individual could not stay alive. The command concerning procreation involves the whole of the human race which is obliged not only to multiply in body but also to grow in spirit. Therefore the human race is sufficiently provided for if some are involved with bodily procreation and others abstain from it to devote themselves to the contemplation of the divine for the improvement and welfare of mankind.

Qu. 154. The Types of Lechery

2   Is Ordinary Fornication a Grave Sin?

A mortal sin is any sin that is committed in direct opposition to human life.[4] Now ordinary fornication involves a disorder that leads to injury to the life of that which would be born as a result of such an act of sexual intercourse. In the case of animals in which the care of the male and female is required to bring up the children we observe that their mating does not take place promiscuously but involves the union of a male with one specific female, or several of them as in the case with birds.This is not the case with animals where the female alone is sufficient to rear the offspring, such as dogs and the like whose intercourse is promiscuous. It is clear that to bring up a child requires both the care of the mother who nourishes him and even more the care of the father to train and defend him and to develop him in internal and external endowments. Therefore promiscuity is contrary to the nature of man. The intercourse of the male must be with a specific female and he should stay with her not for a little while but for a long period of time or even for a whole lifetime. This is why there is a natural human concern among men to be certain

3. I Corinthians, 7:34.
4. A mortal sin means the death (mors) of grace in the soul.

about their offspring because they are responsible for the education of their children. They would not have this certainty if sexual intercourse were promiscuous. This commitment to one woman is called matrimony and therefore is considered to be part of the natural law.* * *

Hence since fornication is promiscuous intercourse outside of marriage it is contrary to the good of the upbringing of offspring, and therefore is a mortal sin. It makes no difference if a person who commits fornication makes some provision for the upbringing of the child since the law provides on the basis of what ordinarily occurs rather than of what might happen in a specific case.

4 May Caresses and Kisses be Mortally Sinful?

A sin may be mortal in two ways. The first is in itself, and kisses, embraces, and caresses are not mortal sins in themselves, since they can take place without libidinous desire or because of the custom of the country or for some requirement or good reason. On the other hand something can be a mortal sin because of its purpose. For example someone who gives alms in order to persuade someone to embrace heresy commits a mortal sin because of his evil intention. We have already said that consent to the pleasure of mortal sin, not merely to the act itself, is a mortal sin. Therefore since fornication is a mortal sin and still more other lustful acts, it follows that consent to the pleasure of these sins is a mortal sin, and not merely consent to the acts themselves. Therefore in so far as kisses and embraces of this kind are engaged in for the purpose of this kind of pleasure it follows that they are mortal sins—and only in this case are they called lustful. Therefore those actions to the degree that they are lustful are mortal sins.

8 Is Adultery a Specific Kind of Lechery?

In adultery one acts in a way that is contrary to chastity and to the good of the continuation of the human race. First, one has sexual relations with a woman who is not joined to oneself in matrimony which is a requirement for the good of the proper upbringing of offspring. Secondly, one has sexual relations with a woman who is joined to someone else in matrimony, thus injuring the offspring of someone else. The same applies to a married woman who is corrupted by the adultery. * * * And so adultery is clearly a specific kind of lechery since it manifests a special disorder in sexual activity.

11 Is Unnatural Vice a Kind of Lechery?

A particular kind of lechery takes place when a special quality of disorder makes a sexual act indecent. This can happen in two ways—first when it is opposed to right reason which generally is the case with all types of lechery, and second because when in addition it is opposed to the natural order of the sex act itself that is appropriate to mankind—and this is called unnatural vice.

This can happen in several ways. First, if orgasm is induced for the sake of sexual pleasure without intercourse, and this is the sin of uncleanness [masturbation] that some call "the softness." Secondly, when intercourse is carried out with a thing belonging to a different species and this is called bestiality. Thirdly, if intercourse is with a person of the same sex, male with male or female with female, as the Apostle [Paul] says and this is called the vice of sodomy.[5] Fourthly, when the natural method of intercourse is not observed either as to the proper organ or utilizing monstrous or bestial techniques of intercourse. * * *

12 Is Unnatural Vice the Worst Sin of all the Types of Lechery?

The principles of reason are those that are in accordance with nature. * * * Reason begins with principles that are based on nature and on the basis of what has been determined by nature determines what it is proper to do. This is true both for the speculative and practical reason. Just as in the area of theory (speculative reason) an error as to the principles that are instilled in man by nature is most serious and reprehensible, so in the area of practice (practical reason) actions that are in violation of what has been determined by nature are also serious and reprehensible.

Since therefore in the case of unnatural vice man violates what has been determined by nature concerning sexuality, this is the most serious sin. After it comes incest which violates the natural reverence which we owe to members of our family. * * * Among the unnatural vices, the least serious is the sin of uncleanness which consists only in not having intercourse with another person. The most serious is that of bestiality because it does not involve the right species. Thus the Gloss on Genesis, "He [Joseph] accused his brothers of the worst sin" says that "They had relations with cattle."[6] After this comes the vice of sodomy since it does not involve the right sex. After this is the sin of not using the right method of sexual intercourse—which is worse if it is not in the right place than if it relates to other aspects of the method of intercourse.[7]

---

5. John Boswell, *Christianity, Social Tolerance, and Homosexuality* (Chicago: University of Chicago Press, 1980), makes an unconvincing—if not specious—argument that Aquinas's condemnation of homosexuality represents a relatively late development in Christian attitudes. He does this by a) misrepresenting St. Paul's rejection of homosexuality in Romans, 1: 26–27 as applying only to such conduct by heterosexuals, b) claiming that the sin of Sodom (Genesis 19) was not sodomy but a breach of hospitality (pp. 92–98) and c) interpreting Aquinas's argument from nature as based on a comparison with the behavior of animals, ignoring the obvious teleological character of his understanding of nature (pp. 318–330). Boswell admits that homosexuality is condemned in the Old Testament (Leviticus 18:22 and 20:13) but dismisses the condemnations as denunciations of "ceremonial uncleanness" (pp. 100–102).

6. Genesis, 37:2. The Gloss was the generally accepted line-by-line commentary.

7. The ranking of the seriousness of various sexual sins was based on the application of a teleological or purposive understanding of nature. It was useful to confessors in assigning the appropriate penance.

III   Part III (1272–1273)

Qu. 8. The Grace of Christ as Head of the Church

3   Is Christ Head of All Mankind?

The difference between the natural body of a man and the mystical body of the church is that the parts of a natural body all exist together at the same time while those of a mystical body do not. They do not by nature since the church is made up of different people from the beginning to the end of the world. They do not by grace because of those who exist at a given time some do not have grace but will have it later, while others possess it now. Thus there can be actual and potential members of a mystical body. Some are potential members who will never become actual members. Others will become members in three ways—by faith, in love on earth, and in the enjoyment of heaven.

Therefore we can say that in general throughout the history of the world, Christ is the head of all men but in different degrees. First and mainly he is the head of those who are united to him in heaven. Secondly he is head of those who are actually united with him in love. Thirdly, of those who are actually united with him in faith. But fourthly [he is head] of those who are not yet actually united with him but will actually be so united according to the divine plan [predestination]. Fifth, he is head of those who are potentially united with him but will never actually be so united—such as the people in this world who are not predestined. When they leave this world they cease entirely to be members of Christ since they are no longer potentially united with him. * * * Those who are members of Christ in an actual union of love are those who are not in the state of mortal sin, while those who are subject to these sins are not actual members of Christ but only potential ones, except perhaps in an imperfect way through a deformed faith which unites them to Christ in a way, although not in the full sense that through Christ a man achieves the live of grace. "For faith without works is dead," says the Epistle of [St.] James.[1] But they do receive a certain vital activity from Christ, in whom they believe—just as if a withered limb were moved by a man. * * *

1. James, 2:20.

Supplement (Posthumous Compilation, 1274ff.)

Qu. 52. *Slavery as an Impediment*

1 *Is Slavery an Impediment to Marriage?*

Obj. 2. What is against nature cannot be an impediment to what is in accordance with nature. But slavery is against nature because as [Pope] Gregory says, it is against nature for one man to have dominion over another.[1] This is also clear from the fact that God said to man that he would have dominion over the fish of the sea, etc.[2] Therefore what is natural cannot be an impediment to marriage.

Obj. 3. If slavery is an impediment, this must be part of either natural law or positive law. It is not part of natural law because, as [Pope] Gregory says, according to natural law all men are equal, and at the beginning of the *Digest* [of Roman Law] it says that slavery is not part of the natural law.[3] Positive law stems from natural law, as Cicero says.[4] Therefore there is no law that says that slavery is an impediment to marriage. * * *

Reply to Obj. 2. Nothing prevents a thing from being contrary to nature in one sense, but not contrary to it in another sense. Corruption and weakness and old age are contrary to nature, as is said in *On the Heavens*,[5] because nature intends things to be perfect. They are not against nature in another sense, however, because nature cannot preserve one thing in being without something else being corrupted. And when nature cannot produce a greater perfection it produces a lesser one. For example when it cannot make a male, it makes a female which is a misbegotten male, as is said in *On the Soul.*[6]

Similarly I say that slavery is against nature in one sense, but not against it in another sense. Natural reason inclines to good, and nature desires that everyone should be good, but if someone sins, nature also is inclined that the sin should be punished. Thus slavery was introduced as a punishment for sin. It is proper that something which is against nature in some way should be an impediment to something that is natural. Thus impotence which is against nature in the way described above is an impediment to marriage.

Reply to Obj. 3. The natural law decrees that a punishment should be inflicted for every offense and that no one who is innocent should be

1. St. Gregory the Great, *Pastoral Rule*, II, 6; available in English in vol. 12 of the *Select Library of Nicene and Post-Nicene Fathers*, Philip Schaff and Henry Ware, eds., (Grand Rapids: Eerdmans, 1956). Pope Gregory was born in 540 and died in 604. His book was used as a guide for bishops during the Middle Ages.

2. Genesis, 1:26.
3. Gregory the Great, *Pastoral Rule*, II, 6; *Digest*, I, i, 1, 4 (Ulpian).
4. Cicero, *Rhetoric*, II, 54.
5. Aristotle, *On the Heavens (De Caelo)*, VI, 3.
6. Aristotle, *On the Generation of Animals*, II, 3.

punished. To specify a punishment according to the condition of the person and his offense is a matter of positive law. Therefore slavery which is a punishment is determined by positive law and is related to natural law as what is specific is related to what is unspecified. The positive law has determined that not knowing that a person is a slave is an impediment to marriage so that no innocent person would be punished—since it would be a punishment for a woman to have a husband who is a slave, and vice versa.

BACKGROUNDS
AND SOURCES

ARISTOTLE

The introduction into the West of the works of Aristotle (384–322 B.C.) in the thirteenth century provided a vast philosophic corpus on many different subjects. Facing the challenge of Aristotelianism to medieval Christianity, Aquinas attempted to make use of its central analytic concepts to construct a new system of theology. From Aristotle's *Physics* he derived a teleological view of nature as purposive and dynamic, as well as the analysis of living things as composites of matter, their underlying substratum, and form, their organizing principle. In Aristotle's *On the Soul*, the soul is described as the form that actualizes and gives substantial form to the body. Aristotle is ambiguous on whether the soul can exist separately from the body, but at least left open this possibility. Aristotle's *Metaphysics* was important in providing Aquinas with the concept of an infinite, eternal, self-moving ("necessary") First Mover who is the source of motion and goodness in the world which he could use in demonstrating the existence of God in the *Summa Theologiae*. Aristotle's *Nicomachean Ethics* argued that man's happiness was to be found in virtue—especially the exercise of his highest faculties of reason which he shares with the Divine. It also outlined a theory of natural justice which could be developed in Aquinas's discussion of natural law where he also drew on Aristotelian theories of a purposive nature ("final causes") to argue for "natural inclinations" as the basis of natural law. Finally, Aristotle's *Politics* provided Aquinas with important elements of his political theory—political life as natural to man, the condemnation of usury (the taking of payment for the lending of money) as unnatural, the defense of private property as natural and useful provided it is used in a way that contributes to the common good, and an argument for the collective wisdom of ordinary men. Aristotle's theory of natural slavery was incorporated in Thomistic thought in an ambiguous fashion, both because it clashed with arguments in the writings of the church fathers, such as Augustine and Gregory the Great, and because it conflicted with the Christian view of the equality of all men in the eyes of God. Yet for Aquinas, Aristotle was "the Philosopher" and his system in revised form became the basis of what is now known as Thomism.

Physics †

Bk. II, ch. 1 [Nature and the Natural]

Of things that exist, some exist by nature, some from other causes. 'By nature' the animals and their parts exist, and the plants and the

† Translated by R. P. Hardie and R. K. Gaye, from Richard McKeon, ed., *The Basic Works of Aristotle* (New York: Random House, 1941), by permission.

simple bodies (earth, fire, air, water)—for we say that these and the like exist 'by nature'.

All the things mentioned present a feature in which they differ from things which are *not* constituted by nature. Each of them has *within itself* a principle of motion and of stationariness (in respect of place, or of growth and decrease, or by way of alteration). * * *

Things 'have a nature' which have a principle of this kind. Each of them is a substance; for it is a subject, and nature always implies a subject in which it inheres.

The term 'according to nature' is applied to all these things and also to the attributes which belong to them in virtue of what they are, for instance the property of fire to be carried upwards—which is not a 'nature' nor 'has a nature' but is 'by nature' or 'according to nature.' * * *

One account of 'nature' is that it is the immediate material substratum of things which have in themselves a principle of motion or change.

Another account is that 'nature' is the shape or form which is specified in the definition of the thing.

For the word 'nature' is applied to what is according to nature and the natural in the same way as 'art' is applied to what is artistic or a work of art. We should not say in the latter case that there is anything artistic about a thing, if it is a bed only potentially, not yet having the form of a bed; nor should we call it a work of art. The same is true of natural compounds. What is potentially flesh or bone has not yet its own 'nature,' and does not exist 'by nature,' until it receives the form specified in the definition, which we name in defining what flesh or bone is. Thus in the second sense of 'nature' it would be the shape or form (not separable ·except in statement) of things which have in themselves a source of motion. (The combination of the two, e.g., man, is not 'nature' but 'by nature' or 'natural'.)

The form indeed is 'nature' rather than the matter; for a thing is more properly said to be what it is when it has attained to fulfilment than when it exists potentially. * * *

We also speak of a thing's nature as being exhibited in the process of growth by which its nature is attained. The 'nature' is this sense is not like 'doctoring,' which leads not to the art of doctoring but to health. Doctoring must start from the art, not lead to it. But it is not in this way that nature (in the one sense) is related to nature (in the other). What grows *qua* growing grows from something into something. Into what then does it grow? Not into that from which it arose but into that to which it tends. The shape then is nature. * * *

Bk. II, ch. 3 [The Four Causes]

In one sense, then, (1) that out of which a thing comes to be and which persists, is called its 'cause', e.g., the bronze of the statue, the silver of the bowl, and the genera of which the bronze and the silver are species.

In another sense (2) the form or the archetype, (i.e., the statement of the essence) and its genera, are called 'causes' (e.g., of the octave of relation of 2:1, and generally number), and the parts in the definition.

Again (3) the primary source of the change or coming to rest; (e.g. the man who gave advice is a cause, the father is cause of the child), and generally what makes of what is made and what causes change of what is changed.

Again (4) in the sense of end or 'that for the sake of which' a thing is done, e.g., health is the cause of walking about. ('Why is he walking about?' we say. 'To be healthy', and, having said that, we think we have assigned the cause.) The same is true also of all the intermediate steps as means towards the end, e.g., reduction of flesh, purging, drugs, or surgical instruments are means towards health. All these things are 'for the sake of' the end, though they differ from one another in that some are activities, others instruments.

This then perhaps exhausts the number of ways in which the term 'cause' is used. * * *

On the Soul

Bk. II, ch. 1 [The Soul and the Body]

* * * the body is the subject or matter, not what is attributed to it. Hence the soul must be a substance in the sense of the form of a natural body having life potentially within it. But substance is actuality, and thus soul is the actuality of a body as above characterized. Now the word actuality has two senses corresponding respectively to the possession of knowledge and the actual exercise of knowledge. It is obvious that the soul is actuality in the first sense, viz., that of knowledge as possessed, for both sleeping and waking presuppose the existence of soul, and of these waking corresponds to actual knowing, sleeping to knowledge possessed but not employed, and, in the history of the individual, knowledge comes before its employment or exercise. * * *

What is soul? It is substance in the sense which corresponds to the definitive formula of a thing's essence. That means that it is 'the essential whatness' of a body. * * * [T]he soul is inseparable from its body, or at any rate certain parts of it are (if it has parts)—for the actuality of some of them is nothing but the actualities of their bodily parts. Yet some may be separable because they are not the actualities of any body at all.

Metaphysics †

Bk. XII, ch. 5 [The Unmoved Mover]

[W]e must assert that it is necessary that there should be an eternal unmovable substance. For substances are the first of existing things, and if they are all destructible, all things are destructible. But it is impossible that movement should either have come into being or cease to be (for it must always have existed), or that time should. For there could not be a before and an after if time did not exist. * * * Since there is something which moves while itself unmoved, existing actually, this can in no way be otherwise than as it is. For motion in space is the first of the kinds of change, and motion in a circle the first kind of spatial motion; and this the first mover *produces*. The first mover, then, exists of necessity; and in so far as it exists by necessity, its mode of being is good, and it is in this sense a first principle. For the necessary has all these senses—that which is necessary perforce because it is contrary to the natural impulse, that without which the good is impossible, and that which cannot be otherwise but can exist only in a single way.

On such a principle, then, depend the heavens and the world of nature. And it is a life such as the best which we enjoy, and enjoy for but a short time (for it is ever in this state, which we cannot be), since its actuality is also pleasure. (And for this reason are waking, perception, and thinking most pleasant, and hopes and memories are so on account of these.) And thinking in itself deals with that which is best in itself, and that which is thinking in the fullest sense with that which is best in the fullest sense. And thought thinks on itself because it shares the nature of the object of thought; for it becomes an object of thought in coming into contact with and thinking its objects, so that thought and the object of thought are the same. For that which is *capable* of receiving the object of thought, i.e., the essence, is thought. But it is *active* when it *possesses* this object. Therefore the possession rather than the receptivity is the divine element which thought seems to contain, and the act of contemplation is what is most pleasant and best. If, then, God is always in that good state in which we sometimes are, this compels our wonder; and if in a better state this compels it yet more. And God *is* in a better state. And life also belongs to God; for the actuality of thought is life, and God is that actuality; and God's self-dependent actuality is life most good and eternal. We say therefore that God is a living being, eternal, most good, so that life and duration continuous and eternal belong to God; for this *is* God. * * *

It is clear then from what has been said that there is a substance which is eternal and unmovable and separate from sensible things. It has been shown also that this substance cannot have any magnitude, but is with-

†Translated by W. D. Ross, from R. McKeon, ed., *The Basic Works of Aristotle* (New York: Random House, 1941), by permission.

out parts and indivisible (for it produces movement through infinite time, but nothing finite has infinite power; and, while every magnitude is either infinite or finite, it cannot, for the above reason, have finite magnitude, and it cannot have infinite magnitude because there is no infinite magnitude at all). But it has also been shown that it is impassive and unalterable; for all the other changes are posterior to change of place.

Nicomachean Ethics †

Bk. I, ch. 7 [Happiness as the Life of Virtue in accord with Reason]

By a different path, therefore, our argument has arrived at the same point; and this we must attempt to explain still farther.

Since ends appear to be more than one, and of these we choose some for the sake of others, as, for instance, riches, musical instruments, and universally all instruments whatever, it is plain that they are not all perfect. But the chief good appears to be something perfect; so that if there is some one end which is alone perfect, that must be the very thing which we are in search of; but if there are many, it must be the most perfect of them. Now we say that the object pursued for its own sake is more perfect than that pursued for the sake of another; and that the object which is never chosen on account of another thing, is more perfect than those which are eligible both by themselves, and for the sake of that other: in fine, we call that completely perfect, which is always eligible for its own sake, and never on account of anything else.

Of such a kind does happiness seem in a peculiar manner to be; for this we always choose on its own account, and never on account of anything else. But honor, and pleasure, and intellect, and every virtue we choose partly on their own account (for were no further advantage to result from them, we should choose each of them), but we choose them also for the sake of happiness, because we suppose that we shall attain happiness by their means; but no one chooses happiness for the sake of these, nor in short for the sake of anything else.

As to the musician, and statuary, and to every artist, and in short to all who have any function or course of action, the good and excellence of each appears to consist in their peculiar function; so would it appear to be with man, if there is any peculiar function belonging to him. Are there, then, certain peculiar functions and courses of action belonging to the carpenter and shoemaker; and is there no peculiar function of man, but is he by nature without a function? or, as there appears to be a certain function peculiarly belonging to the eye, the hand, and the foot, and, to each of the members, in like manner would not one assume a certain function besides all these peculiarly belonging to man?

† Translated by R. W. Browne (London: George Bell & Sons, 1895).

What, then, must this peculiar function be? For life man appears to share in common with plants; but his *peculiar* function is the object of our inquiry: we must, therefore, separate the life of nutrition and growth. Then * * * sensitive life would next follow; but this also he appears to enjoy in common with the horse, the ox, and every animal. There remains, therefore, a certain practical life of a being which possesses reason; and of this one part is, as it were, obedient to reason, the other as possessing it, and exercising intellect. But this life also being spoken of in two ways [according to activity and according to habit], we must take in the sense of activity, for that appears to be more properly called life. Now if the function of man is an activity of the soul according to reason, or not without reason; and if we say that the function of man, and of a good man, is the same generically, as in the case of a harp player and a good harp player (and so, in short, in all cases, superiority in each particular excellence being added to each particular work); for it is the work of a harp player to play, of a good harp player to play well: and if we assume the peculiar function of man to be a kind of life, and this life an activity of the soul and actions performed with reason; and the peculiar function of a good man to be the same things done well, and honorably; and everything to be complete according to its proper excellence: if, I repeat, these things are true, it follows, that man's chief good is "an activity of the soul according to virtue"; but if the virtues are more than one, according to the best and most perfect virtue; and besides this, we must add, in a perfect life: for as neither one swallow, nor one day, makes a spring; so neither does one day, nor a short time, make a man blessed and happy.

Bk. II, ch. 6 [Virtue as the Mean between Extremes]

If, then, every science accomplishes its function well, by keeping the mean in view, and directing its works to it (whence people are accustomed to say of excellent works, that it is impossible to take anything away, or add anything to them, since excess and defect destroy the excellence, but the being in the mean preserves it), and if good artisans, as we may say, perform their function, keeping this in view, then virtue, being, like nature, more accurate and excellent than any art, must be apt to hit the mean. But I mean moral virtue; for it is conversant with passions and actions; and in these there is defect and excess, and the mean; as, for example, we may feel fear, confidence, desire, anger, pity, and, in a word, pleasure and pain, both too much and too little, and in both cases improperly. But the time when, and the cases in which, and the persons towards whom, and the motive for which, and the manner in which, constitute the mean and the excellence; and this is the characteristic property of virtue.

In like manner, in actions there are excess and defect, and the mean; but virtue is conversant with passions and actions, and in them excess is wrong, and defect is blamed, but the mean is praised, and is correct; and both of these are properties of virtue. Virtue, then, is a kind of mean state, being at least apt to hit the mean. Again, it is possible to go wrong in many ways (for evil, as the Pythagoreans conjectured, is of the nature of the infinite, but good of the finite); but we can go right in one way only; and for this reason the former is easy, and the latter difficult; it is easy to miss a mark, but difficult to hit it; and for these reasons, therefore, the excess and defect belong to vice, but the mean state to virtue; for "we are good in one way only, but bad in all sorts of ways."

Virtue, therefore, is a "habit, accompanied with deliberate preference, in the relative mean, defined by reason, and as the prudent man would define it." It is a mean state between two vices, one in excess, the other in defect; and it is so, moreover, because of the vices one division falls short of, and the other exceeds what is right, both in passions and actions, whilst virtue discovers the mean and chooses it. Therefore, with reference to its essence, and the definition which states its substance, virtue is a mean state; but with reference to the standard of "the best" and "the excellent," it is an extreme.

Bk. V, ch. 7 [Natural Justice]

Of the political just, one part is natural, and the other legal. The natural is that which everywhere is equally valid, and depends not upon being or not being received. But the legal is that which originally was a matter of indifference, but which, when enacted, is so no longer; as the price of ransom being fixed at a mina, or the sacrificing of a goat, and not two sheep; and further, all particular acts of legislation; as the sacrificing to Brasidas, and all those matters which are the subjects of decrees. But to some persons all just things appear to be matters of law, because that which is natural is unchangeable, and has the same power everywhere, just as fire burns both here and in Persia; but they see that just things are subject to change. This is not really the case, but only in some sense; and yet with the gods perhaps it is by no means so; but with us there is something which exists by nature; still it may be argued, everything with us is subject to change, yet nevertheless there is that which is by nature and that which is not. Of things contingent, what is natural, and what is not natural, but legal, and settled by agreement (even granting that both are alike subject to change), is evident; and the same distinction will apply to all other cases; for, naturally, the right hand is stronger than the left; and yet it is possible for some people to use both equally. But that justice which depends upon agreement and expediency resembles the case of measures; for measures of wine and corn are not everywhere equal; but where men buy they are larger, and where they sell again smaller. And in like manner, that justice which is not natural, but man's invention, is not everywhere the same; since neither are all political constitutions, although there is one which would be by nature and best everywhere; for there can be but one by nature best everywhere.

Bk. X, ch. 7 [Contemplation as Perfect Happiness]

If happiness be activity according to virtue, it is reasonable to suppose that it is according to the best virtue; and this must be the virtue of the best part of man. Whether, then, this best part be the intellect, or something else—which is thought naturally to rule and govern, and to possess ideas upon honorable and divine subjects; or whether it is itself divine, or the most divine of any property which we possess; the activity of this part according to its proper virtue must be perfect happiness: and that this activity is contemplative has been stated. This also would seem to agree with what was said before, and with the truth: for this activity is the noblest; since the intellect is the noblest thing within us, and of subjects of knowledge, those are noblest with which the intellect is conversant. * * *

If, then, of all courses of action which are according to the virtues, those which have to do with politics and war excel in beauty and greatness; and these have no leisure, and aim at some end, and are not chosen for their own sakes; but the activity of the intellect is thought to be superior in intensity, because it is contemplative; and to aim at no end beyond itself, and to have a pleasure properly belonging to it; and if self sufficiency, and leisure, and freedom from cares (as far as anything human can be set free), and everything which is attributed to the happy man, evidently exist in this activity; then this must be the perfect happiness of man, when it attains the end of life complete; for nothing is incomplete of those things which belong to happiness.

But such a life would be better than man could attain to; for he would live thus, not in so far as he is man, but as there is in him something divine. But so far as this divine part surpasses the whole compound nature, so far does its activity surpass the activity which is according to all other virtue. If, then, the intellect be divine when compared with man, the life also, which is in obedience to that, will be divine when compared with human life. * * * And what was said before will apply now; for that which peculiarly belongs to each by nature, is best and most pleasant to every one; and consequently to man, the life according to intellect is most pleasant, if intellect especially constitutes Man. This life, therefore, is the most happy.

Politics †

Bk. I [Man is by Nature a Political Animal]

1.   Every state is a community of some kind, and every community is established with a view to some good; for men always act in order to obtain that which they think good. But, if all communities aim at some

† Translated by Benjamin Jowett (Oxford: Clarendon Press, 1905).

good, the state or political community, which is the highest of all, and which embraces all the rest, aims at good in a greater degree than any other, and at the highest good.

Some people think that the qualifications of a statesman, king, householder, and master are the same, and that they differ, not in kind, but only in the number of their subjects. For example, the ruler over a few is called a master; over more, the manager of a household; over a still larger number, a statesman or king, as if there were no difference between a great household and a small state. The distinction which is made between the king and the statesman is as follows: When the government is personal, the ruler is a king; when, according to the rules of the political science, the citizens rule and are ruled in turn, then he is called a statesman.

But all this is a mistake; for governments differ in kind, as will be evident to any one who considers the matter according to the method which has hitherto guided us. As in other departments of science, so in politics, the compound should always be resolved into the simple elements or least parts of the whole. We must therefore look at the elements of which the state is composed, in order that we may see in what the different kinds of rule differ from one another, and whether any scientific result can be attained about each one of them.

2.   He who thus considers things in their first growth and origin, whether a state or anything else, will obtain the clearest view of them. In the first place there must be a union of those who cannot exist without each other; namely, of male and female, that the race may continue (and this is a union which is formed, not of deliberate purpose, but because, in common with other animals and with plants, mankind have a natural desire to leave behind them an image of themselves), and of natural ruler and subject, that both may be preserved. For that which can foresee by the exercise of mind is by nature intended to be lord and master, and that which can with its body give effect to such foresight is a subject, and by nature a slave; hence master and slave have the same interest. Now nature has distinguished between the female and the slave. For she is not niggardly, like the smith who fashions the Delphian knife for many uses; she makes each thing for a single use, and every instrument is best made when intended for one and not for many uses. But among barbarians no distinction is made between women and slaves, because there is no natural ruler among them: they are a community of slaves, male and female. Wherefore the poets say—

It is meet that Hellenes should rule over barbarians;

as if they thought that the barbarian and the slave were by nature one.

Out of these two relationships between man and woman, master and slave, the first thing to arise is the family, and Hesiod is right when he says—

First house and wife and an ox for the plough,

for the ox is the poor man's slave. The family is the association established by nature for the supply of men's everyday wants, and the members of it are called by Charondas 'companions of the cupboard,' and by
Epimenides the Cretan, 'companions of the manger.' But when several
families are united, and the association aims at something more than
the supply of daily needs, the first society to be formed is the village.
And the most natural form of the village appears to be that of a colony
from the family, composed of the children and grandchildren, who are
said to be 'suckled with the same milk.' And this is the reason why
Hellenic states were originally governed by kings; because the Hellenes
were under royal rule before they came together, as the barbarians still
are. Every family is ruled by the eldest, and therefore in the colonies of
the family the kingly form of government prevailed because they were
of the same blood. As Homer says:

> Each one gives law to his children and to his wives.

For they lived dispersedly, as was the manner in ancient times. Wherefore men say that the gods have a king, because they themselves either
are or were in ancient times under the rule of a king. For they imagine,
not only the forms of the gods, but their ways of life to be like their own.

When several villages are united in a single complete community,
large enough to be nearly or quite self-sufficing, the state comes into
existence, originating in the bare needs of life, and continuing in existence for the sake of a good life. And therefore, if the earlier forms of
society are natural, so is the state, for it is the end of them, and the
nature of a thing is its end. For what each thing is when fully developed,
we call its nature, whether we are speaking of a man, a horse, or a
family. Besides, the final cause and end of a thing is the best, and to be
self-sufficing is the end and the best.

Hence it is evident that the state is a creation of nature, and that man
is by nature a political animal. And he who by nature and not by mere
accident is without a state, is either a bad man or above humanity; he is
like the

> Tribeless, lawless, heartless one,

when Homer denounces—the natural outcast is forthwith a lover of war;
he may be compared to an isolated piece at draughts.

Now, that man is more of a political animal than bees or any other
gregarious animals is evident. Nature, as we often say, makes nothing
in vain, and man is the only animal whom she has endowed with the
gift of speech. And whereas mere voice is but an indication of pleasure
or pain, and is therefore found in other animals (for their nature attains
to the perception of pleasure and pain and the intimation of them to one
another, and no further), the power of speech is intended to set forth the
expedient and inexpedient, and therefore likewise the just and the unjust.
And it is a characteristic of man that he alone has any sense of good and

evil, of just and unjust, and the like, and the association of living beings who have this sense makes a family and a state.

Further, the state is by nature clearly prior to the family and to the individual, since the whole is of necessity prior to the part; for example, if the whole body be destroyed, there will be no foot or hand, except in an equivocal sense, as we might speak of a stone hand; for when destroyed the hand will be no better than that. But things are defined by their working and power; and we ought not to say that they are the same when they no longer have their proper quality, but only that they have the same name. The proof that the state is a creation of nature and prior to the individual is that the individual, when isolated, is not self-sufficing; and therefore he is like a part in relation to the whole. But he who is unable to live in society, or who has no need because he is sufficient for himself, must be either a beast or a god: he is no part of a state. A social instinct is implanted in all men by nature. * * *

3.   [Natural Slavery]   Seeing then that the state is made up of households, before speaking of the state we must speak of the management of the household. The parts of household management correspond to the persons who compose the household, and a complete household consists of slaves and freemen. Now we should begin by examining everything in its fewest possible elements; and the first and fewest possible parts of a family are master and slave, husband and wife, father and children. We have therefore to consider what each of these three relations is and ought to be: I mean the relation of master and servant, the marriage relation (the conjunction of man and wife has no name of its own), and thirdly, the procreative relation (this also has no proper name). And there is another element of a household, the so-called art of getting wealth, which, according to some, is identical with household management, according to others, a principal part of it; the nature of this art will also have to be considered by us.

Let us first speak of master and slave, looking to the needs of practical life and also seeking to attain some better theory of their relation than exists at present. For some are of the opinion that the rule of a master is a science, and that the management of a household, and the mastership of slaves, and the political and royal rule, as I was saying at the outset, are all of the same. Others affirm that the rule of a master over salves is contrary to nature, and that the distinction between slave and freeman exists by law only, and not by nature; and being an interference with nature is therefore unjust.

4.   Property is a part of the household, and the art of managing the household; for no man can live well, or indeed live at all, unless he be provided with necessaries. And as in the arts which have a definite sphere the workers must have their own proper instruments for the accomplishment of their work, so it is in the management of a household. Now

instruments are of various sorts; some are living, others lifeless; in the rudder, the pilot of a ship has a lifeless, in the look-out man, a living instrument; for in the arts the servant is a kind of instrument. Thus, too, a possession is an instrument for maintaining life. And so, in the arrangement of the family, a slave is a living possession, and property a number of such instruments; and the servant is himself an instrument which takes precedence of all other instruments. * * * Again, a possession is spoken of as a part is spoken of; for the part is not only a part of something else, but wholly belongs to it; and this is also true of a possession. The master is only the master of the slave; he does not belong to him, whereas the slave is not only the slave of his master, but wholly belongs to him. Hence we see what is the nature and office of a slave; he who is by nature not his own but another's man, is by nature a slave; and he may be said to be another's man who, being a human being, is also a possession. And a possession may be defined as an instrument of action, separable from the possessor.

5.   But is there any one thus intended by nature to be a slave, and for whom such a condition is expedient and right, or rather is not all slavery a violation of nature?

There is no difficulty in answering this question, on grounds both of reason and of fact. For that some should rule and others be ruled is a thing not only necessary, but expedient; from the hour of their birth, some are marked out for subjection, others for rule. * * *

It is clear that the rule of the soul over the body, and of the mind and the rational element over the passionate, is natural and expedient; whereas the equality of the two or the rule of the inferior is always hurtful. The same holds good of animals in relation to men; for tame animals have a better nature than wild, and all tame animals are better off when they are ruled by man; for then they are preserved. Again, the male is by nature superior, and the female inferior; and the one rules, and the other is ruled; this principle, of necessity, extends to all mankind. Where then there is such a difference as that between soul and body, or between men and animals (as in the case of those whose business is to use their body, and who can do nothing better), the lower sort are by nature slaves, and it is better for them as for all inferiors that they should be under the rule of a master. For he who can be, and therefore is, another's, and he who participates in rational principle enough to apprehend, but not to have, such a principle, is a slave by nature. Whereas the lower animals cannot even apprehend a principle; they obey their instincts. And indeed the use made of slaves and of tame animals is not very different; for both with their bodies minister to the needs of life. Nature would like to distinguish between the bodies of freemen and slaves, making the one strong for servile labor, the other upright, and although useless for such services, useful for political life in the arts both of war and peace. But the opposite often happens—that some have the souls and others have the bodies of freemen. And doubtless if men differed from one another in the mere forms of their bodies as much as the statues of the gods do from men, all would acknowledge that the inferior class should be slaves of the superior. And if this is true of the body, how much more just that a similar distinction should exist in the soul? But the beauty of the body is seen, whereas the beauty of the soul is not seen. It is clear, then, that some men are by nature free, and others slaves, and that for these latter slavery is both expedient and right.

6.   But that those who take the opposite view have in a certain way right on their side, may be easily seen. For the words slavery and slave are used in two senses. There is a slave or slavery by law as well as by nature. The law of which I speak is a sort of convention—the law by which whatever is taken in war is supposed to belong to the victors. But this right many jurists impeach, as they would an orator who brought forward an unconstitutional measure: they detest the notion that, because one man has the power of doing violence and is superior in brute strength, another shall be his slave and subject. * * *

We see then that there is some foundation for this difference of opinion, and that all are not either slaves by nature or freemen by nature, and also that there is in some cases a marked distinction between the two classes, rendering it expedient and right for the one to be slaves and the others to be masters: the one practising obedience, the others exercising the authority and lordship which nature intended them to have. The abuse of this authority is injurious to both; for the interests of part and whole, of body and soul, are the same, and the slave is a part of the master, a living but separated part of his bodily frame. Hence, where the relation of master and slave between them is natural they are friends and have a common interest, but where it rests merely on law and force the reverse is true. * * *

8.   [Interest-Taking Is against Nature]   Let us now inquire into property generally, and into the art of getting wealth, in accordance with our usual method, for a slave has been shown to be a part of property. * * *

10.   There are two sorts of wealth-getting, as I have said; one is a part of household management, the other is retail trade: the former necessary and honorable, while that which consists in exchange is justly censured; for it is unnatural, and a mode by which men gain from one another. The most hated sort, and with the greatest reason is usury, which makes a gain out of money itself, and not from the natural object of it. For money was intended to be used in exchange, but not to increase at interest. And this term interest, which means the birth of money from money, is applied to the breeding of money because the offspring resembles the parent. Wherefore of all modes of getting wealth this is the most unnatural.

Bk. II, ch. 5 [The Natural Basis of Property]

5.   Next let us consider what should be our arrangements about property. * * * Property should be in a certain sense common, but, as a general rule, private; for, when every one has a distinct interest, men will not complain of one another, and they will make more progress, because every one will be attending to his own business. And yet by reason of goodness, and in respect of use, 'Friends,' as the proverb says, 'will have all things in common.' Even now there are traces of such a principle, showing that it is not impracticable, but, in well-ordered states, exists already to a certain extent and may be carried further. For, although every man has his own property, some things he will place at the disposal of his friends, while of others he shares the use with them. * * * It is clearly better that property should be private, but the use of it common; and the special business of the legislator is to create in men this benevolent disposition. Again, how immeasurably greater is the pleasure, when a man feels a thing to be his own; for surely the love of self is a feeling implanted by nature and not given in vain, although selfishness is rightly censured; this, however, is not the mere love of self, but the love of self in excess, like the miser's love of money; for all, or almost all, men love money and other such objects in a measure. And further, there is the greatest pleasure in doing a kindness or service to friends or guests or companions, which can only be rendered when a man has private property. These advantages are lost by excessive unification of the state. * * *

We see that there is much more quarreling among those who have all things in common, though there are not many of them when compared with the vast numbers who have private property.

Again, we ought to reckon, not only the evils from which the citizens will be saved, but also the advantages which they will lose. The life which they are to lead appears to be quite impracticable. The error of Socrates [in Plato's *Republic*] must be attributed to the false notion of unity from which he starts. Unity there should be, both of the family and of the state, but in some respects only. For there is a point at which a state may attain such a degree of unity as to be no longer a state, or at which, without actually ceasing to exist, it will become an inferior state, like harmony passing into unison, or rhythm which has been reduced to a single foot. The state, as I was saying, is a plurality, which should be united and made into a community by education; and it is strange that the author of a system of education which he thinks will make the state virtuous [Plato], should expect to improve his citizens by regulations of this sort, and not by philosophy or by customs and laws, like those which prevail at Sparta and Crete respecting common meals, whereby the legislator has made property common. Let us remember that we should not disregard the experience of ages; in the multitude of years these things, if they were good, would certainly not have been unknown; for almost everything has been found out, although some-

times they are not put together; in other cases men do not use the knowledge which they have.

Bk. III, ch. 11 [The Collective Wisdom of the Many]

11.   The principle that the multitude ought to be supreme rather
than the few best is one that is maintained, and, though not free from
difficulty, seems to contain an element of truth. For the many, of whom
each individual is but an ordinary person, when they meet together may
very likely be better than the few good, if regarded not individually but
collectively just as a feast to which many contribute is better than a
dinner provided out of a single purse. For each individual among the
many has a share of virtue and prudence, and when they meet together,
they become in a manner one man, who has many feet, and hands, and
senses; that is a figure of their mind and disposition. Hence the many
are better judges than a single man of music and poetry; for some understand one part, and some another, and among them they understand the
whole. There is a similar combination of qualities in good men, who
differ from any individual of the many, as the beautiful are said to differ
from those who are not beautiful, and works of art from realities, because
in them the scattered elements are combined, although, if taken separately, the eye of one person or some other feature in another person
would be fairer than in the picture. Whether this principle can apply to
every democracy, and to all bodies of men, is not clear. Or rather, by
heaven, in some cases it is impossible of application; for the argument
would equally hold about brutes; and wherein, it will be asked, do some
men differ from brutes? But there may be bodies of men about whom
our statement is nevertheless true. And if so, the difficulty which has
been already raised, and also another which is akin to it—viz., what
power should be assigned to the mass of freemen and citizens, who are
not rich and have no personal merit—are both solved. There is still a
danger in allowing them to share the great offices of state, for their folly
will lead them into error, and their dishonesty into crime. But there is a
danger also in not letting them share, for a state in which many poor
men are excluded from office will necessarily be full of enemies. The
only way of escape is to assign to them some deliberative and judicial
functions. For this reason Solon and certain other legislators give them
the power of electing to offices, and of calling the magistrates to account,
but they do not allow them to hold office singly. When they meet together
their perceptions are quite good enough, and combined with the better
class they are useful to the state (just as impure food when mixed with
what is pure sometimes makes the entire mass more wholesome than a
small quantity of the pure would be), but each individual, left to himself, forms an imperfect judgement. On the other hand, the popular
form of government involves certain difficulties. In the first place, it
might be objected that he who can judge of the healing of a sick man

would be one who could himself heal his disease, and make him whole—that is, in other words, the physician; and so in all professions and arts. As, then, the physician ought to be called to account by physicians, so ought men in general to be called to account by their peers. But physicians are of three kinds: there is the ordinary practitioner, and there is the physician of the higher class, and thirdly the intelligent man who has studied the art—in all arts there is such a class, and we attribute the power of judging to them quite as much as to professors of the art. Secondly, does not the same principle apply to elections? For a right election can only be made by those who have knowledge; those who know geometry, for example, will choose a geometrician rightly, and those who know how to steer, a pilot; and, even if there be some occupations and arts in which private persons share in the ability to choose, they certainly cannot choose better than those who know. So that, according to this argument, neither the election of magistrates, nor the calling of them to account, should be entrusted to the many. Yet possibly these objections are to a great extent met by our old answer, that if the people are not utterly degraded, although individually they may be worse judges than those who have special knowledge—as a body they are as good or better.

ST. AUGUSTINE

It is customary to contrast the philosophies of St. Augustine (354–430) and St. Thomas Aquinas, stressing the differences between them. As the following selections from St. Augustine's *City of God* demonstrate, Augustine took a much more negative attitude than did Aquinas towards earthly existence and to the possibilities of using reason to pursue truth and virtue, stressing mankind's radical dependence on God's grace and the negative effects of Original Sin upon human nature. Only faith in God and obedience to his Word enables man to do good, and only in the afterlife is true happiness possible. Aquinas shares with Augustine the Christian belief in the necessity of God's grace for man to do good and in the direct vision of God as man's true fulfillment. (As Augustine put it in his Confessions, "Our hearts will not rest until we rest in Thee"). Yet Aquinas seems more optimistic about the possibilities of reason and nature to work to achieve a semblance of the divinely-intended order ("the Eternal Law") in the world. Aquinas was also obliged to attempt to reconcile Augustine's negative view of the state as essentially coercive, and of slavery as a punishment for sin, with Aristotle's arguments that both institutions were justified by nature—and this was part of a more general effort to combine Augustinian fideism with Aristotelian rationalism. The resulting synthesis still bears significant evidence of the impact of the thinking of the greatest of the Christian Fathers.

The City of God †

Bk. IV, ch. 4 [Kingdoms as Large-Scale Robberies]

Justice being taken away, then, what are kingdoms but great robberies? For what are robberies themselves, but little kingdoms? The band itself is made up of men; it is ruled by the authority of a prince, it is knit together by the pact of the confederacy; the booty is divided by the law agreed on. If, by the admittance of abandoned men, this evil increases to such a degree that it holds places, fixes abodes, takes possession of cities, and subdues peoples, it assumes the more plainly the name of a kingdom, because the reality is now manifestly conferred on it, not by the removal of covetousness, but by the addition of impunity. Indeed, that was an apt and true reply which was given to Alexander the Great by a pirate who had been seized. For when that king asked the man what he meant by keeping hostile possession of the sea, he answered with bold pride, "What thou meanest by seizing the whole earth; but because I do it with a petty ship, I am called a robber, whilst thou who dost it with a great fleet art styled emperor."

Bk. XIV, ch. 28 [The Two Cities]

Accordingly, two cities have been formed by two loves: the earthly by the love of self, even to the contempt of God; the heavenly by the love of God, even to the contempt of self. The former, in a word, glories in itself, the latter in the Lord. For the one seeks glory from men; but the greatest glory of the other is God, the witness of conscience. The one lifts up its head in its own glory; the other says to its God, "Thou art my glory and the lifter up of mine head."[1] In the one, the princes and the nations it subdues are ruled by the love of ruling; in the other, the princes and the subjects serve one another in love, the latter obeying, while the former take thought for all. The one delights in its own strength, represented in the persons of its rulers; the other says to its God, "I will love Thee, O Lord, my strength."[2] And therefore the wise men of the one city, living according to man, have sought for profit to their own bodies or souls, or both, and those who have known God "glorified Him not as God, neither were thankful, but became vain in their imaginations, and their foolish heart was darkened; professing themselves to be wise," —that is, glorying in their own wisdom, and being possessed by pride,— "they became fools, and changed the glory of the incorruptible God into an image made like to corruptible man, and to birds, and four-footed beasts, and creeping things." For they were either leaders or followers of the people in adoring images, "and worshipped and served the creature

† Translated by Marcus Dods (Edinburgh: T. and T. Clark, 1872).

1. Psalms, 3:3.
2. Psalms, 18:1.

more than the Creator, who is blessed for ever."[3] But in the other city there is no human wisdom, but only godliness, which offers due worship to the true God, and looks for its reward in the society of the saints, of holy angels as well as holy men, "that God may be all in all."[4]

Bk. XIX, ch. 6 [Judges Condemn the Innocent]

What shall I say of these judgments which men pronounce on men, and which are necessary in communities, whatever outward peace they enjoy? Melancholy and lamentable judgments they are, since the judges are men who cannot discern the consciences of those at their bar, and are therefore frequently compelled to put innocent witnesses to the torture to ascertain the truth regarding the crimes of other men. What shall I say of torture applied to the accused himself? He is tortured to discover whether he is guilty, so that, though innocent, he suffers most undoubted punishment for crime that is still doubtful, not because it is proved that he committed it, but because it is not ascertained that he did not commit it. Thus the ignorance of the judge frequently involves an innocent person in suffering. And what is still more unendurable—a thing, indeed, to be bewailed, and, if that were possible, watered with fountains of tears—is this, that when the judge puts the accused to the question, that he may not unwittingly put an innocent man to death, the result of this lamentable ignorance is that this very person, whom he tortured that he might not condemn him if innocent, is condemned to death both tortured and innocent, for if he has chosen, in obedience to the philosophical instructions to the wise man, to quit this life rather than endure any longer such tortures, he declares that he has committed the crime which in fact he has not committed. And when he has been condemned and put to death, the judge is still in ignorance whether he has put to death an innocent or a guilty person, though he put the accused to the torture for the very purpose of saving himself from condemning the innocent; and consequently he has both tortured an innocent man to discover his innocence, and has put him to death without discovering it. If such darkness shrouds social life, will a wise judge take his seat on the bench or no? Beyond question he will. For human society, which he thinks it a wickedness to abandon, constrains him and compels him to this duty. * * *

Bk. XIX, ch. 13 [Peace as the Tranquillity of Order]

The peace of the body then consists in the duly proportioned arrangement of its parts. The peace of the irrational soul is the harmonious repose of the appetites, and that of the rational soul the harmony of knowledge and action. The peace of body and soul is the well-ordered and harmonious life and health of the living creature. Peace between

3. Romans, 1:21–25.   4. 1 Corinthians, 15:28.

man and God is the well-ordered obedience of faith to eternal law. Peace between man and man is well-ordered concord. Domestic peace is the well-ordered concord between those of the family who rule and those who obey. Civil peace is a similar concord among the citizens. The peace of the celestial city is the perfectly ordered and harmonious enjoyment of God, and of one another in God. The peace of all things is the tranquillity of order. Order is the distribution which allots things, equal and unequal, each in its own place.

Bk. XIX, ch. 15 [Slavery as Punishment for Sin]

This is prescribed by the order of nature: it is thus that God has created man. For "let them," he says, "have dominion over the fish of the sea, and over the fowl of the air, and over every creeping thing which creepeth on the earth."[5] He did not intend that his rational creature, who was made in his image, should have dominion over anything but the irrational creature—not man over man, but man over the beasts. And hence the righteous men in primitive times were made shepherds of cattle rather than kings of men, God intending thus to teach us what the relative position of the creatures is, and what the desert of sin; for it is with justice, we believe, that the condition of slavery is the result of sin. And this is why we do not find the word "slave" in any part of Scripture until righteous Noah branded the sin of his son with this name. It is a name, therefore, introduced by sin and not by nature. The origin of the Latin word for slave is supposed to be found in the circumstance that those who by the law of war were liable to be killed were sometimes preserved by their victors, and were hence called servants.[6] And these circumstances could never have arisen save through sin. For even when we wage a just war, our adversaries must be sinning; and every victory, even though gained by wicked men, is a result of the first judgment of God, who humbles the vanquished either for the sake of removing or of punishing their sins. Witness that man of God, Daniel, who, when he was in captivity, confessed to God his own sins and the sins of his people, and declares with pious grief that these were the cause of the captivity.[7] The prime cause, then, of slavery is sin, which brings man under the dominion of his fellow—that which does not happen save by the judgment of God, with whom is no unrighteousness, and who knows how to award fit punishments to every variety of offence. But our Master in heaven says, "Every one who doeth sin is the servant of sin."[8] And thus there are many wicked masters who have religious men as their slaves, and who are yet themselves in bondage; "for of whom a man is overcome, of the same is he bought in bondage."[9] And beyond question it is a happier thing to be the slave of a man than of a lust; for even this

---

5. Genesis, 1:26.
6. *Servus*, "a slave," from *servare*, "to preserve."
7. Daniel, 9.

8. John, 8:34.
9. 2 Peter, 2:19.

very lust of ruling, to mention no others, lays waste men's hearts with the most ruthless dominion. Moreover, when men are subjected to one another in a peaceful order, the lowly position does as much good to the servant as the proud position does harm to the master. But by nature, as God first created us, no one is the slave either of man or of sin. This servitude is, however, penal, and is appointed by that law which enjoins the preservation of the natural order and forbids its disturbance; for if nothing had been done in violation of that law, there would have been nothing to restrain by penal servitude. And therefore the apostle admonishes slaves to be subject to their masters, and to serve them heartily and with good-will, so that, if they cannot be freed by their masters, they may themselves make their slavery in some sort free, by serving not in crafty fear, but in faithful love, until all unrighteousness pass away, and all principality and every human power be brought to nothing, and God be all in all.

Bk. XIX, ch. 20 [True Wisdom]

Since, then, the supreme good of the city of God is perfect and eternal peace, not such as mortals pass into and out of by birth and death, but the peace of freedom from all evil, in which the immortals ever abide, who can deny that that future life is most blessed, or that, in comparison with it, this life which now we live is most wretched, be it filled with all blessings of body and soul and external things? And yet, if any man uses this life with a reference to that other which he ardently loves and confidently hopes for, he may well be called even now blessed, though not in reality so much as in hope. But the actual possession of the happiness of this life, without the hope of what is beyond, is but a false happiness and profound misery. For the true blessings of the soul are not now enjoyed; for that is no true wisdom which does not direct all its prudent observations, manly actions, virtuous self-restraint, and just arrangements, to that end in which God shall be all and all in a secure eternity and perfect peace.

Bk. XXI, ch. 16 [Sinful Man and Grace]

But such is God's mercy towards the vessels of mercy which he has prepared for glory, that even the first age of man, that is, infancy, which submits without any resistance to the flesh, and the second age, which is called boyhood, and which has not yet understanding enough to undertake this warfare, and therefore yields to almost every vicious pleasure (because though this age has the power of speech, and may therefore seem to have passed infancy, the mind is still too weak to comprehend the commandment), yet if either of these ages has received the sacraments of the Mediator, then, although the present life be immediately brought to an end, the child, having been translated from the power of darkness to the kingdom of Christ, shall not only be saved from eternal punishments, but shall not even suffer purgatorial torments after death. For spiritual regeneration of itself suffices to prevent any evil consequences resulting after death from the connection with death which carnal generation forms. But when we reach that age which can now comprehend the commandment, and submit to the dominion of law, we must declare war upon vices, and wage this war keenly, lest we be landed in damnable sins. And if vices have not gathered strength, by habitual victory they are more easily overcome and subdued; but if they have been used to conquer and rule, it is only with difficulty and labor they are mastered. And indeed this victory cannot be sincerely and truly gained but by delighting in true righteousness, and it is faith in Christ that gives this. For if the law be present with its command, and the Spirit be absent with his help, the presence of the prohibition serves only to increase the desire to sin, and adds the guilt of transgression. Sometimes, indeed, patent vices are overcome by other and hidden vices, which are reckoned virtues, though pride and a kind of ruinous self-sufficiency are their informing principles. Accordingly vices are then only to be considered overcome when they are conquered by the love of God, which God himself alone gives, and which he gives only through the Mediator between God and men, the man Christ Jesus, who became a partaker of our mortality that he might make us partakers of his divinity. But few indeed are they who are so happy as to have passed their youth without committing any damnable sins, either by dissolute or violent conduct, or by following some godless and unlawful opinions, but have subdued by their greatness of soul everything in them which could make them the slaves of carnal pleasures. The greater number having first become transgressors of the law that they have received, and having allowed vice to have the ascendency in them, then flee to grace for help, and so, by a penitence more bitter, and a struggle more violent than it would otherwise have been, they subdue the soul to God, and thus give it its lawful authority over the flesh, and become victors. Whoever, therefore, desires to escape eternal punishment, let him not only be baptized, but also justified in Christ, and so let him in truth pass from the devil to Christ.

DIONYSIUS THE AREOPAGITE

Dionysius the Areopagite or, as he is sometimes called, Pseudo-Dionysius, was a fifth century Syrian monk who wrote theological works that expressed the Christian message in terms of the Neo-Platonic "light theology," a vision of descending levels of illumination from God through the choirs of angels, the various ranks of society, animals, plants, and lower orders of being. His writings are based on the theological works of the neo-Platonist philosopher, Proclus (418–485), but they would never have had the powerful influence that they exercised on medieval thought had they not, as a result of what appears to have been a deliberate deception on the part of Dionysius, been presented as the works of the "Dionysius the Areopagite" who is mentioned in the Acts of the Apostles as a convert of St. Paul after his sermon on the altar of the Unknown God in Athens (Acts of the Apostles, 17:34). Because of their supposed connection to St. Paul, his works received almost scriptural veneration in the Middle Ages. His writings were translated into Latin in the ninth century, Dante placed him in Paradise next to Thomas Aquinas, and Aquinas cited him no less than one hundred and forty-three times.

Dionysius coined the word, "hierarchy"—literally "rule of the priests" and wrote two influential works on the subject, selections from which are translated below. They gave a theological basis to the hierarchical outlook of the Middle Ages, and reinforced the anti-equalitarian aspects of the medieval order. Their influence on Aquinas was mainly upon his cosmological outlook—his vision of the order of the universe as the action of Divine Goodness enlightening the world—but in at least one case (S.T., I, qu. 108, a. 2) they provided a model for his views on the structure of society. The most important political use of Dionysius was the reference to Dionysian hierarchy in Pope Boniface VIII's bull, *Unam Sanctam* (1302) which argued for the subordination of all earthly rulers to the papacy.

The Celestial Hierarchy †

Chapter III [Hierarchy leads to God]

What I call hierarchy is a sacred order, science, and operation which is as far as possible like the form of the divine and leads through divine enlightenment to the imitation of God. In its simplicity, goodness, and fundamental perfection, the Beauty of God which is free of all dissemblance communicates itself to every being according to its merits, a part of its own Light, and perfects it through a most divine initiative, endowing what it has perfected with its own form in a harmonious and lasting fashion.

The purpose of hierarchy then is to provide to creatures as far as is possible a resemblance with the divine and to unite them with God. For the hierarchy God is the source of all knowledge and every action. It does not cease to contemplate his most divine Goodness. To the degree that it can, it receives his imprint and from its members it forms for itself perfect images of God, spotless and pure mirrors receiving the influence of the Divine Rule, and then, having in holy fashion received the fullness of its splendor, according to the commands of the Divine Rule, capable of freely transmitting that light to its inferiors. * * *

When we speak of hierarchy we mean a certain perfectly holy ordi-

† Translated by the editor from the Greek, Latin, and French texts in *Dionysiaca*, 2 vols (Solesmes: Desclée De Brouwer, 1937).

nation, the image of the splendor of the Divine Rule, extending through the sacred order in its ranks and hierarchical knowledge, the mysterious operations of illumination, and thus in so far as it can be done without sacrilege, tending to resemble the One who is its own beginning. Therefore, for each of the members of the hierarchy perfection consists in the imitation of God to the degree possible, becoming in a way that is a more divine mystery than any other a "collaborator" in the words of the Scriptures [1 Corinthians, 3:9] of God, and as far as possible manifesting in itself the reflection of the action of the Divine.

If for example the hierarchical order demands that some be purified, and others purify, that some receive illumination, and others illuminate, that some receive perfection, and others perfect, each will imitate God in the way appropriate for his proper functioning. It remains to say in what we call human language that the Divine Blessedness remains free of all dissemblance; it shines with the fullness of everlasting light; it is perfect and lacking in no perfection, since it purifies, illumines, and perfects. Still more it is itself holy purity and light, yet transcending purity and light, source in itself of every perfection and perfect from the beginning, and itself the beginning of every hierarchy yet transcending every sacral order. * * * (Dionysius then enumerates the nine angelic ranks: Seraphim, Cherubim, and Thrones; Dominations, Powers, and Virtues; and Principalities, Archangels, and Angels.)

Chapter X [Hierarchies of Angels and Men]

We conclude therefore that the most revered order of the holy spirits that surround God, directed by the illumination which comes to it from the source of all illumination, towards whom it rises without intermediaries, receives purification, illumination, and perfection through the gift of the light of the Divine Rule. * * * After it in proportion to its nature, comes the second order, and after the second, the third, and after the third, the human hierarchy which, in accordance with the prescription of the harmonious source of all ordering, rises in divinely proportioned accord in hierarchical order towards the origin and infinite end of all harmony. * * *

The Ecclesiastical Hierarchy

Chapter I [Definition of Hierarchy]

* * * When we say hierarchy, we mean an ordered collection of all the holy realities, and the term "hierarch" means a Godlike and divine person, instructed in all sacred knowledge, in whom the whole hierarchy that depends on him finds a most pure means of perfection and expression.

The lifegiving source and the beneficent and creative essence of that hierarchy is the Trinity, the sole cause of being, and in its goodness it confers all existence and happiness. But that happy Divine Rule which is transcendent and at the same time truly both one and three, has determined in a way which we do not know, but which is perfectly clear to It, to assure our salvation as well as that of the heavenly spirits. But our salvation is only possible by our becoming like God. To become like God means to resemble God and to unite ourselves to Him as far as we can. The common element in every hierarchy consists therefore in a continual love of God and of the divine mysteries that produces in us in a holy fashion the unifying presence of God himself. But to reach his presence it is necessary to strip ourselves totally and irrevocably of everything that may interfere. * * *

Chapter V [Hierarchy in the Church]

* * * After that celestial hierarchy which is not of this world, the beneficent Divine Rule extending its most holy gifts to mankind, and treating us, in the words of the Scriptures, as little children (Galatians, 4:24), grants us the Hierarchy of the Law [the Old Testament], clothing the truth in obscure images, using representations that are very distant from the original, enigmas that are difficult to resolve, and figures whose meaning can only be perceived with difficulty, while granting only a limited enlightenment in order not to damage the feeble eyes that contemplate them. That Hierarchy of the Law initiated souls into worship in accordance with the spirit. Those who conducted that worship were the men whom Moses—the first to do so as the leader of the high priests of the law—initiated in pious fashion into the mysteries of the sacred tabernacle. In that tabernacle, for the instruction of the others he wrote on the holy institutions of the Hierarchy of the Law, describing the rites of the priesthood as images of that Face that had been revealed to him on Mount Sinai. The initiated are the ones who are raised up to conduct the sacred rites of the Law, in accordance with their capacities in a most perfect initiation.

However, according to Scripture the most perfect revelation takes place in the case of our own hierarchy which proclaims its completion and holy fulfillment. It is both celestial and legal, situated as a mean between the two extremes, sharing with the one intellectual contemplation, and with the other the usage of the varied symbols of the sensible order through which it is raised in a holy way to the divine. Like the other two hierarchies, it is divided into three orders. It includes first the most holy sacraments, then a body of priests charged with distributing the sacred mysteries in conformity with God's will; and lastly the faithful who are led by the priesthood to the holy mysteries in accord with their capacities. As we have seen in the case of the hierarchy of the law, and of the celestial hierarchy, each of the three divisions of our hierarchy has three ranks—the first, the intermediate, and the last, through a power whose purpose is to regulate that order in proportions that are worthy of its sacred object, joining all its elements in a harmonious order which assures their cohesion. * * *

INTERPRETATIONS

The Ingredients of the Thomistic Synthesis

WALTER ULLMANN

The New Orientation †

(Ullmann argues that the acceptance of Aristotelian "naturalism" by Aquinas marks the rebirth of "the political" in the West, and the beginnings of populist or what he calls "ascending" theories of the origin of political authority, as distinct from the prevailing theocratic or "descending" theories of the Middle Ages.)

The accommodation of (Aristotle) to Christian cosmology appeared as one of the urgent tasks in the thirteenth century. Now that his works were available in competent translations the "Great Synthesis" appeared as a feasible undertaking: it was begun by the Dominican Albert the Great and accomplished by his pupil, Thomas Aquinas. It is certainly true that, as one of the eminent experts on Thomas has said, no one before and no one after the thirteenth century had studied Aristotle as Thomas had done.[1] Indeed, the masterly elaboration of Aristotelian ideas and their weaving into the Christian set of ideas presupposed a mind of quite extraordinary width, perception, and depth. The power of his intellect produced a fusion of Christian and Aristotelian themes "which entailed an infinity of nice distinctions in accommodating a pagan philosophy to Christian cosmology."[2] Thomas created a synthesis of disparate and irreconcilable elements, which appeared to deprive Aristotelianism of those ingredients which, from a theocentric point of view, were considered harmful. The effect of this synthesis was that Aristotle could now

† Walter Ullmann, A History of Political Thought in the Middle Ages (Baltimore, Md.: Pelican, 1965, 1970), copyright © 1965 by Walter Ullmann.

Reprinted by permission of Penguin Books Ltd.
1. M. Grabmann.
2. McIlwain.

be fully accepted as part of the contemporary intellectual setting—indeed, one can with every justification speak of Thomism as Christian Aristotelianism [3] within the present context.

The evolutionary concept of nature, physical reality, or actual being (as opposed to an idealized postulate) was Aristotle's basic idea. Frequently enough Thomas referred to the element of growth in nature which he also explained by the same etymology as Ulpian had done long before him, whence Thomas maintained the idea of physical generation of the living organism, and hence of physical birth. In closest dependence on Aristotle he told his readers that the idea of motion was inherent in nature which could be observed in moving bodies, for they must have an "intrinsic beginning" in themselves. His concept of nature was no different from Aristotle's: it designated birth, growth, decay. This "naturalistic" way of thinking—observable, at the very time Thomas wrote, in many other departments to which reference has already been made—was nevertheless a new departure in purely philosophical thought. In fact, the idea of nature as an element that contained its own force and its own principles of operation became a most important instrument in Thomas's system of thought, which enabled him to declare that this or that phenomenon was "according to nature," "above nature," "contrary to nature," and so on. Setting out from the (originally Aristotelian) premises, Thomas had no difficulty in applying them to society and its government. The Aristotelian teleogy regarding the operations of nature and the idea of the state as a product of nature reappeared in the Thomist system; and so did the Aristotelian definition of man as a "political animal," which Thomas improved by designating man also as a social animal, so that his definition was expanded to man being "a political and social animal." This refinement of man as a being which was also a social animal Thomas derived from the ancient (pagan) writer Macrobius who wrote at the end of the fourth century. The concept of man as a political animal signified the entry of the "political" into contemporary vocabulary and thought-processes. Thinking in "political" terms became a new mental category.

What, however, is of immediate interest is that, for Thomas, man and Christian were conceptually different notions. Man was a natural product, and as such demanded attention. His naturalness was his hallmark, and as member of human society he was a social animal. This emphasis on man, on the *homo*, brought forth the Thomist conception of *humanitas* which he considered to be the essential being of man himself. The conception of *humanity* was not in the least original with Thomas—Roman law was perfectly familiar with it, and so were theologians who had discussed the humanity of Christ; shortly before him the idea of humanity was employed by Frederick II in his famous constitutions of Melfi (1231). But, then, there were few terms in the whole Thomist edifice which had no pedigree: this is indeed one of the secrets

3. Grabmann.

of success, that is, to employ more or less well-known terminology and yet to fill it with contents different from the accepted meaning. For nothing facilitates the progress of a new theory better than familiarity with its terminology, however much a familiar term may thereby have changed its meaning. This observation applies to the Thomist *humanitas* and his concept of man. Neither of these (and other concepts, we shall presently meet) was new: each was familiar, and yet the meaning he gave to them did not entirely correspond to the commonly accepted one.

The complement of man in organized society was the citizen. The citizen was man writ large. The citizen was, to Thomas, no longer the subject, the *sub/ditus*, who simply had to obey superior authority. It was Aristotle's definition of a citizen as one who partook in government which supplied the solvent and which made possible the release of the (inferior) subject from (superior) authority. For, we recall, sharing in government was precisely what was denied to the subject, nor had he any share in the making of the law which was given to him. The important point here is that Thomas, by absorbing Aristotle's ideas, effected in the public sphere not so much a metamorphosis of the subject as the re-birth of the citizen who since classical times had been hibernating. It is impossible to exaggerate the significance of the emergence of the concept of citizen: his re-birth was to be of crucial importance. That the "new" concept made rapid headway cannot, in view of the historical situation, cause any surprise. Moreover the distinction drawn by Aristotle between man and the citizen reappeared in Thomas's system:

> It sometimes happens (he said) that someone is a *good citizen* who has not the quality according to which someone is also a *good man*, from which follows that the quality according to whether someone is a good man or a good citizen is not the same.

The significance of this statement does not need any comment. It was the denial of what for want of a better term we have called the totalitarian point of view. It was a major step forward towards a new orientation. What applied to the one need not necessarily apply to the other. The citizen—political man—answered the description of a being different from mere man. Thereby the specter of splitting up man's activities begins to be discernible and herewith the subjection of man to different sets of norms and postulates (political, religious, moral, economic, etc.).

Thomas Aquinas began not only to re-introduce, in theory, the concept of the citizen (as distinct from the subject), but also—and on the same Aristotelian basis—to introduce political science proper. *Scientia politica* to him was knowledge concerning the government of the state, which he called *civitas* or *civilitas*. In fact, both these concepts were intrinsically linked in Thomas's mind. Political science was to him the science of government as far as it related to the natural product, the state. As such it was primarily concerned with practical matters, and not with speculation. It was what he called *operativa*, that is, a science con-

cerning itself with the actual doing of things and with putting theories
into practice. Contrariwise, political science was not a science that merely
recognized things without doing anything about them. And the basis of
this "operative science" was natural-human reason with which man was
endowed by nature. This became the pivotal point in his system. This
human reason received its direction and orientation from concrete experience which, he said, was especially noticeable "in the natural things"
as well as "in moral matters." Still more important, political science had
its working principles within itself—it needed no outside agency to make
it work—and hence he called political science the most practical as well
as the most fundamental and "architectonic" of all the sciences, "aiming
as it did at the perfect good in human affairs." The birth of political
science at once brought forth its human and practical character: it was
human experience that counted and the observation of the natural-human
elements, because political science, as he stressed, was part of the *human*
sciences and therefore "aimed at imitating nature." Reality as it is, and
not as it ought to be, was for Thomas the keynote of the new science.
This realistic approach emerged in his statement, for instance, that "the
law can rightly be changed because of the changes of men's conditions,
according to which different laws are required." This indeed was a breeze
of fresh air.

The introduction of a further new concept, that of the "political government" *(regimen politicum)*, was closely related to the premises upon
which Thomas worked. Perhaps the easiest way in which the full meaning of "political government" can be understood is to contrast it with its
opposite, which was the "regal government" *(regimen regale)*. In fact the
two chief theories of government and law were pretty clearly stated in
these two notions. The "regal government," (i.e. the theocratic form of
government) Thomas considered to be characterized by the king's possessing "full powers" and by his unaccountability for his governmental
actions: this is, as we know, the traditional medieval king. But opposed
to this was the "political government," which for Thomas existed when
the ruler had his powers circumscribed according to the laws of the state.
This ruler, hedged in as he was by the laws of the state—or as Thomas
said in a different context "restricted by positive law"—and little in common with the theocratic ruler. On the contrary, Thomas very clearly
approached the ascending or populist theory, and this quite especially
when he spoke of the *status popularis* in connexion with democracy and
"the will of the people." His definition of democracy left little to be
desired: here operated the will of the people, because "from the members of the people the leaders can be elected and their election belongs
to the people." And at once the principle of representation emerged: the
leader "personifies" the state, so that it can be said that "what the ruler
of the state does, the state itself is said to do." For practical purposes
Thomas held that a mixture of a political and regal government would
be the most suitable.

The advance made by Thomas is so great that any commentary seems superfluous. What had not existed before, a political science, had come into being. Something more must be said about Thomas's concept of the State. It was this which had not existed in men's minds, and it was this which could only come about when Aristotelian ideas were absorbed and his political theory was made the basis of further elaboration. Thomas held that it was man's "natural instinct" which brought forth the state, that is, organized human society. Consequently, to Thomas, the state was a product of nature and therefore followed the laws of nature. It was "natural reason which urges" this human association, and for the working of the state no divine or supra-natural elements were necessary, because it had all the laws of its own operation within itself. Since "nature leaves nothing imperfect," Thomas called the state a perfect community and also "the most perfect human association." What generations of writers and governments had been seeking was now found in the simple application of the concept of nature. The state was, in a word, a natural thing, and herewith the conceptual gulf between it and the Church was opened up: the latter had nothing to do with nature, because it was founded or instituted by divinity. The state was a natural product; the Church a supra-natural product.

Thomas's definition of the state ("the state is nothing but the congregation of men")[4] brought into clear relief its essential difference to its supra-natural counterpart, the Church, which was "the congregation of the faithful." This was the dichotomy between men and the faithful Christian. The state was a matter for man or the citizen only: it had neither in its origin nor in its working anything to do with any ecclesiastical authority. Being a natural product it pursued aims which were inherent in its natural essence, and that aim was the well-being, the welfare, of its members. This aim could be guaranteed only if the state was independent and self-sufficient. The state stood on its own feet, was still a living organism, and not yet an abstraction which it was later to become. Once again, Thomas did not invent the terminology—everyone was familiar with the term *civitas*—but what he did was to give the term a new meaning, and the success of a new theory is assured if it employs familiar terminology. To Thomas the state was a *corpus politicum et morale*, a body politic with moral ends which took into account the social habits and customs of its citizens. The Church on the other hand was a mystical body *(corpus mysticum)*. Thomas gave back to the thirteenth-century world the ancient and yet forgotten concept of the state: it was a human body politic, in which indeed the accent lay on the human, that is, natural qualifications of its citizens.

4. *Civitas est nonnisi congregatio hominum.*

HARRY JAFFA

Thomism and Aristotelianism †

(Jaffa's book undertakes the not difficult task of showing that Aquinas often departs from Aristotle while claiming merely to be interpreting his thought. The selection is devoted mainly to the differences between Aristotle's legal theory and Aquinas's conception of natural law.)

* * * [T]here is nowhere in Aristotle's *Ethics* or *Politics* any mention of natural *law*. There is only a single doubtful mention of natural law in the *Rhetoric*.[1] But in the context of a discussion of the means of forensic persuasion one can draw no serious conclusions from it alone. The reason why there is no mention of natural law in Aristotle may be gathered from Thomas's own definition of law: "Law is nothing else than a certain ordinance of reason for the common good, by him who has the care of the community, and promulgated."[2] There are four criteria for law: that it be reasonable; for the common good; made by one responsible for the community; and promulgated. But of these four criteria only two could possibly be said by Aristotle to emanate from nature: reasonableness and goodness, which are really correlative terms. The other criteria depend upon a *legislator*, which, in the case of a natural law, would mean a divine legislator. An ordinance is imposed, says Thomas, "on others," which would imply providence. Without particular divine providence there can be no doctrine of natural law in the Thomistic sense. But such a natural law doctrine implies divine revelation because the fact (as distinct from the possibility) of divine providence, is evidently not naturally known to all men. But to be binding the natural law must be known in its legal character, that is, it must be known *to be promulgated*. Yet, for one who was perhaps the wisest of the pagans to deny this crucial premise of the natural law—as Aristotle does in denying particular divine providence—would certainly seem to suggest that the legal character of the natural law is most immanifest to unassisted natural reason.

* * * Aristotle begins: "Of political justice [i.e., the politically just, *jus*, the object of justice, distinct from the habit, *justitia*] part is natural, part legal." Thomas, in his comment, says: the citizens do justly what nature imprints on the human mind, and what is laid down by law.[3] But Aristotle has not said anything about nature imprinting or bestowing anything. If it be granted that the principles of justice are implanted in us by habituation in the actions of the virtue, yet this implanting, according

† Harry V. Jaffa, *Thomism and Aristotelianism* (Chicago: University of Chicago Press, 1952). By permission of Harry V. Jaffa.

1. Aristotle, *Rhetoric*, 1373b 1ff.

2. *Summa Theologiae* I–II, qu. 4.

3. *Commentary on the Nicomachean Ethics*, para. 1017ff.

to Aristotle, is the result of moral education, and not any action of nature. But the subject of this chapter is not the virtue of justice, not that whereby any principles could be said to be imprinted, but the *justum politicum*, the politically just. Then Aristotle continues, "natural, that which has everywhere the same force and does not exist by people's thinking this or that." And Thomas: " '*Justum naturale*' is what has everywhere the same power and virtue *for tending towards the good and turning away from the evil.*"[4] Again, Thomas imputes an active agency to natural right, where Aristotle speaks only of its intrinsic rightness. * * * And then comes the following crucial passage of the commentary: "For just as in speculative matters there are certain things naturally known, as indemonstrable principles, and others closely following upon them *(propinqua)*; and certain things that the industry of men finds out, and what follow upon them; *thus also* in matters of action there are certain principles *naturally known, as if (quasi)* indemonstrable principles and [others] linked to them, as, evil is to be avoided, no one is to be unjustly harmed, one should not steal, and the like. Others are thought out by the industry of men, which are here called legally just." Thus Thomas apparently takes Aristotle's statement, to the effect that what is naturally right or just does not depend on opinion, as an outright endorsement of his own doctrine that there is a natural habit of the understanding, by which *we know* what is, in principle, right and wrong according to nature. * * *

In the most enigmatic passage of the *Nicomachean Ethics* Aristotle says "with us there is something that is just even by nature, yet all of it is changeable; but still some is by nature, some not by nature. It is evident which sort of thing, among things capable of being otherwise, is by nature and which is not but is legal and conventional, assuming that both are equally changeable. And in all other things the same distinction will apply; by nature the right hand is stronger, yet it is possible that all men should come to be ambidextrous."[5] Thomas's accounting for the mutability of natural right follows one very simple principle: natural right is true for the most part, but is not true in a few cases; for the same reason that nature generally succeeds in its intentions for the most part, but fails in a few cases. Thomas first gives the example of the man who has had a sword deposited with him, "and nothing seems more just than that a deposit should be returned"; yet a sword should not be returned to a man who demands it in a rage; nor should money be returned to a traitor to his country, who would use it to buy arms.[6] That deposits be returned is naturally just in most cases, but the rule is altered in the few.[7] The reason why this is so, according to Thomas, is as follows: "It is to be noted that the natures *(rationes)* of changeable things are unchangeable, thus anything natural to us as pertaining to the very nature of man, in no way may be changed. But what follows *(consequuntur)*

4. *Commentary on the Nicomachean Ethics*, para. 1017ff.

5. Aristotle, *Nicomachean Ethics*, 1135a.

6. *Commentary on the Nicomachean Ethics*, para. 1025.

7. *Ibid.*, para. 1028.

our nature, as dispositions, actions, motions, are changed in a few cases. And similarly those things which pertain to the nature of justice itself in no way can be changed, for example that one should not steal, which is to do what is unjust. But those things which follow are changed in the minor part."

That this explanation is quite inadequate we may now see. According to the English translation, Aristotle says that the naturally and the legally just are equally changeable. Thomas's text says they are "*ambo mobilia similiter*" (i.e., both similarly changeable, or both changeable in like manner). The force of this we would construe in the same way as the English text. The point is that Aristotle makes no distinction between the changeability of natural and legal right. Thomas, however, emphasizes that natural right changes only "*in paucioribus*" and "*in minori parte.*" The example of the change in the relative dexterity of the right and left hands is remarkable for its amoral connotation. Thomas's examples are not of this character. His examples and his explanation presuppose a failure of nature which causes a departure from the rule. Aristotle's example could be interpreted as suggesting a possible perfection of nature: although most men are naturally right-handed (or left-handed), it might be thought *better* to be ambidextrous. That men should be ambidextrous is a natural possibility, a possibility that may be realized under favorable circumstances.

*   *   *

The lack of connection of Aristotle's doctrine of natural right, with the Catholic Natural Law, as expressed by Thomas, can be readily inferred from some of the precepts which supply the content of the latter and which are most widely known today. In the best polity described in Books 7 and 8 of the *Politics* it is explicitly stated that it is the function of the legislator, to "direct his attention above all to the education of the youth; for the neglect of education does harm to the constitution. The citizen should be moulded to suit the form of government under which he lives."[8] As, according to Aristotle, the political community is the most perfect kind of human community, the art of "politike" is supreme over "oekonomike," and the statesman to the head of the household. The family is prior to the state in order of generation, but not in order of perfection. It is with a view to the perfection of the latter that the life of the former must be regulated, and the notion that the head of the family has an independent natural right to educate his children, because the family is "prior" to the state, is entirely alien to Aristotle's thought. Similarly with birth control. Aristotle explicitly says that population limits shall be decided by law, and abortion procured, if necessary, to keep within the limits set.[9] It is reasonable to assume that, if he sanctions abortion, he would not object to easier methods of keeping population within limits, by preventing unnecessary conceptions. In the passage just

8. Aristotle, *Politics*, 1337a 10.   9. Aristotle, *Politics*, 1335b 22ff.

referred to Aristotle also requires exposure of deformed children which, under the headings of euthanasia, would be absolutely forbidden by the Catholic Natural Law. These instances, however, do not mean that the practices Aristotle considered fitting for the best polity would be universally applicable; certainly birth control would be forbidden where population was a radical necessity; and education under parental guidance might be considered preferable to that of an inefficient public school system. There is no rule or precept of natural right, according to Aristotle, which may not change with circumstances.

That there is no evidence that Aristotle held to the notion that there was a habit of the principles of practical reason comparable to intuitive reason, we have seen. We shall briefly present evidence that such could not have been his view, and that from his point of view the only possible natural habit of understanding is that of the speculative principles. We quoted above the passage in which Aristotle said that the mass of mankind do not have even a notion of what is by nature noble.[1] We may also note the passage in the *Politics* in which Aristotle clearly says that the virtue of the subject, as distinct from that of the ruler, is only true opinion. "The subject," says Aristotle, "corresponds to the maker of flutes and the ruler to the flute-player who uses them."[2] The man who possesses the virtue of a ruler is the one whom Aristotle calls a good man; but he must possess the virtue of practical wisdom. However, only a few people can be expected to be wise, although many can be virtuous (i.e., as subjects). Yet if all had a habit whereby they *knew*, in principles, what was good and bad, the many too could become good. This is what Thomas implies is the case, but it is explicitly denied when Aristotle says that the most that the many can hope for is true opinion. * * *

We said that Thomas rarely, if ever, attempts to explain any statements of Aristotle except in terms of other of his statements; and that nothing extraneous to the *Ethics* is permitted to serve as the basis for interpretation of the *Ethics*. We must, perforce, now qualify this by saying that, although Thomas never appeals to any *non-Aristotelian principles* to interpret Aristotle's words, he nonetheless imputes non-Aristotelian principles to Aristotle, although treating them as if they were Aristotelian. We concluded then that Thomas's assumption as to the harmony of natural and revealed doctrine, at least in so far as Aristotle is to be considered a representative of the former, is entirely unwarranted. Thomas's "success" in creating the appearance of such harmony is due, we believe, entirely to his imputation to Aristotle of such non-Aristotelian principles as the following:

1. Belief in divine particular providence.
2. Belief that perfect happiness is impossible in this life.
3. Belief in the necessity of personal immortality to complete the happiness intended, evidently, by nature.

1. Aristotle, *Nicomachean Ethics*, 1095b 20.   2. Aristotle, *Politics*, 1277b 25.

4. Belief in personal immortality.
5. Belief in the special creation of individual souls.
6. Belief in a divinely implanted "natural" habit of the moral principles.

St. Thomas and Platonism

FERNAND VAN STEENBERGHEN

Thomism as a New Philosophy †

(Van Steenberghe, a professor at Louvain, argues for a substantial Platonic element in Aquinas's philosophy—particularly his conception of God as Creative Being in which all created things participate—thus Christianizing the Platonic doctrine of participation in the Ideas and in Being itself.)

He first made contact with Aristotle when he was a student of the liberal arts in Naples, from 1239 to 1244. He was a youngster, barely fifteen years of age when he received lessons from master Martin (of Dacia?), professor of grammar and logic, and then from master Peter of Ireland, professor in the natural sciences. Later, from 1245 to 1252, he studied for seven years under the direction of Albert the Great and this gave him the chance of broadening and deepening the philosophical knowledge he had acquired in Naples. At the same time, he began his studies in the various branches of theology, using Holy Scripture, the works of the Fathers, the *Sentences* of Peter Lombard, and no doubt other more recent theological works. During this comparatively long period of training, Thomas Aquinas made many reflections, meditations and comparisons, and when we come to read his first writings, we feel we are in the presence of a man who has already choosen the path he is to tread—a man who has already made the fundamental decisions.

Thomas Aquinas made his master's ideas on the autonomy and hierarchy of the sciences his own. In philosophy, he was the first among thirteenth century thinkers to break with the hesitant and wavering attitude of his contemporaries, the first, that is, who firmly adopted the essential intuitions of Aristotelianism, after purging them of later corruptions. Among these fundamental intuitions must be counted especially the theory of knowledge, the doctrine of act and potency, and hylo-

† Fernand van Steenberghe, *Aristotle in the West* (Louvain: E. Nauwelaerts, 1955). By permission of the publisher.

morphism.[1] In the field of knowledge St. Thomas definitely opted for Aristotle's intellectualistic empiricism, rejecting any special illumination at the level of natural consciousness and any direct intuition of spiritual realities. His theory of knowledge took as its basis the doctrine of abstraction, to which was added Aristotelian logic. In metaphysics, he adopted the important doctrine of act and potency which Aristotle had made the key-stone of his moderate dynamism, but, as we shall see, St. Thomas brought out the profound metaphysical signification of this doctrine. In natural philosophy, he re-established the hylomorphic theory in its authentic form, eliminating all Stoic and neo-Platonic excrescences which were threatening to stifle it; such were, for example, *rationes seminales*, spiritual matter, and the plurality of substantial forms.

We should, however, be flying in the face of historical truth if we were to present St. Thomas's philosophy as Aristotelianism pure and simple, or even if we were to explain it as a preference for Aristotle over Plato.[2] A quick glance over the Thomistic system is sufficient for us to see that St. Thomas, following in this the example of his Arab and Latin predecessors, borrowed neo-Platonic elements to widen Aristotelianism; his system, like theirs, is a "neo-Platonizing" Aristotelianism. But his originality and superiority lay in the rigor of his criticism and in the perfect coherence and depth of his philosophical synthesis, in which Platonic, Aristotelian, neo-Platonic, and Christian elements were all given a single, solid foundation. This new philosophy, therefore—*the first really original philosophy produced by the thirteenth century and, even, by Christian civilization in general*—cannot be given any satisfactory label based on its historical sources. Only one term [is] apt enough to express the profoundly personal philosophical attitude of St. Thomas—he created *Thomism.* * * *

St. Thomas unifies Platonism and Aristotelianism in a higher synthesis, by taking the original step of *transposing* the doctrine of participation. At the level of metaphysical causality, Platonic participation is expressed by St. Thomas's doctrine of the real composition of *esse* [being] and *essentia* [essence] in the finite being, and by the total dependence of the finite being on the creative influx of the Infinite Being. The composition of *esse* and *essentia* in turn gives rise to an extension of the Aristotelian notion of act and potency, these notions being used from now on to explain the ontological structure of the composite finite being. All things considered, we can see in Thomism Greek thought rejuvenated and deepened in a highly original way. * * * [A]s far as the principal sources are concerned, Thomism is a form of Platonism with Aristotelian specifications, rather than the reverse.

These opinions on St. Thomas's metaphysics seem to be quite cor-

---

1. Hylomorphism—the metaphysical doctrine, derived from Aristotle, that beings are composed of matter *(hylē)* and form *(morphē)* [Editor].

2. Cf. E. Gilson, *Pourquoi saint Thomas a critiqué saint Augustin*, pp. 125–126. M. Gilson's expression would no doubt be acceptable if they were limited to the domain of knowledge; but we cannot admit that Plato and Aristotle are "rigorously antinomic" in their "metaphysics." On the contrary, we think that St. Thomas's fundamental merit is in seeing their profound agreement.

rect. To realize the depth of the abyss which separates Thomistic from Aristotelian metaphysics, it is sufficient to consider the judgments which each system makes about God and His attributes. Aristotle presents us with *Actus Purus*, which is eternal thought, the supreme cause of movement. For this, St. Thomas substitutes the *Esse Subsistens*, which is the creative cause, the infinitely perfect exemplar and final end of creation, the universal providence that governs the world and calls all created persons to an immortal destiny. Thus, those attributes which are essential to the God of Christianity are discovered at the summit of metaphysics, in the supreme Being, whose existence is affirmed as the metaphysical implication of the reality of which we have experience.

This system of metaphysics has equally remarkable results in psychology and ethics. To keep to the essentials, St. Thomas's solution to the problem of man's nature goes beyond all the suggested solutions recorded earlier in the history of philosophy. He teaches: that the substance of man is one, being a hylomorphic composition; that the soul is spiritual, and is both a substantial and a subsistent form; that in human activity there is a parallel unity and composition, the spiritual element being always in association with the material element in our present state here below. This solid but very subtle doctrine, which corresponds completely with our experience and with the data of our consciousness, has immeasurable repercussions in all departments of psychology, ethics, and even theology. But to formulate it in Aristotelian terms, it was necessary to go beyond Aristotelianism itself and to solve the problem of man by referring it to God's metaphysical causality.

St. Thomas's Christian Aristotelianism is therefore a remarkable extension and transfiguration of the peripatetic philosophy,[3] so much so that it becomes a philosophy in its own right, transcending its historical sources.

ETIENNE GILSON

The Christian Philosophy of St. Thomas Aquinas†

(Gilson, one of the leading twentieth century interpreters of Thomism, distinguishes between the hierarchical thinking of the neo-Platonists who influenced Aquinas and that contained in Aquinas's own thought. The difference is explained by the fact that "St. Thomas's God was not the God of Plotinus but the Christian God of Augustine." Gilson also summarizes Aquinas's epistemology or theory of knowledge.)

3. i.e., Aristotelianism—traditionally believed to have been taught by Aristotle while walking around (*peripateō*).
† From Etienne Gilson, *The Christian Philosophy* of *St. Thomas Aquinas* (New York: Random House, 1956). Copyright © 1956 by Etienne Gilson. Reprinted by permission of Random House, Inc.

* * * This world of becoming which grows active in order to find itself, these heavenly spheres continually seeking themselves in the successive points of their orbits, these human souls which capture and assimilate being by their intellect, these substantial forms forever searching out new matters in which to realize themselves, do not contain in themselves the explanation of what they are. If such beings were self-explaining, they would be lacking nothing. Or, inversely, they would have to be lacking nothing before they could be self-explaining. But then they would no longer move in search of themselves. They would repose in the integrity of their own essence realized at last. They would cease to be becoming and enjoy the fulness of being.

It is, therefore, outside the world of potency and act, above becoming, and in a being which is what it is totally, that we must look for the cause of the universe. But this being which thought can reach is obviously of a different nature than the being we have been talking about, for if it were not different from the being which experience gives, there would be no point in positing it. Thus the world of becoming postulates a principle removed from becoming and placed entirely outside it.

But then a new problem arises. If the being we postulate from experience is radically different from the one given to us in experience, how can we know it through this experience and how shall we even explain it in terms of this experience? Nothing can be deduced or inferred about a being from some other being which does not exist in the same sense as the first one does. Our thought would be quite inadequate to proceed to such a conclusion unless the reality in which we moved formed, by its hierarchical and analogical structure, a sort of ladder leading toward God.

It is precisely because every operation is the realization of an essence, and because every essence is a certain quantity of being and perfection, that the universe reveals itself to us as a society made up of superiors and inferiors. The very definition of each essence ranks it immediately in its proper place in this hierarchy. To explain the operation of an individual thing, not only must we have the notion of this individual, but we must also have the definition of the essence which it embodies in a deficient manner. And the species itself is not enough because the individuals which go to make up the species are ceaselessly striving to realize themselves. Thus it becomes necessary either to renounce trying to account for this operation or else to seek for its explanation at a higher level, in a superior grade of perfection.

From here on, the universe appears essentially a hierarchy and the philosophical problem is to indicate its exact arrangement and to place each class of beings in its proper grade. To do this, one principle of universal value must always be kept in mind: that the greater or less can only be appraised and classified in relation to the maximum, the relative in relation to the absolute. Between God who is Being, pure and simple, and complete nothingness, there come near God pure intelligence known as angels and near nothingness material forms. Between angels and material nature come human creatures on the borderline between spirits and bodies. Thus the angels reduce the infinite gap separating man from God and man fills in the gap between angels and matter.

Each of these degrees has its own mode of operation since each being operates according as it is in act and as its degree of actuality merges with its degree of perfection. The orderly and arranged hierarchy of beings is thus made complete by the orderly and arranged hierarchy of their operations, and in such a way that the bottom of the higher degree invariably comes into close contact with the top of the lower. Thus the principle of continuity gives precision and determination to the principles of perfection. Actually, both of these principles but express the higher law governing the communication of being. There is no being save the divine being in which all creatures participate; and creatures only differ from one another by reason of their greater or lesser degree of participation in the divine being. Their perfection must, accordingly, be measured by the distance separating them from God. It is in thus differentiating themselves from one another that they arrange themselves into a hierarchy.

If this is true, it is analogy alone which enables our intelligence to arrive at a transcendent God from sensible things. It is analogy, too, which alone permits us to say that the universe has its existence from a transcendental principle and yet is neither confused with it nor added to it. The similarity of the analogue has, of course, to be explained, and it can only be explained by means of what the analogue imitates: "For (being) is not said of many equivocally, but analogically, and thus must be reduced to unity."[1] But at the same time that it possesses enough of its model's being to require it as its cause, it possesses it in such a manner that the being of this cause does not become involved in that of the thing caused. And because the word "being" signifies two different modes of existence when applied to God and to creatures, no problem of addition or subtraction can arise. The being of creature is only an image, an imitation of the divine being. Even as reflections appear about a flame, increasing, decreasing and disappearing, without the substance of the flame being affected, so the likenesses freely created by the divine substance owe all their being to this substance. They subsist only through it, yet borrow nothing from its *per se* mode of being, a mode very different from their own. They neither add to it nor subtract from it even in the least degree.

These two principles, analogy and hierarchy, enable us to explain the creature through a transcendent Creator. They also permit us to maintain relations between them and to extend bonds between them which become the constitutive principles of created essences and the laws which serve to explain them. Whatever physics or natural philosophy ultimately shows to be the nature of things, it has necessarily to remain

---

1. Plotinus—neoplatonist pagan philosopher (205–270) whose *Enneads* expressed the neoplatonic theory of the world as emanation of the One (God) [*Editor*].

subordinate to a metaphysics of being. If creatures are similitudes in what concerns their basic origin, then it is to be expected that analogy will serve to explain the universe just as it explains creation. To account for the operation of a being, we shall always have to show that its operation is based, beyond its essence in its act-of-being. And to give account of this essence will always be to show that a definite degree of participation in being, corresponding exactly to what this essence is, ought to have a place in our universe. But why was such a determined similitude required by a universe like ours? It is because the similitudes of any model can only be essentially different if they are more or less perfect. A finite system of images of an infinite being must have all the real degrees of likeness which can appear within the bounds assigned to the system by the free will of the Creator. The metaphysical explanation of a physical phenomenon must always be concerned with putting an essence in its place in a hierarchy.

This sense of hierarchy shows the profound influence of the Pseudo-Dionysius on the thought of St. Thomas.[2] There is no denying this influence; and it explains why some have wished to rank the author of the *Summa Theologiae* among the disciples of Plotinus. Only when we strictly limit its range does such a thesis become acceptable. The Areopagite furnishes the framework of the hierarchy. He firmly implants in thought the need for a hierarchy. He makes it impossible not to consider the universe as a hierarchy. But he left for St. Thomas the task of completing it; and even though Dionysius assigns the various grades in the hierarchy, he does not know the law which governs their arrangement and distribution.

But is it true to say that St. Thomas thought of the content of this universal hierarchy in a neo-Platonic spirit? If we except with numerous reservations the case of pure spirits, it is quite apparent that the answer is no. The God of St. Thomas the Christian is the same as St. Augustine's. That St. Augustine was under neo-Platonic influence does not mean that his God could be confused with the God of Plotinus. Between Plotinian speculation and the theology of the Fathers of the Church there stands Jehovah, the personal God who acts by intelligence and will, and who freely places outside himself that real universe which his wisdom chose from an infinity of possible universes. Between this freely created universe and God the Creator there is an impassable abyss and no other continuity than the continuity of order. Properly speaking, the world is an ordered discontinuity. Must we not see that we are here far removed from neo-Platonic philosophy? To make of St. Thomas a Plotinian, or even a neo-Platonizer, is to confuse him with the adversaries he resisted so energetically.

The distance between the two philosophers is no less noticeable when

2. Pseudo-Dionysius or Dionysius the Areopagite—Christian monk (c. A.D. 500) who through his works, *The Celestial Hierarchy*, *The Ecclesiastical Hierarchy*, and *The Divine Names*, transmitted a Christianized neoplatonism to the Middle Ages. He was endowed with a quasi-Scriptural authority because he was believed to have been converted by St. Paul [*Editor*].

we move from God to man. We said that St. Thomas's God was not the God of Plotinus but the Christian God of Augustine. Neither is St. Thomas's man the man of Plotinus. The opposition is particularly sharp right at the heart of the problem: in the relation between soul and body, and in the doctrine of knowledge which results from this. In Platonism there is the affirming of the extreme independence and almost complete aseity[3] of the soul; this allows for Platonic reminiscence and even for the momentary return to the One through the ecstatic union. But in Thomism there is a most energetic affirming of the physical nature of the soul and vigilant care to close all paths which might lead to a doctrine of direct intuition of the intelligible in order to leave open no other road than that of sense knowledge. Platonism locates mystical knowledge in the natural prolongation of human knowledge; in Thomism, mystical knowledge is added to and co-ordinated with natural knowledge, but is not a continuation of it. All we know about God is what our reason teaches us about Him after reflecting upon the evidence of the senses. If we want to find a neo-Platonic doctrine of knowledge in the Middle Ages, we will have to look elsewhere than in St. Thomas.

This becomes clearer when we put aside the consideration of this particular problem and examine directly the Thomistic hierarchy of the universe. We have had a great deal to say about God and His creative power, about the angels and their functions, about man and his operations. We have considered, one after the other, all creatures endowed with intellect, and the First Intelligence itself. What we have seen is that the nature and compass of the many kinds of knowledge it has been given to us to acquire have varied very considerably according to the greater or less perfection of the reality which was its object. One who wishes to extract a clear notion of the spirit of Thomistic philosophy must first examine the ladder of being, and then inspect the values which locate each order of knowledge in its proper degree.

What is knowing? It is apprehending what is. There is no other perfect knowledge. Now it is immediately apparent that all knowledge, properly so-called, of the higher degrees in the universal hierarchy is relentlessly refused us. We know that God and pure intelligences exist, but we do not know what they are. There is no doubting, however, that the awareness of a deficiency in our knowledge of God leaves us with a burning desire for higher and more complete knowledge. Nor can it be doubted that, if knowing consists in grasping the essence of the object known, God, angels and, generally speaking, anything of the purely intelligible order, is by definition beyond the grasp of our intellect. This is why, instead of having an institution of the Divine Essence, we have but a vast number of concepts which, taken together, are a confused sort of imitation of what would have been a true notion of the Divine Essence. When all that we have been able to say about such a subject is put

---

3. separateness [Editor].

together, the result is a collection of negations or analogies, nothing more.

Where, then, does human knowledge find itself at home? When is it in the presence of its own object? Only at that point where it comes into contact with the sensible. And although it does not here totally penetrate the real, because the individual as such implies or presupposes matter and is therefore beyond expression, still reason is in control of the field in which it is working. In order to describe man, that is, the human composite, to describe the animal and its operations, the heavenly bodies and their powers, mixed bodies or the elements, rational knowledge remains proportioned to the order or rank of the objects it is exploring. Although its content is incomplete, it is nevertheless positive. What is original and truly profound in Thomism is not an attempt either to establish science more solidly or to extend it. St. Thomas places the proper object of the human intellect in the sensible order, but he does not consider the study of this order to be the highest foundation of the knowing faculty. The proper object of the intellect is the quiddity[4] of the sensible, but its proper function is to make the sensible intelligible. From the particular object on which its light falls it draws something universal. It can do this because this particular object carries the divine image naturally impressed upon it as the mark of its origin. The intellect is, in the proper sense of the term, born and made for the universal. Hence its straining toward that object which is by definition vigorously inaccessible, the Divine Being. Here reason knows very little, but what little it knows surpasses in dignity and value any other kind of certitude.

St. Thomas and Augustinian Christianity

FREDERICK COPLESTON, S.J.

Aquinas and Augustine †

(Copleston argues against the belief that Aquinas's philosophy marks a break with that of St. Augustine. Rather, he says, Aquinas "expresses Augustine in Aristotelian categories.")

4.   It is sometimes said that St. Thomas differs from St. Augustine in that while the latter considers man simply in the concrete, as man

4. Latinized word for "whatness" [Editor].

† Frederick Copleston, S.J., A History of Philoso- phy, vol. II (London: Burnes Oates, 1950). By permission of Search Press Ltd.

called to a supernatural end, St. Thomas distinguishes two ends, a supernatural end, the consideration of which he assigns to the theologian, and a natural end, the consideration of which he assigns to the philosopher. Now, that St. Thomas distinguishes the two ends is quite true. In the *De Veritate*[1] he says that the final good as considered by the philosopher is different from the final good as considered by the theologian, since the philosopher considers the final good *(bonum ultimum)* which is proportionate to human powers, whereas the theologian considers as the final good that which transcends the power of nature, namely life eternal, by which he means, of course, not simply survival but the vision of God. This distinction is of great importance and it has its repercussion both in morals, where it is the foundation of the distinction between the natural and the supernatural virtues, and in politics, where it is the foundation of the distinction between the ends of the Church and the state and determines the relations which should exist between the two societies; but it is not a distinction between two ends which correspond to two mutually exclusive orders, the one supernatural, the other that of "pure nature": it is a distinction between two orders of knowledge and activity in the same concrete human being. The concrete human being was created by God for a supernatural end, for perfect happiness, which is attainable only in the next life through the vision of God and which is moreover, unattainable by man by his own unaided natural power; but man can attain an imperfect happiness in this life by the exercise of his natural powers, through coming to a philosophic knowledge of God through creatures and through the attainment and exercise of the natural virtues.[2] Obviously these ends are not exclusive, since man can attain the imperfect felicity in which his natural end consists without thereby putting himself outside the way to his supernatural end; the natural end, imperfect beatitude, is proportionate to human nature and human powers, but inasmuch as man has been created for a supernatural final end, the natural end cannot satisfy him, as St. Thomas argues in the *Contra Gentiles;*[3] it is imperfect and points beyond itself.

How does this affect the question of the relation between theology and philosophy? In this way: Man has one final end, supernatural beatitude, but the existence of this end, which transcends the powers of mere human nature, even though man was created to attain it and given the power to do so by grace, cannot be known by natural reason and so cannot be divined by the philosopher; its consideration is restricted to the theologian. On the other hand, man can attain through the exercise of his natural powers to an imperfect and limited natural happiness in this life, and the existence of this end and the means to attain it are discoverable by the philosopher, who can prove the existence of God from creatures, attain some analogical knowledge of God, define the natural virtues and the means of attaining them. Thus the philosopher may be said to con-

1. *De Veritate*, 14:3.
2. Cf. *In Boethium de Trinitate*, 6, 4, 5; *In I Sent.*,

prol., I, I; *De Veritate*, 14:2; *S.T.*, Ia, IIae, 5, 5.
3. 3, 27ff.

sider the end of man in so far as this end is discoverable by human reason (i.e. only imperfectly and incompletely). But both theologian and philosopher are considering man in the concrete: the difference is that the philosopher, while able to view and consider human nature as such, cannot discover his supernatural vocation; he can only go part of the way in discovering man's destiny, precisely because man was created for an end which transcends the powers of his nature. It is, therefore, not true to say that for St. Thomas the philosopher considers man in a hypothetical state of pure nature, that is, man as he would have been, had he never been called to a supernatural end: he considers man in the concrete, but he cannot know all there is to be known about that man in the concrete. When St. Thomas raises the question whether God could have created man in *puris naturalibus*[4] he is asking simply if God could have created man (who even in this hypothesis was created for a supernatural end) without sanctifying grace, that is to say, if God could have first created man without the means of attaining his end and then afterwards have given it; he is not asking if God could have given man a purely natural ultimate end, as later writers interpreted him as saying. Whatever, then, the merit of the idea of the state of pure nature considered in itself may be (this is a point I do not propose to discuss), it does not play a part in St. Thomas's conception of philosophy. Consequently he does not differ from St. Augustine so much as has been sometimes asserted, though he defined the spheres of the two sciences of philosophy and theology more clearly than Augustine had defined them: what he did was to express Augustinianism in terms of the Aristotelian philosophy, a fact which compelled him to utilize the notion of natural end, though he interpreted it in such a way that he cannot be said to have adopted a starting-point in philosophy totally different from that of Augustine.

* * *

6.   When one looks back on the thirteenth century from a much later date, one does not always recognize the fact that St. Thomas was an innovator, that his adoption of Aristotelianism was bold and 'modern.' St. Thomas was faced with a system of growing influence and importance, which seemed in many respects to be incompatible with Christian tradition, but which naturally captivated the minds of many students and masters, particularly in the faculty of arts at Paris, precisely because of its majesty, apparent coherence and comprehensiveness. That Aquinas boldly grasped the bull by the horns and utilized Aristotelianism is the building up of his own system was very far from being an obscurantist action: it was, on the contrary, extremely 'modern' and was of the greatest importance for the future of Scholastic philosophy and indeed for the history of philosophy in general. That some Scholastics in the later Middle Ages and at the time of the Renaissance brought

4. *In 2 Sent.*, 29, 1, 2; *ibid.*, 29, 2, 3; *S.T.*, Ia, 95, 1, 4; *Quodlibet*, 1, 8.

Aristotelianism into discredit by their obscurantist adherence to all the Philosopher's dicta, even on scientific matters, does not concern St. Thomas: the plain fact is that they were not faithful to the spirit of St. Thomas. The Saint rendered, to any count, an incomparable service to Christian thought by utilizing the instrument which presented itself, and he naturally interpreted Aristotle in the most favorable sense from the Christian standpoint, since it was essential to show, if he was to succeed in his undertaking, that Aristotle and Averroes did not stand or fall together. Moreover, it is not true to say that St. Thomas had no sense of accurate interpretation: one may not agree with all his interpretations of Aristotle, but there can be no doubt that, given the circumstances of the time and the paucity of relevant historical information at his disposal, he was one of the most conscientious and the finest commentators of Aristotle who have ever existed.

In conclusion, however, it must be emphasized that though St. Thomas adopted Aristotelianism as an instrument for the expression of his system, he was no blind worshipper of the Philosopher, who discarded Augustine in favor of the pagan thinker. In theology he naturally treads in the footsteps of Augustine, though his adoption of the Aristotelian philosophy as an instrument enabled him to systematize, define and argue logically from theological doctrines in a manner which was foreign to the attitude of Augustine: in philosophy, while there is a great deal which comes straight from Aristotle, he often interprets Aristotle in a manner consonant with Augustine or expresses Augustine in Aristotelian categories, though it might be truer to say that he does both at once. For instance, when treating of divine knowledge and providence, he interprets the Aristotelian doctrine of God in a sense which at least does not exclude God's knowledge of the world, and in treating of the divine ideas he observes that Aristotle censured Plato for making the ideas independent both of concrete things and of an intellect, with the tacit implication that Aristotle would not have censured Plato, had the latter placed the ideas in the mind of God. This is, of course, to interpret Aristotle *in meliorem partem*[5] from the theological standpoint, and although the interpretation tends to bring Aristotle and Augustine closer together, it most probably does not represent Aristotle's actual theory of the divine knowledge. * * *

But what I am suggesting is that St. Thomas is speaking pretty well as St. Augustine might speak, that he is considering man in the concrete, as called to a supernatural end and that when he says that man has a natural desire to know the essence of God, he does not mean to imply that man in a hypothetical state of nature would have had such a natural desire, whether absolute or conditional, of seeing God, but simply that the term of the natural movement of the human intellect towards truth is *de facto* the vision of God, not because the human intellect can of itself see God, whether in this life or the next, but because *de facto* the

5. in a more favorable way [*Editor*].

only end of man is a supernatural end. I do not think that St. Thomas is considering the hypothetical state of nature at all, when he speaks of the *desiderium naturale*,[6] and if this is so, it obviously means that his moral theory is not and cannot be a purely philosophical theory. His moral theory is partly theological and partly philosophical: he utilizes the Aristotelian ethic but fits it into a Christian setting. After all, Aristotle was himself considering man in the concrete, as far as he knew what man in the concrete actually is, and St. Thomas, who knew much better than Aristotle what man in the concrete actually is, was fully justified in utilizing the thought of Aristotle when he believed it to be correct and found it compatible with his Christian standpoint. * * *

6. natural desire [*Editor*].

Thomism and Politics

AQUINAS AS MEDIEVAL CONSERVATIVE

KATHERINE ARCHIBALD

The Concept of Social Hierarchy in the Writings of St. Thomas Aquinas †

(Writing from the point of view of an American committed to social and political equality, and what more recently would be called a feminist out-look, Archibald has highlighted the anti-equalitarian and undemocratic [as well as sexist] attitudes in Aquinas's theory. To make her argument, Professor Archibald has equated medieval serfs with slaves in Aquinas's theory, although legally serfdom had a different status from slavery in the Middle Ages. She also overstates the degree to which Aristotelian and medieval notions of fixed hierarchies in society override Aquinas's Christian belief in the responsibility of the individual soul to God.)

To organize in proper sequence the diversity of the universe, St. Thomas turns to a number of traditional capacities and characteristics presumed to exist in totality and perfection in the Deity and to be more and more partially and imperfectly present in the descending order of creatures. God is pure spirit, pure act, the unmoved mover, the uncaused cause. Hence the more adulterated with matter, the more weakened with potency a creature is, the less it moves itself and the more it is moved by others, the less it causes and the more it is caused, the lower in the scale the creature stands. Laboring thus with metaphysical justifications, St. Thomas emerges finally with the traditional order of creatures and creation: inanimate nature at the base, plants following, animals next (divided in turn into those that are capable of self-motion and those that are not), and spiritual or intellectual substances at the crown.[1] The basic dichotomy

† *The Historian*, vol. II (1949–50). By permission of Phi Alpha Theta. 1. *Summa contra Gentiles* (S.C.G.), II, 95.

in this series is the again traditional metaphysical division of the universe into the realm of mind, spirit, soul, and the realm of matter or the animal.

Man, in this universe, is placed halfway between the realms of spirit and matter. He is a composite of animal and soul and contains within his own nature an hierarchy of powers. Rightly organized, this hierarchy is capped by reason. The soul must rule the body, and within the soul, with its nutritive, sensitive, and rational levels, reason must dominate. When man is thus composed within himself, he is ordered in accordance with Divine reason; he is virtuous.[2] Man's infinite sins have therefore a common source, which is the rebellion of man's lower faculties against the rightful rule of reason.[3] Rebelling against reason, man rebels against God. Reason, moreover, is that capacity which most particularly links him to the realm of spirit and ultimately to the Pure Intelligence which is the Deity.[4]

In designating man as a rational animal, St. Thomas defines the human species. But to assert that all men are rational is for St. Thomas merely to delimit the human from the subhuman level and not to establish the unvarying equality of humanity within itself. Diversity exists within the human species; individualism exists. Permeated as he is with the viewpoint of hierarchy, St. Thomas conceives a difference and inequality as virtually synonymous. Expanding fully the implications of this concept, he develops an hierarchical structure which from one viewpoint may be compared, not so much to a pyramid, as to a totem pole of status, whose length is exactly equivalent to the extent of human differences.

Since the human soul constitutes the form of man and is single and specific in its nature,[5] St. Thomas seeks the source of human diversity in the matter which enters into the construction of the human composite. Every human organism is conceived and develops in the womb with its own peculiar complement of fleshly skills and sensory equipment. And each soul, while retaining the specific character and the basic style of all human souls, is nonetheless tailored to fit, at the point of its introduction into the embryonic organism, the particular shape of a particular body.[6] Even when the body dies and the soul survives alone for a period while awaiting reunion with a spiritualized body on the Day of Judgment, even then each soul is individual and different since it retains the fit and the proportion which marked it in its life of union with the flesh.[7] All these differences, furthermore, between body and body, soul and soul, and one human composite and another, are differences, not of simple variety, but of value, of better and worse, of more or less perfect. For differences, wherever they exist in the Thomistic universe, are vertically, and not horizontally ordered; differences are typically in-

2. S.C.G., III, 121.
3. St. Thomas Aquinas, *Summa Theologiae* (S.T.), I–II, qu. 71, a.2.
4. S.T., II–II, qu. 2, a. 3.
5. S.T., I–II, qu. 63, a. 1.

6. St. Thomas Aquinas, *Commentary on the Sentences* (S.C.G.), (Vives ed., Paris, 1880), II, d. 32, qu. 2, a. 3.
7. S.C.G., II, 81.

equalities, and inequalities, in the long run, are matters of greater or less goodness. * * *

In accordance with his emphasis on reason and intelligence as chief among human abilities, St. Thomas tends to point to intellect as the hallmark of a human being's excellence.[8] Since he also tends to connect reason and morality, the more intelligent man becomes the more virtuous man as well. "Now," St. Thomas asserts, "the virtues are nothing but those perfections whereby reason is directed to God, and the inferior powers regulated according to the dictate of reason. . . ."[9] The Angelic Doctor continues a further tradition common among philosophers in pursuit of an intellectual elite in that he joins excellence of mind and soul with an excellence of body compatible with a life of physical ease and leisure rather than with a life of manual toil. The fine mind, he declares, is found, not in the strong-muscled and broad-shouldered body, but in the body with soft flesh and delicate sensitivities.[1]

The differences which make an almost infinite hierarchy of human individuals are solidified and organized in human society into differences of authority and status. Man is by nature social; only the man who is in some sense either beyond or beneath the human level can live in solitude.[2] And society is by nature hierarchical. The multitude of individuals in any given society, St. Thomas writes, would be hopelessly confused if that society were not divided into different orders which are ranked hierarchically.[3] Society, in being hierarchical, not only reflects the fact of human differences, but also, as part of a pyramidal universe, contains its own rationale of status. God's universe is ordered. And inequality is the essence of order. "It belongs to divine providence that order be preserved in the world;" St. Thomas observes, "and suitable order consists in a proportionate descent from the highest to the lowest. . . ."[4]

So germane to society is inequality that even in the society of the State of Innocence, which St. Thomas pictures as very numerous, since the processes of reproduction were normally active while the hand of death was stayed, even in the society of Eden, there was inequality of status, as between husband and wife, father and child, ruler and ruled. * * *

St. Thomas's effort to reproduce in the society of fallen man the hierarchical pattern of the universe is clearly seen in his prescription for the good political society or state. Although he speaks without negativism of Aristotle's aristocracy and polity (the latter of which is, after all, little more than a broadened aristocracy), his unequivocal preference, as he shows in his *De Regimine Principum*, is for monarchy. As God, by being One, brings the diversity of the universe to a single point, so the ruler, by being one, brings to a point of unity the diversity of society and thus assures peace for all its members.[5] Again the structure of the pyramid

8. S.T., I, qu. 85, a. 7.
9. S.T., I, qu. 95, a. 3.
1. S.T., I, qu. 85, a. 7.
2. S.T., II–II, qu. 188, a. 8, resp. 5.
3. S.T., I, qu. 108, a. 2.

4. S.C.G., III, 78.
5. St. Thomas Aquinas, *De Regimine Principum* (English translation, *On the Governance of Rulers*, by Gerald B. Phelan, Toronto, 1935), I, 2.

emerges, and beneath the capstone of the monarch the orders of the secular world are ranged in layers of status, the bulk of which increases the farther from the top they lie.

The Angelic Doctor apparently assumes that under the guidance of Divine Providence the position of ruler will be for the most part occupied by a man whose intelligence and virtue are such that he is fit to rule. The assumption forms a necessary basis for his support of monarchy as the most desirable type of government and forms the basis, too, for his acceptance of absolutism as the pattern of control. * * *

Although it is the welfare of the community which is the proper goal of government—and hence there is a positive correlation between the consent of the community to be ruled for its own good and monarchical authority—St. Thomas nowhere provides a firm foundation for the idea of the "natural" or "original" right of the people as against the power of the king. He follows closely the Aristotelian concept that, since political relationship is grounded in nature, the real foundation of the order of dominance and subordination must be sought in the natural inequality of men. On the whole, then, he who leads is wiser and better than he who follows, and rebellion on the part of the follower is treason and sin. * * *[6]

Manual labor, in the literal sense of the work with the hands, is, in St. Thomas's view, the mark *par excellence* of servile or semi-servile status. Though St. Thomas concedes that all useful human labor has dignity, he constructs an elaborate scale of greater or lesser dignity for various kinds of labor, a scale which reaches up to the life of contemplation at its peak and down through grades of less involvement of the intellect and more involvement of the body to manual labor at the base. The division which St. Thomas makes between the liberal and the servile arts is in keeping with this scale and the concepts it embodies. The liberal arts, which are declared to be nobler than the arts necessary to the sustenance of the body, derive their name, St. Thomas states, from the fact that they pertain chiefly to the soul, which in man is free.[7] But in St. Thomas's society these arts were also chiefly restricted in their practice to free men. The servile arts are so called because they pertain primarily to the body, and the body is in a certain sense in servitude to the soul.[8] But they were also linked in thirteenth century Europe to a class whose status was servile.

Manual labor, in the Thomistic synthesis, has gained somewhat in honor over its place in Aristotelian attitudes. It has assumed, as one of its possible functions, the subjugation of the body, through punishing and exhausting it, to the rightful rule of reason, and a well-born man may obtain favor in God's eyes by humbling himself to the extent of working with his hands.[9] But this is a voluntary abasement equivalent to

6. In fact Aquinas gives the people a wider role than Archibald claims. See S.T., I–II, qu. 105, a. 1 (p. 58), and allows for resistance to the ruler in specified circumstances, (S.T., II–II, qu. 42, a. 2

(p. 65) [Editor].
7. S.T., II–II, qu. 57, a. 3, resp. 3.
8. Ibid.
9. S.T., I–II, qu. 30, a. 3.

King Louis IX's washing the feet of beggars as a token of humility. To work with one's hands of necessity is to find oneself, in the Christian world of St. Thomas, either in the lowest strata of the free or, more generally, in the vast anonymity of the servile mass.

The servile status in which, without effort at distinction, St. Thomas groups both serf and slave, is asserted to have come into existence at the time of the Fall.[1] It is in some sense punitive, as, indeed, manual labor, which is the particular burden appertaining to servility, is also punitive.[2] Servility is further associated with positive rather than with natural law.[3] The very fact, however, that St. Thomas assumes the serf to be not a serf by nature but by way of punishment for original sin and/or by way of social convenience makes all the more astonishing his complacent approval of servility as the status of what was in his time by far the majority of the population of Europe. * * *

St. Thomas preserves certain minimal rights to the slave or serf; the right to self-preservation in terms of the animal necessities of food and rest and the right to reproduce, with the implied right of marriage.[4] The strength of the marriage bond on the servile level is considerably weakened, however, by the prescription that concealment of servile status by one of the parties to the marriage contract, the other being free, is grounds for annulment of the marriage.[5] The man of servile status cannot enter Orders unless and until his freedom be obtained.[6] This mass of the unfree, this great majority of the populace, are, of course, to be excluded from participation and even apparently from consideration in the political life of the state. "For if men assembled merely to *live,* then animals and serfs would form a part of the civil body," St. Thomas writes in his *De Regimine Principum*[7] (borrowing almost word for word a phrase from Aristotle's *Politics*).[8] But the end of the state is not mere animal livelihood; it is the enjoyment of God to be achieved through virtuous living.[9]

1. *Commentary on the Sentences,* II, d. 44, qu. 1, a. 3. [By her use of the term "servility" Archibald confuses the status of serf and slave—and makes it appear that Aquinas consigns "the majority of the population of Europe" to the status of Aristotle's natural slave, little better than that of an animal. In fact, the two situations were very different, and Aquinas is talking about slaves, not serfs. As Marc Bloch has noted: "(The) serf, so despised and placed in a state of strict dependence, was not at all a slave. He did not present the same legal characteristics, since he could possess land by rental or even as full-fledged property to give, sell, and under certain conditions, inherit; since, also, he served at the host and sat at tribunals; and since above all his obligations were, in principle and except when violated, strictly limited by custom. Even less did he represent the characteristics of the slave's economic order, because his labor power did not belong to his lord * * * Serfdom was something quite different from slavery. *Servus* and the Latin derivatives of the world had, as we have seen, slipped bit by bit into a meaning vastly different from their ancient content." Marc Bloch,

Slavery and Serfdom in the Middle Ages (Berkeley, Cal., University of California Press, 1975) 22–23—*Editor.*]

2. S.T., II–II, qu. 164, a. 2, resp. 3.

3. S.T., III, qu. 52, a. 1, resp. 2. The third part of the *Summa Theologica* remained unfinished at the death of St. Thomas. Its completion, presumably from notes and instructions left by the master, was accomplished by a disciple, Reginald of Piperno, and is known as the *Supplementum.* In accordance with the practice of other students of the subject, I have treated the *Supplementum* as an integral part of the *Summa* and of St. Thomas's thought.

4. *Sent.,* IV, d. 36, qu. 1, a. 2.

5. S.T., III, qu. 52, a. 1.

6. S.T., III, qu. 39, a. 3.

7. *On Kingship* I, 14. (Italics in translation.)

8. Aristotle, *The Politics* (English translation by H. Rackham, London, 1932), Bk. III, ch. v. [Note that Aquinas, writing in Latin, uses *servi*—slaves—which Archibald translates as "serfs"—a status that Aristotle never knew—*Editor.*]

9. *De Reg.,* I, 14.

Serfs, therefore, along with animals, are not part of the political body. * * *

The woman's society, like that of the serf, is in St. Thomas's view essentially the society of the family. By the very fact of this limitation of realm St. Thomas reinforces his rigid doctrine of the unqualified inferiority of woman to man. From the elaborate Thomistic analysis, woman, as a group and generality, emerges inferior to man in every aspect of her being. Physiologically she is inferior, since St. Thomas perpetuates the Aristotelian concept of woman as a misshapen or half-formed man.[1] The relative weakness of her reason is emphasized,[2] and from this weakness follows the greater susceptibility of her soul to the disorder of sin.[3] God is asserted to have created her as a helpmate for man in only one essential function, the process of reproduction. Another man, St. Thomas asserts, would have been more suitable as a helpmate in all other regards.[4] And even in the process of generation her role is that of the inferior; man is the active principle of generation, woman the passive; man provides the form of the newly created being, woman only the matter.[5]

Woman's status is in accord with her asserted incapacities. As a child she is subject to her father. As an adult, she is subject to her husband, whose power over her is limited only by the absence of the power of life and death. The husband is specifically permitted to correct his wife with corporal punishment in case of need.[6] He is assigned control over the financial affairs of the household, and the wife is cautioned, along with children and serfs, not to give alms without her husband's permission.[7] The woman's authority over her children, which is at the start a secondary authority in the line of family command, is further weakened by St. Thomas's contention that, absolutely speaking, the father is to be loved by his children more than is the mother. "For father and mother," he asserts, "are loved as principles of our natural origin. Now the father is principle in a more excellent way than the mother, because he is the active principle, while the mother is a passive and material principle."[8]

Although the subjection of the wife is modified by the assurance that she is not a slave in the home of her husband,[9] woman, in a different instance, is compared with a slave to her own limitation and the slave's advantage. Whereas the slave, it is stated, is not necessarily a slave by nature, the woman, in whatever circumstance she may find herself, is always by her nature a subject.[1] For the slave there is the possibility of escape from dependence and tutelage to freedom; for the woman, there is none. * * *

In considering the highest possible life for man on earth, St. Thomas provides a certain escape from pyramids of family, Church, and state, an escape, in a sense, for the rarest of the chosen, from all society. In

1. *S.T.*, I, qu. 99, a. 2, resp. 1.
2. *S.C.G.*, III, 123.
3. *S.T.*, III *(Supple.)*, qu. 62, a. 5, resp. 5.
4. *S.T.*, I, qu. 92, a. 1.
5. *S.C.G.*, IV, 11; *S.T.*, II–II, qu. 26, a. 10, resp. 1.
6. *S.T.*, III, qu. 62, a. 2, resp. 1.
7. *S.T.*, II–II, qu. 32, a. 8.
8. *S.T.*, II–II, qu. 26, a. 10.
9. *S.T.*, I, qu. 92, a. 1, resp. 2.
1. *S.T.*, III, qu. 39, a. 3, resp. 4.

choosing the life on earth which is most like the life of eternity, in selecting the labor which lifts man farthest from the level of the animal and nearest to the level of the divine, he turns to the life and labor of contemplation. "Now the contemplative life," he declares "pertains directly and immediately to the love of God. . . . On the other hand, the active life is more directly concerned with the love of our neighbor, because it is *busy about serving.* . . . Wherefore the contemplative life is generally of greater merit than the active life."[2] He is careful to make the contemplative life, however, no universal prescription for all men. Only those may turn to it, he states, whose physical requirements are provided for by other means than the need for personal labor and who have no family responsibilities. * * *

In summing up the structure of society, as St. Thomas presents it, it is easy to observe that he has in part simply outlined the pattern of living of thirteenth century Europe and has then proceeded to defend that pattern as proper for all societies and times. There is, however, a deeper stream of argument as well. For St. Thomas is defending not just his own specific society nor societies like his own in other places and eras but the structure of hierarchy, status, and privilege as such. This structure is developed, furthermore, in terms of a specifically gifted, divinely sponsored, and leisured elite ruling with stable power over a dull-witted and sodden-souled mass of manual workers—ruling in this fashion, finally, because the mass is presumably incapable of managing itself.

THE TRANSMISSION OF THOMISM

PAUL OSKAR KRISTELLER

The Thomist Tradition †

(Kristeller's concise summary of the history of Thomist influence underscores the fact that it is only in the sixteenth, and in particular, the late nineteenth centuries that Aquinas comes to be regarded as the single most representative and important medieval thinker. As he points out, the principal instruments of transmission of the Thomist tradition have been the Dominican and Jesuit orders, and the papacy from Pope Leo XIII to Pope John XXIII.)

---

2. *S.T.*, II–II, qu. 182, a. 2. (Italics in translation.)

† Paul Oskar Kristeller, *Medieval Aspects of*

Renaissance Learning (Durham, N.C.: Duke University Press, 1974). Copyright 1974 © Duke University Press, by permission.

Great caution should be exercised in examining the history of St. Thomas's tradition and influence. The first thing to avoid—and this has not always been done— is to attribute to his influence the presence in the thought of the following centuries of a large number of ideas which are indeed found in his work, but which are not in fact peculiar to him. Rather, they are common to many other medieval thinkers or they are derived from ancient sources just as accessible to his successors as to himself. It is also advisable to point out that a great number and a great variety of problems and doctrines in his very vast work are not closely linked one with another. The attempt has been often made to establish a clear distinction between orthodox Thomists and eclectic Thomists. If by orthodox is meant the thinker who is content to reaffirm the doctrines contained in the master's work without adding anything, it is indeed difficult to find any Thomist other than Saint Thomas himself. It is important to distinguish clearly those authors who rely principally on his authority and who tend to support most of his major and characteristic doctrines from those who combine his ideas with other ideas that are either original or from another source, or who are content simply to borrow certain of his ideas or assertions without giving them a central position in their own writings or thought. When dealing with the history of Thomism, it is obviously necessary to consider all of these various factors.

In tracing Saint Thomas's influence on the centuries following him, it is necessary to distinguish the authority attributed to the Saint and to his doctrine by the Dominican Order, of which he had been a member, from that accorded him by theologians of the Catholic Church in general who were not Dominicans and, finally, from that ascribed to him by those philosophers and other scholars not especially concerned with theology. * * *

The event which did most to determine Saint Thomas's role in the Church outside his order was his canonization, declared in 1323 by John XXII after a long process. A consequence of the canonization was the revocation by the bishop of Paris of the condemnation of those of Saint Thomas's positions which had been included in the condemnation of 1277.[1] There is no doubt that the canonization contributed in an indirect, but effective, manner to the increase of the Saint's doctrinal authority among theologians and scholars outside the Dominican Order. The Dominicans immediately instituted an office for the new saint, whose feast-day was fixed as March 7, and already in the fourteenth century there were sermons containing eulogies to him.

What may be called the second period of the history of Thomism is marked by the tendency to adopt the *Summa Theologiae* instead of the

---

1. In 1277 after Aquinas's death the bishop of Paris condemned as heretical 219 propositions including at least four identified with Aquinas's teach-ing—on the unity of the world, the individuation of spirits and bodies, the localization of spiritual substances, and the operation of the will [*Editor*].

Sentences as the basic text in theology.[2] This movement, whose existence must be established from school and university documents, as well as from manuscript and printed commentaries, began according to the results of the most recent research with which I am acquainted, in the Dominican convents of Germany during the second half of the fifteenth century and a little later in Italy. It spread, thanks to Dominican professors, from the convents to the universities, especially in Germany. Then, it was introduced at the University of Paris by Peter Crockaert around 1510 and at Salamanca by his student, Francis de Vitoria, around 1530. During the sixteenth century, the *Summa* was also adopted as a text by the theologians of the new order of the Jesuits in their college and university teaching, and their example was followed by other Catholic theologians. The study of university documents and the compilation of a bibliography of the commentaries are not yet completed, but we have the impression both that the use of the *Summa*, especially in Spain, Portugal, and their colonies, was very widespread after the second half of the sixteenth century, although study of the *Sentences* had not been completely abandoned, and also that the Franciscans in particular never forsook their Scotist orientation.[3] The notable importance accorded Saint Thomas at the Council of Trent is an indication that his authority had become more general, if not exclusive, in the area of Catholic theology. To the same period, namely to the sixteenth century and the first half of the seventeenth century, also belong numerous commentaries on the *Summa* and on some other works, in particular on the *Summa contra Gentiles* and the *De ente et essentia*. A complete inventory of these published and unedited commentaries has yet to be made, but their importance may be appreciated if we consider the influence exercised by the commentaries of Cardinal Cajetan, Sylvester of Ferrara, Francis of Vitoria and the other theologians of Salamanca and Coimbra, as well as by those of John of St. Thomas.

Although it is a subject not lacking in interest, the influence that Saint Thomas exerted, outside theological and even Catholic circles, on medieval philosophy and on early modern philosophy has not yet been sufficiently studied. I am referring here, of course, to an influence exercised by means of texts and particular doctrines rather than to a solid current of thought. Saint Thomas's prestige, however, was always great, and beginning with the sixteenth century it often happened—as it never did during the Middle Ages—that the ordinary reader who was not a theologian, and even the reader who was neither a Catholic nor a philosopher, considered Saint Thomas to be the sole representative of medieval philosophy and theology who deserved to be excluded from the general contempt for that tradition.

The third period in the history of Thomism is that in which we are

2. The *Sentences* (*Sententiae*—opinions) *of Peter Lombard* was the standard medieval theological text. Aquinas's first work—the equivalent of his doctoral dissertation—was his *Commentary on the Sentences* [*Editor*].

3. i.e., their commitment to the theology of Duns Scotus, a contemporary of Aquinas [*Editor*].

still living today. It began in 1879 with the encyclical *Aeterni Patris.*
Saint Thomas thereby became the principal master in Catholic schools,
not only in theology but also in philosophy. This event must have had
a profound influence on the teaching of these subjects in all Catholic
institutions, and it did have very salutary effects on Catholic scholarship,
particularly in the area of the history of medieval philosophy and theology. I am sure I will be allowed to note, however, that the position of
Thomism, even within the Catholic Church, has since 1879 become
very different from what it had been previously. In order to form a correct idea of the history of Thomism and of Saint Thomas's influence
during the periods prior to 1879, it is necessary to get a clear idea of the
facts that I have attempted to outline and to distinguish various levels of
influence according as this influence has been felt in theology or philosophy within the Dominican Order, outside this order but within the
Catholic Church, or outside the Catholic Church itself. * * *

THOMISM AND EARLY MODERN POLITICAL THOUGHT— ENGLAND AND SPAIN

RICHARD HOOKER

The Laws of Ecclesiastical Polity †
Book I—Laws in General

(Hooker was an Anglican clergyman who published the first books of *The
Laws of Ecclestical Polity* in 1593, as a defense of the Elizabethan religious
settlement against Puritan criticisms. He took over with slight modifications
the Thomist theory of law and linked it to ideas of community consent to
government that were later given a more individualist emphasis in Locke's
Second Treatise which often refers to "the judicious Hooker.")

This law therefore we may name eternal, being "that order which
God before all ages hath set down with himself, for himself to do all
things by."
III.   I am not ignorant that by "law eternal" the learned for the
most part do understand the order, not which God hath eternally pur-
posed himself in all his works to observe, but rather that which with
himself he hath set down as expedient to be kept by all his creatures,

---

† Richard Hooker, *Works*, vol. I (Oxford, 1841).

according to the several conditions wherewith he hath endued them.[1] They who thus are accustomed to speak apply the name of Law unto that only rule of working which superior authority imposeth: whereas we somewhat more enlarging the sense thereof term any kind of rule or canon, whereby actions are framed, a law. Now that law which, as it is laid up in the bosom of God, they call Eternal, receiveth according unto the different kinds of things which are subject unto it different and sundry kinds of names. That part of it which ordereth natural agents we call usually Nature's law; that which Angels do clearly behold and without any swerving observe is a law Celestial and heavenly; the law of Reason, that which bindeth creatures reasonable in this world, and with which by reason they may most plainly perceive themselves bound; that which bindeth them, and is not known but by special revelation from God, Divine law; Human law, that which out of the law either of reason or of God men probably gathering to be expedient, they make a law. * * *

9.   Laws of Reason have these marks to be known by. Such as keep them resemble most lively in their voluntary actions that very manner of working which Nature herself doth necessarily observe in the course of the whole world. The works of Nature are all behoveful, beautiful, without superfluity or defect; even so theirs, if they be framed according to that which the Law of Reason teacheth. Secondly, those Laws are investigable by Reason, without the help of Revelation supernatural and divine. Finally, in such sort they are investigable, that the knowledge of them is general, the world hath always been acquainted with them; according to that which one in Sophocles observeth concerning a branch of this Law, "It is no child of to-day's or yesterday's birth but hath been no man knoweth how long sithence." It is not agreed upon by one, or two, or few, but by all. Which we may not so understand, as if every particular man in the whole world did know and confess whatsoever the Law of Reason doth contain; but this Law is such that being proposed no man can reject it as unreasonable and unjust. Again, there is nothing in it but any man (having natural perfection of wit and ripeness of judgment) may by labour and travail find out. And to conclude, the general principles thereof are such, as it is not easy to find men ignorant of them. Law rational therefore, which men commonly use to call the Law of Nature, meaning thereby the Law which human Nature knoweth itself in reason universally bound unto, which also for that cause may be termed most fitly the Law of Reason; this Law, I say, comprehendeth all those things which men by the light of their natural understanding evidently know, or at leastwise may know, to be beseeming or unbeseeming, virtuous or vicious, good or evil for them to do. * * *

We all make complaint of the iniquity of our times: not unjustly; for the days are evil. But compare them with those times wherein there were

---

1. This definition of the eternal law is quoted by John Locke and attributed to Aquinas in Locke's early (1664) *Essays on the Law of Nature*, Essay 1, edited by W. von Leyden (Oxford: Clarendon Press, 1954), 117 [*Editor*].

no civil societies, with those times wherein there was as yet no manner of public regiment established, with those times wherein there were not above eight persons righteous living upon the face of the earth: and we have surely good cause to think that God hath blessed us exceedingly, and hath made us behold most happy days.

4.   To take away all such mutual grievances, injuries, and wrongs, there was no way but only by growing unto composition and agreement amongst themselves, by ordaining some kind of government public, and by yielding themselves subject thereunto; that unto whom they granted authority to rule and govern, by them the peace, tranquillity, and happy state of the rest might be procured. Men always knew that when force and injury was offered they might be defenders of themselves; they knew that howsoever men may seek their own commodity, yet if this were done with injury unto others it was not to be suffered, but by all men and by all good means to be withstood; finally they knew that no man might in reason take upon him to determine his own right, and according to his own determination proceed in maintenance thereof, inasmuch as every man is towards himself and them whom he greatly affecteth partial; and therefore that strifes and troubles would be endless, except they gave their common consent all to be ordered by some whom they should agree upon: without which consent there were no reason that one man should take upon him to be lord or judge over another; because, although there be according to the opinion of some very great and judicious men a kind of natural right in the noble, wise, and virtuous, to govern them which are of servile disposition;[2] nevertheless for manifestation of this their right, and men's more peaceable contentment on both sides, the assent of them who are to be governed seemeth necessary.

To fathers within their private families Nature hath given a supreme power; for which cause we see throughout the world even from the foundation thereof, all men have ever been taken as lords and lawful kings in their own houses. Howbeit over a whole grand multitude having no such dependency upon any one, and consisting of so many families as every politic society in the world doth, impossible it is that any should have complete lawful power, but by consent of men, or immediate appointment of God; because not having the natural superiority of fathers, their power must needs be either usurped, and then unlawful; or, if lawful, then either granted or consented unto by them over whom they exercise the same, or else given extraordinarily from God, unto whom all the world is subject. It is no improbable opinion therefore which the arch-philosopher was of, that as the chiefest person in every household was always as it were a king, so when numbers of households joined themselves in civil society together, kings were the first kind of governors amongst them.[3] Which is also (as it seemeth) the reason why the name of Father continued still in them, who of fathers were made rulers; as

---

2. Aristotle, *Politics*, III and IV [*Editor*].   3. Aristotle, *Politics*, I, 2 [*Editor*].

also the ancient custom of governors to do as Melchisedec, and being kings to exercise the office of priests, which fathers did at the first, grew perhaps by the same occasion.

Howbeit not this the only kind of regiment that hath been received in the world. The inconveniences of one kind have caused sundry others to be devised. So that in a word all public regiment of what kind soever seemeth evidently to have risen from deliberate advice, consultation, and composition between men, judging it convenient and behoveful; there being no impossibility in nature considered by itself, but that men might have lived without any public regiment. Howbeit, the corruption of our nature being presupposed, we may not deny but that the Law of Nature doth now require of necessity some kind of regiment, so that to bring things unto the first course they were in, and utterly to take away all kind of public government in the world, were apparently to overturn the whole world.

5.   The case of man's nature standing therefore as it doth, some kind of regiment the Law of Nature doth require; yet the kinds thereof being many, Nature tieth not to any one, but leaveth the choice as a thing arbitrary. At the first when some certain kind of regiment was once approved, it may be that nothing was then further thought upon for the manner of governing, but all permitted unto their wisdom and discretion which were to rule; till by experience they found this for all parts very inconvenient, so as the thing which they had devised for a remedy did indeed but increase the sore which it should have cured. They saw that to live by one man's will became the cause of all men's misery. This constrained them to come unto laws, wherein all men might see their duties beforehand, and know the penalties of transgressing them. * * *

FRANCISCO SUAREZ, S.J.

Political Authority and Community Consent †

(Suarez was a Spanish Jesuit theologian whose major treatise, *On Laws and God the Lawgiver*, published in 1612, attempted to apply Thomist thought to the problems of post-Reformation Europe, including new forms of relations among nations to which the *jus gentium* was applied in ways that anticipated later developments in international law. In the following selection he argues, as did other Jesuit writers of the Counter-Reformation, that the civil ruler derives his authority from the consent of the community, acting as "a single mystical body," (i.e. in a corporate capacity). On the significance of the revival of Thomism for the development of constitutionalism see Quentin Skinner, *The Foundations of Modern Political Thought*, vol. II [Cambridge: Cambridge University Press, 1978], ch. 5.)

† Francisco Suarez, *On Laws and God the Lawgiver* in F. Suarez, *Selections*, vol. II (Oxford: Claren- don Press, 1944). By permission of the publisher.

1.   The reason for doubt on this point is the fact that the power in question dwells either in individual men; or in all men, that is to say, in the whole body of mankind collectively regarded.

The first alternative cannot be upheld. For it is not true that every individual man is the superior of the rest; nor do certain persons, [simply] by the nature of things, possess the said power in a greater degree than other persons [on some ground apart from general superiority], since there is no reason for thus favoring some persons as compared with others. * * *

We must say that this power, viewed solely according to the nature of things, resides not in any individual man but rather in the whole body of mankind. This conclusion is commonly accepted and certainly true. It is to be deduced from the words of St. Thomas (S.T., I–II, qu. 90, a. 3, resp. 2 and qu. 97, a. 3, resp. 3) in so far as he holds that the prince has the power to make laws, and that this power was transferred to him by the community. * * *

The basic reason in support of the first part of the conclusion is evident, and was touched upon at the beginning of our discussion, namely, the fact that in the nature of things all men are born free; so that, consequently, no person has political jurisdiction over another person, even as no person has dominion over another; nor is there any reason why such power should, [simply] in the nature of things, be attributed to certain persons over certain other persons, rather than *vice versa*. One might make this assertion only: that at the beginning of creation Adam possessed, in the very nature of things, a primacy and consequently a sovereignty over all men, so that [the power in question] might have been derived from him, whether through the natural origin of primogeniture, or in accordance with the will of Adam himself. * * * However, by virtue of his creation only and his natural origin, one may infer simply that Adam possessed domestic—not political—power. For he had power over his wife, and later he possessed the *patria potestas*[1] over his children until they were emancipated. In the course of time, he may also have had servants and a complete household with full power over the same, the power called 'domestic.' But after families began to multiply, and the individual heads of individual families began to separate, those heads possessed the same power over their respective households. Political power, however, did not make its appearance until many families began to congregate into one perfect community. Accordingly, since this community had its beginning, not in the creation of Adam nor solely by his will, but rather by the will of all who were assembled therein, we are unable to make any well-founded statement to the effect that Adam, in the [very] nature of things, held a political primacy in the said community. For such an inference cannot be drawn from natural principles, since it is not the progenitor's due, by the sole force of natural law, that he shall also be king over his posterity.

1. paternal authority [*Editor*].

But, granted that this inference does not follow upon natural principles, neither have we sufficient foundation for the assertion that God has bestowed such power upon that [progenitor], through a special donation or act of providence, since we have had no revelation to this effect, nor does Holy Scripture so testify to us.

*   *   *

4.   From the foregoing, it is easy to deduce the second part of the assertion, namely, that the power in question resides, by the sole force of natural law, in the whole body of mankind [collectively regarded].

The proof is as follows: this power does exist in men, and it does not exist in each individual, nor in any specific individual, as has also been shown; therefore, it exists in mankind viewed collectively, for our foregoing division [into the two alternatives] sufficiently covers the case.

However, in order that our argument may be better understood, it must be noted that the multitude of mankind is regarded in two different ways.

First, it may be regarded simply as a kind of aggregation, without any order, or any physical or moral union. So viewed, [men] do not constitute a unified whole, whether physical or moral, so that they are not strictly speaking one political body, and therefore do not need one prince, or head. Consequently, if one regards them from this standpoint, one does not as yet conceive of the power in question as existing properly and formally; on the contrary, it us understood to dwell in them at most as a fundamental potentiality, so to speak.

The multitude of mankind should, then, be viewed from another standpoint, that is, with regard to the special volition, or common consent, by which they are gathered together into one political body through one bond of fellowship and for the purpose of aiding one another in the attainment of a single political end. Thus viewed, they form a single mystical body which, morally speaking, may be termed essentially a unity; and that body accordingly needs a single head. Therefore, in a community of this kind, viewed as such, there exists in the very nature of things the power of which we are speaking, so that men may not, when forming such a group, set up obstacles to the power; and consequently, if we conceive of men as desiring both alternatives—that is to say, as desirous of so congregating, but on the condition (as it were) that they shall not be subject to the said power—the situation would be self-contradictory, and such men would accordingly fail to achieve any [valid end]. For it is impossible to conceive of a unified political body without political government or disposition thereto; since, in the first place, this unity arises, in a large measure, from subjection to one and the same rule and to some common superior power; while furthermore, if there were no such government, this body could not be directed towards one [common] end and the general welfare. It is then, repugnant to natural reason to assume the existence of a group of human beings united in the form of a single political body, without postulating the existence of some common power which the individual members of the community are bound to obey; and therefore, if this power does not reside in any specific individual, it must necessarily exist in the community as a whole.

5.   To what has been said above, we should add the statement that the power in question does not reside in the multitude of mankind by the very nature of things in such wise that it is necessarily one sole power with respect to the entire species, or entire aggregate, of men existing throughout the whole world; inasmuch as it is not necessary to the preservation or welfare of nature, that all men should thus congregate in a single political community. On the contrary, that would hardly be possible, and much less would it be expedient. For Aristotle (*Politics*, Bk. VII, ch. iv) has rightly said that it is difficult to govern aright a city whose inhabitants are too numerous; accordingly, this difficulty would be still greater in the case of a kingdom excessively large, and therefore, it would be greater by far (we are referring to civil government) if the whole world were concerned.

Consequently, it seems to me probable that the power of which we speak never existed in this fashion in the whole assemblage of mankind, or that it so existed for an exceedingly brief period; and that, on the contrary, soon after the creation of the world, mankind began to be divided into various states in each one of which this power existed in a distinct form. * * *

It may be concluded from the foregoing that this power to make human laws of an individual and special nature, laws which we call civil, as if to indicate that they are ordained for one perfect community—it may be concluded, I say—that this power never existed in one and the same form throughout the whole world of men, being rather divided among various communities, according to the establishment and division of these communities themselves. Thus we also conclude that—before the coming of Christ, at least—this civil power did not reside in any one specific man with respect to the whole world. For at no time did all men agree to confer the power upon a particular ruler of the entire world, neither have we any knowledge of its bestowal upon some particular individual by God. * * *

LEO XIII

Human Liberty †

(Writing in 1888, shortly after the official adoption of Thomism as the basis for theological instruction in Catholic seminaries, Pope Leo XIII uses Aquinas's thought to criticize contemporary European liberalism, arguing that the existence of objective truth which can be known by reason and revelation means that there must be limits on freedom of speech, worship, and the press.)

8.　　Foremost in this office comes the *natural law*, which is written and engraved in the mind of every man; and this is nothing but our reason, commanding us to do right and forbidding sin. Nevertheless, all prescriptions of human reason can have force of law only inasmuch as they are the voice and the interpreters of some higher power on which our reason and liberty necessarily depend. For, since the force of law consists in the imposing of obligations and the granting of rights, authority is the one and only foundation of all law—the power, that is, of fixing duties and defining rights, as also of assigning the necessary sanctions of reward and chastisement to each and all of its commands. But all this, clearly, cannot be found in man, if, as his own supreme legislator, he is to be the rule of his own actions. It follows, therefore, that the law of nature is the same thing as the *eternal law*, implanted in rational creatures, and inclining them *to their right action and end*; and can be nothing else but the eternal reason of God, the Creator and Ruler of all the world. To this rule of action and restraint of evil God has vouchsafed to give special and most suitable aids for strengthening and ordering the human will. The first and most excellent of these is the power of his divine *grace*, whereby the mind can be enlightened and the will wholesomely invigorated and moved to the constant pursuit of moral good, so that the use of our inborn liberty becomes at once less difficult and less dangerous. Not that the divine assistance hinders in any way the free movement of our will; just the contrary, for grace works inwardly in man and in harmony with his natural inclinations, since it flows from the very Creator of his mind and will, by whom all things are moved in conformity with their nature. As the Angelic Doctor [St. Thomas] points out, it is because divine grace comes from the Author of nature that it is

† From Etienne Gilson, ed., *The Church Speaks to the Modern World* (New York: Doubleday, 1954).　Copyright © 1954 by Doubleday and Co., Inc. Reprinted by permission of the publisher.

so admirably adapted as to be the safeguard of all natures, and to maintain the character, efficiency, and operations of each.

* * *

15.   What *naturalists* or *rationalists* aim at in philosophy, that the supporters of *liberalism*, carrying out principles laid down by naturalism, are attempting in the domain of morality and politics. The fundamental doctrine of rationalism is the supremacy of the human reason, which, refusing due submission to the divine and eternal reason, proclaims its own independence, and constitutes itself the supreme principle and source and judge of truth. Hence, these followers of liberalism deny the existence of any divine authority to which obedience is due, and proclaim that every man is the law to himself; from which arises that ethical system which they style *independent* morality, and which, under the guise of liberty, exonerates man from any obedience to the commands of God, and substitutes a boundless license. The end of all this is not difficult to foresee, especially when society is in question. For, when once man is firmly persuaded that he is subject to no one, it follows that the efficient cause of the unity of civil society is not to be sought in any principle external to man, or superior to him, but simply in the free will of individuals; that the authority in the State comes from the people only; and that, just as every man's individual reason is his only rule of life, so the collective reason of the community should be the supreme guide in the management of all public affairs. Hence the doctrine of the supremacy of the greater number, and that all right and all duty reside in the majority. But, from what has been said, it is clear that all this is in contradiction to reason. To refuse any bond of union between man and civil society, on the one hand, and God the Creator and consequently the supreme Law-giver, on the other hand, is plainly repugnant to the nature, not only of man, but of all created things; for, of necessity, all effects must in some proper way be connected with their cause; and it belongs to the perfection of every nature to contain itself within that sphere and grade which the order of nature has assigned to it, namely, that the lower should be subject and obedient to the higher.

* * *

18.   There are others, somewhat more moderate though not more consistent, who affirm that the morality of individuals is to be guided by the divine law, but not the morality of the State, so that in public affairs the commands of God may be passed over, and may be entirely disregarded in the framing of laws. Hence follows the fatal theory of the need of separation between Church and State. But the absurdity of such a position is manifest. Nature herself proclaims the necessity of the State providing means and opportunities whereby the community may be enabled to live properly, that is to say, according to the laws of God. For, since God is the source of all goodness and justice, it is absolutely ridiculous that the State should pay no attention to these laws or render

them abortive by contrary enactments. Besides, those who are in authority owe it to the commonwealth not only to provide for its external well-being and the conveniences of life, but still more to consult the welfare of men's souls in the wisdom of their legislation. But, for the increase of such benefits, nothing more suitable can be conceived than the laws which have God for their author; and, therefore, they who in their government of the State take no account of these laws abuse political power by causing it to deviate from its proper end and from what nature itself prescribes. And, what is still more important, and what We have more than once pointed out, although the civil authority has not the same proximate end as the spiritual, nor proceeds on the same lines, nevertheless in the exercise of their separate powers they must occasionally meet. For their subjects are the same, and not infrequently they deal with the same objects, though in different ways. Whenever this occurs, since a state of conflict is absurd and manifestly repugnant to the most wise ordinance of God, there must necessarily exist some order or mode or procedure to remove the occasions of difference and contention, and to secure harmony in all things. This harmony has been not inaptly compared to that which exists between the body and the soul for the well-being of both one and the other, the separation of which brings irremediable harm to the body, since it extinguishes its very life.

*   *   *

23.   We must now consider briefly *liberty of speech*, and *liberty of the press*. It is hardly necessary to say that there can be no such right as this, if it be not used in moderation, and if it pass beyond the bounds and end of all true liberty. For right is a moral power which—as We have before said and must again and again repeat—it is absurd to suppose that nature has accorded indifferently to truth and falsehood, to justice and injustice. Men have a right freely and prudently to propagate throughout the state what things soever are true and honorable, so that as many as possible may possess them; but lying opinions, than which no mental plague is greater, and vices which corrupt the heart and moral life, should be diligently repressed by public authority, lest they insidiously work the ruin of the state. The excesses of an unbridled intellect, which unfailingly end in the oppression of the untutored multitude, are no less rightly controlled by the authority of the law than are the injuries inflicted by violence upon the weak. And this all the more surely, because by far the greater part of the community is either absolutely unable, or able only with great difficulty, to escape from illusions and deceitful subtleties, especially such as flatter the passions. If unbridled license of speech and of writing be granted to all, nothing will remain sacred and inviolate; even the highest and truest mandates of natures, justly held to be the common and noblest heritage of the human race, will not be spared. Thus, truth being gradually obscured by darkness, pernicious and manifold error, as too often happens, will easily prevail. Thus, too, license will gain what liberty loses; for liberty will ever be more free and

secure in proportion as license is kept in fuller restraint. In regard, however, to all matters of opinion which God leaves to man's free discussion, full liberty of thought and of speech is naturally within the right of every one; for such liberty never leads men to suppress the truth, but often to discover it and make it known.

24.   A like judgment must be passed upon what is called *liberty of teaching*. There can be no doubt that truth alone should imbue the minds of men, for in it are found the well-being, the end, and the perfection of every intelligent nature; and therefore nothing but truth should be taught both to the ignorant and to the educated, so as to bring knowledge to those who have it not, and to preserve it in those who possess it. For this reason it is plainly the duty of all who teach to banish error from the mind, and by sure safeguards to close the entry to all false convictions. From this it follows, as is evident, that the liberty of which We have been speaking is greatly opposed to reason, and tends absolutely to pervert men's minds, in as much as it claims for itself the right of teaching whatever it pleases—a liberty which the state cannot grant without failing in its duty. And the more so because the authority of teachers has great weight with their hearers, who can rarely decide for themselves as to the truth or falsehood of the instruction given to them. * * *

LEO XIII

Rerum Novarum—The Condition of Labor †

(Writing in 1891, Pope Leo uses natural law arguments to defend private property against Marxist criticisms, but is critical of the abuses of contemporary capitalism, asserting the natural right of the working man to receive a just wage and to establish trade unions and other associations in pursuit of a decent standard of living. One of the results of the encyclical was to encourage the development of Catholic trade unions in many European countries.)

2.   But all agree, and there can be no question whatever, that some remedy must be found, and quickly found, for the misery and wretchedness which press so heavily at this moment on the large majority of the very poor. The ancient workmen's Guilds were destroyed in the last century, and no other organization took their place. Public institutions and the laws have repudiated the ancient religion. Hence by degrees it has come to pass that Working Men have been given over, isolated and defenseless, to the callousness of employers and the greed of unrestrained competition. The evil has been increased by rapacious Usury, which, although more than once condemned by the Church, is

† From *Seven Great Encyclicals* (Glen Rock, N.J.: Paulist Press, 1963). Copyright © 1963 by the Missionary Society of St. Paul the Apostle in the State of New York. Reprinted by permission of Paulist Press.

nevertheless, under a different form but with the same guilt, still prac-
ticed by avaricious and grasping men. And to this must be added the
custom of working by contract, and the concentration of so many branches
of trade in the hands of a few individuals, so that a small number of very
rich men have been able to lay upon the masses of the poor a yoke little
better than slavery itself.

3.　　To remedy these evils the *Socialists*, working on the poor man's
envy of the rich, endeavor to destroy private property, and maintain that
individual possessions should become the common property of all, to be
administered by the state or by municipal bodies. They hold that, by
thus transferring property from private persons to the community, the
present evil state of things will be set to rights, because each citizen will
then have his equal share of whatever there is to enjoy. But their pro-
posals are so clearly futile for all practical purposes, that if they were
carried out the working man himself would be among the first to suffer.
Moreover they are emphatically unjust, because they would rob the lawful possessor, bring the state into a sphere that is not its own, and cause
complete confusion in the community.

Private Ownership

4.　　It is surely undeniable that, when a man engages in remunerative
labor, the very reason and motive of his work is to obtain property, and
to hold it as his own private possession. If one man hires out to another
his strength or his industry, he does this for the purpose of receiving in
return what is necessary for food and living; he thereby expressly proposes to acquire a full and real right, not only to the remuneration, but
also to the disposal of that remuneration as he pleases. Thus, if he lives
sparingly, saves money, and invests his savings, for greater security, in
land, the land in such a case is only his wages in another form; and,
consequently, a working man's little estate thus purchased should be as
completely at his own disposal as the wages he receives for his labor. But
it is precisely in this power of disposal that ownership consists, whether
the property be land or movable goods. The *Socialists*, therefore, in
endeavoring to transfer the possessions of individuals to the community,
strike at the interests of every wage earner, for they deprive him of the
liberty of disposing of his wages, and thus of all hope and possibility of
increasing his stock and of bettering his condition in life.

5.　　What is of still greater importance, however, is that the remedy
they propose is manifestly against justice. For every man has by nature
the right to possess property as his own. This is one of the *chief points of
distinction* between man and the animal creation. For the brute has no
power of self-direction, but is governed by two chief instincts, which
keep his powers alert, move him to use his strength, and determine him
to action without the power of choice. These instincts are self-preservation and the propagation of the species. Both can attain their purpose by
means of things which are close at hand; beyond their surroundings the

brute creation cannot go, for they are moved to action by sensibility alone, and by the things which sense perceives. But with man it is different indeed. He possesses, on the one hand, the full perfection of animal nature, and therefore he enjoys, at least as much as the rest of the animal race, the fruition of the things of the body. But animality, however perfect, is far from being the whole of humanity, and is indeed humanity's humble handmaid, made to serve and obey. It is the mind, or the reason, which is the chief thing in us who are human beings; it is this which makes a human being human, and distinguishes him essentially and completely from the brute. And on this account—viz., that man alone among animals possesses reason—it must be within his right to have things not merely for temporary and momentary use, as other living beings have them, but in stable and permanent possession; he must have not only things which perish in the using, but also those which, though used, remain for use in the future.

The Power of Reason

6.   This becomes still more clearly evident if we consider man's nature a little more deeply. For man, comprehending by the power of his reason, things innumerable, and joining the future with the present—being, moreover, the master of his own acts—governs himself by the foresight of his counsel, under the eternal law and the power of God, whose Providence governs all things. Wherefore it is in his power to exercise his choice not only on things which regard his present welfare, but also on those which will be for his advantage in time to come. Hence man can possess not only the fruits of the earth, but also the earth itself; for of the products of the earth he can make provision for the future. Man's needs do not die out, but recur; satisfied today, they demand new supplies tomorrow. Nature, therefore, owes to man a storehouse that shall never fail, the daily supply of his daily wants. And this he finds only in the inexhaustible fertility of the earth.

Nor must we, at this stage, have recourse to the state. Man is older than the state and he holds the right of providing for the life of his body prior to the formation of any state.

7.   And to say that God has given the earth to the use and enjoyment of the universal human race is not to deny that there can be private property. For God has granted the earth to mankind in general; not in the sense that all without distinction can deal with it as they please, but rather that no part of it has been assigned to any one in particular, and that the limits of private possession have been left to be fixed by man's own industry and the laws of individual peoples. Moreover, the earth, though divided among private owners, ceases not thereby to minister to the needs of all; for there is no one who does not live on what the land brings forth. Those who do not possess the soil, contribute their labor; so that it may be truly said that all human subsistence is derived either from labor on one's own land, or from some laborious industry which is

paid either in the produce of the land itself or in that which is exchanged for what the land brings forth.

The Law of Nature

Here, again, we have another proof that private ownership is according to nature's law. For that which is required for the preservation of life and for life's well-being, is produced in great abundance by the earth, but not until man has brought it into cultivation and lavished upon it his care and skill. Now, when man thus spends the industry of his mind and the strength of his body in procuring the fruits of nature, by that act he makes his own that portion of nature's field which he cultivates— that portion on which he leaves, as it were, the impress of his own personality; and it cannot but be just that he should possess that portion as his own, and should have a right to keep it without molestation.

*   *   *

Socialism Rejected

11.   The idea, then, that the civil government should, at its own discretion, penetrate and pervade the family and the household, is a great and pernicious mistake. True, if a family finds itself in great difficulty, utterly friendless, and without prospect for help, it is right that extreme necessity be met by public aid; for each family is a part of the commonwealth. In like manner, if within the walls of the household there occur grave disturbance of mutual rights, the public power must interfere to force each party to give the other what is due; for this is not to rob citizens of their rights, but justly and properly to safeguard and strengthen them. But the rulers of the state must go no further: nature bids them stop here. Paternal authority can neither be abolished by the state nor absorbed; for it has the same source as human life itself; "the child belongs to the father," and is, as it were, the continuation of the father's personality; and, to speak with strictness, the child takes its place in civil society not in its own right, but in its quality as a member of the family in which it is begotten. And it is for the very reason that "the child belongs to the father," that, as St. Thomas Aquinas says, "before it attains the use of free-will, it is in the power and care of its parents."[1] The Socialists, therefore, in setting aside the parent and introducing the providence of the state, act *against natural justice*, and threaten the very existence of family life.

*   *   *

Employer and Employee

15.   The great mistake that is made in the matter now under consideration, is to possess oneself of the idea that class is naturally hostile

1. *Summa Theologica*, II–II, qu. 10, a. 12.

to class; that rich and poor are intended by nature to live at war with one another. So irrational and so false is this view, that the exact contrary is the truth. Just as the symmetry of the human body is the result of the disposition of the members of the body, so in a state it is ordained by nature that these two classes should exist in harmony and agreement, and should, as it were, fit into one another, so as to maintain the equilibrium of the body politic. Each requires the other; capital cannot do without labor nor labor without capital. Mutual agreement results in pleasantness and good order; perpetual conflict necessarily produces confusion and outrage. Now, in preventing such strife as this, and in making it impossible, the efficacy of Christianity is marvelous and manifold.

* * *

19.   The chief and most excellent rule for the right use of money is one which the heathen philosophers indicated, but which the Church has traced out clearly, and has not only made known to men's minds, but has impressed upon their lives. It rests on the principle that it is one thing to have a right to the possession of money, and another to have a right to use money as one pleases. Private ownership, as we have seen, is the natural right of man; and to exercise that right, especially as members of society, is not only lawful but absolutely necessary. "It is lawful," says St. Thomas Aquinas, "for a man to hold private property; and it is also necessary for the carrying on of human life."[2] But if the question be asked, How must one's possessions be used? the Church replies without hesitation in the words of the same holy Doctor: "Man should not consider his outward possessions as his own, but as common to all, so as to share them without difficulty when others are in need. Whence the Apostle saith, Command the rich of this world . . . to give with ease, to communicate."[3] True, no one is commanded to distribute to others that which is required for his own necessities and those of his household; nor even to give away what is reasonably required to keep up becomingly his condition in life; "for no one ought to live unbecomingly."[4] But when necessity has been supplied, and one's position fairly considered, it is a duty to give to the indigent out of that which is over.

* * *

Just Wages

34.   We now approach a subject of very great importance and one on which, if extremes are to be avoided, right ideas are absolutely necessary. Wages, we are told, are fixed by free consent; and, therefore, the employer when he pays what was agreed upon, has done his part, and is

2. S.T., II–II, qu. 66, a. 2.   4. S.T., II–II, qu. 32, a. 6.
3. S.T., II–II, qu. 65, a. 2.

not called upon for anything further. The only way, it is said, in which injustice could happen, would be if the master refused to pay the whole of the wages, or the workman would not complete the work undertaken; when this happens the state should intervene, to see that each obtains his own, but not under any other circumstances.

This mode of reasoning is by no means convincing to a fair-minded man, for there are important considerations which it leaves out of view altogether. To labor is to exert one's self for the sake of procuring what is necessary for the purposes of life, and most of all for self-preservation. "In the sweat of thy brow thou shalt eat bread."[5] Therefore, a man's labor has two notes or characters. First of all, it is *personal*; for the exertion of individual power belongs to the individual who puts it forth, employing this power for that personal profit for which it was given. Secondly, a man's labor is *necessary*; for without the results of labor a man cannot live; and self-conservation is a law of nature, which it is wrong to disobey. Now, if we were to consider labor merely so far as it is *personal*, doubtless it would be within the workman's right to accept any rate of wages whatever; for in the same way as he is free to work or not, so he is free to accept a small remuneration or even none at all. But this is a mere abstract supposition; the labor of the working man is not only his personal attribute, but it is *necessary*; and this makes all the difference. The preservation of life is the bounden duty of each and all, and to fail therein is a crime. It follows that each one has a right to procure what is required in order to live; and the poor can procure it in no other way than by work and wages.

Let it be granted, then, that, as a rule, workman and employer should make free agreements, and in particular should freely agree as to wages; nevertheless, there is a dictate of nature more imperious and more ancient than any bargain between man and man, that the remuneration must be enough to support the wage-earner in reasonable and frugal comfort. If through necessity or fear of a worse evil, the workman accepts harder conditions because an employer or contractor will give him no better, he is the victim of force and injustice. In these and similar questions, however—such as, for example, the hours of labor in different trades, the sanitary precautions to be observed in factories and workshops, etc.— in order to supersede undue interference on the part of the State, especially as circumstances, times and localities differ so widely, it is advisable that recourse be had to societies or boards such as We shall mention presently, or to some other method of safeguarding the interests of wage-earners; the state to be asked for approval and protection.

Benefits of Property Ownership

35.   If a workman's wages be sufficient to enable him to maintain himself, his wife, and his children in reasonable comfort, he will not

5. Genesis, 3:1.

find it difficult, if he is a sensible man, to study economy; and he will not fail, by cutting down expenses, to put by a little property: nature and reason would urge him to do this. We have seen that this great labor question cannot be solved except by assuming as a principle that private ownership must be held sacred and inviolable. The law, therefore, should favor ownership, and its policy should be to induce as many people as possible to become owners.

Workmen's Associations

36.   In the first place—employers and workmen may themselves effect much in the matter of which we treat, by means of those institutions and organizations which afford opportune assistance to those in need, and which draw the two orders more closely together. Among these may be enumerated: societies for mutual help; various foundations established by private persons for providing for the workman, and for his widow or his orphans, in sudden calamity, in sickness, and in the event of death; and what are called "patronages," or institutions for the care of boys and girls, for young people, and also for those of more mature age.

The most important of all are Workmen's Associations; for these virtually include all the rest. History attests what excellent results were effected by the Artificer's Guilds of a former day. They were the means not only of many advantages to the workmen, but in no small degree of the advancement of art, as numerous monuments remain to prove. Such associations should be adapted to the requirements of the age in which we live—an age of greater instruction, of different customs, and of more numerous requirements in daily life. It is gratifying to know that there are actually in existence not a few societies of this nature, consisting either of workmen alone, or of workmen and employers together; but it were greatly to be desired that they should multiply and become more effective. We have spoken of them more than once; but it will be well to explain here how much they are needed, to show that they exist by their own right, and to enter into their organization and their work.

These lesser societies and the society which constitutes the state differ in many things, because their immediate purpose and end is different. Civil society exists for the common good, and, therefore, is concerned with the interests of all in general, and with the individual interests in their due place and proportion. Hence, it is called *public* society, because by its means, as St. Thomas Aquinas says, "Men communicate with one another in the setting up of commonwealth." But the societies which are formed in the bosom of the state are called *private*, and justly so, because their immediate purpose is the private advantage of the associates. "Now, a private society," says St. Thomas again, "is one which is formed for the purpose of carrying out private business; as when two or three enter into partnership with the view of trading in conjunction."

*　*　*

38.   Particular societies, then, although they exist within the state, and are each a part of the state, nevertheless cannot be prohibited by the state absolutely and as such. For to enter into a "society" of this kind is the natural right of man; and the state must protect natural rights, not destroy them; and if it forbids its citizens to form associations, it contradicts the very principle of its own existence; for both they and it exist in virtue of the same principle, viz., the natural propensity of man to live in society.

There are times, no doubt, when it is right that the law should interfere to prevent association; as when men join together for purposes which are evidently bad, unjust, or dangerous to the state. In such cases the public authority may justly forbid the formation of association, and may dissolve them when they already exist. But every precaution should be taken not to violate the rights of individuals, and not to make unreasonable regulations under the pretense of public benefit. For laws only bind when they are in accordance with right reason, and therefore with the eternal law of God.

PIUS XI

Quadragesimo Anno—Reconstructing the Social Order †

(As the Latin title states, the encyclical was published in 1931, the fortieth anniversary of *Rerum Novarum*. It repeated Leo's rejection of the Marxist theory of class conflict, and argued that functional groups in the various industries and professions should be given a certain autonomy by the government in regulating the problems of their respective groups. Applying papal teaching, Catholic-influenced political parties such as the Christian Democrats and leaders such as Charles De Gaulle have supported the creation of bodies such as the Economic and Social Council in post-war France, and the restructured Senate unsuccessfully proposed by De Gaulle in 1969. More authoritarian versions of the same idea have appeared in the corporatist structures of Spain under Franco and Portugal under Salazar.)

Authority of the State

49.   It follows from the twofold character of ownership, which We have termed individual and social, that men must take into account in this matter not only their own advantage but also the common good. To define in detail these duties, when the need occurs and when the natural law does not do so, is the function of the government. Provided that the

† From *Seven Great Encyclicals* (Glen Rock, N.J.: Paulist Press, 1963). Copyright © 1963 by the Missionary Society of St. Paul the Apostle in the State of New York. Reprinted by permission of Paulist Press.

natural and divine law be observed, the public authority, in view of the common good, may specify more accurately what is licit and what is illicit for property owners in the use of their possessions. Moreover, Leo XIII had wisely taught that "the delimiting of private possession has been left by God to man's industry and to the laws of individual peoples."[1]

History proves that the right of ownership, like other elements of social life, is not absolutely rigid, and this doctrine we ourselves have given utterance to on a previous occasion in the following terms: "How varied are the forms which the right of property has assumed! First, a primitive form in use among untutored and backward peoples, which still exists in certain localities even in our own day; then, that of the patriarchal age; later came various tyrannical types (we use the word in its classical meaning); finally, the feudal and monarchic systems down to the varieties of more recent times."[2]

It is plain, however, that the state may not discharge this duty in an arbitrary manner. Man's natural right of possessing and transmitting property by inheritance must be kept intact and cannot be taken away by the state from man. "For man is older than the state."[3] Moreover, "the domestic household is antecedent logically as well as in fact, to the civil community."[4]

The prudent pontiff had already declared it unlawful for the state to exhaust the means of individuals by crushing taxes and tributes. "The right to possess private property is derived from nature, not from man; and the state has by no means the right to abolish it, but only to control its use and bring it into harmony with the interests of the public good."[5]

However, when civil authority adjusts ownership to meet the needs of the public good it acts not as an enemy, but as the friend of private owners; for thus it effectively prevents the possession of private property, intended by Nature's Author in His Wisdom for the sustaining of human life, from creating intolerable burdens and so rushing to its own destruction. It does not therefore abolish, but protects private ownership, and far from weakening the right of private property, it gives it new strength.

Obligations Regarding Superfluous Income

50.   At the same time a man's superfluous income is not left entirely to his own discretion. We speak of that portion of his income which he does not need in order to live as becomes his station. On the contrary, the grave obligations of charity, beneficence and liberality which rest upon the wealthy are constantly insisted upon in telling words by Holy Scripture and the Fathers of the Church.

51.   However, the investment of superfluous income in developing favorable opportunities for employment, provided the labor employed

1. *Rerum Novarum*, p. 3.
2. Allocution to Italian Catholic Action, May 6, 1926.
3. *Rerum Novarum*, p. 4.
4. *Rerum Novarum*, p. 4.
5. *Rerum Novarum*, p. 23.

produces results which are really useful, is to be considered, according to the teaching of the Angelic Doctor[6] an act of real liberality particularly appropriate to the needs of our time.

Titles in Acquiring Ownership

52.   The original acquisition of property takes place by first occupation and by industry, or, as it is called, specification. This is the universal teaching of tradition and the doctrine of our predecessor, despite unreasonable assertions to the contrary, and no wrong is done to any man by the occupation of goods unclaimed and which belong to nobody. The only form of labor, however, which gives the workingman a title to its fruits is that which a man exercises as his own master, and by which some new form or new value is produced.

*   *   *

Harmony Between Ranks in Society

81.   Now this is a major and pressing duty of the state and of all good citizens: to get rid of conflict between "classes" with divergent interests, and to foster and promote harmony between the various "ranks" or groupings of society.

82.   It is necessary, then, that social policy be directed toward the re-establishment of functional groups. Society today continues in a strained and hence unstable and uncertain condition, for it relies upon "classes" with diverse interests and opposing each other, and hence prone to enmity and strife.

83.   Labor, indeed, as has been well said by our predecessor in his encyclical, is not a mere chattel, since the human dignity of the workingman must be recognized in it, and consequently it cannot be bought and sold like any piece of merchandise. Nonetheless the demand and supply of labor divides men on the labor market into two classes, as into two camps, and the bargaining between these parties transforms this labor market into an arena where the two armies are engaged in combat. To this grave disorder which is leading society to ruin a remedy must evidently be applied as speedily as possible. But there cannot be question of any perfect cure, except this opposition be done away with, and well ordered members of the social body come into being: functional "groups," namely, binding men together not according to the position they occupy in the labor market, but according to the diverse functions which they exercise in society. For as nature induces those who dwell in close proximity to unite into municipalities, so those who practice the same trade or profession, economic or otherwise, constitute as it were fellowships or bodies. These groupings, autonomous in character, are considered by

6. Summa Theologiae, II–II, qu. 134.

many to be, if not essential to civil society, at least a natural accompaniment thereof.

84.   Order, as the Angelic Doctor well defines, is unity arising from the apt arrangements of a plurality of objects; hence, true and genuine social order demands various members of society, joined together by a common bond.[7] Such a bond of union is provided, on the one hand by the common effort of employers and employees of one and the same "group" joining forces to produce goods or give service; on the other hand, by the common good which all "groups" should unite to promote, each in its own sphere, with friendly harmony. Now this union will become powerful and efficacious in proportion to the fidelity with which the individuals and the "groups" strive to discharge their professional duties and to excel in them.

85.   From this it is easy to conclude that in these associations the common interest of the whole "group" must predominate: and among these interests the most important is the directing of the activities of the group to the common good. Regarding cases in which interests of employers and employees call for special care and protection against opposing interests, separate deliberation will take place in their respective assemblies and separate votes will be taken as the matter may require.

*   *   *

Catholic and Socialist Are Opposing Terms

120.   If, like all errors, socialism contains a certain element of truth (and this the sovereign pontiffs have never denied), it is nevertheless founded upon a doctrine of human society peculiarly its own, which is opposed to true Christianity. "Religious socialism," "Christian socialism" are expressions implying a contradiction in terms. No one can be at the same time a sincere Catholic and a true socialist.

JOHN XXIII

Mater et Magistra—Christianity and Social Progress †

(By the time of the publication of *Mater et Magistra* in 1961, the expansion of the welfare state and the nationalization of some industries in Western Europe had made Pius XI's absolute condemnation of socialism passé, and Pope John's encyclical accepts a large increase in government intervention in the economy and society. However he reaffirms Pius XI's recommendation that lower associations be encouraged to carry out public functions, and

7. *Summa contra Gentiles,* III, 71; *Summa Theologiae,* I, qu. 63, a. 2.
† From *Seven Great Encyclicals* (Glen Rock, N.J.: Paulist Press, 1963). Copyright © 1963 by the

Missionary Society of St. Paul the Apostle in the State of New York. Reprinted by permission of the Paulist Press.

endorses worker participation in ownership and management as an appropriate contemporary application of man's natural need for freedom and responsibility.)

53.   This intervention of public authorities that encourages, stimulates, regulates, supplements, and complements, is based on the *principle of subsidiarity* as set forth by Pius XI in his Encyclical *Quadragesimo Anno:* "It is a fundamental principle of social philosophy, fixed and unchangeable, that one should not withdraw from individuals and commit to the community what they can accomplish by their own enterprise and industry. So, too, it is an injustice and at the same time a grave evil and a disturbance of right order, to transfer to the larger and higher collectivity functions which can be performed and provided for by lesser and subordinate bodies. Inasmuch as every social activity should, by its very nature, prove a help to members of the body social, it should never destroy or absorb them. . . ."

*   *   *

59.   One of the principal characteristics of our time is the multiplication of social relationships, that is, a daily more complex interdependence of citizens, introducing into their lives and activities many and varied forms of association, recognized for the most part in private and even in public law. This tendency seemingly stems from a number of factors operative in the present era, among which are technical and scientific progress, greater productive efficiency, and a higher standard of living among citizens.

*   *   *

82.   Justice is to be observed not merely in the distribution of wealth, but also in regard to the conditions under which men engage in productive activity. There is, in fact, an innate need of human nature requiring that men engaged in productive activity have an opportunity to assume responsibility and to perfect themselves by their efforts.

83.   Consequently, if the organization and structure of economic life be such that the human dignity of workers is compromised, or their sense of responsibility is weakened, or their freedom of action is removed, then we judge such an economic order to be unjust, even though it produces a vast amount of goods, whose distribution conforms to the norms of justice and equity.

*   *   *

Participation of Workers in Medium-size and Large Enterprises

91.   Furthermore, as did our predecessors, we regard as justifiable the desire of employees to be partners in enterprises with which they are associated and wherein they work. We do not think it possible, however,

to decide with certain and explicit norms the manner and degree of such partnerships, since this must be determined according to the state of the individual productive enterprises. For the situation is not everywhere the same, and, in fact, it can change suddenly within one and the same enterprise. Nevertheless, we do not doubt that employees should have an active part in the affairs of the enterprise wherein they work, whether these be private or public. But it is of the utmost importance that productive enterprises assume the character of a true human fellowship whose spirit suffuses the dealings, activities and standing of all its members.

92. This requires that mutual relations between employers and directors on the one hand and the employees of the enterprise on the other, be marked by mutual respect, esteem, and good will. It also demands that all collaborate sincerely and harmoniously in their joint undertaking, and that they perform their work not merely with the objective of deriving an income, but also of carrying out the role assigned them and of performing a service that results in benefit to others. This means that the workers may have a say in, and may make a contribution toward, the efficient running and development of the enterprise.

* * *

115. It is especially appropriate that today, more than heretofore, widespread private ownership should prevail, since, as noted above, the number of nations increases wherein the economic systems experience daily growth. Therefore, by prudent use of various devices already proven effective, it will not be difficult for the body politic to modify economic and social life so that the way is made easier for widespread private possession of such things as durable goods, homes, gardens, tools requisite for artisan enterprises and family-type farms, investments in enterprises of medium or large size. All of this has occurred satisfactorily in some nations with developed social and economic systems.

Public Property

116. Obviously, what we have said above does not preclude ownership of goods pertaining to production of wealth by states and public agencies, especially "if these carry with them power too great to be left in private hands, without injury to the community at large. * * *"[1]

117. It seems characteristic of our times to vest more and more ownership of goods in the state and in other public bodies. This is partially explained by the fact that the common good requires public authorities to exercise ever greater responsibilities. However, in this matter, the *principle of subsidiarity*, already mentioned above, is to be strictly observed. For it is lawful for states and public corporations to expand their domain of ownership only when manifest and genuine requirements of the common good so require, and then with safeguards, lest

---

1. Encyclical Letter *Quadragesimo Anno*; A.A.S., XXIII (1931), p. 214.

the possession of private citizens be diminished beyond measure, or, what is worse, destroyed.

118.   Finally, we cannot pass over in silence the fact that economic enterprises undertaken by the state or by public corporations should be entrusted to citizens outstanding in skill and integrity, who will carry out their responsibilities to the commonwealth with a deep sense of devotion. Moreover, the activity of these men should be subjected to careful and continuing supervision, lest, in the administration of the state itself, there develop an economic imperialism in the hands of a few. For such a development is in conflict with the highest good of the commonwealth.

Social Function of Property

119.   Our predecessors have always taught that in the right of private property there is rooted a social responsibility. Indeed, in the wisdom of God the Creator, the over-all supply of goods is assigned, first of all, that all men may lead a decent life. * * *

120.   Although in our day, the role assigned the state and public bodies has increased more and more, it by no means follows that the social function of private ownership is obsolescent, as some seem to think. For social responsibility in this matter derives its force from the very right of private property. Furthermore it is quite clear that there always will be a wide range of difficult situations, as well as hidden and grave needs, which the manifold providence of the state leaves untouched, and of which it can in no way take account. Wherefore, there is always wide scope for humane action by private citizens and for Christian charity. Finally, it is evident that in stimulating efforts relating to spiritual welfare, the work done by individual men or by private civic groups has more value than what is done by public authorities. * * *

JOHN XXIII

Pacem in Terris—Peace on Earth †

(Issued in 1963, as one of the last official statements of Pope John, *Pacem in Terris* in effect reversed Leo's criticisms of liberal theories of natural rights. Most important it committed the church to freedom of worship, both privately and publicly, quoting Leo XIII in support of a doctrine that he repeatedly condemned. Subsequent papal documents since the Second Vatican

† From *Seven Great Encyclicals* (Glen Rock, N.J.: Paulist Press, 1963). Copyright © 1963 by the Missionary Society of St. Paul the Apostle in the State of New York. Reprinted by permission of Paulist Press.

Council have largely abandoned the vocabulary of Thomistic natural law in discussing social and moral issues.)

Order in Human Beings

4. How strongly does the turmoil of individual men and peoples contrast with the perfect order of the universe! It is as if the relationships which bind them together could be controlled only by force.

5. But the Creator of the world has imprinted in man's heart an order which his conscience reveals to him and enjoins him to obey: *They show the work of the Law written in their hearts. Their conscience bears witness to them.*[1] And how could it be otherwise? For whatever God has made shows forth His infinite wisdom, and is manifested more clearly in the things which have greater perfection.

6. But fickleness of opinion often produces this error: many think that the relationships between men and states can be governed by the same laws as the forces and irrational elements of the universe, whereas the laws governing them are of quite a different kind and are to be sought elsewhere, namely, in the nature of man, where the Father of all things wrote them.

7. By these laws men are most admirably taught, first of all how they should conduct their mutual dealings; then how the relationships between the citizens and the public authorities of each state should be regulated; then how states should deal with one another; and finally how, on the one hand individual men and states, and on the other hand the community of all peoples, should act toward each other, the establishment of such a world community of peoples being urgently demanded today by the requirements of the universal common good.

Every Man is a Person with Rights and Duties

8. In the first place, it is necessary to speak of the order which should exist between men.

9. Any human society, if it is to be well-ordered and productive, must lay down as a foundation this principle: that every human being is a person; his nature is endowed with intelligence and free will. By virtue of this, he has rights and duties of his own, flowing directly and simultaneously from his very nature, which are therefore universal, inviolable and inalienable.

10. If we look upon the dignity of the human person in the light of divinely revealed truth, we cannot help but esteem it far more highly; for men are redeemed by the blood of Jesus Christ, they are by grace the children and friends of God and heirs of eternal glory.

---

1. Romans, 2:15.

Rights

The Right to Life and a Worthy Manner of Living

11.   Beginning our discussion of the rights of man, we see that every man has the right to life, to bodily integrity, and to the means which are necessary and suitable for the proper development of life; these are primarily food, clothing, shelter, rest, medical care, and finally the necessary social services. Therefore a human being also has the right to security in cases of sickness, inability to work, widowhood, old age, unemployment, or in any other case in which he is deprived of the means of subsistence through no fault of his own.

Rights pertaining to Moral and Cultural Values

12.   By the natural law every human being has the right to respect for his person, to his good reputation; the right to freedom in searching for truth and in expressing and communicating his opinions, and in pursuit of art, within the limits laid down by the moral order and the common good; and he has the right to be informed truthfully about public events.

13.   The natural law also gives man the right to share in the benefits of culture, and therefore the right to a basic education and to technical and professional training in keeping with the stage of educational development in the country to which he belongs. Every effort should be made to ensure that persons be enabled, on the basis of merit, to go on to higher studies, so that, as far as possible, they may occupy posts and take on responsibilities in human society in accordance with their natural gifts and the skills they have acquired.

The Right to Worship God according to an Upright Conscience

14.   Every human being has the right to honor God according to the dictates of an upright conscience, and therefore the right to worship God privately and publicly.[2] For, as Lactantius so clearly taught: *We were created for the purpose of showing to the God who bore us the submission we owe Him, of recognizing Him alone, and of serving Him. We are obliged and bound by this duty to God; from this religion itself receives its name.*[3] And on this point Our Predecessor of immortal memory, Leo XIII, declared: *This genuine, this honorable freedom of the sons of God, which most nobly protects the dignity of the human person, is greater than any violence or injustice; it has always been sought by the Church, and always most dear to Her. This was the freedom which the Apostles claimed with intrepid constancy, which the Apologists defended with their*

---

2. In 1965 the Second Vatican Council issued a Declaration on Religious Freedom, formally endorsing the right to the public and private exer-

cise of religious freedom [*Editor*].
3. *Divinae Institutiones*, Bk. IV, c. 28, 2; PL. 6, 535.

writings, and which the Martyrs in such numbers consecrated with their blood.[4]

The Right to Choose Freely One's State of Life

15.   Human beings have the right to choose freely the state of life which they prefer, and therefore the right to establish a family, with equal rights and duties for man and woman, and also the right to follow a vocation to the priesthood or the religious life.

16.   The family, grounded on marriage freely contracted, monogamous and indissoluble, should be regarded as the first and natural cell of human society. To it should be given every consideration of an economic, social, cultural and moral nature which will strengthen its stability and facilitate the fulfillment of its specific mission.

17.   Parents, however, have the prior right in the support and education of their children.

Rights pertaining to Economic Life

18.   We turn now to the sphere of economic affairs. Human beings have the natural right to free initiative in the economic field, and the right to work.

19.   Indissolubly linked with those rights is the right to working conditions in which physical health is not endangered, morals are safeguarded, and young people's normal development is not impaired. Women have the right to working conditions in accordance with their requirements and their duties as wives and mothers.

20.   From the dignity of the human person, there also arises the right to carry on economic activities according to the degree of responsibility of which one is capable. Furthermore—and this must be specially emphasized—there is the right to a proper wage, determined according to criterions of justice, and sufficient, therefore, in proportion to the available resources, to provide for the worker and his family a manner of living in keeping with the dignity of the human person. In this regard, our predecessor Pius XII said: *To the personal duty to work imposed by nature, there corresponds and follows the natural right of each individual to make of his work the means to provide for his own life and the lives of his children; so profoundly is the empire of nature ordained for the preservation of man.*[5]

21.   The right to private property, even of productive goods, also derives from the nature of man. This right, as we have elsewhere declared, *is an effective aid in safeguarding the dignity of the human person and the free exercise of responsibility in all fields of endeavor. Finally, it*

4. Encyclical Letter *Libertas praestantissimum, Acta Leonis XIII,* VIII (1888), pp. 237–38.
5. Cf. Pius XII's *Radio Broadcast* on the Feast of Pentecost, June 1, 1941, A.A.S., XXXIII (1941), p. 201.

strengthens the stability and tranquillity of family life, thus contributing to the peace and prosperity of the commonwealth.[6]

22.　　　However, it is opportune to point out that there is a social duty essentially inherent in the right of private property.[7]

NEO-THOMISM AND CHRISTIAN DEMOCRACY IN EUROPE AND LATIN AMERICA

JACQUES MARITAIN

The Rights of Man; Church and State †

(Jacques Maritain, the French neo-Thomist philosopher, was one of the most important influences in promoting the acceptance of liberal democracy and religious pluralism by European Catholics and the papacy who had been alienated by the anti-clericalism of continental liberalism. He did this by reinterpreting the traditional Thomist teachings to justify support for human rights and freedom of worship, so that the modern secular democratic state was seen as more faithful to the principles of Christianity and man's "natural inclinations" than the hierarchical corporatism of the Middle Ages which continued to influence the thinking of Catholic conservatives.)

There are imperceptible transitions (at least from the point of view of historical experience) between Natural Law, the Law of Nations, and Positive Law. There is a dynamism which impels the unwritten law to flower forth in human law, and to render the latter ever more perfect and just in the very field of its contingent determinations. It is in accordance with this dynamism that the rights of the human person take political and social form in the community.

Man's right to existence, to personal freedom, and to the pursuit of the perfection of moral life, belongs, strictly speaking, to natural law.

The right to the private ownership of material goods pertains to natural law, insofar as mankind is naturally entitled to possess for its own common use the material goods of nature; it pertains to the Law of Nations, or *jus gentium*, in so far as reason necessarily concludes that for the sake of the common good those material goods must be privately owned, as a result of the conditions naturally required for their management and for human work (I mean human work performed in a genuinely human manner, ensuring the freedom of the human person in the

6. Encyclical Letter *Mater et Magistra*, A.A.S., LIII (1961), p. 428.
7. *Ibid.*, p. 430.
† Jacques Maritain, *Man and the State* (Chicago:

University of Chicago Press, 1950). Copyright © 1950 by the University of Chicago. Reprinted by permission of the publisher.

face of the community). And the particular modalities of the right to private ownership, which vary according to the form of a society and the state of the development of its economy, are determined by positive law.

The freedom of nations to live unburdened by the yoke of want or distress ("freedom from want") and the freedom for them to live unburdened by the yoke of fear or terror ("freedom from fear"), as President Roosevelt defined them in his Four Points, correspond to requirements of the Law of Nations which are to be fulfilled by positive law and by a possible economic and political organization of the civilized world. The right of suffrage granted to each one of us for the election of the officials of the State arises from positive law, determining the way in which the natural right of the people to self-government has to apply in a democratic society.

As I just put it, the historical climate of modern civilization, in contradistinction to medieval civilization, is characterized by the fact that it is a "lay" or "secular," not a "sacral" civilization. On the one hand the dominant dynamic idea is not the idea of strength or fortitude at the service of justice, but rather that of the conquest of freedom and the realization of human dignity. On the other hand the root requirement for a sound mutual cooperation between the Church and the body politic is not the unity of a religio-political body, as the *respublica Christiana* of the Middle Ages was, but the very unity of the human person, simultaneously a member of the body politic and of the Church, if he freely adheres to her. The unity of religion is not a prerequisite for political unity, and men subscribing to diverse religious or non-religious creeds have to share in and work for the same political or temporal common good. Whereas "medieval man," as Father Courtney Murray puts it, [1] entered the State (what State there was) to become a 'citizen,' through the Church and his membership in the Church, modern man is a citizen with full civic rights whether he is a member of the Church or not."

Hence many consequences derive. First, the political power is not the secular arm [2] of the spiritual power, the body politic is autonomous and independent within its own sphere. Second, the equality of all members of the body politic has been recognized as a basic tenet. Third, the importance of the inner forces at work in the human person, in contradistinction to the external forces of coercion; the freedom of individual conscience with regard to the state; the axiom—always taught by the Catholic Church, but disregarded as a rule by the princes and kings of old—that faith cannot be imposed by constraint [3]—all these assertions

1. John Courtney Murray "Governmental Repression of Heresy" *Proceedings of the Catholic Theological Society*, 1949, p. 57.
2. On the question of the "secular arm" see *ibid.*, pp. 62ff.; Journet, *L'Église du Verbe Incarné*, pp. 249, 317–26. Be it noted in passing that the stock phrase "recourse to the secular arm," that is, to civil law, to enforce, in certain circumstances dealing with the public order and the temporal domain, a canonic regulation concerning the members of the Church, means something quite different from the concept of the political power as being the secular arm or instrument of the Church. In a pluralistic society it is but normal that the particular regulations of an autonomous body may be sanctioned by civil law, from the civil society's own viewpoint, when the interests of the common good are concerned.
3. See Journet, *L'Église du Verbe Incarné*, pp. 261–64.

have become, more explicitly than before, crucial assets to civilization, and are to be especially emphasized if we are to escape the worst dangers of perversion of the social body and of state totalitarianism. Fourth, a reasoned-out awareness has developed, at least in those of the civilized world where love for freedom is still treasured—and is growing all the keener as freedom is more threatened—with regard to the fact that nothing more imperils both the common good of the earthly city and the supra-temporal interests of truth in human minds than a weakening and breaking down of the internal springs of conscience. Common consciousness has also become aware of the fact that freedom of inquiry, even at the risk of error, is the normal condition for men to get access to truth, so that freedom to search for God in their own way, for those who have been brought up in ignorance or semi-ignorance of Him, is the normal condition in which to listen to the message of the Gospel and the teachings of the Church, when grace will illumine their hearts.

Such a body politic Christianly inspired, such a political society really and vitally Christian, by virtue of the very spirit that would animate it and give shape to its structure—let us say, a political society evangelically Christian—would have its own social and political morality, its own conception of justice and civic friendship, temporal common good and common task, human progress and civilization, vitally rooted in Christian awareness. Considering now a new and particularly difficult issue, which deals with the temporal society itself in its proper order and life, and with its legislation, we may ask ourselves what kind of notions this legislation would call into play when it comes to matters of conscience or questions directly concerned with personal creeds and standards as well as with civil law. At this point we have to maintain that the legislation of the Christian society in question could and should never *endorse* or *approve* any way of conduct contrary to Natural Law. But we have also to realize that this legislation could and should *permit* or *give allowance to* certain ways of conduct which depart in some measure from Natural Law, if the prohibition by civil law of these ways of conduct were to impair the common good, either because such prohibition would be at variance with the ethical code of communities of citizens whose loyalty to the nation and faithfulness to their own moral creed, however imperfect it may be, essentially matter to the common good, or even because it would result in a worse conduct, disturbing or disintegrating the social body, for a great many people whose moral strength is not on a level with the enforcement of this prohibition.[4]

---

4. Thomas Aquinas states the principles of the matter in a basically significant article: "Law," he says, "is established as a certain rule and measure of human acts. Now every measure must be homogeneous with the thing measured. . . . Hence it is necessary that even laws be imposed on men according to the condition of them: for, as Isidore puts it (*Etym.*, Bk. V, c. 21) law must be possible, *both with regard to nature and to fatherland's custom.*

"Now the power or ability to act proceeds from the inner disposition or *habitus* of the subject: for the same thing is not possible to the one who does not possess virtue, and to the virtuous man; just as to the child and to the perfect man (the grownup). As a result, we do not have the same law laid down for children and for adults; and many things are permitted to children which for adults are punished by the law or held to be shameful. Similarly, many things must be permitted to men who are

I would say, therefore, that in the matters we are considering, civil legislation should adapt itself to the variety of moral creeds of the diverse spiritual lineages which essentially bear on the common good of the social body—not by endorsing them or approving of them, but rather by giving allowance to them. In other words, civil law would only lay down the regulations concerned with the allowance of the actions sanctioned by those various moral codes, or grant such actions the juridical effects requested by their nature; and consequently the State would not take upon itself the responsibility for them, or make them valid by its own pronouncement, but only register (when the matter is of a nature to require a decision of civil authorities) the validity acknowledged to them by the moral codes in question.

Thus, in the sense which I just defined, a sound application of the pluralist principle and of the principle of the lesser evil would require from the State a juridical recognition of the moral codes peculiar to those minorities comprised in the body politic whose rules of morality, though defective in some regard with respect to perfect Christian morality, would prove to be a real asset in the heritage of the nation and its common trend toward good human life. Such recognition would not be grounded on a right, I know not what, of which any moral way of life whatsoever would be possessed with regard to civil law, but on the requirements of the political common good, which in a democratic society demands on the one hand a particular respect for the inner forces and conscience of the human subject, and, on the other hand, a particular care not to impose by force of law rules of morality too heavy for the moral capacity of large groups of the population. It would be up to the political wisdom of the lawmaker, furthermore, to determine what communities of citizens could enjoy the pluralistic legal status which I have described.

As a result, I would see, in some conceivable future society, the laws of the body politic recognizing in such matters—not by virtue of a right belonging to any moral way of life whatever, but by virtue of the free decisions of political wisdom—the moral codes to which the consciences of the main spiritual stocks or lineages that make up the national community and its complex moral heritage are attached; of course on the condition that the body politic, while granting such freedoms to its own parts, were heedful of the moral interests of the whole, and made as restricted as possible, in actual existence, the derogations to the highest requirements of Natural Law which the legislators would allow as a lesser evil for the sake of the common good. The final objective of law is to make men morally good. Civil law would adapt itself, with a view to the

---

not perfected by virtue, which could not be tolerated in virtuous men.

"Now human law is laid down for the multitude, the major part of which is composed of men not perfected by virtue. Consequently, all and every vice, from which virtuous men abstain, is not prohibited by human law, but only the gravest vicious actions, from which it is possible for the major part of the multitude to abstain and mainly those—like homicide, theft, etc.—which are harmful to others, and without the prohibition of which human society could not be preserved" (*Summa Theologicae*, I–II, qu. 96, a. 2).

maximum good of which the multitude is capable, to various ways of life sanctioned by various moral creeds, but it should resist changes which were requested through sheer relaxation of morality and decaying mores. And it should always maintain a general orientation toward virtuous life, and make the common behavior *tend*, at each level, to the full accomplishment of moral law.

* * *

This Christian political society would realize that there is only one temporal common good, that of the body politic, as there is only one supernatural common good, that of the Kingdom of God, which is suprapolitical. Once the political society had been fully differentiated in its secular type, the fact of inserting into the body politic a particular or partial common good, the temporal common good of the faithful of one religion (even though it were the true religion), and of claiming for them, accordingly, a privileged juridical position in the body politic, would be inserting into the latter a divisive principle and, to that extent, interfering with the temporal common good.

JAIME CASTILLO

Natural Law and Communitarianism†

(Jaime Castillo is the principal theoretician of the Chilean Christian Democratic Party. The Christian Democratic theory of communitarianism is an attempt to develop a "third position" alternative to laissez-faire capitalism and Marxist socialism, along the lines of the papal criticisms of both systems.)

Property and Natural Law

In response to those who claim that private property is a matter of natural law, we hold that that system is not required by natural law but only conforms to it when at a given time it is the best method to regulate and permit the most efficient use of all the goods of the earth. * * *

What is a matter of natural law is what we call the right of common use, that the enjoyment of goods is a demand of human nature because man should satisfy his needs with the goods which have been placed at his disposal.

Nevertheless, there are those who, without denying that the right of common use is essential and permanent and that systems of appropriation are mutable, would deny the existence of natural law itself. In my

† Translated by the editor from *Propriedad y Sociedad Communitaria* (Instituto de Estudios Politicos, Santiago, Chile, 1966), in Paul E. Sigmund, ed., *The Ideologies of the Developing Nations* (revised edition). Copyright © 1967 by Frederick A. Praeger, reprinted by permission of Holt, Rinehart and Winston.

opinion to deny the theory of natural law is as absurd as claiming to deny the theory of being. It is an impossible claim. And if we deny the existence of the natural law we will of necessity develop the same solution under a different name. Ultimately it seems to me that discussion on this matter is a dispute over terms rather than over concepts.

What is meant by natural law has to be conceived, it seems to me, as that minimum of rational terminology which is necessary to explain an obvious fact—that there exists in human nature a certain need to use and dispose of things in a way which accords with the ethical and social character of every human act. The formula, natural law, therefore expresses something very minimal and perhaps excessively vague—that man proceeds in accordance with the integrity of his being. To concretize a theoretical system to reflect this exigency is inevitable from the point of view of logic, but it runs the risk of seeming to set down in precise terms what is a complex of visions. These then become for some a substitute for reality, abstractions in the bad sense of the word. The polemics of those who in their turn develop another set of abstractions or ideological fetishes exaggerate the problem and prevent simply and authentic reflection. * * *

The Communitarian Society

First, in a communitarian society there will be the full realization of community in the sense which we explained above. There will be a plenitude of human life in common. It will be a fraternal society [in which] the highest human values will prevail. This is the same as saying that the full human life of each man will be realized in its plenitude.

Second, the communitarian society will give preference to social values over those of the individual. On this point I must also refer to something which we have debated elsewhere—the opposition of communitarianism and socialism. I have said it already—I think that both terms point to the same thing. At least their relation is very intimate. Nevertheless, I personally think that the term *communitarianism* is an expression which is more vivid, more vigorous, and more expressive of our thinking. In addition, the term *socialism* implies certain doctrinal principles which are questionable as far as we are concerned and which are also linked to the experiences of totalitarian collectivism. Therefore, I prefer to use the term *communitarianism*. In any case the idea is the same, but to use the term *communitarian socialism* is to involve oneself in an unnecessary redundancy and at the same time to create certain doubts on our part.[1]

The communitarian society will possess a structure which is in

1. This is a reference to the increasing use during the 1960s of the term "communitarian socialism" by the left wing of the Chilean Christian Democratic Party in order to indicate their opposition to the continued existence of "capitalist" property relationships in Chile. The left Christian Democrats split from the party in 1969 and 1971 and supported the Marxist-dominated coalition behind Salvador Allende.

accordance with what has been said above. Its decisive characteristic will be a communitarian type of property holding (by communities of workers, cooperatives, and other social forms), but it will allow for personal property when it has a social function as well as for the retention of some property by the national community. The dichotomy between capital and labor will be superseded by communitarian relationships, i.e., by uniting labor and capital in the hands of the workers themselves. * * *

JULIO SILVA SOLAR

St. Thomas and Property—A View From the Christian Left in Chile†

(The following selection is a rarity—a radical interpretation of Aquinas. It argues that since St. Thomas described property and slavery as additions to the natural law for human convenience, and slavery has been rejected, it is time to recognize that private property in the ownership of capital goods is also no longer defensible because of the contradictions which it has produced between the increasing concentration of ownership in the hands of the few and the collective character of modern economic production. Silva Solar's thinking is symptomatic of the radicalization of a segment of Latin American Catholicism in the 1960s. Its dialectical argument also presages the later movement of many leftist Catholics in Latin America toward Marxist modes of analyses.)

Thomas Aquinas, one of the most important church theologians, defends property in a certain way as an institution arguing that it is something that is permissible. Before Saint Thomas there had been doubts as to whether it was allowed by natural law or whether only a community of goods was admitted. However if we analyze things we see that there is not a real difference between the two approaches, at least as to their basic view.

For Saint Thomas the community of goods is part of the natural law, as to proprietorship over inferior beings and goods for use for man's benefit. However, private property, that is "the distinction of possessions, is not part of natural law but rather is a good derived from human agreement which is a matter of positive law." Now positive law is subordinated to natural law. "Human law," says St. Thomas, "may not violate natural law or divine law."[1] The natural law in this area, determines that goods are ordered to the satisfaction of men—of all men, so that appropriation or division of goods, that is, private property which proceeds from human or positive law remains subject to the earlier precept.

† Selected and translated by the editor from Juan Silva Solar and Jacques Chanchol, *El Desarrollo de la Nueva Sociedad en America Latina* (Santiago: Editorial Universitaria, 1969). Reprinted by permission of the publisher.
1. S.T., II–II, qu. 66, a. 2; II–II, qu. 66, a. 7.

The foundation of property—what makes it licit—is that in practice it turns out to be an instrument or institution that is effective in making goods fulfill their natural end of serving all men. The common good and nothing else is the supreme norm that justifies (or condemns) it. St. Thomas believes that it is useful for the common good and we will see what his reasons are for this. In any case only to the extent that it is useful for the common good does there cease to be a contradiction between the natural law (goods at the service of the community) and the positive law (private property). It is in this sense, St. Thomas concludes, that property is not contrary to natural law.

In another text St. Thomas says that "Property and slavery were not imposed by nature but by the reason of man for usefulness to human life."[2] Its justification depends, then, on its usefulness. It is noteworthy that in this text St. Thomas links property with slavery as institutions of the positive law that are useful to men. It would not be strange then that if slavery has ceased to be useful to human life, the same thing should occur with property. What is certain is that both receive the same treatment from St. Thomas. The truth is that like slavery, property is a positive institution that is a product of history, neither sacred, nor eternal, nor natural. Like it too, it is a product of social development and will disappear as a result of that same development just as slavery has disappeared. The image of property as an absolute institution inseparable from man is nothing but a myth created under the influence of the large propertyholders who have dominated society.

Hardly a hundred years ago slavery was abolished in the United States and serfdom in Russia. This indicates both the persistence of this type of institution that today appears to us so repugnant, and the power and speed of the movement of social emancipation in our time. Something that had appeared immutable is now clearly seen despite its long duration as transitory. What appeared sacred is generally rejected. The same thing will occur with private property and its modern slave, the wage laborer. Let no one doubt this! * * * The reasons given by St. Thomas for thinking that property was convenient are the classic ones—we give more attention to taking care of our own things than those that are communally owned; good administration and order in human affairs requires a division of labor; there is more peace when each one is content with his own goods. We see that possession, administration, and labor are closely united in the conception of St. Thomas.

These links have been lost completely in the modern economy and therefore the reasons given by St. Thomas in favor of property do not appear to us to have validity, at least as far as the goods are concerned that constitute capitalist property. What do we see today? The overwhelming majority is dispossessed of existing goods. Their own things to which they could devote care and administration have no meaning for them, nor do particular goods that would produce content and social

2. *S.T.*, I–II, qu. 94, a. 5.

peace. Far from that, the masses are discontent and their discontent has produced the great social revolutions of our century. A certain kind of private property, capitalist property, the ownership of the capital goods that require collective labor, has separated man from the means of production, from the product of his labor, and from the land on which he works, in general from the goods of civilization and culture—all this under the domination of the capitalist.

*   *   *

The land and productive goods that by their very nature can only be exploited collectively, to which the associated labor of many men is applied in the modern economy will become the property of the whole community where no one lives without working, or of communities of workers. In the communitarian regime capital in all its forms will pass into the hands of organized labor. That is its essence.

Theoretically, then, we can say that it will be a form of socialism—a communitarian socialism different from state socialism, in which the principle of the self-management of the workers both in the factory and in the economy as a whole will be fundamental. The state will exercise a subsidiary function supporting self-management. At the outset its role will no doubt be larger and more varied, doing what is necessary—directing, organizing, planning etc., and, of course, operating in the particular area of the state sector of the economy.

PAUL E. SIGMUND

Thomistic Natural Law and Social Theory †

(After analyzing the components of Aquinas's system of natural law and observing that his syncretism led him to a "moderate" political position, the editor surveys the influence of Thomism on modern Catholic political and social thought, concluding that it has become less important in recent years.)

The most influential previous Christian work with implications for political thought, Augustine's *City of God*, was more an expression of an attitude than a systematic attempt to develop an analysis of politics and society. The concept of the two cities implies a relativity of the political order and a pessimism about the possibility of achieving the peace that is the "tranquillity of order" (*City of God*, 19,13) in this world, yet in the same work the Christian emperor is urged to act as a minister of God in spreading the true religion (5,24). Augustinianism has been viewed as related to an attitude of rejection of politics, to a "realistic" pessimism about the inevitability of power politics, and to attempts to

† Reprinted from *Calgary Aquinas Studies*, edited by Anthony Parel, pp. 67–76, by permission of the publisher; copyright © 1978 by Pontifical Institute of Medieval Studies, Toronto.

create a papal world-state.[1] These interpretations exaggerate and perhaps distort the political implications of Augustine's writings, but the fact that both the theocrat and the Machiavellian can be related to Augustine's political thought demonstrates how ambiguous is the political application of his writings.

It is only with Saint Thomas that a systematic attempt is made to relate the Christian message to classical social, political, and legal thought in a philosophical way. As is well known, the occasion for that attempt was a second confrontation of Christianity with classical culture—in this case, the sudden reintroduction into Western Europe of the corpus of Aristotle's writings. However, as an examination of Aquinas's natural law theory demonstrates, the Thomistic synthesis involved much more than a combination of Aristotelianism and Christianity. It also drew on Roman legal thought and the Stoic natural law conception embodied therein; it placed law, politics, and society in a Neoplatonic hierarchical framework; and it reflected a knowledge of medieval political institutions and controversies, as well.

The combination of these often conflicting theories into a single system was motivated by a fundamental belief in the ultimate possibility of the resolution of conflicting theories, itself the result of Christian faith in a rational God who has created an ordered and purposive universe the nature of which can be understood, if only in a limited fashion, by man's reason. The Thomistic theory of natural law is a good example of Aquinas's synthetic approach. Thus the hierarchical relationship of eternal, natural, and human law, as well as Aquinas's belief in a natural hierarchy in society, in the church, and among the angels show evidence of Neoplatonic influences as mediated by Dionysius and the *Liber de Causis*.[2] In order to harmonize the conflicting formulations of the theory contained in Title 1 of the *Digest* of Roman law in which Ulpian had asserted that natural law was "that which nature has taught all animals" while Gaius had described it as a law laid down by natural reason for all mankind, Aquinas distinguishes the various levels of natural law corresponding to that which man shares with all substances, other animals, and man alone.[3] The carefully nuanced discussion of whether the king is free from the law (*legibus solutus*) again reflects controversy surrounding a Roman law text.[4] The subtle analysis of the relation of divine and natural law indicates Aquinas's awareness of the confusion in the treatment of that relationship in the *Decretum* of Gratian.[5] The numerous references to the role of the community in the making of law, and possibly calling the ruler to account reflect a knowledge of contemporary political practice and the common medieval belief in the (ultimate) derivation of law and government from the people as a whole.

1. Cf. H. X. Arquillière, *L'augustinisme politique*, 2nd ed. (Paris: J. Vrin, 1955); John Neville Figgis, *The Political Aspects of S. Augustine's "City of God"* (London: Longmans, Green, 1921); Reinhold Niebuhr, *Christian Realism and Political*

Problems (New York: Scribner, 1953), ch. 9.
2. S.T., I, qu. 108, a. 4; S.C.G., IV, 76.
3. S.T., I–II, qu. 94.
4. S.T., I–II, qu. 96, a. 5.
5. S.T., I–II, qu. 91, a. 4.

The most interesting part of the Thomistic synthesis, however, is the use which he makes of the Aristotelian belief in immanent purposes in nature as the core of his theory of natural law. Alexander Passerin D'Entrèves is right in relating this belief to Aquinas's explicitly stated assumption of Divine Providence,[6] but it is important to emphasize that Providence is described as "a *rational* governance of created things" and that rational creatures are said to share in the divine reason by purposive action in accordance with natural inclinations to "appropriate" actions and goals.[7] How does man determine what are the natural inclinations to fitting actions and goals? He considers the goals (we might say, needs) he has in common with all substances such as self-preservation; with all animals—sex and child-rearing; and as a rational man—to know God and live in society—and on the assumption of a purposive nature created by a rational God proceeds to derive certain norms or laws.[8] The process of derivation is not a strictly logical or deductive one but involves the use of *synderesis* or direct moral intuition to arrive at basic principles and the exercise of the practical reason to apply those principles to varying and contingent circumstances.[9] In this description of the natural law Aquinas takes a number of Aristotelian concepts and combines them in a way which is different from the way that Aristotle himself used them. Whether or not he was faithful to the spirit of Aristotle may be argued, but a comparison of Aquinas's discussion of natural law with the relevant passages in Aristotle's *Nicomachean Ethics* and *Politics* reveals that Aquinas has combined quite disparate elements in Aristotle—the *phronesis* of the *Ethics*, the description of final causality in the *Physics*, its ethico-political application in the discussions of government, slavery, property, and usury in Book I of the *Politics*, the ambiguous treatment of natural justice in Book 5 of the *Ethics*, and the description of law as reason in Book 3 of the *Politics*—into a new synthesis that makes the determination of natural ends a central consideration in the development of Aquinas's theory of natural law.

This has been the traditional understanding of Aquinas's natural law in theory and I believe that it is the correct one. Those who see in his theory either an attempt to build a deductive theory on the model of a logical system (Morton White) or who maintain that Thomistic natural law involves intuitive perceptions of what is good which, once they are expressed rationally, become *jus gentium* rather than natural law (Jacques Maritain), or that natural law is really "the traditional pragmatism . . . not a set of generalizations but a set of individual intelligent actions" (Michael Novak) either misunderstand what Aquinas plainly says or simply wish to add the weight of St. Thomas's authority to their own ethical theories.[1] Aquinas states explicitly that adultery, homosexuality, usury,

6. *S.T.*, I–II, qu. 91, a. 1.
7. *S.T.*, I–II, qu. 91, a. 7.
8. *S.T.*, I–II, qu. 94, a. 2.
9. *S.T.*, I, qu. 79, a. 12; I–II, qu. 94.
1. Morton White, *Religion, Politics and the Higher*

Learning (Cambridge, Mass.: Harvard University Press, 1959), 124ff.; Jacques Maritain, *Man and the State* (Chicago: University of Chicago Press, 1951), ch. 4; Michael Novak, *A Time to Build* (New York: Macmillan, 1967), 342.

drunkenness, gluttony, suicide, murder, and the breaking of promises are opposed to nature and therefore forbidden.[2] His argument is not deductive, intuitive, or pragmatic, but teleological—in terms of the nature and purpose of man in relation to a given type of action. Those purposes can come in conflict, as Aquinas recognizes, and this is why he allows for a variety of ways of applying the precepts of natural law, but he believes that those conflicts are not irreconcilable, and that apparent contradictions can be resolved by the use of reason. The effort of the philosopher (or better, the moral theologian because his reason should be guided by faith) is to order those claims, to see what is the legitimate basis and the extent of each of them, and to harmonize them—because such a harmony is both possible and necessary.

When one emphasizes, as I have, the syncretism and the central position of final causality in Aquinas's natural law theory, it is easy to see why I described him earlier as a moderate in political philosophy. Aquinas's tendency to ascribe a cosmic purposiveness to human conduct combines with his optimism about the possibility of synthesis of conflicting positions in a rational system to lead him to take an intermediate or moderate position wherever he can. To give just a few examples: the state has a natural justification and infidel (but not heretic) rulers have a right to rule but the church has a higher goal and the pope has a special position which combines both spiritual and temporal powers;[3] the best form of government is a constitutional monarchy, preferably elective in form with a role for the *populus*;[4] unjust laws do not oblige but it is better to tolerate an evil ruler or have him removed by higher authority than to produce the social ills that result from revolution;[5] property is an addition to the natural law which is now "necessary to human life"[6] but the wealthy property holder is obliged by natural law to provide for the poor, and the starving man may take what he needs to stay alive;[7] slavery is the result of sin and it is useful for the slave to have the guidance of a wiser master, but "all men are equal by nature" and the slave's rights of self-preservation, marriage and family life are not subject to abridgement;[8] usury and prostitution are wrong but may be tolerated to avoid greater evils.[9] On warfare, Aquinas opposes individual violence or private warfare but espouses the just war theory, provided that it is carried out "from a desire for peace."[1] Society is hierarchically and organically structured and divided into classes[2] and government is based on natural differences of capacity among men[3] but as noted above, "all men are equal by nature" and "all should have some part in government."[4]

2. *S.T.*, I–II, qu. 94, a. 3; II–II, qu. 47, a. 2; qu. 64, a.5; qu. 78; qu. 88, a. 3; qu. 148, a. 2; qu. 154, a. 2.
3. *S.T.*, I, qu. 96, a. 4; II–II, qu. 10, a. 10; qu. 12, a. 2; *On Kingship*, 14; *S.T.*, II–II, qu. 60, a. 6; *Commentary on the Sentences*, D. 44, qu. 3, a. 4.
4. *S.T.*, I–II, qu. 95, a. 4; I–II, qu. 105, a. 1.
5. *On Kingship*, 6.

6. *S.T.*, II–II, qu. 66, a. 2.
7. *S.T.*, II–II, qu. 66, a. 7.
8. *S.T.*, II–II, qu. 57, a. 3; qu. 104, a. 5.
9. *S.T.*, II–II, qu. 78, a. 1; qu. 10, a. 11.
1. *S.T.*, II–II, qu. 40, a. 1.
2. *S.T.*, I, qu. 108, a. 4.
3. *S.T.*, I, qu. 96, a. 3; *S.C.G.*, III, 81.
4. *S.T.*, II–II, qu. 105, a. 1.

More generally the philosophical assumptions of Aquinas and those influenced by him are likely to lead them to take a moderate position in political and social theory, and extreme political positions such as papal theocracy, divine right monarchy, absolute popuar sovereignty, or modern totalitarianism are completely opposed to the basic method and content of their theory. Here as elsewhere Aquinas and his followers are faithful to their mentor, Aristotle, in the belief that in ethics and politics virtues lie in the happy medium ("mean").

Yet having said this, have we said very much? For are not most political and social controversies located somewhere other than at the extremes? The conflict between left and right, liberal and conservative, is the basic stuff of modern politics and if we look at the continuing influence of Saint Thomas on social thought, and in particular his influence since the end of the nineteenth century from the point of view of a liberal-conservative dichotomy, I think we may draw some interesting conclusions. For scholasticism in general and Thomistic natural law theory in particular provided the conceptual framework on which were erected the papal critiques of liberalism, industrial capitalism, and socialism, and the ideologies and programs for both right-wing authoritarians and center-left Christian Democrats in Europe and Latin America. Regimes and parties of the moderate (and sometimes, as in Chile since the coup, not-so-moderate) right and moderate left have drawn their inspiration from the Thomistic vision of society and politics, as transmitted and reinterpreted by Catholic writers and by the papacy itself.

If we analyze the social thought contained in the two influential papal social encyclicals, *Rerum Novarum* of Leo XIII (1891) and *Quadragesimo Anno* of Pius XI (1931) we see the papal response to modern industrialism couched in terms of an approach to private property which consciously adopts an intermediate position between what is described as the excessive individualism of liberal capitalism and the statist collectivism of socialism. In terms that recall Saint Thomas's discussion, the social encyclicals defend private property as fulfilling a natural need in man, but limited by its social aspect.[5] The popes endorse the "natural" right of the worker to form associations to protect his right to a living wage for himself and his family, and advocate intermediate structures of decision making based on Pius XI's principle of "subsidiarity" (lower associations should be encouraged and the state should only intervene as a last resort) and the formal recognition of labor-management associations ("orders") in each industry, trade, or profession which will be self-regulating, although "coordinated" by the state.

The nature of that recognition and "coordination" is, of course, crucial to whether a system built on this model results in a quasi-fascist corporatism á la Spain or Portugal or Austria in the early thirties or in

---

5. Leo XIII, however, uses a labor theory argument for private property, the best known formulation of which appears in John Locke's *Second Treatise of Civil Government*, ch. 5. Did Leo derive his argument indirectly from Locke, or did Locke borrow it from the scholastics?

an effort to institutionalize the democratic representation of functional groups as in the Economic and Social Council in the Fourth and Fifth Republics in France (and in De Gaulle's unsuccessful effort to restructure the French Senate in 1969). Both corporatism and pluralism can claim to be inspired by a Thomistic natural law theory—although were it not for the statist character which it seems to acquire in modern practice, the corporatist version would seem to be closer to the social thought of Saint Thomas, given his belief in order, hierarchy, and integration in a harmonious and non-conflictual structure. On the other hand, the papal theory has inspired the European and Latin American Christian Democrats to propose the creation of worker-managed and owned factories which in some versions (e.g., some of the Chilean Christian Democrats) have a considerable similarity to the Marxist-inspired Workers Councils of Yugoslavia. Similar Catholic theories also influenced the Peruvian military in drawing up the Industrial Community Law in 1970 providing for the gradual transformation of most companies in Peru into worker-management cooperatives, and the Social Property Law of 1974 mandating the establishment of worker self-managed factories. The Peruvian National System of Social Mobilization (*Sinamos*) and the Chilean Christian Democrats' 1964 program of *Promoción Popular* are two contrasting examples of Catholic-influenced efforts to encourage, finance, (and control?) intermediate organizations between the individual and the state.[6]

The political institutions advocated by neo-Thomists since the revival of interest in Aquinas's thought also cover a broad range on the left-right spectrum. A straight reading of Aquinas indicates a clear preference for a limited monarchy, but neo-Thomists such as Mortimer Adler, Jacques Maritain, and Yves Simon have drawn the conclusion that democratic government is the logical conclusion to be drawn from Saint Thomas's natural law theories. The argument is based on a teleological analysis of human freedom which is only implicitly present in Aquinas's thought, but which provided a philosophical basis for the long-overdue accommodation between the Catholic Church and liberal democracy in France, Italy, and Latin America which only was brought to completion in the middle of this century. In the thought of Maritain, Saint Thomas's teleological argument derived from natural inclinations received a thoroughgoing reworking to produce a Thomistic theory of human rights which claimed an ontological foundation more lasting, and in the case of the property right, a formulation more applicable to contemporary conditions, than those of the natural rights theorists of the eighteenth century.

The philosophers of Christian Democracy did not go uncriticized by Catholics of a more conservative orientation who also claimed to base

6. For examples of the divergent interpretations of neo-Thomistic social thought in Latin America, see Paul E. Sigmund, ed., *Models of Political Change in Latin America* (New York: Praeger, 1970), 310–316, and id., *The Ideologies of the Developing Nations*, 2nd rev. ed. (New York: Praeger, 1972), 407–410, 454–465.

their thinking on Saint Thomas. To give one example drawn from Latin America, Christian Democratic theories were attacked in Chile as opposed to Saint Thomas's belief in order and hierarchy, since they were based instead on "the equalitarian liberalism of the French Revolution, poorly disguised by the varnish of Christianity concocted by the philosophical talent of Maritain."[7]

Maritain himself had difficulty with the relation of the liberal democratic state to religion. While he was able to argue for religious pluralism on Thomist grounds he could not accept a state that was neutral between religion and irreligion. The papacy did not endorse religious freedom until Pope John's encyclical, *Pacem in Terris*, in 1963 and the Declaration on Religious Freedom of the Second Vatican Council in 1965. The natural law doctrine of Aquinas as reinterpreted by the neo-Thomists provided much of the argument for religious liberty, but it was difficult to reverse the traditional teaching of the papacy (and of Aquinas's own statements) on the duties of the state to the true religion. As in the corporatist-pluralist debate and the controversy over equalitarian democracy, Aquinas's teaching could be cited by both liberals and conservatives.

From the perspective of the mid-seventies, one may now ask whether the Second Vatican Council did not mark the end of the period in which Thomistic natural law theories exercised an important influence on Catholic social thought. The negative reaction of Jacques Maritain in *The Peasant of the Garonne* to the new theology of the 1960s indicated that he was aware of what those changes might mean for Thomism, as well as for Catholicism. Already in Pope Paul VI's encyclical, *Populorum Progressio*, one is struck by the absence of the natural law vocabulary used in earlier papal documents and by the fact that Pope Paul does not follow Leo XIII and Pius XI in advocating a third position between simplistically portrayed caricatures of individualist capitalism and collectivist socialism. The ecumenism which was encouraged by the council also resulted in an increased attention to the bases of Catholic social thought in scripture and the early Church which echoed Protestant criticisms of the corruption of the Christian message resulting from the introduction of Greco-Roman elements. In philosophy, greater attention is now given by Catholic thinkers to the epistemological criticisms of natural law which have been current in modern philosophy since Hume. Probably the most important source of attacks on teleological natural law theories came in the course of the dispute over the papal condemnation, principally on natural law grounds, of artificial birth control. Scholastic natural law was criticized for its dualism—the artifi-

---

7. Jorge Ivan Hübner Gallo, "Catholic Social Justice, Authoritarianism and Class Stratification" in *The Conflict Between Church and State in Latin America*, ed. Fredrick B. Pike (New York: Knopf, 1964), 199. Thomistic theories of democracy appear in Mortimer Adler, *A Dialectic of Morals* (Notre Dame, Ind.: The Review of Politics, University of Notre Dame, 1941), ch. 7; Yves Simon, *Philosophy of Democratic Government* (Chicago: University of Chicago Press, 1951); and Jacques Maritain, *The Rights of Man and Natural Law* (New York: C. Scribner's Sons, 1943), and id. *Man and the State*, ch. 2–6.

cial division which it implies between the natural and supernatural—its legalism, its excessively abstract analysis of the procreative function apart from the needs of the human person as a whole, and its lack of a scriptural foundation. It was not long until one of the *periti* at the council could write, "While I affirm the reality called 'natural law' it seems to me that it is neither natural nor law."[8]

At the same time the Christian Democratic parties of Europe and Latin America, recognizing that their Catholic associations, while helpful in providing an inspirational base and in attracting the young, were preventing them from broadening their appeal to non-Catholics, became increasingly secular in tone and uninspired in ideology and programs, often losing their more innovative and reform-minded members to movements further to the left, especially those of Marxist inspiration. In Europe, the Christian Democratic parties became identified with the establishment right, losing the reformist impulse which had characterized them following World War II.[9] In Latin America, Christians for Socialism, Third World Priests, and Marxist-Christian dialogues replaced the earlier search for specifically Christian solutions to contemporary problems drawn from Thomistic social and political thought. In areas of Catholic culture, there is now a new openness and willingness to discuss a wider range of alternatives on both left and right outside the (relatively broad) boundaries set by the natural law formulations. Whether this is a positive development depends on one's concept of the relation of religion and politics, but it may mean the end of the last vestige in Europe and North America of the moderating influence of the natural law tradition.

On the other hand, as the Peruvian experiments in worker participation and the Chilean debates on the same topic indicate, it may be a little premature to announce the death of social and political thought inspired by Thomistic natural law concepts. Indeed, the renewed interest in corporatism on the part of students of the developing nations may indicate that new versions of Thomist-inspired social thought may have a special applicability in the Third World and may adopt forms which are closer to the conservative than to the liberal interpretations of Thomism, and more authoritarian than libertarian in content.[1]

8. Gregory Baum, "Remarks on Natural Law" in *Natural Law in Political Thought*, ed. Paul E. Sigmund (Cambridge, Mass.: Winthrop Publishers, 1971), 203. For criticism of the natural law basis of the papal position on birth control, see Louis K. Dupré, *Contraception and Catholics: A New Appraisal* (Baltimore: Helicon Press, 1964), and G. Egner, *Contraception vs. Tradition: A Catholic Critique* (New York: Herder and Herder, 1967), ch. 3. See also John T. Noonan, *Contraception* (Cambridge, Mass.: Harvard University Press, 1965), ch. 15.

9. The recent controversies in Germany over the expansion of worker participation in management (*Mitbestimmungsrecht*) from one-third to one-half

of company boards of directors indicate that the reformist aspects of Catholic social thought continue to exercise some influence in Europe.

1. Corporatism derives from many other sources besides Saint Thomas, but it shares Saint Thomas's emphasis on the need for unity and hierarchy as well as his belief in a "natural" order of harmonious cooperating parts in society and politics. For a discussion which emphasizes the importance of Catholic social thought for Latin American corporatism, see Howard Wiarda, "Toward a Framework for the Study of Political Change in the Iberic-Latin Tradition: the Corporative Model," *World Politics*, 25 (1972–1973), 206–250. For an attempt to relate the natural law

It would be unfortunate if Thomistic thought no longer gave rise to new social and political formulations, because, along with Marxism and the liberal humanism of the enlightenment, Christianity has been a principal source of symbols and motivation for the transformation of society, especially in times of crisis, and the Thomistic formulation of Christian social and political theory remains one of the more appealing, moderate, and flexible ways to relate the Christian message to contemporary politics and society. More fundamentally, the belief that it exemplifies that human beings can perceive a purposive order and essential regulative principles for their life in community is one that has attracted man throughout the ages—and if that belief disappears one has reason to fear for the future of democracy—or even of our civilized life together.

---

tradition to contemporary protest movements in the West on the basis of a theory of "human needs and potentialities," see the concluding chapter in my *Natural Law in Political Thought*, (Cambridge, Mass.: Winthrop Publishers, 1971; reissued, Washington, D.C.: University Press of America, 1981).

Thomistic Natural Law

JOHN FINNIS

Nature, Reason, and God in Aquinas †

(John Finnis, an Oxford philosopher, has written *Natural Law and Natural Rights*, an account which is much influenced by Aquinas's approach. In the following selection he explains Aquinas's concept of Eternal Law in terms intended to make it more understandable to modern readers. He then compares Aquinas's view of the relation of nature and God with those of Plato and Aristotle and explains how man participates in natural law through his reason and natural inclinations. Note that Finnis emphasizes the accessibility of "the general principals of practical reasonableness" to every person.)

"God" is a term burdened with varying associations. So the argument set out in the preceding section terminates in the affirmation of the existing, not of God (since I do not know what the reader understands by "God"), but of D, of which all that has been affirmed is that it is a state of affairs which exists simply by being what it is, and which is required for the existing of any other state of affairs (including the state of affairs: D's causing all caused states of affairs).

And beyond this the argument will not, I think, take us. Still, it is philosophically possible to speculate that D's causing of all caused states of affairs, being an uncaused causing which determines between contingent possibilities, is in some respects analogous to the free choices of human persons. Of course, human choosing, unlike D's causing, requires many prerequisites; so the analogy must be imperfect. But the analogy may be justified in as much as human persons, by free acts of thinking, choosing, and using or making, bring into being entities (e.g., arguments, friendships, poems, and constitutions) that simply would not exist but for these not-wholly-determined human acts.

If there is any such analogy, then, D's uncaused causality can be described as an *act*, and can be thought of as presupposing something like our *knowledge* of the alternative possibilities available to be brought to realization by choice and creation. We only act freely when we know what the possibilities are, and when we know what we are doing. This

† John Finnis, *Natural Law and Natural Rights* (Oxford: Clarendon Press, 1982). By permission of the publisher.

knowledge is propositional: we can say what we are up to in doing what we are doing. The Augustinian and Thomistic speculation on Eternal Law is a development of the analogy in this respect: what we do is guided, shaped, directed by the formally (and often chronologically) prior plan we have in mind: if we are trying to get the members of a community themselves to act in the way we have it in mind for them to act, our plan of action can be presented as a law of their actions. So too the ensemble of caused states of affairs can be thought of as a quasi-community of entities or states of affairs which exist in intelligible orders in accordance with physical and other laws of nature (both "classical" and statistical), with principles of logic and theoretical rationality, with requirements of practical reasonableness for human flourishing, and with the flexible norms of arts and technologies. Thus the theory of Eternal Law proposes that the laws, principles, requirements, and norms of the four orders be regarded as holding for their respective orders precisely because they express aspects, intelligible to us, of the creative intention which guides D's causing of the categorially variegated "community" of all entities and all states of affairs in all orders.

The purport of the theory of Eternal Law can easily be misunderstood. *First*, it must not be treated as a theory which could guide investigation and verification of suggested norms in any of the four orders; rather it is a speculation about why those norms whose holding has been appropriately verified or established do hold. *Secondly*, the creative "plan" of D which the theory hypothesizes (by a speculative inference not altogether unlike "reading off" an artist's or architect's intention from his work) must not be imagined on some single model of "law" or "norm" drawn from any one of the four orders; rather, it must comprise elements as categorially diverse as the four orders which we directly understand. As it is a mistake to confuse the laws in human legal systems with laws of nature such as the classical and statistical laws of physics, so it is a mistake to suppose that the Eternal Law could be described on the model of any of the norms of any of the four orders. *Thirdly*, the sense of "eternal" must not be misunderstood. To exist, it requires nothing other than to be what it is; thus D cannot be incomplete, cannot be changing in any sense of "change" that we could apply to contingent entities or states of affairs in any of the four orders. But, for just the same reason, D cannot be "static" or "unchanging" in any sense applicable to such contingent entities or states of affairs. To say that D is eternal, and to call the act(s) and intension(s) of D eternal, is simply a way of indicating that D (and anything that can be predicated of D) neither develops nor declines, that D is outside the range of application of the concepts of change and changelessness, and hence of time. *Fourthly*, the speculation that the norms intelligible to us in any of the four orders are expressions or indications of D's creative plan in no way warrants the further speculation that D's creative plan is understood by us. All that we *know* about D is that D has what it takes to bring it about that every state of affairs which exists exists. But what states of affairs do in fact exist is not at all fully explained by the laws and norms of natural sciences, or of reasoning, or human arts, or of practical reasonableness and human flourishing. Much is coincidental, "fortuitous". Yet every state of affairs, however "fortuitous," requires D's creative causality if it is to exist. So the speculation of the "plan" of that causality, i.e. on Eternal Law, suggests that much of that Law is quite unknown to us. * * *

Plato and Aristotle do not use the existence of God or the gods as an argument to justify their claim that there are objective norms of human flourishing and principles of human reasonableness. But their arguments in justifying that claim, and their reflection upon the nature, point, and source of those (and all such) arguments, lead them to affirm that there is a transcendent source of being (i.e., of entities and states of affairs, and of their existing) and in particular of our capacity and desire to understand being (or nature) and its many forms of good. Thus in realizing one's nature, in flourishing (*eudaimonia*), and (what is the same thing from another aspect) in recognizing the authoritativeness of practical reasonableness, its principles, and its requirements, one is responding to the divine pull and recognizing the mastery of God. So when Plato speaks of God's law, his meaning is rather close to what a Christian theologian, such as Aquinas, means in speaking of natural law as the Eternal Law in so far as it is addressed to human practical reasonableness.

> God, as the old saying says, holds in his hand the beginning, end, and middle of all that is, and straight he travels to the accomplishment of his purpose, as is (his) nature (*kata physin*); and always by his side is Right (*dike:* justice) ready to punish those who disobey the divine law (*theiou nomou*). Anyone who wants to flourish (*eudaimonesein*) follows closely in the train of Right, with humility. . . . What line of conduct, then, is dear (*phile*) to God and a following of him? . . . Well, it is God who is for us the measure (*metron*) of all things; much more truly so than, as they (sophists, notably Protagoras) say, man. So to be loved by such a being, a man must strive as far as he can to become like that being; and, following out this principle, the person who is temperate-and-ordered is dear to God, being like him.[1]

Plato has no conception corresponding to Aquinas's differentiated concept of divine law, i.e. the law which supplements the natural law and is promulgated by God for the regulation of the community or communities (Israel and then the universal Church) constituted through God's public self-revelation and offer of friendship. For Plato, while he would affirm that God can be apprehended by us in the act and experience of human understanding, has no conception of a revelation accessible to men without the effort of rational dialectic and contemplation—of the

1. *Laws*, IV, 715e, 716d. See also *Republic*, VI, 600b.

sort of empirical revelation, for instance, that would be 'folly to the Greeks' (but would be offered to them none the less).[2]

In short, Plato and Aristotle consider that what I have called a speculative analogue model of D's nature and causality is in some measure verified in the experience of the true philosopher.[3] By this belief they are encouraged to treat reason as more than a skill, knack, or characteristic that men, unlike animals, happen to have; and to treat the nature or reality that both includes and is illuminated by man's understanding as more than a fortuitous agglomeration of entities and states of affairs devoid of any significance that could attract human admiration and allegiance. Practical reasonableness gains for them the significance of a partial imitation of God; the basic values grasped by practical reason gain an objectivity; and practical reason's methodological requirements of constancy and impartiality are reinforced by the worth of adopting a viewpoint of the God who "contemplates all the time and all existence."

For Aquinas, there is nothing extraordinary about man's grasp of the natural law; it is simply one application of man's ordinary power of understanding. None-the-less his account of this practical *participatio* of the Eternal Law draws attention to some related points worth recapitulating here.

Aquinas begins by drawing a sharp distinction (which runs through all his work) between the intelligent nature of human beings, and the intelligible but not intelligent nature of animals, vegetables, and the rest of "nature." The latter participate in the Eternal Law "somehow"[4] since that is the ultimate source of all their tendencies (*inclinationes*) (which have and follow intelligible patterns). Human beings, on the other hand, provide for themselves (and for others); so we can say that man is not only subject to God's providence, but is actually a participant (*particeps*) in it. In brief, animals (and the rest of "lower creation") are *not* subject to natural law. And their nature is not a basis for inference about the principles of human reasonableness.

Next, Aquinas specifies the basic manner in which the eternal reason is participated in us: through our "natural inclination to the due (*debitum*) act and the due end." This terse formulation needs expansion. It is elaborated a few pages later, when he explains that amongst our natural inclinations is the inclination to act *secundum rationem*, i.e. reasonably.[5] But the formula also looks right back to the beginning of Aquinas's discussion of human self-direction.[6] There his first exploration is of our inclination towards our last (or all-embracing) and (*ultimus*

---

2. As by Paul: 1 Corinthians 1: 22–24. Of course, on Aquinas's view, this revelation does not oppose reason; in going beyond what is accessible either to argument or to meditative rational experience, the revealed truths, he thinks, incorporate truths accessible to reason and answer questions raised, pressed, but found insoluble by reason. Correspondingly, the divine (i.e., revealed) law, for Aquinas, incorporates and repromulgates many elements of natural law: S.T., I–II, qu. 100, a. 1,3;

qu. 99, a.2.
3. Plato adds that every human being possesses the capacity of learning this truth: *Republic*, VII, 518; cf. VI, 505.
4. Aliqualiter: S.T., I–II, qu. 91, a. 2c; in resp. 3 he remarks that their participation can be called (a following of) law only metaphorically (*per similitudinem*).
5. S.T., I–II, qu. 94, a. 3c.
6. See S.T., I–II, Prologue, and qu. 1–5.

finis), a completeness of flourishing (*beatitudo*) which will be found when our natural desire for understanding (i.e. for the satisfaction of our reason) is satisfied by that undying contemplation of God which, he says, can be anticipated only on the basis of revelation and can be attained only by a divine gift. Finally, the formula in the discussion of natural law looks forward to his resumption of the Aristotelian mediation on the divine causality that underpins all our inclinations and capacities, including our desire to know and to be intelligent, reasonable, responsible, and our capacity to choose freely and responsibly. All these themes Aquinas draws together in explaining this aspect of the participation of Eternal Law in us as natural law: "every activity of reason and of will derives, in us, from that which is according to nature. . . ." For all reasoning derives from principles (or sources: *principiis*) naturally [7] known; and all desire for things which are for an end derives from natural desire for an end beyond which is no further end (*ultimus finis*); and so it must be that the first directing of our acts towards an end (or: the end) is through natural law.

Having thus stressed the inclinations which, prior to any rational control of ours, underlie all our effort, including our effort to make our efforts intelligent and reasonable, Aquinas turns to that aspect of our participation of God's practical reason which I mentioned earlier: our power of understanding. For, by this power, we grasp the basic forms of good (and thus the basic principles of natural law); the data for this act of understanding include the desires and inclinations which we experience, but like all understanding, this act of understanding goes beyond the data as experienced, to concepts accessible or available not to experience but only to understanding. I have already indicated (briefly!) Aquinas's general account of the source of our power of illuminating the data of imagination and experience by the insights of common sense, natural science, philosophy, and practical reasonableness. So now he cites again the words of Psalm 4:7, and adds that "the light of natural reason, whereby we discern what is good and what is bad (which is what natural law concerns), is simply the impress in us of the divine light." [8]

MORTIMER ADLER AND BILL MOYERS

A Dialogue on the Nature of Goodness†

(Mortimer Adler was one of the leaders of the neo-Thomist revival at the University of Chicago, along with its president, Robert M. Hutchins. More

---

7. But not without experience; for the intelligence of each of us starts as a *tabula rasa*: S.T., I, qu. 79, a. 2c. Like Aristotle (*Post Anal.* B, c. 19: 99b14–100b17), Aquinas has no truck with 'innate ideas.'

8. S.T., I–II, qu. 91, a. 2c. Some people are more receptive of this light than others, though every

(sane and conscious) person grasps the general principles of practical reasonableness: qu. 93, a. 2.

† From *Six Great Ideas, III: Goodness.* Television transcript, copyright © 1982, JCS Productions. Reprinted by permission of Bill Moyers, Producer and Director.

recently he has promoted the Great Books movement and helped to organize the Aspen Institute to discuss the Great Ideas. In this selection, taken from the Public Broadcasting System television series, *Six Great Ideas*, produced by Bill Moyers, Adler argues, in Thomistic natural law terms, that goodness is based on the nature of man.)

DR. ADLER: I'm using the word "goodness" in the moral sense of what is good for human beings. Good for them—it makes them good men and women, makes their lives good lives or bad lives.

MOYERS: Isn't it true that what is good for you is not necessarily good for me?

DR. ADLER: Most of the things we call good or bad are—correspond to—the things we like or dislike—

MOYERS: Matters of taste?

DR. ADLER: Matters of taste. If I like fish, and I say, "I like fish, and I find it good," and you say, "I like meat," that's a difference of opinion and is not arguable. I don't have to say to you, "Bill, you ought to like meat; I like meat, and you ought to like meat." That's a nonsensical statement. There's no meaning to the "ought" there. But if I said to you, "Bill, I think you're wasting your time; you aren't trying to get more knowledge. You're playing most of your time here, indulging in all kinds of sports and activities but aren't improving your mind—I think you ought to spend more time learning." There's an "ought."

MOYERS: "Ought." Which means?

DR. ADLER: When I say "ought," whenever I use the word "ought," I'm referring to a basic need that I think you are morally obliged to fulfill.

MOYERS: But how, when you say you ought to do this, or you ought to do that, can you prove the truth or falsity of that statement in regard to my need? How do you know my need?

DR. ADLER: Well, I don't know your need individually, Bill; I know the needs that are common to all human beings. The only way that I can make any moral judgments that have universal validity is if the needs I'm talking about are common to all human beings. We have an animal part of our nature, and we have animal needs, what we call biological needs—the needs for food and drink and sleep, take those three for a moment. They are life sustaining, and insofar as I would say that life is a fundamental good for a living thing, we need the things that sustain life. And every human being needs them, every human being, not just you and I, not just Americans, not just Frenchmen, not just Asiatics— all human beings everywhere at all times. Now, you say, "Are there needs that point to real goods beyond the biological level?" Yes, I think man is by nature a political animal; and therefore being a citizen, I mean, having suffrage, having a voice in his own government, is a real good and meets the need of a political animal. I think man has by nature freedom of choice, and he therefore needs freedom of action. Because if he had freedom of choice and didn't have that freedom of action, the freedom of choice would be nugatory, you couldn't carry out your choices, you see. So that our right to liberty is based upon our need for that freedom of action, which is the liberty we are concerned with, in order to fulfill the freedom of choice—the choices we've made freely.

MOYERS: But the Communists would say to that, "You're not speaking for what is a basic need in our society, because as long as we meet the basic biological needs of the people, the other needs are relative to your own society."

DR. ADLER: I would say they're wrong. I have to say I think the Communist failure to recognize the human need for freedom, political freedom and individual freedom of action, is an error on the part of the totalitarian state.

MOYERS: You're saying then, that some things are good for us regardless of what people think about them?

DR. ADLER: Precisely, I'm saying there are some moral truths—not everything, one man's meat is another man's poison is quite right. Your fish and my meat, okay. But for a smaller number of real goods—a very small number, I'd say less than a dozen—I can make, I think, moral judgments about what human beings ought to seek and ought to do, that I think can be shown to be true and true for all men everywhere.

MOYERS: You said real goods.

DR. ADLER: Real goods.

MOYERS: As opposed to—

DR. ADLER: Apparent goods. Now, the difference is that an apparent good is something you call good because you want it or like it. It is good because you want it. In the case of real goods, your need for it—what you need—the good itself is that which you need. It corresponds to a need.

MOYERS: You need it because you're human.

DR. ADLER: That's right.

MOYERS: Give me an example.

DR. ADLER: Well, I would say that when I say I like vanilla ice cream, and I think it's good and I call it good because I like it, that's an apparent good. I dislike pistachio—I don't like it, and I don't call it good. But if I say, "I desire as much knowledge as I can get, and I'm going to make every effort to get as much knowledge as I can," I'm talking about a good that I feel obliged, under obligation, to pursue, to seek, to acquire—

because I think it's really good for me because it fulfills a basic human need that I have. All the real goods are goods that we are obliged to seek, to desire, reach out for, because they satisfy our fundamental need to fulfill our potentialities.

MOYERS: But not all of us feel obliged to seek knowledge.

DR. ADLER: I didn't say that everyone feels obliged; I say they ought to seek knowledge, and the obligation is upon them. If I make the moral judgment, every human being should seek knowledge, I can defend that judgment.

MOYERS: Defend it.

DR. ADLER: Well, a moral judgment can't be true in the way in which a statistical statement or a scientific statement is true. When we talked about truth, you and I, Bill, we said that such descriptive truths are true because, in that case, what the mind thinks conforms to the way things are, to reality.

MOYERS: That mountain is 6,000 feet high, we can prove that.

DR. ADLER: That's right. It either is or is not, and the statement is either true or false descriptively, right? When I say you ought to seek knowledge, there's no conformity between my statement "ought" and reality, there are no oughts or ought nots in reality. The only philosopher who ever solved the problem of how to make prescriptive judgments, or how to explain the truth or falsity of prescriptive judgments, was Aristotle. And in one paragraph he says, on the one hand our theoretical statements, our descriptive statements are true by the agreement of the mind with reality. But when we say "ought" or "ought not," when we make prescriptive judgments, "The truth lies in conformity to right desire." I puzzled about that for a long time; that'd be fine if I knew what "right desire" is. Now, what's right desire? Well, right desire is what I ought to desire. Well, what ought I desire? Then I found the answer: I ought to desire what I need. Tell me have you ever thought of something and said, "Well, that man has a wrong need"? Wrong wants, I understand, I can point to lots of people who I think want the wrong thing, but can a person need something—can a person need by nature something that is bad for his nature? I think not. Every need is a right desire, for something that is really good for the person that needs it. And since we all have the same human nature, and our potentialities are the same, our inherent natural needs are the same—that is the basis of our moral judgments.

MOYERS: All right, let's see if we can make this more concrete for people by playing "Fill in the blank."

DR. ADLER: All right.

MOYERS: And I will call out the blank and you fill it in with only what you consider to be those needs all of us need because we are human, right?

DR. ADLER: Right.

MOYERS: Men and women need . . .

DR. ADLER: Food.

MOYERS: Because . . .

DR. ADLER: They're human, human animals.

MOYERS: Men and woman need . . .

DR. ADLER: Friends.

MOYERS: Because . . .

DR. ADLER: They're social animals, they need to associate with their fellow human beings.

MOYERS: Men and woman need . . .

DR. ADLER: Liberty.

MOYERS: Because . . .

DR. ADLER: By nature they have free choice, and they need liberty of action in order to execute their free choice.

MOYERS: Men and women need . . .

DR. ADLER: Knowledge.

MOYERS: Because . . .

DR. ADLER: Because they have minds that are empty, just as their stomachs are empty, and that those minds crave filling just as their stomachs crave filling. What filling the mind craves—tends toward—is knowledge.

MOYERS: Men and women need . . .

DR. ADLER: Peace. A civil society in which there is peace.

MOYERS: Because . . .

DR. ADLER: That peace provides them with the conditions of life that they need in order to pursue happiness.

MOYERS: When you talk about the biological needs, you don't mention sex, and it seems to me that food is necessary for an individual to survive, but sex is necessary for the race to survive, and therefore, sex is as important to the race as food is to the individual.

DR. ADLER: Sex is a very complex thing. Since sex can take place without reproduction, without the reproduction of the race, we have to separate sex from reproduction. The question is whether or not the deprivation of sex—I'm glad you mentioned it, because one of the things I should have said was pleasure—all human beings need pleasure.

MOYERS: Because . . .

DR. ADLER: Because they are animals that suffer pleasure and pain and pleasure is a fulfilling experience, as pain is a disturbing and distressing experience. Now, pleasures are of various kinds—the pleasures of the flesh and the pleasures of the spirit. I would include sexual pleasure among the pleasures, but I don't think it's the only pleasure men need. They can't be deprived of pleasure and lead good lives, but I cannot bring myself to think that a life of sexual deprivation is a life that is prevented from being a good one.

MOYERS: But don't they need it because they're human, and that the need for sex is as genetically coded as the need for food?

DR. ADLER: No. I don't think so. The evidence on that, I would say, is that a man who starves, dies; the man who doesn't sleep, becomes so weak and emaciated that his health is ruined and his health and vigor is lost. But does the deprivation of the particular fleshly pleasure that is sex produce the same deteriorating or destructive effects as the deprivation of food, sleep, and drink? I just raise the question.

MOYERS: It seems to me that for a man who deals in empirical evidence and logic, it is really quite arbitrary to say that all human beings everywhere at all times have certain basic needs, and therefore they ought to satisfy those needs in order to lead a good life.

DR. ADLER: I'm saying it because we are all members of the same species. That means we all have the same fundamental potentialities. Those same fundamental potentialities are tendencies—every potentiality tends to its own realization and fulfillment. And the things I call the inherent natural desires or natural needs are our common human potentialities. If we were not social animals that have the potentiality of living with and associating with our fellow human beings, I would not say that such fellowship was a natural need. If we didn't have intellects that could know, I would not say that knowledge was a natural need. If we didn't have the power of free choice, I would not say liberty of action was a natural need. If we didn't have bodies and spirits that could be pleased and displeased, I wouldn't say pleasure was a natural need. In other words, I am looking at human beings and saying, here are five, six or seven—not even a dozen, I would think—maybe nine or ten aspects or tendencies of human life that tend toward fulfillment everywhere. And I would say these natural needs are the common human aspirations.

MOYERS: How did we get from a discussion of goodness to a discussion of needs?

DR. ADLER: The question is, are there any prescriptive statements, statements that say you ought to do this, you ought to seek that, that have truth? Now, that's how we got to it. In time, moral philosophy has decided that no value judgments and no prescriptive oughts and ought nots are true or false, because the theory of our contemporary philosophers about the truth is that all truth is descriptive. And if a statement isn't descriptive, it can't be true. Now, an "ought" statement is not descriptive, it is prescriptive.

MOYERS: Define prescriptive.

DR. ADLER: It says "ought," it's an injunction, it's a command. It's a direction of action, with a moral obligation. The word "ought" has a full sense of moral obligation.

MOYERS: You're morally obligated—

DR. ADLER: To do.

MOYERS: To eat.

DR. ADLER: You're morally obligated to seek knowledge, you're morally obligated to exercise political liberty.

MOYERS: Because these are essential to—

DR. ADLER: Your human nature.

MOYERS: Well, what happens when we want more than we need and what does that have to do with goodness?

DR. ADLER: Let me give you a concrete example. I can easily imagine a parent saying to a child, "You ought to seek as much schooling as you can get, not as little as you can get away with." And the child listens to it, pays lip service to it, and goes to college and stays in college, but while there fritters away his time in various forms of play and recreation, and above all, sleeps a great deal—sleeps over the weekend and stays in bed late when he can, often cuts classes to do that, because he indulges his desire for the pleasures of slumber.

MOYERS: But you say sleep is necessary.

DR. ADLER: Sleep is a good that we need, but we can often want more than the real good—more of the real good than we need it, see. A certain amount of sleep, just as a certain amount of pleasure, is a real good, but an immoderate pursuit of pleasure is wanting more pleasure than you need. And wanting more of a good than you really need can often interfere with attaining a good that you do need. For example, this student that we're talking about who is not paying attention to his studies, who is not doing the work he should be doing in college because he's overindulging in pleasure, overindulging in eating, overindulging in drinking, overindulging in play and in sleeping, is interfering with the use of his opportunity to increase the goods of his mind.

MOYERS: So he's seeking the wants at the expense of his need.

DR. ADLER: His need, that's precisely it.

MOYERS: What are the practical applications of thinking about goodness?

DR. ADLER: Of all the great ideas, the one that has the most obvious practical applications, because of our whole life is concerned with good and evil. Everything we do is exercising choices, preferring this to that, preferring doing this to that, feeling the obligation to do this rather than that, having remorse because one did the wrong thing. I can't think of any moment of life in which good and evil doesn't obtrude upon us. We aren't aware of the fact that we're using those terms, but every action that we make is in terms of good and evil, right and wrong.

MOYERS: How does one teach his children to have a respect for the right choice, and to nurture that child into making the right choice?

DR. ADLER: It's very hard. I've had a number of sons, two sets of them as a matter of fact, by two marriages, and in all four cases, two and two, I've tried to talk to them about the long-term future. I have said, "When you make a choice now between this and that, ask yourself which of the things you choose will work out best in the long run."

MOYERS: But no one can know that.

DR. ADLER: Well, let's get back to this student in college who is having a wonderful time playing around, having lots of fun, indulging in a variety of pleasures which are evanescent, and sacrificing the goods of his mind by not studying. Now, what's the effect of that going to be upon him when he gets to be 30, 40, when his skills are poor, when his knowledge is inadequate? He has wasted very precious years of his life because he didn't think about what's good for him in the long run. I know, it's very hard for the young to think about their later lives. The thing that fascinates me is the time when you should think about your life as a whole is when you have your life as a whole before you, that's when you're young. Yet as you get older and older, you tend to be able to think more and better about your life as a whole when you have very little of it left. It's paradoxical, but true. If you could reverse that, if older people from their experience could really persuade younger people how to think about their life as a whole, the history of the human race would be different. . . .

Discussion

DR. ADLER: And just as in the case of descriptive truth there is a distinction between what we do think from moment to moment and what we ought to think, if we wish to think truly rather than falsely, so there is a distinction between what we do actually desire from moment to moment and what we ought to desire, if we wish to desire what is really good for us and to avoid what is really bad for us. Those who say, and you all know the saying, that one man's meat is another man's poison, are recognizing the subjective aspect if they say that's all there is to it. They are then taking the view that value judgments cannot be either true or false objectively and that there are no valid "oughts" in the sphere of human conduct. This seems to be the position, by the way, that Montaigne took in a little essay, and echoed by Hamlet in Shakespeare's play. Montaigne said, "There is nothing good or evil but thinking makes it so." In other words, it's the individual judgment, and nothing but the individual judgment, that confers goodness or badness on the object thought about, desired or wanted. The question I want to ask you is, do you accept or reject Montaigne's position?

BETTY SUE FLOWERS (Associate Dean of Graduate Studies, the University of Texas):   When you look at cultures, individual acts are judged quite differently in different cultures. There is a sense in which by thinking we can call anything good or anything bad. . . . So that it is in fact from one point of view true that there's nothing good or bad but thinking makes it so, because any value you find in one culture might not be a value in another culture.

DR. ADLER: But, if you were to think well of my distinction between that which is merely apparently good because thinking makes it so, and that which is really good no matter what you think, because of your innate, inherent, natural desires or needs. . . . I said a little earlier that all men by nature desire to know, we have a need for knowledge; that there are some human beings who even make the mistake that they don't need it, and avoid learning. They're wrong, because they don't want what they need, and what they need is really good for them. If they want wealth or power or something else, they want the wrong thing, not the right thing.

ALAN BULLOCK (Fellow of the British Academy):   One of my concepts of goodness—terrestrial goodness, not theological goodness—is goodness in itself and for itself. Virtue is its own reward. I can't take this view of the terrestrial life as being adequately covered by animal needs.

DR. ADLER: I didn't say that. I didn't say that terrestrial happiness was on a biological level. And I would like to say that I think you're wrong that virtue is its own reward. It is a good—moral virtue is a good—but it's a means, it's a means, not an end. It's a means to happiness either in this life or the next. In the next life, when it has as its end the happiness in heaven the souls have in the vision of God, the virtue is at a higher level—a heroic virtue—and the theological virtues are involved, not just the simple moral virtues.

SOEDJATMOKO (Indonesian philosopher/Rector, United Nations University, Tokyo): I want to point out that it is possible to look at the human person—and some cultures do it and some religions do it—as free from the concept of original sin, free from the fall from paradise, and so forth. The point I want to make is that there are many cultures where evil is accepted as an inevitable accompaniment of good. This lesson we all now have to learn. First that it is not of the greatest importance that our truth is true—that there are multiple truths, and that we will have to reconcile those multiple truths at the point where our survival as the human race and as civilized human beings, where some transcendental conception of man that takes him beyond the animal level becomes possible. The point is the multiplicity of truths, of the various aspects of truth, and the need for us, all of us, to learn whatever the strength of our conviction of our own truths, to give room to the truth of others.

DR. ADLER: Look, may I make a comment on that, please? The deepest difference between East and West is on this very point. In the West in one of the great disputations of the Middle Ages, St. Thomas defended against many opponents the doctrine of the unity of truth. And his point is, truth is a very complex whole, but all the parts of it must hang together. That unity which embraces all truth must include no conflicting truth. There cannot be conflicting truths within the unity of truth. He did this in defense of the Christian position against the Averroists, who thought there were two truths, truth of religion on the one hand, truth of science on the other, and the left hand and the right hand didn't have to get together. For St. Thomas, there can be no conflict between science and religion. If there's truth of science and truth of religion, they must cohere and be consistent, otherwise they can't be parts of the unity of truth. Now, I may be wrong, but in the Eastern view of these matters, when you and other Easterners, if I may say so, speak about the multiplicity of truths, you are willing to embrace in that multiplicity conflicting truths. I'm not saying for a moment who's right, I'm only saying this is as fundamental a difference between the Far East and the West as any I know. And I do think, I have to say, that one of us is right and one of us is wrong. Which, I will not know.

SOEDJATMOKO: There are cultures that put different value on the capacity of reason to comprehend truth. There are other ways of directly relating to reality, including absolute reality—through the artistic eye, through the mystic, through the religious view and so forth. As a result, in many of the non-western civilizations, people have felt no need to be consistent—to construct, to develop a construct of the mind that is— that has an inner coherence and inner logic. So that is to say, that may not be the problem, the problem may be a false issue. The real problem now is, can we develop a new consensus, moral consensus, on a global scale and on a trans-generational scale, that will allow our children and grandchildren to live as decent human beings.

DR. ADLER: I share your hope.

MOYERS: How can one be so presumptuous as to make judgments about what is good for other people in other cultures that are not Western?

DR. ADLER: The only way that one can make those judgments on the philosophical level—because as I have to be quite open about the diversity of religious beliefs and the diversity of things that go beyond the natural place, the hereafter; the obligations of one's life come from transcendental sources, not the sources of our nature. The presumption, I think, is minimized by the fact that it relies upon the common nature that all of us share.

MOYERS: You mean what we all are as humans?

DR. ADLER: Human beings, yes. For example—

MOYERS: That being human goes beyond being Western.

DR. ADLER: If I say slavery is universally bad, the life of the free man is universally good for man, I don't apologize for it—if that's a Western idea, I say it's a human idea. It applies to all human beings everywhere. And any Eastern civilization, or any civilization anywhere, that denies that, I think is wrong, and I don't hesitate to say that other civilizations are wrong.

MOYERS: But that brings us back to the beginning of the circle, which is, who is to decide what is right and wrong, what is good or evil?

DR. ADLER: Our problem is to find out what is really good for every human being. How do we find that out? I say there is no way of finding it out except by looking to human nature. If I abandon the notion of human nature, if I abandon the notion that human nature is the same wherever men are, that is the common constant throughout the human life on earth, I have no basis for moral judgments at all. I want to be perfectly clear with you, if I give up the notion of human nature and natural needs, I have no basis whatsoever for any universally valid moral judgment.

MOYERS: What about human rights—because many societies do not accept, as Jimmy Carter learned, our definition of human rights?

DR. ADLER: If I may say so, I think the only word that you used there that I would quarrel with is "our" definition. The definition of human rights is identical with the definition of human needs. Anything that a human being needs as a condition of his leading a good life he has a right to.

MOYERS: Which is more important by your philosophy, to know what is good to have, or to know what is right to do?

DR. ADLER: In a sense something I've just said implicitly answers your question. I don't think we can ever know what is right or wrong in our conduct to others unless we know what is really good for ourselves to have. It's only by my knowing that freedom is a real good for me, that I know that slavery is wronging somebody else. It's only when I know that having a moderate supply of external goods is a real good for me as a condition of a good life, that I know that grinding poverty and destitution is wrong for others—they have a right to a minimum—at least a decent minimum of wealth. Only when I know what is really good for me, that I should pursue or ought to pursue, do I know what is right for everybody else to have and am obligated to do my best to act justly toward them.

MOYERS: And is this knowledge the work of philosophy?

DR. ADLER: It seems to me this is what moral philosophy is about.

JACQUES MARITAIN

Natural Law †

(The most influential contemporary restatement of Thomistic natural law is contained in the writings of the French philosopher, Jacques Maritain. The following selection illustrates the way he has updated and changed Aquinas's theory to make it applicable to contemporary experience.)

Shall we try to reestablish our faith in human rights on the basis of a true philosophy? This true philosophy of the rights of the human person is based upon the true idea of natural law, as looked upon in an ontological perspective and as conveying through the essential structures and requirements of created nature the wisdom of the Author of Being.

The genuine idea of natural law is a heritage of Greek and Christian thought. It goes back not only to Grotius, who indeed began deforming it, but, before him to Suarez and Francisco de Vitoria; and further back to St. Thomas Aquinas (he alone grasped the matter in a wholly consistent doctrine, which unfortunately was expressed in an insufficiently clarified vocabulary,[1] so that its deepest features were soon overlooked and disregarded); and still further back to St. Augustine and the Church Fathers and St. Paul (we remember St. Paul's saying: "When the Gentiles who have not the Law, *do by nature* the things contained in the Law, these, having not the Law, are a law unto themselves . . .");[2] and even further back to Cicero, to the Stoics, to the great moralists of antiquity and its great poets, particularly Sophocles. Antigone, who was aware

† Jacques Maritain, *Man and the State* (Chicago: University of Chicago Press, 1950). Copyright © 1950 by the University of Chicago. Reprinted by permission of the publisher.
1. Especially because the vocabulary of the *Commentary on the Sentences*, as concerns the "pri-
mary" and "secondary" precepts of Natural Law, is at variance with the vocabulary of the *Summa Theologica*, I–II, qu. 94. Thomas's respect for the stock phrases of the jurists also causes some trouble, particularly when it comes to Ulpian.
2. Paul, Romans, 2:14.

that in transgressing the human law and being crushed by it she was obeying a better commandment, the *unwritten and unchangeable laws*, is the eternal heroine of natural law: for, as she puts it, they were not, those unwritten laws, born out of today's or yesterday's sweet will, "but they live always and forever, and no man knows from where they have arisen."[3]

The First Element (Ontological) in Natural Law

Since I have not time here to discuss nonsense (we can always find very intelligent philosophers, not to quote Mr. Bertrand Russell, to defend it most brilliantly) I am taking it for granted that we admit that there is a human nature, and this human nature is the same in all men. I am taking it for granted that we also admit that man is a being gifted with intelligence, and who, as such, acts with an understanding of what he is doing, and therefore with the power to determine for himself the ends which he pursues. On the other hand, possessed of a nature, or an onto-logic structure which is a locus of intelligible necessities, man possesses ends which necessarily correspond to his essential constitution and which are the same for all—as all pianos, for instance, whatever their particular type and in whatever spot they may be, have as their end the production of certain attuned sounds. If they do not produce these sounds they must be tuned, or discarded as worthless. But since man is endowed with intelligence and determines his own ends, it is up to him to put himself in tune with the ends necessarily demanded by his nature. This means that there is, by the very virtue of human nature, an order or a disposi-tion which human reason can discover and according to which the human will must act in order to attune itself to the essential and necessary ends of the human being. The unwritten law, or natural law, is nothing more than that.

The example that I just used—taken from the world of human work-manship—was purposely crude and provocative; yet did not Plato him-self have recourse to the idea of any work of human art whatever, the idea of the Bed, the idea of the Table, in order to make clear his theory (which I do not share) of eternal Ideas? What I mean is that every being has its own natural law, as well as it has its own essence. Any kind of thing produced by human industry has, like the stringed instrument that I brought up a moment ago, its own natural law, that is, the *normality of its functioning*, the proper way in which, by reason of its specific construction, it demands to be put into action, it *"should"* be used. Confronted with any supposedly unknown gadget, be it a corkscrew or a peg-top or a calculating machine or an atom bomb, children or scien-

---

3.   "Nor did I deem
Your ordinance of so much binding force,
As that a mortal man could overbear
The unchangeable unwritten code of Heaven;
This is not of today and yesterday,
But lives forever, having origin

Whence no man knows; whose sanctions I were
   loath
In Heaven's sight to provoke, fearing the will
Of any man."
   (Sophocles *Antigone* II. 452–60, George
   Young's translation)

tists, in their eagerness to discover how to use it, will not question the existence of that inner typical law.

Any kind of thing existing in nature, a plant, a dog, a horse, has its own natural law, that is, the *normality of its functioning*, the proper way in which, by reason of its specific structure and specific ends, it *"should"* achieve fulness of being either in its growth or in its behavior. Washington Carver, when he was a child and healed sick flowers in his garden, had an obscure knowledge, both by intelligence and congeniality, of that vegetative law of theirs. Horse-breeders have an experiential knowledge, both by intelligence and congeniality, of the natural law of horses, a natural law with respect to which a horse's behavior makes him a *good horse* or a *vicious horse* in the herd. Well, horses do not enjoy free will, their natural law is but a part of the immense network of essential tendencies and regulations involved in the movement of the cosmos, and the individual horse who fails in that equine law only obeys the universal order of nature on which the deficiencies of his individual nature depend. If horses were free, there would be an ethical way of conforming to the specific natural law of horses, but that horsy morality is a dream because horses are not free.

When I said a moment ago that the natural law of all beings existing in nature is the proper way in which, by reason of the specific nature and specific ends, they *should* achieve fulness of being in their behavior, this very word *should* had only a metaphysical meaning (as we say that a good or a normal eye "should" be able to read letters on a blackboard from a given distance). The same word *should* starts to have a *moral* meaning, that is, to imply moral obligation, when we pass the threshold of the world of free agents. Natural law for man is *moral* law, because man obeys or disobeys it freely, not necessarily, and because human behavior pertains to a particular, privileged order which is irreducible to the general order of the cosmos and tends to a final end superior to the immanent common good of the cosmos.

What I am emphasizing is the first basic element to be recognized in natural law, namely the *ontological* element; I mean the *normality of functioning* which is grounded on the essence of that being: man. Natural law in general, as we have just seen, is the ideal formula of development of a given being; it might be compared with an algebraical equation to which a curve develops in space, yet with man the curve has freely to conform to the equation. Let us say, then, that in its ontological aspect, natural law is an *ideal order* relating to human actions, a *divide* between the suitable and the unsuitable, the proper and the improper, which depends on human nature or essence and the unchangeable necessities rooted in it. I do not mean that the proper regulation for each possible human situation is contained in the human essence, as Leibniz believed that every event in the life of Caesar was contained beforehand in the idea of Caesar. Human situations are something existential. Neither they nor their appropriate regulations are contained of that essence. Any given situation, for instance the situation of Cain with regard to Abel, implies a relation to the essence of man, and the possible murder of the one by the other is incompatible with the general ends and innermost dynamic structure of that rational essence. It is rejected by it. Hence the prohibition of murder is grounded on or required by the essence of man. The precept: thou shalt do no murder, is a precept of natural law. Because a primordial and most general end of human nature is to preserve being— the being of that existent who is a person, and a universe unto himself; and because man insofar as he is man has a right to live.

Suppose a completely new case or situation, unheard of in human history: suppose, for instance, that what we now call *genocide* were as new as that very name. In the fashion that I just explained, that possible behavior will face the human essence as incompatible with its general ends and innermost dynamic structure: that is to say, as prohibited by natural law. The condemnation of genocide by the General Assembly of the United Nations has sanctioned the prohibition of the crime in question by natural law—which does not mean that that prohibition was part of the essence of man as I know not what metaphysical feature eternally inscribed in it—nor that it was a notion recognized from the start by the conscience of humanity.

To sum up, let us say that natural law is something both *ontological* and *ideal*. It is something *ideal*, because it is grounded on the human essence and its unchangeable structure and the intelligible necessities it involves. Natural law is something *ontological*, because the human essence is an ontological reality, which moreover does not exist separately, but in every human being, so that by the same token natural law dwells as an ideal order in the very being of all existing men.

In that first consideration, or with regard to the basic *ontological* element it implies, natural law is coextensive with the whole field of natural moral regulations, the whole field of natural morality. Not only the primary and fundamental regulations but the slightest regulations of natural ethics mean conformity to natural law—say, natural obligations or rights of which we perhaps have now no idea, and of which men will become aware in a distant future.

An angel who knew the human essence in his angelic manner and all the possible existential situations of man would know natural law in the infinity of its extension. But we do not. Though the Eighteenth Century theoreticians believed they did.

The Second Element (Gnoseological) in Natural Law

Thus we arrive at the *second* basic element to be recognized in natural law, namely natural law *as known*, and thus as measuring in actual fact human practical reason, which is the measure of human acts.

Natural law is not a written law. Men know it with greater or less difficulty, and in different degrees, running the risk of error here as elsewhere. The only practical knowledge all men have naturally and infallibly in common as a self-evident principle, intellectually perceived by virtue of the concepts involved, is that we must do good and avoid evil. This is the preamble and the principle of natural law; it is not the law itself. Natural law is the ensemble of things to do and not to do which follow therefrom in *necessary* fashion. That every sort of error and deviation is possible in the determination of these things merely proves that our sight is weak, our nature coarse, and that innumerable accidents can corrupt our judgment. Montaigne maliciously remarked that, among certain peoples, incest and thievery were considered virtuous acts. Pascal was scandalized by this. All this proves nothing against natural law, any more than a mistake in addition proves anything against arithmetic, or the mistakes of certain primitive peoples, for whom the stars were holes in the tent which covered the world, prove anything against astronomy.

Natural law is an unwritten law. Man's knowledge of it has increased little by little as man's moral conscience has developed. The latter was at first in a twilight state. Anthropologists have taught us within what structures of tribal life and in the midst of what half-awakened magic it was primitively formed. This proves merely that the knowledge men have had of the unwritten law has passed through more diverse forms and stages than certain philosophers or theologians have believed. The knowledge which our own moral conscience has of this law is doubtless still imperfect, and very likely it will continue to develop and to become more refined as long as humanity exists. Only when the Gospel has penetrated to the very depth of human substance will natural law appear in its flower and its perfection.

So the law and the knowledge of the law are two different things. Yet the law has force of law only when it is promulgated. It is only insofar as it is known and expressed in assertions of practical reason that natural law has force of law.

At this point let us stress that human reason does not discover the regulations of natural law in an abstract and theoretical manner, as a series of geometrical theorems. Nay more, it does not discover them through the conceptual exercise of the intellect, or by way of rational knowledge. I think that Thomas Aquinas's teaching, here, should be understood in a much deeper and more precise fashion than is usual. When he said that human reason discovers the regulations of natural law through the guidance of the *inclinations* of human nature, he means that the very mode or manner in which human reason knows natural law is not rational knowledge, but knowledge *through inclination.*[4] That

---

4. This is, in my opinion, the real meaning implied by St. Thomas, even though he did not use the very expression when treating of Natural Law. Knowledge through inclination is generally understood in all his doctrine on Natural Law. It alone makes this doctrine perfectly consistent. It alone squares with such statements as the following ones: "Omnia illa ad quae homo *habet naturalem inclinationem, ratio naturaliter apprehendit ut bona,* et per consequens ut opere prosequenda; et contraria eorum, ut mala et vitanda" (S.T., I–II, qu. 94, a. 2); "Ad legem naturae pertinet omne illud

ad quod homo inclinatur secundum naturam. . . . Sed, si loquamur de actibus virtuosis secundum seipsos, prout scilicet in propriis speciebus considerantur, sic *non* omnes actus virtuosi sunt de lege naturae. Multa enim secundum virtutem fiunt *ad quae natura non primo inclinat; sed per rationis inquisitionem ea homines adinvenerunt,* quasi utilia ad bene vivendum" (S.T., I–II, qu. 94, a. 3). The matter has been somewhat obscured because of the perpetual comparison that St. Thomas uses in these articles between the speculative and the practical intellect, and by reason of which he speaks

kind of knowledge is not clear knowledge through concepts and conceptual judgments; it is obscure, unsystematic, vital knowledge by connaturality or congeniality, in which the intellect, in order to bear judgment, consults and listens to the inner melody that the vibrating strings of abiding tendencies make present in the subject.[5]

When one has clearly seen this basic fact, and when, moreover, one has realized that St. Thomas's views on the matter call for an historical approach and a philosophical enforcement of the idea of development that the Middle Ages were not equipped to carry into effect, then at last one is enabled to get a completely comprehensive concept of Natural Law. And one understands that the human knowledge of natural law has been progressively shaped and molded by the inclinations of human nature, starting from the most basic ones. Do not expect me to offer an a priori picture of those genuine inclinations which are rooted in man's being as vitally permeated with the preconscious life of the mind, and which either developed or were released as the movement of mankind went on. They are evinced by the very history of human conscience. Those inclinations *were really genuine* which in the immensity of the human past have guided reason in becoming aware, little by little, of the regulations that have been most definitely and most generally recognized by the human race, starting from the most ancient social communities. For the knowledge of the primordial aspects of natural law was first expressed in social patterns rather than in personal judgments: so that we might say that our knowledge has developed within the double protecting tissue of human inclinations and human society.

With regard to the second basic element, the element of knowledge which natural law implies in order to have force of law, it thus can be said that natural law—that is, natural law *naturally known*, or, more exactly, natural law *the knowledge of which is embodied in the most general and most ancient heritage* of mankind—covers only the field of ethical regulations of which men have become aware by virtue of knowledge *through inclination*, and which are *basic principles* in moral life—progressively recognized from the most common principles to the more and more specific ones. * * *

Let us now discuss further some problems which deal with human rights in general. My first point will relate to the distinction between Natural Law and Positive Law. One of the main errors of the rationalist philosophy of human rights has been to regard positive law as a mere transcript traced off from natural law, which would supposedly prescribe

of the *propria principia* of Natural Law as "*quasi conclusiones principiorum communium*" (I–II, qu. 94, a. 4). As a matter of fact, those *propria principia* or specific precepts of Natural Law are in no way conclusions rationally deduced; they play in the practical realm a part *similar* to that of conclusions in the speculative realm. (And they appear as inferred conclusions in the "after-knowledge" of the philosophers who have to reflect upon and explain the precepts of Natural Law.)

5. For criticisms of Maritain's theory of knowledge through inclination as contrary to Aquinas's view, see Paul Ramsey, *Nine Modern Moralists* (Englewood Cliffs, N.J.: Prentice-Hall, 1962), ch. 8, ("Jacques Maritain is a revisionist among theorists of natural law; and a rather radical one") as well as, by implication, D. J. O'Connor, *Aquinas and Natural Law* (London: Macmillan, 1967), ch. 7, [*Editor*].

in the name of Nature all that which positive law prescribes in the name of society. They forgot the immense field of human things which depend on the variable conditions of social life and on the free initiative of human reason, and which natural law leaves undetermined.

As I have pointed out, *natural law* deals with the rights and the duties which are connected in a *necessary* manner with the first principle: "Do good and avoid evil." This is why the precepts of the unwritten law are in themselves or in the nature of things (I am not saying in man's knowledge of them) universal and invariable.

Jus gentium, or the *Law of Nations*, is difficult to define exactly, because it is intermediary between natural law and positive law. Let us say that in its deepest and most genuine meaning, such as put forward by Thomas Aquinas, the law of nations, or better to say, the common law of civilization, differs from natural law because it is *known*, not through inclination, but through the *conceptual exercise of reason*, or through rational knowledge,[6] in this sense it pertains to positive law, and formally constitutes a juridical order (though not necessarily written in a code). But as concerns its content, *jus gentium* comprises both things which belong also to natural law (insofar as they are not only known as rationally inferred, but also known through inclination) and things which—though obligatory in a universal manner, since concluded from a principle of natural law—are beyond the content of natural law (because they are *only* rationally inferred, and not known through inclination). In both cases *jus gentium* or the common law of civilization deals, like natural law, with rights and duties which are connected with the first principle in a necessary manner. And precisely because it is known through rational knowledge, and is itself a work of reason, it is more especially concerned with such rights and duties as exist in the realm of the basic natural work achieved by human reason, that is, the state of civil life.

Positive Law, or the body of laws (either customary law or statute law) in force in a given social group, deals with the rights and the duties which are connected with the first principle, but in a *contingent* man-

---

6. According to St. Thomas (S. T., I–II, qu. 95, a. 4) *jus gentium*—which he sharply distinguishes from natural law and connects rather with positive law—is concerned with all things that derive from natural law as *conclusions* from principles.

Yet he also teaches that the *propria principia* of Natural Law are like conclusions derived from *principia communia* (S.T., I–II, qu. 94, a. 4–6). And assuredly the *propria principia* of natural law belong to Natural Law, not to *jus gentium!* Well, in qu. 95, a. 2, St. Thomas gives the prohibition of murder as an example of a conclusion derived from a principle of natural law ("do nobody evil"), and pertaining to what is defined as *jus gentium* in art. 4. It is obvious, however, that the prohibition of murder, which is inscribed in the Decalogue, is a precept of natural law. What then?

The only way to realize the inner consistency of all that, and correctly to grasp the Thomistic distinction between Natural Law and *jus gentium*, is

to understand that a precept which is *like* a conclusion derived from a principle of natural law but which in actual fact is *known through inclination, not through rational deduction*, is part of *natural law*; but that a precept which is *known through rational deduction, and as a conclusion conceptually inferred* from a principle of natural law, is part of *jus gentium*. The latter pertains to positive law more than to natural law precisely by virtue of the manner in which it is known and because of the intervention of human reason in the establishment of the precepts conceptually concluded (whereas the *only* reason on which natural law depends is divine Reason). The prohibition of murder, in so far as this precept is *known by inclination*, belongs to natural law. The same prohibition of murder, if this precept is known as a conclusion *rationally* inferred from a principle of natural law, pertains to *jus gentium*.

ner, by virtue of the determinate ways of conduct set down by the reason and the will of man when they institute the laws or give birth to the customs of a particular society, thus stating of themselves that in the particular group in question certain things will be good and permissible, certain other things bad and not permissible.

But it is by virtue of natural law that the Law of Nations and positive law take on the force of law, and impose themselves upon the conscience. They are a prolongation or an extension of natural law, passing into objective zones which can less and less be sufficiently determined by the essential inclinations of human nature. For it is *natural law itself which requires that whatever it leaves undetermined shall subsequently be determined*, either as a right or a duty existing for all men, and of which they are made aware, not by knowledge through inclination, but by conceptual reason—that's for *jus gentium*—or—this is for positive law—as a right or a duty existing for certain men by reason of the human and contingent regulations proper to the social group of which they are a part. * * *

KAI NIELSEN

An Examination of the Thomistic Theory of Natural Moral Law †

(Nielsen's attack on Aquinas and Maritain is perhaps typical of the attitude of contemporary philosophers. It identifies Aquinas's moral theory with his outmoded scientific views, questions how one can distinguish natural from unnatural inclinations, objects to the belief that there is an essential human nature, and cites Hume to prove that the Thomistic belief in a purposive nature confuses statements of fact and statements of value which are logically distinct.)

Aquinas and contemporary Thomists like Maritain and Copleston give a large place to reason in their Christian ethical theory. They argue that if man doubts God's revealed Word, he can by the use of his reason come to know that God exists and that there are certain natural moral laws carrying obligations. By his reason alone, man can know certain natural goods. Aquinas's approach here bears the stamp of Aristotle's "commonsensical philosophy of ethics."

Though "metaphysical ethics" is now out of fashion in most quarters, Aquinas's theory has no plausibility at all apart from his conception of the nature of the universe. In evaluating Aquinas's ethics we must keep constantly in mind his physics and cosmology. As Copleston remarks, Aquinas "sees the moral life in the general setting of the providential

† *Natural Law Forum*, IV, 1 (1959). By permission.

government of creatures" (p. 212),[1] that is to say, Aquinas, like Aristotle, thinks the universe is purposive. It has a destiny and a rationale. The universe is not just some vast machine or conglomeration of atoms swirling in the void. The end of all activities in nature, says Aquinas, is God. In medieval physics, it is believed that all natural motions are just so many attempts to reach the changeless. Sublunar substances seek reestablishment in their proper places. Celestial motions cannot falter; they return upon themselves in perfect circles. Nevertheless, they are still motions. Only God is absolutely motionless and changeless. All motions and all things try to attain God, the motionless or changeless Being. We know that knowledge of and union with God is man's highest good; all other goods are finally instrumental to that good. But as Sisyphus sticks to his job with his stone, we ineluctably quest for that highest good. We know God exists, but we contingent, changing creatures never obtain God or knowledge of His essence in this life. But, unlike Sisyphus, we mortals have a surcease from striving, for after death there is a complete apprehension of God in His very essence.

Maritain emphasizes that conceptions of the natural moral law cannot be secularized, as in Grotius or Paine, without cutting out their very heart. The natural moral law theory only makes sense in terms of an acceptance of medieval physics and cosmology. If we give up the view that the universe is purposive and that all motions are just so many attempts to reach the changeless, we must give up natural moral law theories. One might say, as a criticism of the Thomistic doctrine of natural moral law, that since medieval physics is false then it follows that natural moral law theory must be false. While agreeing with this criticism, I think it is too short and too easy a way out to carry complete conviction. Contemporary Thomists would like to say that somehow the medieval view of cosmology or metaphysics is distinct from physics, and though the physics is false, the cosmology is still true. This seems to me just an evasion. If the word 'cosmology' means anything at all, it seems only to denote bad armchair physics. The so-called disciplines of cosmology and metaphysics have made no progress in discovering the categorial features of the world. This is so partly because of the very unsettled and indefinite signification of the words 'cosmology' and 'metaphysics.' In such a situation, it seems to me quite unrealistic to think we can use such disciplines as a basis for anything very substantial. * * *

Let us now consider difficulties in Maritain's conception of "knowledge through inclination." First, the work of philosophical analysts like Ryle and Wittgenstein makes it questionable whether one can sensibly speak of a kind of knowing "inexpressible in words and notions." To call something that cannot be conceptualized or expressed "knowledge" seems like an early retreat into a kind of obscurity that makes philosophical appraisal impossible. How can we, if we doubt there is really such a kind of knowing, rationally resolve this doubt? Or, even more basically, what

1. F. C. Copleston, *Aquinas* (Baltimore, Md.: Penguin Books, 1955).

is it that Maritain is claiming? It is a truism to say that in philosophical *appraisal* we must necessarily deal with what is expressible.

My second critical point about his doctrine of knowledge through inclination is connected with the last part of my second positive point. In effect, Maritain sets forth a naturalistic theory at the foundation of natural moral law: what man strives for is good and what man avoids is bad. But at the same time he claims that only a supernatural sanction will do for morality and will avoid the chaos of our time. Yet, on his doctrine of knowledge through inclination and on his natural moral law theory, the man in moral perplexity needs only to observe the desires and wishes of his fellow man and by seeing what they generally seek he will know what is good and what he ought to do. * * *

Let us now consider the actual precepts of the natural moral law. "Good is to be done and gone after, and evil is to be avoided" is the primary natural moral law from which all others are derived, and it is the first principle of practical reason. Aquinas and his contemporary followers insist that all the other natural laws are based on this vacuous first principle of natural moral law. This, of course, is a very weak base indeed. For, unless we assign some denotation to the word "good," as used above, this first principle of the natural moral law we cannot determine what the denotata or criteria of application of "good" will be. All we can conclude from this primary principle is that if something is good we have to seek it. It does not tell us what to seek. (Is Aquinas's statement here really anything more than a bit of linguistic information, disguised because it is stated in the material mode? Is Aquinas, here, really saying anything more than "If we call something 'good' then we must also say that it is something that is to be sought, everything else being equal"? But this informs us about our linguistic behavior; it hardly gives us the foundation of an objective rational ethic that will save us from the "dark night of subjectivity.")

Our knowledge of the other natural moral laws is much less certain. We know them (as Maritain most emphatically argues) immediately and nonconceptually by natural inclination. They are the ends we necessarily seek in virtue of our very humanity. We might list the ones Aquinas mentions, stating them clearly as normatives, so as to bring out their moral force.

1.   Life ought to be preserved.
2.   Man ought to propagate his kind.
3.   Children ought to be educated.
4.   Men ought to know the truth about God.
5.   Man ought to live in society.
6.   Ignorance ought to be avoided.
7.   Offense ought not to be given unnecessarily.

These are all supposedly based, in some manner, on man's natural inclinations. It is claimed they are based on human nature. However, according to Aquinas, not all our inclinations are natural inclinations, for some can be "corrupted by vicious habits," and again the natural knowledge of good in them (people with vicious habits) is "darkened by passions and habits of sin." Aquinas is contending that there are some cross-cultural or pan-human characteristics that we might use in constructing a definition of "human nature." Like Plato, Aquinas is claiming that man is distinguished from the other animals by his ability to reason. If man examines his natural inclinations, he will discover that there are certain unalterable pan-human natural moral laws. Copleston states Aquinas's argument here in the following manner: "For although man cannot read off, as it were, eternal law in God's Mind, he can discern the fundamental tendencies and needs of his nature, and by reflecting on them he can come to know the natural moral law." (p. 213) Copleston continues: "Every man possesses also the light of reason, whereby he can reflect on these fundamental inclinations of his nature and promulgate to himself the natural moral law. . . ." (p. 213) Purely natural man is not left in ignorance of the eternal law which is the ultimate rule of all conduct. The natural law part of the eternal law is not simply a Divine Fiat. Rather, we moral agents recognize its inherent rationally binding force. Though the first principle of natural law only tells us that good is to be done and evil is to be avoided, we give concrete content or non-zero denotation to our concept of good and evil "by examining the fundamental natural tendencies or inclinations of man." (p. 215) By examining man's nature and natural inclinations one can discern the good for man in the natural order.

Now, St. Thomas does distinguish between primary and secondary precepts of the natural moral law. The secondary precepts are not relative. But they do have only a limited contextual application, that is, they apply only to certain classes of acts. As Copleston remarks, what Aquinas means in saying that they can be changed is that such natural moral laws are altered when the circumstances of the act may be such that it no longer falls into the class of actions prohibited by the precept. Copleston uses the following example: "We can say in general that if someone entrusts his property to us for safekeeping and asks for it back, we ought to return it. No sensible man would say that if someone entrusts us with a knife or a revolver and asks for it back when he is in a state of homicidal mania, we are obliged to return it." (p. 219) Copleston then generalizes: "In its general form, however, the precept remains valid. We can say with truth that Aquinas believed in a set of unalterable moral precepts." (p. 219)

As clear as Aquinas's kind of theory may seem the first time around, it becomes far more difficult to comprehend after a closer look. Its taxonomic structure hides fundamental confusions, though on Aquinas's behalf it must be said that they were confusions which might naturally arise in his cultural context.

In pointing up these difficulties, I shall first turn to two standard difficulties that have been traditional stumbling blocks for students of natural moral law theories. I do not think these are the most basic difficulties, but I do think these standard difficulties are genuine and need looking into. I doubt that they can be answered satisfactorily from within the Thomistic position of natural moral law. I shall examine them first and then turn to what I regard to be the two more philosophically interesting and more basic difficulties in the natural moral law theory.

The first standard difficulty emerges when we compare the natural moral law theory with some of the things now being said in social psychology. It is frequently said that *from the point of view of science*, there is no such thing as an essential human nature which makes a man a man. The concept of human nature is a rather vague cultural concept; it is not a scientific one. While I think this criticism is surely debatable, it does raise a problem for the natural moral law theory since it is clear that the statement, "there is an essential human nature," is not the obvious, self-evidently true statement Aquinas and his contemporary followers take it to be.

The second standard criticism is a stronger one. It appeals to the facts of cultural relativity. If we go to actual cultures and study them, we find that all of the natural moral laws listed above by Aquinas are broken somewhere by some people. If it is answered, "Well, most cultures obey the above rules," two replies can be made.

First, it can be said that the reply in itself assumes that what most people find natural and better, is natural and better. To assume this, however, is to presuppose the value of a naive kind of democracy; we determine what is good by counting noses or by a Gallup Poll. Moral issues become vote issues. Aquinas, of course, would not wish to say they are "vote issues." Moreover, why must we accept this "democratic" standard as our ultimate standard? If we say that people simply do accept it, we not only make a statement that is anthropologically false, but we also go in a circle. We use our democratic standard to establish our democratic standard. Secondly, it is the case that for the natural moral laws which are fairly concrete, there is not this majority agreement. If we turn to the more general natural moral laws, we find that they are so vague that they hide all sorts of differences that both parties would regard as crucial. As anthropologists, like Ralph Linton, have pointed out, all cultures have a concept of murder. But if we try to give the concept of murder some specific content which would cover its use in all cultures, we run into difficulty. While all cultures agree that murder is wrong, this is completely compatible with the Eskimos' killing members of their family if they do not feel they can make it through the winter; or with infanticide in Polynesia and Greece; or with the old Scandinavian habit of clubbing one's older ancestors to death so that they may go to Valhalla. But for these people this killing is not murder which is by implicit definition wrong. Just what will count as murder in the given culture varies radically. To say that all cultures have a concept of murder tends to obscure basic radical moral differences. To suggest that these are just indeterminate expressions of the basic moral law blurs a crucial way in which our judgments of good and evil are relative.

There are two more basic difficulties with Thomistic natural moral law theory that I would like to consider now. First, even if it is the case (contrary to what was said above) that there is basic cross-cultural universal acceptance of certain fundamental moral beliefs and/or attitudes, it would *not* follow that the Thomistic natural moral law ethic had been established. This agreement could be explained at least as adequately by a theological voluntarism, the kind of meta-ethic offered by Russell and Hume, or by a Deweyian kind of naturalism. Russell, for example, would not talk of an apprehension of natural moral law emanating from God. He could explain the same facts by saying that those common moral ideals are expressions of commonly held attitudes or commonly felt emotions. They express the common decisions we men make in virtue of our common interests and similar make-up. Recalling that Aquinas and Maritain must invoke the strange doctrine of "knowledge through inclination," it might well be argued that Russell's kind of theory is to be preferred because it is simpler. Applying Ockham's razor, we might naturally remark that Aquinas's "hypothesis" is one we can well dispense with.

The same point can be put differently. Because we have (if we have) a common human nature and in accordance with it make certain common moral appraisals, it does not follow that there is a natural moral law in the Thomist's sense. Even if it is true "that all men share some very vague ideas about the good for man, precisely because they are men who possess certain natural tendencies and inclinations in common," this does not serve as a proof that these shared ethical ideals are *God—given* rather than man-made. It does not even serve to make such a belief plausible. One can accept some pan-human agreement about what man's good is without being committed to Aquinas's moral philosophy. As a matter of fact, Erich Fromm makes a similar argument from a naturalistic and neo-Freudian point of view.

It must be added that this form of "natural moral law" based on universally shared attitudes is not enough for Aquinas, for it does not establish that they are self-evident, unchanging moral laws. Thomists need a stronger basis than the unity of human nature to establish their natural moral law theory. If there is no unity or common human nature, the Thomists are clearly wrong; but if there is a unity or common nature to the human animal, it does not follow that the Thomists are right.

I suggest, finally, that the whole theory rests on the confusion between *what ought to be* and *what is*. As Hume made us realize, the statement, "Man ought not to steal," is quite different from the statement, "Man does steal." Men steal when they ought not. Sentences with an "ought" in them belong to a different *logical type* than sentences with an "is" in them. From factual statements alone, including statements of fact about human nature, we cannot deduce or derive any "ought" statement whatsoever. Values and facts are distinct, and Aquinas and his followers are not clear about this distinction, precisely because they looked upon nature as purposive, as having some kind of moral end in itself. This conception of a purposive nature is not only false but it also serves to obfuscate the basic distinction between facts and values that is so essential if we are to understand the nature of moral argument and decision. * * *

VERNON J. BOURKE

Natural Law, Thomism—and Professor Nielsen †

(Bourke replies to Neilsen by arguing for teleology or "end-directedness in the activities of men and of other things in nature." He also argues for a bridge between fact and value either through belief in God as a source of moral obligation or through pursuit of moral goodness as a conditional necessity for individual and social fulfillment.)

* * * If Thomistic natural law thinking today requires acceptance of Aristotle's *Physics*, then I do not favor such thinking.

Here we come to the heart of the matter. Probably Neilsen does not see much difference between a medieval physics and a metaphysics. They talk about natures in both. Yet the Thomist metaphysician makes the greatest effort to understand the judgment that being is not confined to bodily existents. The kind of natural law reasoning identified with much present-day Thomism centers on another metaphysical judgment: that there are certain specific "natures" (say, dog, tree, man) which can be understood universally. These natures are not regarded as existing individual things, nor are they fictions of the human mind. What, then, are they? To answer this question is difficult, because of the weight of much modern thinking which tends to discredit the notion of a universal.

Take the judgment: "water freezes at 32 degrees F., under certain conditions of pressure and purity." What is the meaning of "water" in this proposition? Of course it is an object of thought but the point is that the judgment is not arbitrary. The judgment implies that a number of things, recognizable as "waters" in different times and places, behave in this way. If someone finds a new kind of "water" that does not freeze in this way, then he has found a new nature. Much physical science still deals precisely with such natures. This is so of the descriptive rather than the mathematical sciences. The ordinary chemist is not interested simply in the sulphuric acid in his own bottle. He desires to know certain properties typical of this acid, whenever and wherever it is found. Water is a universal object of study and understanding (and practical use); it is real or thingish, because there are many individual instances of existing "waters." A circle is also a universal object of understanding but it is not real, because there are no instances of circles existing as individual things. This is the reason why physical science is not mathematics.

No Thomist professes to have an exhaustive knowledge of the real "natures" of things. Nor do I know any serious representatives of Thomism who claims to be able to deduce the rules of natural law from his knowledge of the "nature" of man. Other natures than that of man are involved in human activity. To put it very briefly: it is a different matter, consciously and deliberately, to drink water, liquor, and sulphuric acid. Our variables are three different liquids that produce different results within the man who performs much the same action in drinking them.

It is practical and morally advisable to know which of these liquids to drink. Such information does not enable us to judge immediately that natural law "tells us" that a man ought to drink water and not acid. Unfortunately, many Catholic writers have fallen into the habit of speaking as if it did. Notice that I have passed over the problem of what to say about drinking liquor: it is obviously much more complicated. Circumstances, other things than the natures of man and liquor, must be known before one could make a practical judgment on it. There are many fringe cases like this, where the average person is frankly puzzled at times in trying to determine what is right. It is not advisable to give the impression that mere adherence to natural law thinking provides immediate and infallible judgments on all moral issues. On the other hand, there are some actions that are, under usual circumstances, suitable for a man to do; and others are not. These homely examples illustrate the first point that I wish to make: "natures"—in the realistic sense suggested above—are important to our understanding of the theory of natural law. More than human nature is involved. And we do not learn about these "natures" from Aristotle's *Physics* but from our own experience of reality.

At this point it may be helpful to distinguish two kinds of knowledge of natural law: a) the way in which most men (not moral scientists) may grasp natural moral law; and b) the way in which a moral expert reflects on, and endeavors to offer a scientific or philosophical explanation of natural law. This distinction is important to our reading of Maritain. He writes, of course, as a moral expert but about what he sometimes calls "natural" (untrained, unreflective, non-philosophical) moral knowledge. When Maritain speaks of nonconceptual, connatural knowledge, or knowledge by inclination, he is talking about level a) above. He is asserting that the ordinary person grasps certain natural law notions of attitudes in a vague, nonreflective manner. This ordinary grasping is a combination of low-grade cognitive and affective activity. Sometimes it is close to animal feeling. Such a "natural" knower is related to the moral scientist in somewhat the same way that a natural singer is to a trained teacher of singing.

Maritain is trying to describe the bases within the moral agent for his own moral decisions. Maritain cannot make these ordinary moral experiences any clearer than they actually are in the average person. Consider the so-called synderesis principle: *Good should be done; evil should be avoided*. To say with Maritain that this generalized rule is known to all men is not to claim that all, or even most, men can and will state the rule, when called upon to justify their moral decisions. Rather, Maritain's view is (and it is the position of most Thomists) that practically all men show some concern (both affective and cognitive) for right and wrong. I say most men. Some unwary Thomists may say that all men do. However, as Hobbes and Locke and Nielsen, and others, have said, there are some classes of men who do not show that they can discriminate between right and wrong. These atypical people are: very young children, fools, and certain highly sophisticated ethicians. I think we can exclude the first two classes: time will cure the children; and insane people are not regarded as responsible, legally or morally, precisely because they lack an awareness of such values. The professors of ethics are not the ordinary people that Maritain is talking about. I realize that I am passing over the really difficult point, here. Some appeal to what is "normal" is made, consciously or unconsciously, in talking about such exceptions. This introduces the notion of what a nature is for, of finality in natures.

Thomists think that every action and every real thing that exists has some end. This is teleology. It is Aristotle's old theory of final causality. For Aquinas, finality has a different explanation, however, from that given by Aristotle. St. Thomas took it that God is the creator and providential governor of man and his universe. Aristotle did not. In the Thomistic view, God's intelligence directs all natural things and actions, in an orderly way, to their ends, just as an archer aims his arrow at the target. All finite natures have, in this position, a vector quality which God gives to them. This is true of man's nature, too. However, Aquinas thought that men control some of their activities and may direct them toward the end of man, if they wish. Man is free. Otherwise, man would be a physical but not a moral agent.

Is there evidence of end-directedness in the activities of men and of other things in nature? That there is some such evidence is not usually disputed. The biological and social disciplines make considerable use of purposive analyses. The concept of the "function" of a physiological member is teleological. Oddly, most evolutionary theories introduce some surreptitious notions of purpose. Self-perfectionism is an internal form of teleology: it is the kind of finality that we find in the biology of Aristotle. At one point, Nielsen remarks that anthropology does not back up the Thomistic notion of a purposive human nature. I can hardly think that he is serious about this. Without quoting chapter and verse, I should like to remind him that there is a strong movement in recent American anthropology in this direction. Some of the leading names in the field (Kluckhohn, Malinowski, Kroeber, Redfield, Evans-Pritchard, Montague) see man as a very distinctive nature. Indeed, one of the basic assumptions of anthropology is that man is the only culture-producing animal.

There is, finally, a point of criticism that is found throughout Nielsen's appraisal of Thomistic natural law theory: you can't get an *ought* from an *is*. The fact that things exist or happen in a certain way does not mean that they should do so. This is a well-known dilemma in contemporary ethics and value theory.

I think that this difficulty is set up by taking the terms *is* and *ought* (or fact and value) in a narrow, unrealistic sense.

Consider the *ought* part of it, first. This term expresses some sort of obligation or necessity. The necessity implied cannot be absolute, in the sense that agents who come under it must do what is required and cannot do otherwise. One does not tell a man that he ought to obey the "law" of gravity—he cannot avoid it. But the foregoing use of "absolute" in connection with necessity is only one way of employing the term. In the time of Kant (when most philosophers were theists and very conscious of the weight of moral duty) one could talk about an "absolute" moral necessity in a different way. God was there as an absolute lawgiver, dwelling in power and majesty above all men. In such a view, God may function as an absolute Monarch: what He requires *ought* to be done, or else. To many thinkers in the eighteenth and the nineteenth century, the "or else" implied very real sanctions. If you didn't obey God's commands you ended in Hell. This sort of *ought* is compatible with human freedom (and so, is not a type of physical necessity) but it is an obligation imposed on all men whether they choose to recognize it or not. (Parenthetically, it is well to note that the Thomist thinks that God does so command men, and that it is not possible for men to evade moral duty by not thinking of it; but the forces of this necessity is lost if God is left out of the picture.)

What Kant did with this has caused trouble in philosophy ever since. He tried to see whether you could retain this strong meaning of the moral ought, even if you ignored sanctions (punishments and rewards), and even if you ignored God as the absolute Lawmaker. He asked the odd question: Can man find within himself a sufficient source for such a duty, such an absolute ought? (This is one of those Irish questions to which Kant was addicted—something like his question: how can we know a thing-in-itself if we define the *Ding-an-sich* as that which is outside knowledge?) Ever since Kant's time, moral philosophers have been plagued by this question: How to find an absolute *ought*, if we do away with absolutes?

It seems rather obvious to me that, without God in one's moral view, the moral ought can only represent a conditional necessity. Kant saw this and introduced God as guarantor of the *summum bonum*. Otherwise, ought names an "if A, then B" sequence. Some British writers on ethics ridicule the idea that a moral ought is anything like the statement that a carpenter ought to use a certain tool to achieve a desired result. However, a conditional necessity is difficult to construe in the practical order, unless we introduce the notion of the utility of certain means to achieve a given end. That is probably why most British ethicians have still a lingering respect for social utilitarianism. The good of society is a respectable goal and may be used to decide many moral questions. It does not help, however, with some of the most difficult questions of private morality.

If we bracket the existence of God as moral legislator, then we must reduce our meaning of the moral *ought* to the notion of utility for a certain end. One way of putting this is to admit that no man is forced to work for happiness, or well-being, or self-perfection. Any person may reject the whole concept of working for an end that is suitable to his nature. In doing so, he has repudiated the only basis on which a moral ought can be given a workable meaning, apart from divine law. To me, a naturalistic moral *ought* means that a person must do certain actions and avoid others, or take the consequences of an unfulfilled and imperfect human life. This is a reason for trying to do one's best but it is not an absolute one.

* * * G. E. Moore made the naturalistic fallacy famous. In doing so, he perpetuated a far more dangerous moral fallacy: the notion that, if good is not a natural property, it must be a nonnatural one. These are not the only alternatives. Good, right, wrong, and other such moral terms name complex relations, not properties. It takes understanding to grasp them. Thomism has a long and perhaps overcomplicated explanation of the working of the human intellect. It differs radically from most modern theories of knowledge. What is essential in it is the claim that man knows on two levels: he senses individuals and he understands universals.

In regard to the philosophy of law, the understanding of universal relations, meanings, implications, tendencies, goods, obligations is of primary importance. So it appears to a Thomist. A law is not sense "fact"; whatever else it is, a law is some sort of universal. It applies to many possible subjects, in a variety of circumstances. Clearly a theory of knowledge that reduces all human experience to atomized, isolated, unrelated sense impressions cannot give an account of law. Nor can it account for obligation, moral or legal.

I am far from suggesting that Thomism offers a fully developed explanation of all that natural law implies. More attention to the multiple experiences of modern life is needed. More cooperation with social scientists is advisable. Modern Thomists are not yet doing a proper job of making their position clear to their colleagues. Nielsen does a real service in demanding a better presentation of the natural law theory. Of course, communication is a two-way affair; it cannot all be accomplished by Thomists. To me it is encouraging to see a non-Thomist offering a searching criticism of Thomism.

REINHOLD NIEBUHR

Christian Faith and Natural Law †

(A leading twentieth century Protestant theologian, Niebuhr criticizes Thomistic natural law as too dependent on a natural justice that is difficult, if not impossible, to achieve in a sinful world. He argues for a more open notion of justice related to the Christian doctrine of supernatural love.)

* * * The facts of human history are more complex than either the traditional Catholic or Protestant doctrines of natural order and natural law suggest.

According to Thomistic doctrine, the Fall robbed man of a *donum superadditum*[1] but left him with a *pura naturalia*,[2] which includes a capacity for natural justice. What is lost is a capacity for faith, hope, and love—that is, the ability to rise above the natural order and have communion with divine and supernatural order, to know God and, in fellowship with him, to be delivered of the fears, anxieties, and sins which result from this separation from God. The fallen man is thus essentially an incomplete man, who is completed by the infusion of sacramental grace, which restores practically, though not quite, all of the supernatural virtues which were lost in the Fall. The Fall does not seriously impair man's capacity for natural justice. Only this is an incomplete perfection, incapable of itself to rise to the heights of love.

According to Protestant theology, the Fall had much more serious consequences. It left man "totally corrupt" and "utterly leprous and unclean." The very reason which in Catholic thought is regarded as the instrument and basis of natural justice is believed in Protestant thought to be infected by the Fall and incapable of arriving at any true definition of justice. Calvin is slightly more equivocal about the effects of sin upon reason than Luther, and as a consequence Calvinism does not relegate the natural law and the whole problem of justice so completely to the background as does Lutheranism. Nevertheless, the theory of total depravity is only slightly qualified in Calvinism.

I should like to maintain that the real crux of the human situation is missed in both the Catholic and the Protestant version of the effect of sin upon man's capacity for justice. Something more than a brief paper would be required to prove such a thesis; I must content myself therefore with suggesting the argument in general outline.

The Biblical conception of man includes three primary terms: (a) he is made in the image of God, (b) he is a creature, and (c) he is a sinner. His basic sin is pride. If this pride is closely analyzed, it is discovered to be man's unwillingness to acknowledge his creatureliness. He is betrayed

† Reinhold Niebuhr, "Christian Faith and Natural Law," *Theology*, XL, 236 (Feb. 1940). Reprinted by permission of the Society for Promoting Christian Knowledge.

1. super-added gift [*Editor*].
2. purely natural characteristics [*Editor*].

by his greatness to hide his weakness. He is tempted by his ability to gain his own security to deny his insecurity, and refuses to admit that he has no final security except in God. He is tempted by his knowledge to deny his ignorance. (This is the source of all "ideological taint" in human knowledge.) It is not that man in his weakness has finite perspectives that makes conflicts between varying perspectives so filled with fanatic fury in all human history; it is that man denies the finiteness of his perspectives that tempts him to such fanatic cruelty against those who hold convictions other than his own. The quintessence of sin is, in short, that man "changes the glory of the incorruptible God into the image of corruptible man." He always usurps God's place and claims to be the final judge of human actions.

The loss of man's original perfection therefore never leaves him with an untarnished though incomplete natural justice. All statements and definitions of justice are corrupted by even the most rational men through the fact that the definition is colored by interest. This is the truth in the Marxist theory of rationalization and in its assertion that all culture is corrupted by an ideological taint. The unfortunate fact about the Marxist theory is that it is used primarily as a weapon in social conflict. The enemy is charged with this dishonesty, but the Marxist himself claims to be free of it. This is, of course, merely to commit the final sin of self-righteousness and to imagine ourselves free of the sin which we discern in the enemy. The fact that we do not discern it in ourselves is a proof of our sin and not of our freedom from sin. Christ's parable of the mote and the beam is a perfect refutation of this illusion.

The fact remains, nevertheless, that reason is not capable of defining any standard of justice that is universally valid or acceptable. Thus Thomistic definitions of justice are filled with specific details which are drawn from the given realities of a feudal social order and may be regarded as "rationalizations" of a feudal aristocracy's dominant position in society. (The much-praised Catholic prohibition of usury could be maintained only as long as the dominant aristocratic class were borrowers rather than lenders of money. When the static wealth of the landowners yielded to the more dynamic wealth of the financiers and industrialists, the prohibition of usury vanished. Catholics hold Protestantism responsible for this development, but it is significant that the Catholic Church makes no effort to impose the prohibition of usury upon its own bourgeois members.)

Bourgeois idealists of the eighteenth century invented new natural law theories and invested them with bourgeois rather than feudal-aristocratic content. The natural law of the eighteenth century was supposed to be descriptive rather than prescriptive. It was, more exactly, a "law of nature" rather than a "law of reason." But its real significance lay in its specific content. The content of this law justified the bourgeois classes in their ideals, just as the older law justified the feudal aristocrats. In short, it is not possible to state a universally valid concept of justice from any particular sociological locus in history. Nor is it possible to avoid either making the effort or making pretenses of universality which human finiteness does not justify. This inevitable pretense is the revelation of "original sin" in history. Human history is consequently more tragic than Catholic theology assumes. It is not an incomplete world yearning for completion, and finding it in the incarnation. It is a tragic world, troubled not by finiteness so much as by "false eternals" and false absolutes, and expressing the pride of these false absolutes even in the highest reaches of its spirituality. It is not the incarnation as such that is the good news of the gospel, but rather the revelation of a just God who is also merciful; this is the true content of the incarnation. That is, it is the atonement that fills the incarnation with meaning.

But Catholic thought not only fails to do justice to the positive character of the sinful element in all human definitions and realizations of natural justice. It also fails to do justice to the relation of love to justice. In its conception, natural justice is good as far as it goes, but it must be completed by the supernatural virtue of love. The true situation is that anything short of love cannot be perfect justice. In fact, every definition of justice actually presupposes sin as a given reality. It is only because life is in conflict with life, because of sinful self-interest, that we are required carefully to define schemes of justice which prevent one life from taking advantage of another. Yet no scheme of justice can do full justice to all the variable factors which the freedom of man introduces into human history. Significantly, both eighteenth century and medieval conceptions of natural law are ultimately derived from Stoic conceptions. And it is the very nature of Stoic philosophy that it is confused about the relation of nature to reason. This confusion is due to the fact that it does not fully understand the freedom of man. In all Greco-Roman rationalism, whether Platonic, Aristotelian, or Stoic, it is assumed that man's freedom is secured by his rational transcendence over nature. Since reason and freedom are identified, it is assumed that the freedom that man has over nature is held in check and disciplined by his reason. The real situation is that man transcends his own reason, which is to say that he is not bound in his actions by reason's coherences and systems. His freedom consists in a capacity for self-transcendence in infinite regression. There is therefore no limit in reason for either his creativity or his sin. There is no possibility of giving a rational definition of a just relation between man and man or nation and nation short of a complete love in which each life affirms the interests of the other. Every effort to give a definition of justice short of this perfect love invariably introduces contingent factors, conditions of time and place, into the definition.

Love is the only final structure of freedom. Human personality as a system of infinite potentialities makes it impossible to define absolutely what I owe to my fellow man, since nothing that he now is exhausts what he might be. Human personality as capacity for infinite self-transcendence makes it impossible from my own standpoint to rest content in any ordered relation with my fellow men. There is no such relation that I cannot transcend to imagine a better one in terms of the ideal of love. Provisional definitions of justice short of this perfect love, are, of course, necessary. But they are much more provisional than any natural law theory, whether medieval or modern, realizes. The freedom of man is too great to make it possible to define any scheme of justice absolutely in terms of "necessary" standards.

According to Catholic theology, it is this structure of ultimate freedom that is lost in the Fall just as the accompanying virtue of love is lost. The real situation is that "original justice" in the sense of a mythical "perfection before the Fall" is never completely lost. It is not a reality in man but always a potentiality. It is always what he ought to be. It is the only goodness completely compatible with his own and his fellow man's freedom—that is, with their ultimate transcendence over all circumstances of nature. Man is neither as completely bereft of "original justice" nor as completely in possession of "natural justice" as the Catholic theory assumes * * * all human life stands under an ideal possibility purer than the natural law, and * * * at the same time it is involved in sinful reality much more dubious than the natural justice that Catholic thought declares to be possible. * * *

Contemporary Problems in Thomistic Ethics

THE JUST WAR AND SELF-DEFENSE

PAUL RAMSEY

War and the Christian Conscience †

(In the discussion of St. Thomas in his book, Ramsey argues that Aquinas's analysis of the morality of self-defense is influenced by a Christian ethic of "justice transformed by love." He also analyzes the principle of double effect, often attributed to Aquinas, and concludes that saturation bombing as well as, *a fortiori*, nuclear counter-cities strategies are contrary to Thomistic— and Christian—ethics.)

* * * If a man, in self-defense, uses more than necessary violence, it will be unlawful: whereas if he repel force with moderation his defense will be lawful, because according to the jurists, *it is lawful to repel force by force, provided one does not exceed the limits of a blameless defense.* Nor is it necessary for salvation that a man omit the act of self-defense in order to avoid killing the other man, since one is bound to take more care of one's own life than of another's. But as it is unlawful to take a man's life, except for the public authority acting for the common good, as stated above, it is not lawful for a man to intend killing a man in self-defense, except for such as have public authority, who while intending to kill a man in self-defense refer this to the public good, as in the case of a soldier fighting against the foe, and in the minister or the judge struggling with robbers, although even these sin if they be moved by private animosity (*S.T., II–II, qu. 64, a.7*).

† Paul Ramsey, *War and the Christian Conscience: How Shall Modern War Be Conducted Justly?* (Durham, N.C.: Duke University Press, 1961). Copyright © 1961 by Duke University Press. Reprinted by permission of the publisher.

This is a remarkable passage, deserving close scrutiny. In it Aquinas does *not* say that, because of the principles of natural justice, an unjust assailant may be killed without more ado or more to think about. The only case in which it is right to intend to kill even an unjust assailant would seem to be when, in acting for the public defense, one refers this intentional killing as a means to the public good. Aquinas does not require, as Augustine does, the individual who is unjustly attacked to omit the *act* of private self-defense; but he does require him to omit directing his *intention* against even an unjust man. This "doubling" of the will's intention for love's sake produces, as we shall see, the first formulation of the rule of "double effect." No more than Augustine does Aquinas first justify direct killing in self-defense. He does not say that it is intrinsically right to intend to kill an onrushing, unjust assailant, and then apply this general rule to the case of action in defense of the common good. Intending to kill a man as a means to the public good is clearly an exception to the basic rule (which still remains in force) that no Christian shall intend to kill any man.

Instead, in terms of the ethical standard he has in mind, the only case of direct, intentional killing Aquinas, no less than Augustine, finds warranted he regards as an exception to the rule. "It it not lawful for a man to intend killing a man in self-defense," he says without any qualification, "except for such as have public authority," or who are acting for the public authority charged with preserving the common good. These "while intending to kill a man in self-defense refer this to the public good." Such would still be a direct intention to kill, even though as a means referred to the public good as an end. Shall we say that in this instance, it is right to do evil that good may come of it? Or that, in this instance alone as an exception, the means used—the direct killing of the unjust aggressor—should be judged to be right in itself?

Be that as it may, it is significant that Aquinas has much the same trouble in his Christian conscience as Augustine did when dealing with the case of private self-defense. He does not subsume the just war and domestic police action, along with action to be approved when an individual's life or property are attacked, all under the same rubric of the intrinsic justifiability of killing an unjust aggressor, nor even under the principle that "one is bound to take more care of one's own life than of another's," which has in Aquinas's thought a controlling position it did not have for Augustine. For only in taking responsibility for the public good to which one has allegiance more than for the public good of another, is the direct killing of an unjust aggressor justified; while this is not the case in taking more care of one's own life than of another's. No matter how many canonists may have declared it always to be right, as a general principle, to defend, with every proportionate and necessary means, justice against injustice, it is clear that Aquinas still thinks about these questions from the point of view of love, or of love-transformed-justice, even if not to the measure this was operative in Augustine's thought. In order to wrest from his ancient moral heritage practical, down-to-earth conclusions, while as a Christian unable to depart wholly from it, this great Doctor of the Church was driven to formulate, for the first time clearly, the principle of the double effect.

This principle has two aspects, one subjective and primary, the other objective and secondary. As to the first, Aquinas observes that one and the same action may have two effects, only one of which is intended, the other unintended or beside the intention of the other (the good) effect. In the case of private self-defense, the intention is ordered directly to the good of saving one's own life, while the other effect, unavoidably associated with the first, the slaying of the aggressor, is beside the intention. No more in Aquinas (who allows killing the onrushing assailant) than in Augustine (who does not) is the direct intention to kill justified on the part of a Christian or a truly "just" and "wise" man. This is, indeed, a justice and a wisdom schooled by Jesus Christ; and, indeed, the "law" has been transformed by love in reaching the conclusion that, under these conditions, self-defense is not "unlawful."

* * *

In an excellent article that deserves to be better known in Protestant circles on "The Morality of Obliteration Bombing,[1] Fr. John C. Ford vigorously opposes that barbaric departure from the tradition of civilized warfare which bears the name of "strategic" or "area" bombing. In order to do this effectively he found it necessary to reject any such interpretation of the rule of double effect, when applied to the killing of innocent people, as would "find a simple solution to the moral problem merely by advising the air strategist to let go his bombs, but withhold his intention."[2]

* * *

Area bombing, unlike the destruction of a specific target, cannot be regarded as "twofold in its immediate efficiency," either in fact or (by a subterfuge) in intention. It *de facto* contributes as a means to the victory (the good) desired, even if by a great deal of peculiar psychological effort it may not be explicitly willed as a means. A man could not, even if he wanted to, avoid the direct willing of an evil effect so immediately consequent upon his action as this is;[3] moreover, he would not if he could, and there is plenty of evidence that he does not endeavor to do so. Thus Fr. Ford states together the first two points in the logic of his argument, which is more succinctly expressed elsewhere: "It is my contention that the civil and military leaders who would plan and execute the dropping of a series of high megaton H-Bombs on an area like Moscow or New York: (1) *would not* in practice avoid the direct intention of violence to the innocent; (2) *could not* if they would; and (3) even if they would and could avoid it, would have no proportionate justifying reason for per-

1. *Theological Studies*, V, 3 (Sept., 1944), pp. 261–309.

2. *Ibid.*, p. 289.

3. *Ibid.*, p. 290.

mitting the evils which this type of all-out nuclear warfare would let loose."[4]

Even to devise a policy of area bombing contains the implicit distinction between this and the aim of only allowing the death of many innocent people while destroying specific military targets, and only by explicitly rejecting the latter as not enough does a policy of obliteration come to be adopted by our military leaders. The objective immorality of such a policy seems evident, and the measure of this is taken from the fact that the rule of the double effect cannot rightly be applied to the killing of the innocent in this manner. Indeed, the reverse relation between the two effects or two intentions is more likely the case. "When an entire city is destroyed by such means," Fr. Ford quotes John K. Ryan with approval,

> the military objectives are destroyed indirectly and incidentally as parts of a great civil center, rather than vice versa. It is the case of the good effect coming along with, or better, after and on account of the evil instead of a case where the evil is incidental to the attainment of a good. . . . It is hardly correct to think and speak of the damage done to life and property in such situations as being 'incidental destruction.' Rather it is the realistic interpretation of this situation to hold that any good gained is incidental to the evil. . . . The evil effect is first, immediate and direct, while any military advantage comes through and after it in a secondary, derivative, and dependent way.[5]

CONTRACEPTION

JOHN T. NOONAN, JR.

Aquinas on Contraception†

(According to Noonan, Aquinas's treatment of contraception agrees with that of his predecessors that only acts of coitus that are open to generation

---

4. John C. Ford: "The Hydrogen Bombing of Cities," *Theology Digest*, Winter, 1957, p. 7. This article (now reprinted as chap. vii in the symposium *Morality and Modern Warfare*, ed. Wm. J. Nagle, Baltimore: Helicon Press, 1960, pp. 98–103) contains the substance of Fr. Ford's address to the conference on ethics and nuclear weapons sponsored by the Church Peace Union in 1957. Criticisms of his remarks on that occasion were written by John Cogley, *Commonweal*, Dec. 13, 1957 ("the problem he spoke about is not the moral problem that actually faces our political and military leaders") and by William Lee Miller, in the first issue of *Worldview*, Jan., 1958 (who unfortunately opens by saying, "he granted that it is often necessary to do evil in order to do good").

5. John K. Ryan, *Modern War and Basic Ethics* (Milwaukee: The Bruce Publishing Co., 1944), 105 f., quoted by J.C. Ford, "The Morality of Obliteration Bombing," *loc. cit.*, pp. 291–292.

†John T. Noonan, Jr., *Contraception, A History of Its Treatment by Catholic Theologians and Canonists*, (Cambridge, Mass.: Harvard University Press, 1966). Copyright © 1966 by the President and Fellows of Harvard College. Reprinted by permission of the publisher.

are natural. However, Aristotle's influence led him to take a more favorable view of sexual pleasure, opening the possibility of a revision of the traditional teachings.)

Thomas identifies an intention to have intercourse for the sake of health as an intention against nature. He is defending the proposition that only a procreative purpose excuses coitus, and he is faced with the objection that an act generally good can become evil only through an evil intention. Hence, if marital coitus is good, a sufficiently good intention is the purpose of health. He replies, "Although it is not evil in itself to intend to keep oneself in good health, this intention becomes evil if one intends health by something that is not naturally ordained for that purpose; for instance, if one sought only bodily health by the sacrament of baptism; and the same applies to the act of coitus" (*On the Sentences*, IV, qu. 31, a. 2, 2, reply to obj. 4). This answer identifies the objective and subjective requirements of lawful coitus. Coitus is naturally ordained for procreation, and nothing else.

In the somewhat later *Summa Against the Gentiles*, however, Thomas teaches that "if, *per accidens*, generation cannot follow from emission of the seed, this is not against nature, nor a sin, as if it happens that the woman is sterile" (*S.C.G.*, III, 122). The last statement reflects his settled opinion and the prevailing opinion generally. Intercourse of the pregnant, intercourse of the sterile, intercourse of those lacking a conscious procreative purpose—all these sexual but unprocreative acts are not classified as unnatural. This usage points to what is meant by nature here. In the acts of nonprocreative intercourse accepted as natural, semen can be deposited in the vagina. In the acts stamped as unnatural, insemination has been made impossible. What is taken as sacral is the act of coitus resulting in insemination. The same standard appears in the test for validity of a marriage: it is not inability to generate, but inability to complete coitus, which is ground for nullity. * * *

It would, however, be incorrect to suppose that the value placed on insemination in coitus had no reference to its ultimate generative effect. If coitus was taken as sacred, it was because generation was only achievable through this means. If coitus was to be regarded as an unalterable process because of its generative consequences, but not every act of coitus was generative, then a discrimination had to be made between the normal or per se and the accidental. This discrimination was made by Thomas. He postulated as normal an act of coitus which led to generation. This norm was not derived from any statistical compilation. It was the product of intuition, the same intellectual process by which Lactantius had concluded that the purpose of the sexual members was to generate. Because the sexual act might be generative, and because generation was an important function, the theologian intuited that generation was the normal function. A typical or essential act of coitus, which was generative, was therefore supposed. Other acts of coitus which did not achieve this purpose were regarded as generically generative but accidentally frustrated. There were thus three types of seminal ejaculation: (1) acts in which insemination was impossible; these were unnatural; (2) acts in which insemination was possible and conception resulted; these were natural and normal; (3) acts in which insemination was possible, but conception did not occur; these were normal, but accidentally different from the norm.

Thus, in *Evil*, Thomas showed that every act of lechery was mortally sinful because each such act lacked direction to the generation and education of offspring. The objection was made: "It is manifest that from the copulation of a woman who is aged or sterile, generation of offspring cannot follow. But yet this sometimes can be done without mortal sin in the state of matrimony. Therefore also other acts of lechery, from which the generation and due education of offspring do not follow, may be done without mortal sin" (*Evil*, 15.2, obj. 14). Thomas replied that "the common law is given not according to particular accidents, but according to common consideration." An act in which generation could not follow "according to the common species of the act" was lechery and sin. This kind of act was distinguished from an act affected by a particular circumstance, such as "old age or infirmity."

Did it make sense to postulate one type of coitus as normal, and to treat every variation from it as accidental, even cases in which it was known that conception was impossible? Did it make sense to say that old age was an "accidental" exception to the ability to generate? Thomas did not ask these questions. Part of the essence of animal sexual behavior was seen by him as generative, and this fixed essence guided his analysis. The postulation of the generative act of coitus as the norm was fundamental to his moral judgments.

*   *   *

The rehabilitation of pleasure as a positive value, however, had to wait for the triumph of Aristotelian influence. This work was largely the task of Thomas Aquinas.

Aristotle had analyzed pleasure as a subjective sense accompanying the performance of acts. Pleasure was not an act, and consequently was not the immediate object of moral judgment in the Aristotelian system, where acts were what were judged. Acts and pleasure, however, were inseparably joined, "since without activity pleasure does not arise, and every activity is completed by the attendant pleasure" (*Nicomachean Ethics*, 1174b). A judgment of the act carried with it a judgment on the attendant pleasure. "The pleasure proper to a worthy activity is good and that proper to an unworthy activity bad" (1175b).

As early as the *Commentary on the Sentences* in 1255, Thomas adopted this position. He worked from Robert Grosseteste's translation of the *Ethics*, where *delectatio*, delight, is the term for the Greek *hedone*, translated in modern English as pleasure.[1] "Delight," Thomas taught, "follows operation." "The same judgment is to be made about the delight and the operation" (*On the Sentences*, IV, qu. 31, a. 2, 3). Delight is the complement and the crown of each act, or, Thomas said, echoing Aristotle, "Delight is the perfection of operation" (IV, qu. 49, a. 3, 4, 3).

The Aristotelian propositions on pleasure were specifically related by Thomas to the pleasure present in sexual intercourse. As matrimonial coitus is good, so is the pleasure experienced in it: "The delight which occurs in the matrimonial act, although it is most intense in quantity, does not exceed the limits fixed by reason before its commencement, although during this delight reason cannot set the limits" (IV, qu. 31, a. 2, 1, reply to obj. 3). The pleasure experienced in coitus in Paradise would have been still greater than that known by fallen man.

A more thorough rejection of the notion that sexual pleasure was sinful in itself would be difficult to image. Thomas even went further than a strict interpretation of Aristotle would have suggested in declaring that God had placed delight in the coital act as an inducement to perform it: "To impel man to the act whereby the deficiency of the species is aided, He put delight in copulation" (*On the Sentences*, IV, qu. 31, a. 1, 1, reply to obj. 1).

If pleasure was good, if sexual pleasure in particular was good, why was it not lawful to seek such pleasure? Why was it, according to Thomas, at least venial sin to seek pleasure? A contradiction existed between the statement that God intends sexual pleasure to be an inducement and the statement that to act for sexual pleasure in marriage is evil. But Thomas's statement on inducement was a departure from the Aristotelian principle, according to which pleasure itself was always attendant upon some act: one acted for the act itself, the pleasure followed. A more truly Aristotelian course was chosen by Thomas in discussing temperance in the *Summa Theologica*: "All the pleasurable objects that are at man's disposal are directed to some necessity of this life as to their end. Therefore temperance takes the needs of this life as the rule for the pleasureable objects of which it makes use, and uses them only as much as the needs of this life require" (II–II, qu. 141, a. 6). If the virtuous, temperate man acts only for needs, he will experience pleasure as he satisfies the needs, but he will not act for pleasure itself.

Yet, with pleasure rehabilitated, the question might have been raised whether pleasure itself was not sometimes a need. Aristotle himself has presented Aquinas with one form of this question. He had said that man might seek amusement *(paidia)* "as a sort of relaxation." Such amusement, like rest, might be sought for the sake of health. Aquinas commented on this passage in a translation where amusement appears as *ludus* (game). He noted that "a game or rest is not the end, because rest

1. Aristotle, *Nicomachean Ethics*, trans. W. D. Ross, *Works*, vol. IX (Oxford, 1926). Robert Grosseteste's translation is reproduced in St. Thomas, *In X libros ethicorum ad Nicomachum*, in *Opera*, ed., P. Maré and S.E. Fretté (Paris, 1871–1882), vol. XXV.

is for operation, so that a man after it may work more vigorously" (*On the Nicomachean Ethics*, 10. 9). In other words, he agreed that a game or rest was not the last end, but could be a means to another end. In the *Summa Theologica*, this view of a game was applied generally to the delightful, and Thomas quoted from the *Nicomachean Ethics*, 3.11: "The temperate man desires delightful things for the sake of health or for the sake of a sound condition of body" (*S.T.*, II–II, qu. 141, a. 6, reply to obj. 2). The question was again silently present, If pleasure were good, why could not sexual delight be sought, not as a last end, but as an intermediate value? * * *

PIUS XI

Casti Connubii—Christian Marriage †

(The Catholic opposition to artificial birth control, principally on Thomistic natural law grounds, was given authoritative expression in the encyclical of Pius XI in 1930. It was reaffirmed in 1968 by Pope Paul VI in the encyclical, *Humanae Vitae.*)

53.   And now, Venerable Brethren, we shall explain in detail the evils opposed to each of the benefits of matrimony. First consideration is due to the offspring, which many have the boldness to call the disagreeable burden of matrimony and which they say is to be carefully avoided by married people not through virtuous continence (which Christian law permits in matrimony when both parties consent) but by frustrating the marriage act. Some justify this criminal abuse on the ground that they are weary of children and wish to gratify their desires without their consequent burden. Others say that they cannot on the one hand remain continent nor on the other can they have children because of the difficulties whether on the part of the mother or on the part of family circumstances.

54.   But no reason, however grave, may be put forward by which anything intrinsically against nature may become conformable to nature and morally good. Since, therefore, the conjugal act is destined primarily by nature for the begetting of children, those who in exercising it deliberately frustrate its natural power and purpose, sin against nature, and commit a deed which is shameful and intrinsically vicious.

55.   Small wonder, therefore, if Holy Writ bears witness that the Divine Majesty regards with greatest detestation this horrible crime and at times has punished it with death. As St. Augustine notes, "Intercourse even with one's legitimate wife is unlawful and wicked where the con-

† From *Seven Great Encyclicals*, (Glen Rock, N.J.: Paulist Press, 1963). Copyright © 1963 by the Missionary Society of St. Paul the Apostle in the State of New York. Reprinted by permission of Paulist Press.

ception of the offspring is prevented. Onan, the son of Juda, did this and the Lord killed him for it." [1]

56.   Since, therefore, openly departing from the uninterrupted Christian tradition some recently have judged it possible solemnly to declare another doctrine regarding this question, the Catholic Church, to whom God has entrusted the defense of the integrity and purity of morals, standing erect in the midst of the moral ruin which surrounds her, in order that she may preserve the chastity of the nuptial union from being defiled by this foul stain, raises her voice in token of her divine ambassadorship and through Our mouth proclaims anew: any use whatsoever of matrimony exercised in such a way that the act is deliberately frustrated in its natural power to generate life is an offense against the law of God and of nature, and those who indulge in such are branded with the guilt of a grave sin.

GERMAIN GRISEZ

A New Formulation of a Natural Law Argument against Contraception †

(Instead of arguing from the naturally given structure of the sexual act, as many Catholic moralists had done, Grisez draws on Aquinas [S.T., I–II, qu. 94, a. 2] to argue that practical reason recognizes that "the good of the initiation of human life . . . is a fundamental human good" and that contraception violates that good. Grisez rejects what he calls "genital automatism" in favor of "fully human acts of authentic sexual love," which presuppose such self-control that true self-giving is possible and contraception is unnecessary. For brevity, more than half of Grisez's arguments for his view have been deleted from the article reprinted here.

In later writings, Grisez and others developed his ideas in ways which were attacked by many other proponents of a natural-law theory, especially those who more closely follow Aristotle and St. Thomas. For an update of parts of the theory most often criticized, see Germain Grisez, Joseph Boyle, and John Finnis, "Practical Principles, Moral Truth, and Ultimate Ends," American Journal of Jurisprudence, xxxii [1987]. For a full statement of Grisez's developed views: The Way of the Lord Jesus, vol. 1, Christian Moral Principles [Chicago: Franciscan Herald Press, 1983].)

"The naturally given structure of the sexual act"—that is a phrase one often encounters in discussions of contraception. The contention here is that there is no such thing, if we are talking about the human act; for human acts have their structure from intelligence. Just insofar as an

1. Genesis, 38:8–10.
†The Thomist, XXX, 4 (October 1966) by permis-

sion of the Dominican Fathers, Province of St. Joseph.

human acts have their structure from intelligence. Just insofar as an action is considered according to its naturally given structure, it is to that extent not considered as a *human act*—i.e., as a moral act—but rather as a physiological process or as instinctive behavior. Action with a given structure and acts structured by intelligence differ as totally as nature differs from morality. Nature has an order which reason can consider but cannot make and cannot alter. Morality has an order which reason institutes by guiding the acts of the will.

* * *

It is vital to see that the structure of the sexual act is not naturally given [because] only after gaining this insight can the true issue be appreciated. That issue concerns the principles according to which a human being ought to structure his sexual conduct. Because this structure will be the work of intelligence, and because its realization can be accomplished only through free choice, either intelligence must know immediately what the structure should be, or the structure will have to be articulated from some prior knowledge. The latter is evidently the case: the structure of human sexual acts is articulated through a rational process. Reason proceeds from some principles of action and concludes to the formulation of possible acts about which it also pronounces the judgment: Such and such ought (or ought not) to be done.

Our problem, then, takes us right to the central question of ethical theory: What is the ultimate standard of right and wrong in human acts, and how is this standard to be applied?

* * *

I would suggest that the only adequate ultimate standard for right and wrong in human acts is the total possible good that man can in any way attain. This total possibility is in a certain sense given, for man does not exist of himself but is created in intelligence and freedom, with an innate capacity for indefinite self-transcendence. At the same time, this total possibility is not some definite end, established by nature, that could ever be attained by some efficient means. For this very reason, human intelligence must contrive the structure of human acts, but only freedom can effectively execute the order which intelligence proposes, because a finite nature does not include any necessary and inerrant means for attaining a perfection that is inherently indefinite and open to the infinite.

Given the task of contriving human existence in the light of the possibility of infinite self-transcendence, human reason must start somewhere to give its first direction. Intelligence looks to experience, not because naturally given inclinations must be followed, but rather because no human act is possible if there is no inclination to use as its vehicle. Practical reason, which must project goals toward which it will direct action, must form its initial insights concerning all possible goals of human action by referring to the several modes of inclination that are naturally given in human nature.

Thus it is that the tendency to self-preservation is transmuted by the alchemy of intelligence into a self-evident principle of practical reason: Human life is a good to be preserved. The tendency may be egoistic; the principle is non-discriminatory. The tendency is dispersed among many physiological and psychological drives; the principle is understood more or less clearly as expressing an intelligible goal, which man makes his own, toward which all those drives are disposed.

A number of fundamental categories of human goods are understood in this way. There are not many modes of human good altogether: human life, which includes health and safety; all the arts and skills that can be cultivated simply for the sake of their very exercise; beauty and other objects of esthetic experience; theoretical truth in its several varieties; friendship, both relationship in immediate liasons and organization in larger communities; the use of intelligence to direct action; the effective freedom to do what one chooses with the whole force of an integrated personality; and a proper relationship to the fundamental principles of reality—i.e., to God.

In this list of basic human goods I think we must include, as a distinct item and not merely as an aspect of the good of human life as such, the value of the initiation of human life. This good consists not merely in generation, but in the initiation of human life on all its many levels, for physiological, psychological, moral, and spiritual life each must be initiated and the initiation of human life is not complete until the new person is equipped with the starting points from which he can proceed to live on all of these levels. Once his life is begun, each person has as his own task to carry on and to develop his life in cooperation with others. Consequently, as childhood progresses passivity gives place to activity and dependency to autonomy in cooperative relationships.

There are several reasons for thinking that the good of the initiation of human life, the procreative good, is a fundamental human good and that it is distinct from the good of human life as such.

In the first place, the procreative good is peculiar inasmuch as it is always an object for action whose end is a person other than the agent. One can pursue the good of human life, on the other hand, in a manner that is directly self-regarding, and on the level of natural inclination the good of life as such is represented by the drives which insure self-preservation. Only indirectly can one pursue the procreative good in a manner that is self-regarding, since the good primarily accrues to a person other than the agent himself, and on the level of natural inclination the good of procreation is represented by drives that do not promote self-preservation—which, in fact, often conflict with it—although these drives do yield satisfaction for the agent as well as the achievement of a fundamental human good in another person.

In the second place, the procreative good is the object of the ultimate function of all human organisms precisely insofar as they are organisms. The work of procreation is the work of maturity and full power; every other function leads on to this one while for the agent organism as such this function leads to nothing beyond itself. The good of human life, on the other hand, is the goal of the weakest and most primitive functions of the organism. Now, man, of course, is incomparably more than any other organism. But man is in truth an organized body, and his perfection as such cannot be reduced to any higher plane of his existence, as if the highest plane could save everything below by using it as a means or by encompassing it in a more eminent mode. The simply physiological process of human reproduction already is incomparably more important than the process of reproduction in other animals by the mere fact that the former terminates in the existence of a human person while the latter terminates in the being of a beast. Man is not an incarnate spirit; he is a rational animal. The dualism implied in the definition of man as incarnate spirit threatens to become a totalitarianism which will distort the true shape of man's nature and thus destroy the only solid foundation for a realistic personalism. And Christian personalism must be realistic, as has been declared repeatedly in the past against gnostics, manichees, cathars, and jansenists.

In the third place, we can discern the status of procreation among basic human goods because a whole domain of human action is devoted to the work of procreation. Having a family of one's own—this is one, though not the only, unquestioned goal that most people have in life. The most universal and ancient human institutions are founded in the light of this good, for they are instituted to promote it. Marriage varies greatly from culture to culture, but anthropologists have no difficulty in picking out the phenomena to be recorded in all their variety under this heading. They are the regular phenomena connected with having and raising children. The problem of population itself is proof of the fundamental and universal drive, for even in the most primitive cultures there are means—birth control, abortion, and infanticide—to limit population. And sexual activity almost everywhere flourishes outside marriage as well as within it. But people want children and they usually devote considerable effort to bringing up their children. From the point of view of egoistic theories of human action, the whole business will have to be explained by some implausible account, or it may be absurd, but nevertheless it goes on, for very few people really are consistently egoistic.

Now someone may be willing to grant the primary and distinct place of procreation among a group of fundamental human goods, and he may grant us as well that these goods provide the starting point for practical reason when it sets out to articulate possible human acts. But he still will ask how these fundamental goods provide a practical standard of right and wrong. How, he will wish to know, do the principles that render human acts possible determine that a proposed act will fall in one or the other of these contrary moral classes?

* * *

The attempt to determine right and wrong in human acts by an appeal to their concrete consequences * * * seems to me to rest upon a misconception of the very nature of morality and its essential conditions. Moral acts are man's own contrivance; moral agency is the adventure of human existence. It follows that the moral standard cannot be simply factual, whether the facts be past, present, or predicted. The moral standard must be ideal. Moral acts are the creatures of freedom; to judge right and wrong by actual consequences would be to reduce morality to technique. Moral life is a progress open toward infinite self-transcendence; if the ultimate principle for our discrimination of right and wrong were actual consequences human life would have finite limits. Man not only must be engaged in his present act, he also must be detached from its particular effects, or he shall never attain beyond a finite good. Moral life is autonomous and moral maturity is perfect autonomy—self directedness—but if the standard were concrete consequences man would always have to look for signs outside himself to use for his norm. That is all human action could amount to if man's intelligence were no more than a better way of doing the work of instinct, if man's will were capable only of following paths laid out for it by nature, and incapable of proposing its own destination to itself.

Instead of the measure of actual effects, I defend a quite different way in which fundamental human goods determine the rightness and wrongness of human acts. The fundamental human goods must be viewed as participations in Goodness Itself, which is the only adequate norm of a will open to infinite self-transcendence. The fundamental human goods make it possible for practical reason to begin its work, and to articulate possible lines of action. They underlie the structure of every human act that anyone proposes to do. And every act that is fully human therefore will be good, provided only that it does not involve the will in setting itself against some human good. For one would never be willing to oppose any fundamental human good unless he had been willing, at least implicitly, to substitute some single good or some one kind of good for the true and only adequate norm, Goodness Itself.

The good man need not pursue every possible good—in fact, he cannot do so. But he must avoid directly violating any of the fundamental goods. Thus some kinds of acts are intrinsically immoral, for some kinds of acts necessarily include in themselves a turning against some basic good, an aversion which also inevitably implies an aversion from Goodness Itself.

*　*　*

Now let us consider contraception. I do not think of contraception as if it were an act already given, the moral judgment on which would be made apart from and after the understanding of the act. No, I am concerned with a human act, an act which is performed through a specific choice. It is a mode of behavior selected by someone engaging in sexual intercourse to prevent or to make improbable the initial attainment of the procreative good that otherwise would follow from his sexual act.

The very meaning of this act includes a basic human good. The act precisely is a choice to behave in a way effectively contrary to that good.

I do not condemn contraception because of its bad consequences. No doubt it sometimes has bad consequences for various human goods, and then if those consequences are noticed, this sort of behavior will be condemned more easily. But I point to something bad that is essential to the act. Contraception involves setting the will directly against a basic human good, and this implies foreclosure against some aspect of human good as good and a consequent aversion from Goodness Itself. That first bad consequence is that one who chooses contraception loses purity of heart. He is willing to violate one good when only a principle seems to be at stake, and thus in principle he is willing to violate other goods, for there is no more compelling reason not to violate other goods unless it be a consideration of balanced consequences. One cannot make just one exception to the principle that he will adhere to goods as such and be faithful in regarding them as his norm. The very same considerations which lead one to violate a fundamental good by approving contraception tell equally in favor of violating another fundamental good—life itself—in difficult cases. Either one admits intrinsic immorality or one rejects it. Either one admits that human practical wisdom is bound by the basic human goods that man can discern, or one claims sufficient knowledge of the ultimate end of man to employ it as a standard for moral judgment. Either one admits he is a creature or one claims to be God.

*   *   *

However, if someone does choose to engage in sexual activity which may lead to conception, he already has defined his action in the light of the procreative good. Not that in every act of intercourse this good must necessarily be sought nor that it can always actually follow. No one claims that either is the case. But an act is not fully human if it is not fully understood, and such sexual activity cannot be understood without understanding its reference to procreation. Indeed, there would be no point in trying to prevent conception if one did not see the relevance of one's action to it. In such a case, therefore, an act that does nothing except insofar as it effectively prevents conception is formulated precisely as contraprocreative.

*   *   *

Nor is it any help to assert that the good one hopes to promote is procreation itself—i.e., the education of previously born children. For this good is not really promoted by the contraceptive act. The act of contraception itself happens to be singularly sterile. Contraception never educated anyone, although in the order of actual effects contraception undoubtedly can be an efficient way of preventing births which ought not occur, and where the "ought not" is determined by a sound judgment of the good of children previously born. But killing the innocent also can save lives. Lying about fundamental truths can perhaps serve the truth, at least scientists working under tyrants have thought so. Even oppression is claimed by many to be necessary for freedom. One need not look beyond the sad history of America's treatment of its native population for a plausible instance. Are we to approve life-saving abortion, truth-serving lies, liberating oppression? If not, there is no better reason to approve procreative contraception.

* * *

Sexual capacity emerges at puberty and breaks upon the growing personality with a power that is almost explosive. Perhaps even for physiological reasons, it is difficult to integrate this new function. Moreover, human sexual capacity is extremely plastic, and psychologically it is available for use as a sphere of displacement into a mechanical self-gratification which allows one more or less completely to avoid facing the risks and opportunities of a fully human life. Sex is the first good we encounter which we can form as an idol to replace in our hopes and dreams the fullness of perfection really to be found only through infinite self-transcendence. At least as things go at present, the sexual mechanism almost always is set into play to afford such a displacement and it gains a more or less firm hold on the emerging moral consciousness of the child. Thus moral intelligence is confronted with an incomprehensible sphere organized by the semi-human acts of sexual automatism.

Such pseudo-sex begins easily with masturbation, for if the child shrinks from trying to master the obstacles in the way of self-transcendence, he can at least find solace in the self-gratification of worshiping his own phallic idol. If girls seem to masturbate less than boys, this may be mainly because the whole of a woman's body is her sexual instrument, and so the perversion of sex into a mechanism for self-gratification is more generalized in girls than in boys. This pseudo-sexual activity persists in adolescent sexual acts, such as heterosexual petting and sometimes also homosexual activities. The same perversion of true sexual love most commonly matures into a habit of regular and mechanical sexual acts which is supported by the practice of contraception.

Such semi-human pseudo-sexual acts are altogether different from the free gift of one's whole bodily self in genuine marital love, but for almost all of us the complete exclusion of automatism from true sexual love is a long and hard struggle. The remedy for the difficulties of marriage is love, and more and more genuine love, including the perfection of fully human acts of authentic sexual love. That perfection, which promises ever grander fulfillments of our human desire for ecstasy—fulfillments such as contraceptive couples will never experience—that perfection, which carries with it freedom for the sexual act in the joyous ability of perfect self-restraint without the slightest repression—that perfection is too lovely, too truly and humanly spontaneous to be confused with genital automatism. Genital automatism expressing itself in semi-human pseudo-sexual acts is an enemy of reason and of moral law, but only because it is an enemy of genuine sexual love, whose spontaneity is that of choosing to give a gift, and not that of a compulsive urge for self-gratification.

LOUIS DUPRÉ

A Thomistic Argument against the Ban on Contraception †

(The opening of internal debate within Catholicism associated with the Second Vatican Council—1962–1965—included criticisms of the orthodox position on contraception. Louis Dupré, a professor of philosophy at Georgetown University, used Thomistic natural law arguments to argue that contraception is permissible in individual cases by married couples for serious reasons.)

The first thing which strikes one, and which makes a dialogue on this subject with non-Catholics very difficult, is that most arguments refer to the natural law, a principle which non-Catholics should be able to understand as well as Catholics. Yet, as it turns out, only Catholic Christians seem to have an insight into this point of the natural law. One sometimes wonders whether this emphasis on natural law is not simply due to the absence of any valid argument in Holy Scripture to support the Catholic position.

The most common argument based on natural law starts with the major premise that it is evil to separate an act which pursues a good of vital importance from its natural end. The minor premise states then that with the use of contraceptives the marriage act is always frustrated from its natural end. The conclusion follows that it therefore is always morally evil to use contraceptives and (because of the principle that in sexual matters "non datur parvitas materiae"—the matter is always serious), mortal sin is involved.[1]

The first problem that arises is: What is the natural end of sexual intercourse? The answer that it is procreation is correct, but the implications of this finality are by no means as simple as the argument seems to assume. That *nature's* intrinsic purpose in sexual activity is procreation does not imply that every single act must necessarily lead to pro-

---

† Louis Dupré, *Contraception and Catholics*, (Baltimore, Md.: Helicon Press, 1964). By permission of the publisher.

1. This argument is proposed in different ways by various authors, but is always based on the intrinsic finality of the act of sexual intercourse. It will suffice here to quote one of the most respected textbooks in moral theology, Génicot-Salsmans's *Institutiones Theologiae Moralis*, Vol. II (Bruges, 1951), p. 460: "Malitia huius peccati in eo est quod completus usus venereorum seiungitur a fine suo naturali." "The moral evil of this sin consists in the fact that a complete use of sexuality is severed from its natural end." Also Merkelbach, *Summa Theologiae Moralis*, 3 (Brussels, 1954), n. 955: "Onanism and any other kind of coitus that deprives the act of its natural relationship to generation is intrinsically against nature."

creation, since nature itself does not attain this end in each individual act. It does so only in a small percentage of cases. The argument, therefore, should not be based on the actual effectiveness of the single act: "nature" has arranged things in such a way that a plurality of acts is required to make its intrinsic finality effective.

There is a difference between the intrinsic finality of nature as a whole and that of the individual act of intercourse; the latter, we recognize, does not attain its end in an absolute way, since nature itself has made ample provision for exceptions in the attainment of its end. The intrinsic finality of nature must be actualized if nature is to continue its existence, but this actualization is not bound to any individual act. This distinction between the absolute end of nature and the individual acts by which that end is achieved is both important and traditional. Without it we would be hard-pressed to assert that marital intercourse is morally licit in cases when the act will certainly not have its "natural" effect: during pregnancy, during menstruation, after menopause, in the event of sterility. Moreover, although at one time it was, it is no longer considered immoral if—because of "serious motives such as those that are frequently included in what are called 'indications' (whether medical, eugenic, economic or social)" [2]—married couples systematically and intentionally avoid conception by the rhythm method, although this is a deliberate attempt to have the act only under circumstances in which it cannot attain its natural end.

Here one might object that in rhythm at least the *course of nature* is respected, and consequently that in this case the individual intention is not incompatible with the intrinsic finality of the act. But the fact that nature is not effective in all its acts does not justify deliberate interfering in such a way that a particular act, which might have been effective, will now certainly be frustrated from its effect. The objection amounts to this, that one should not interfere with the course of nature in the attainment of its essential ends.

Now, if one understands by "nature" man's given biological apparatus, this is a strange way of reasoning indeed, for man constantly interferes with this nature in the most radical way, and no one ever thinks of calling this immoral. [3] No Roman Catholic today objects to vaccina-

---

2. Pius XII, *Address to the Italian Catholic Union of Midwives* (Oct. 29, 1951).

3. "Frustration of nature far from being immoral is man's vocation. In the march of physical science and technology it means the progressively rational control of nature by man and for man. Man has always frustrated nature from the time he invented the first tool and will continue to do so until on his last day on earth he lays down his latest invention. And every canal and every dam that man has built are monumental frustrations of nature's even flow. Fundamentalists, of course, will always greet each new tool with the cry 'Violation of nature' just as they did, for example, when drugs were introduced to lessen the pains of childbirth.

When nature is deficient in doing what it should for human welfare, human art makes up for that deficiency. If this be frustration of nature the human cry is 'Give us more of it.' " Dr. Frederick Flynn, "Natural Law and the Overpopulation Problem," *The Catholic Messenger*, Davenport, Iowa, June 16, 1960.

The word "frustration" is unfortunate, since man's conscious intervention in all the cases which Dr. Flynn mentions is directed toward the perfection of nature's harmony, the realization of its immanent designs. Because of this confusion the quoted text is not immediately applicable to the present case. It must first be proved that birth regulation is more than a "frustration" of nature.

tions, injections of hormones, plastic surgery and amputation, when the good of *man* is at stake. Nor probably, will he object to medical intervention in order to induce regularity in a woman's cycle, an indication that in sexual life too, the Catholic is willing to accept interference.[4] Where, then, does the difference lie between all these interventions and artificial birth control?

That there is an essential difference between the artificial prevention of a physical evil, small-pox for example, and the interference with nature in the process of procreation is obvious enough: in the first case one helps or corrects physical nature to achieve its intrinsic end, in the other, one frustrates it from achieving this end; at least in a single, particular act. It is also clear that in a process as important as life itself, reasons serious enough to justify interference with the course of nature in other domains would not be sufficient to justify interference in the process of procreation. It is a substantial leap, however, from these considerations to the assertion that, in the case of marital intercourse, the individual acts by which man's nature attains its vital ends are an *absolute,* unrelated to the totality of his spiritual life. Unfortunately, moralists in the past have been all too inclined to take this leap and to condone any kind of birth regulation as long as the material aspect of the sexual relations were "in order." Professor Janssens justly condemns this "terrible physicism, completely closed to true morality."

In areas other than the sexual, moral theologians habitually avoid the dangerous abstraction of taking an act out of its human context. In explaining the Fifth Commandment, which is no less basic than the Sixth, they immediately grant that the preservation of life itself, the most basic end of man's nature, is not always an absolute value: moral theology has no qualms about killing in a just war or in self-defense, although the question of capital punishment is in a state of flux. It tells us that under certain circumstances a Christian has the right and even the obligation to lay down his life for higher values. Those who have done so are venerated as heroes and saints. Why, then, should this nature, or, more correctly, one particular act out of the many by which it attains its purpose, become an absolute in marital intercourse?

Such a way of reasoning about nature contains, I feel, two basic flaws. It confuses man's biological structure with his human nature and it takes human nature as a static unchangeable thing rather than as a principle of development.

*   *   *

St. Thomas himself makes a distinction in the natural law between general principles which are the same at all times and for all men, and the conclusions, the practical applications derived from these principles, which are true only *ut in pluribus*—in the majority of cases.[5] This dis-

---

4. It should be remarked that, thus far, no absolutely reliable method for regulating the ovulatory cycle is available and that many physicians doubt whether it will be in the near future.

5. *Summa Theologiae,* I–II, qu. 94, a. 4.

tinction could never settle the dispute about contraception, since the whole question is whether artificial birth control goes against the first principles of the natural law or against a derived conclusion which could possibly allow for exceptions.[6] But it would seem that any concrete application of a general principle places it automatically among the "conclusions" in a situation where opposite principles meet. This by no means diminishes the obligatory character of the concrete moral precept; it merely takes it out of the irenic but abstract realm of universal ethical values and puts it in a situation where it is almost never alone in determining a line of action. Nor does it mean that every concrete ethical rule allows for exceptions, for certain precepts (as, for example, the one which forbids adultery) will never enter into conflict with others. It does follow, however, that in the application of an ethical principle circumspection is demanded lest other principles become jeopardized.

It seems that the traditional arguments against contraception take the marital act out of its concrete situation, and then place this isolated, abstract act under an equally abstract moral precept. To be sure, the general precept of procreation remains valid and will always remain valid. But does it apply to every single act individually, regardless of the circumstances? Of course, no circumstances will ever make a good act out of a bad one. The whole question is, however: What makes the act good or bad? If the use of contraceptives is *destructive of an absolute value of man*, it is certainly evil, and no circumstances can ever change this fact. But whether it is destructive of such a value or not depends upon the circumstances in which the contraceptives are used. Father Francis Connell writes about the morality of actions of the bodily functions: "There is no act which is intrinsically wrong if it is considered *merely in itself*, without any modifying circumstances. In other words, when we say that an action is intrinsically evil from the moral standpoint, we mean that the physical action *in a certain circumstance or certain cir-*

---

6. I am not sure that St. Thomas would consider every precept of the natural law which has to do with man's sexual life a primary precept rather than a secondary, as we tend to do. Discussing polygamy, he writes in his *Summa Theologiae*, III, Supplement, qu.65: "Now, whatever renders an action improportionate to the end which nature intends to obtain by a certain work is said to be contrary to the natural law. But an action may be improportionate either to the principal or the secondary end, and in either case this happens in two ways. First, on account of something which wholly hinders the end. . . . Secondly, on account of something that renders the attainment of the principal or secondary end difficult, or less satisfactory, for instance, eating inordinately in respect of undue time. Accordingly, if an action be improportionate to the end, through altogether hindering the principal end directly, it is forbidden by the first precepts of the natural law, which hold the same place in practical matters as the general concepts of the mind in speculative matters. If, however, it be in any way improportionate to the secondary end, or again to the principal end, as rendering its attainment difficult, or less satisfactory, it is forbidden, not indeed by the first precepts of the natural law, but by the second, which are derived from the first, even as conclusions in speculative matters receive our assent, by virtue of self-known principles; and thus the act in question is said to be against the law of nature."

Applying this to the Patriarchs of the Old Testament, he continues in the next article: "As stated above, plurality of wives is said to be against the natural law, not as regards its first precepts, but as regards the secondary precepts, which, like conclusions, are drawn from its first precepts. Since, however, human acts must needs vary according to the various conditions of persons, times, and other circumstances, the aforesaid conclusions do not proceed from the first precepts of the natural law, so as to be binding in all cases, but only in the majority; for such is the entire matter of Ethics, according to the Philosopher. Hence, when they cease to be binding it is lawful to disregard them."

cumstances is opposed to the natural law of God and may never be allowed."[7] The use of contraceptives, then, becomes morally qualified by the situation in which the value of procreation may morally be obtained. For a woman in danger of being raped, to use contraceptives is morally good, since she is not in a situation in which procreation constitutes a morally pursuable value. When married couples choose to have intercourse, on the contrary, they are unquestionably in the *objective* situation—and the only one—in which the continuation of human life is a basic value to be pursued.

Does this necessarily imply, however, that procreation is always, for every married couple, under all circumstances, an absolute value? Can it still be called an absolute value when other values of equal or greater importance are being jeopardized, as, for example, the essential well-being of the living?

ABORTION

JOHN T. NOONAN, JR.

Aquinas on Abortion †

(As he had done with contraception—and earlier with usury—Noonan studied the attitudes of Catholic moralists through the ages towards abortion. He finds that Aquinas did not believe that the human fetus had a soul until some time after conception and therefore did not consider abortion in the first stages of pregnancy as murder. He also sees Aquinas's teaching on self-defense as possibly permitting therapeutic abortion to save the life of the mother, and analyzes the Christian teaching in universal moral terms.)

St. Thomas Aquinas was clear that there was actual homicide when an ensouled embryo was killed.[1] He was equally clear that ensoulment did not take place at conception. There was sin, but not the sin of destroying a man in destroying the *conceptus* in its early stage, for "seed and what is not seed is determined by sensation and movement"; this

7. *The American Ecclesiastical Review*, June 1964. The great moral authority of its author as well as the fact that he is firmly opposed to any form of contraception gives this statement all the more weight.

† John T. Noonan, Jr., "An Almost Absolute Value in History" in John T. Noonan, Jr., ed., *The Morality of Abortion*, (Cambridge, Mass.: Harvard University Press, 1970). Copyright © 1970

by the President and Fellows of Harvard College. Reprinted by permission of the publisher.

1. *Summa Theologica*, II–II, qu. 64, a. 8, reply to objection 2. The topic was "whether one who kills a man by chance incurs the guilt of homicide?" Like the Septuagint version of Exodus, Thomas held that striking a pregnant woman was an illicit deed, and if the death of either the woman or an ensouled fetus followed, it was homicide.

phrase seems to mean that, at the early stage, seed is being destroyed, not man.[2] The result was that there was a period of fetal existence where Thomas's later writing did not specify the offense involved in fetal destruction yet where, according to his clear opposition to contraception, he believed a sin was being committed.[3] It was, however, according to both Albert and Thomas, mortal sin to have intercourse in pregnancy with the risk of abortion. Moreover, both accepted Avicenna's opinion that such risk was especially acute at the beginning. Hence, even in the early state of pregnancy, they held the life of the fetus more valuable than the obligation of the marital debt.

As for deliberate abortion, Thomas considered only one case where justification was alleged, but it was the case with the greatest appeal in a theologically-oriented society: the case of abortion for the child's own good, abortion to baptize the child. In medieval society this case had the appeal of abortion of a defective child in a modern society. In the medieval case it would have been to prevent the child from suffering eternal loss of happiness, as in the modern case it would be to prevent the child from suffering the loss of secular happiness. Why not "split the mother" and extract the fetus, so that, baptized, he "may be freed from eternal death"? To this appeal Thomas replied, "Evils are not to be done that good may come from them, Romans 3; and therefore a man ought rather to let the infant perish than that he himself perish, committing the criminal sin of homicide in the mother."[4] The text cited from St. Paul was in itself not decisive; the reference was to a rejection by Paul of his opponents' charge that "we do evil that good may come" (Romans, 3:8). What was decisive was the perception that God's providence could not be anticipated by a paternalism which would have permitted man to act as God in determining human life and assuring its salvation.

The case of abortion for the child's own good was rejected. What of abortion to save the mother? Thomas did not face the case expressly, but he posed broader principles of relevance; and, as the case itself was known as a medical problem from Avicenna, it cannot be supposed that he was unaware of the relation of the principles to therapeutic abortion.[5] The question was put, "Is it lawful for someone to kill someone in defending himself?" The case posed was not, as many later interpreters would have it, a case of unjust aggression. When Thomas wanted to characterize

---

2. The passage occurs in explaining why Aristotle accepted a lesser evil in accepting abortion, *In octo libros Politicorum* 7.12.

3. Aquinas, like all medieval moral theologians, followed St. Augustine and Gratian's *Decretum* in holding that abortion before the embryo was "formed," "animated," or "vivified" was a serious sin because "against nature" but not subject to penance or punishment as murder. Following Aristotle the period of animation ("ensoulment") was set at forty days for the male embryo and eighty days for the female. See Germain G. Grisez, *Abortion, The Myths, The Realities, and the Arguments* (New York, Corpus Books, 1966), ch. 4.

For discussion by Aquinas see his *Commentary on the Sentences of Peter Lombard*, IV, D. 31, qu. 2, expos. text. and the original text in the *Sentences*, IV, D. 31, c. 4 [*Editor*].

4. *Commentary on the Sentences*, I–I, qu. 3 resp. 4.

5. A leading teacher at Paris in the late twelfth century, Peter Cantor, had condemned the opinion of some that a woman could "procure a poison of sterility" to prevent conception when childbirth would be fatal to her. Peter said simply, "This is prohibited in every case" (*Summa de sacramentis*, 350, ed., Jean-A. Dugauquier, Louvain, 1965, III[2] 463–64).

the one being killed he used the terms "sinner" and "innocent." Here the one killed was merely "someone." His answer to the question was, "If someone kills someone in defense of his own life, he will not be guilty of homicide."[6] The conclusion was based on the principle that "nothing prevents there being two effects of a single act." One effect could be "in intention," the other "beyond intention;" and by intention Thomas meant the mental state of the person killing, for the act itself had as *finis operis* the double end of preservation of life and the killing of another. The act was lawful, because "what was intended was the preservation of one's own life." This intention was not sinful, for it is "natural to everyone to preserve himself as far as he can." The justification was necessary. Fornication, for example, was a lesser sin, but was always mortal, for "it is not ordered to the preservation of one's own life from necessity like the act from which homicide sometimes follows." Put another way, every lie is a sin, and homicide is a worse sin than lying; yet, unlike lying, homicide can sometimes be lawfully done "as when a judge kills a thief." Hence one can say, "Homicide imports not the killing of a man;" it imports "the undue killing of a man." You can then conclude, "Homicide is never lawful, although it is sometimes lawful to kill a man."

From these principles, that all killing is not forbidden, that one may lawfully act to preserve one's own life, and that an indifferent act may be justified by a good intention, an argument could be made to justify abortion to save the life of the mother. Much would depend on how absolutely Thomas meant his declaration in other contexts that "in no way is it lawful to kill the innocent."[7] If the statement held literally, it would seem to preclude capital punishment for a repentant thief, who has become innocent, as most men become innocent, by repentance; yet Thomas justified capital punishment. Applying the principle absolutely, he would have held sinful many acts in warfare such as the killing of enemy soldiers who were in good faith or the killing of infants in attacking a fortress. It cannot be said definitively how Thomas would have answered in these cases or in the case of therapeutic abortion to save the mother's life. * * *

This review of current controversy over the humanity of the fetus emphasizes what a fundamental question the theologians resolved in asserting the inviolability of the fetus. To regard the fetus as possessed of equal rights with other humans was not, however, to decide every case where abortion might be employed. It did decide the case where the argument was that the fetus should be aborted for its own good. To say a being was human was to say it had a destiny to decide for itself which could not be taken from it by another man's decision. But human beings with equal rights often come in conflict with each other, and some decision must be made as whose claims are to prevail. Cases of conflict

6. S.T., II-II, qu. 64, a. 7.
7. S.T., II-II, qu. 64, a. 6. The thrust of this article is the distinction between "sinners" who may be killed by public authority and the "innocent" who may not.

involving the fetus are different only in two respects: the total inability of the fetus to speak for itself and the fact that the right of the fetus regularly at stake is the right to life itself.

The approach taken by the theologians to these conflicts was articulated in terms of "direct" and "indirect." Again, to look at what they were doing from outside their categories, they may be said to have been drawing lines or "balancing values." "Direct" and "indirect" are spatial metaphors; "line-drawing" is another. "To weigh" or "to balance" values is a metaphor of a more complicated mathematical sort hinting at the process which goes on in moral judgments. All the metaphors suggest that, in the moral judgments made, comparisons were necessary, that no value completely controlled. The principle of double effect was no doctrine fallen from heaven, but a method of analysis appropriate where two relative values were being compared. In Catholic moral theology, as it developed, life even of the innocent was not taken as an absolute. Judgments on acts affecting life issued from a process of weighing. In the weighing, the fetus was always given a value greater than zero, always a value separate and independent from its parents. This valuation was crucial and fundamental in all Christian thought on the subject and marked it off from any approach which considered that only the parents' interests needed to be considered.

Even with the fetus weighed as human, one interest could be weighed as equal or superior: that of the mother in her own life. The casuists between 1450 and 1895 were willing to weigh this interest as superior. Since 1895, that interest was given decisive weight only in the two special cases of the cancerous uterus and the ectopic pregnancy. In both of these cases the fetus itself had little chance of survival even if the abortion were not performed. As the balance was once struck in favor of the mother whenever her life was endangered, it could be so struck again. The balance reached between 1895 and 1930 attempted prudentially and pastorally to forestall a multitude of exceptions for interests less than life.

The perception of the humanity of the fetus and the weighing of fetal rights against other human rights constituted the work of the moral analysts. But what spirit animated their abstract judgments? For the Christian community it was the injunction of Scripture to love your neighbor as yourself. The fetus as human was a neighbor; his life had parity with one's own. The commandment gave life to what other would have been only rational calculation.

The commandment could be put in humanistic as well as theological terms: Do not injure your fellow man without reason. In these terms, once the humanity of the fetus is perceived, abortion is never right except in self-defense. When life must be taken to save life, reason alone cannot say that a mother must prefer a child's life to her own. With this exception, now of great rarity, abortion violates the rational humanist tenet of the equality of human lives.

Selected Bibliography

A good general bibliography on Aquinas appears in Mary T. Clark, ed. *An Aquinas Reader*, Garden City, N.Y.: Doubleday Image Book, 1972. 553–575. The most widely available collections of St. Thomas's writings in English are A.C. Pegis, ed. *The Basic Writings of St. Thomas Aquinas*. 2 vols. New York: Random House, 1945, and A.C. Pegis, ed. *An Introduction to St. Thomas Aquinas*, New York: Modern Library, 1948. The *Summa Against the Gentiles* has been published in a translation by A.C. Pegis, et al., 3 vols. Garden City, N.Y.: Doubleday, 1955–57, (Book I, paperback reprint, Notre Dame, Ind.: Notre Dame Press, 1975). An earlier translation was carried out by the English Dominicans, 5 vols. New York: Benziger, 1924ff. The English Dominicans have also translated the *Summa Theologiae*, 22 vols. London: Burnes, Oates, 1924ff. but this rather literal translation has been superseded by a much more colloquial and free translation in a projected 60 volumes by the Blackfriars of Cambridge, New York: McGraw Hill, 1963ff. Questions 1–13 and 14–23 of Part I of the Blackfriars' edition have been published in paperback as Thomas Aquinas, *Summa Theologiae*, vol. I–II, New York: Doubleday Image Books, 1969–71. An unsatisfactory translation of *On Kingship* by G.B. Phelan and I.T. Eschmann, Toronto: Pontifical Institute of Medieval Studies, 1935, is less useful than the perhaps excessively loose version by J.G. Dawson contained in A.P. D'Entreves, ed. *Aquinas, Selected Political Writings*, Oxford: Blackwells, 1948, which also has excerpts from the *Summa* and other works. The only other collection of Aquinas's political writings is D. Bigongiari, *The Political Writings of St. Thomas Aquinas*, New York: Hafner, 1953. It uses the English Dominicans' translation with minor corrections. The ethical parts of the *Summa Theologiae* have been translated by J.G. Rickaby in *Aquinas Ethicus*, 2 vols. London: Burnes, Oates, 1896, and Aquinas's *Commentary on the Nicomachean Ethics* has been translated by C.I. Litzinger, 2 vols. Chicago: Regnery, 1964.

RECOMMENDED FOR FURTHER READING:

Armstrong, R.A. *Primary and Secondary Precepts in Thomistic Natural Law Teaching*, The Hague: Martinus Nijhoff, 1966.

Bourke, Vernon. *Aquinas' Search for Wisdom*, Milwaukee: Bruce, 1965.

Chenu, M.D. *Toward Understanding St. Thomas*, Chicago: Regnery, 1964.

Copleston, F.C. *Aquinas*, Baltimore: Penguin Books, 1955.

D'Arcy, Martin C. *Thomas Aquinas*, Westminster, Md.: Newman Press, 1953.

Finnis, John. *Natural Law and Natural Rights*, Oxford: Clarendon Press, 1982.

Gilby, Thomas. *The Political Thought of St. Thomas Aquinas*, Chicago: University of Chicago, 1958.

Gilson, Etienne. *The Christian Philosophy of St. Thomas Aquinas*, New York: Random House, 1956.

Kenny, Anthony, ed. . *Aquinas, A Collection of Critical Essays*, Notre Dame, Ind.: Notre Dame Press, 1976.

Maritain, Jacques. *Man and the State*. Chicago: University of Chicago Press, 1951.

———. *The Rights of Man and the Natural Law*, New York: Scribner Sons, 1943.

McInerny, Ralph. *St. Thomas Aquinas*, Notre Dame, Ind.: Notre Dame Press, 1982.

Parel, Anthony, ed. *Calgary Aquinas Studies*, Toronto: Pontifical Institute of Medieval Studies 1978.

Pieper, Josef. *A Guide to Thomas Aquinas*, New York: Pantheon, 1962; reprinted, Notre Dame, Ind.: Notre Dame Press, 1987.

Rahner, Karl. *Nature and Grace*, New York: Sheed and Ward, 1963.

Sigmund, Paul E. *Natural Law in Political Thought*, Cambridge, Mass.: Winthrop Press, 1971. (reprinted, Washington, D.C.: University Press of America, 1981).

Tooke, Joan. *The Just War in Aquinas and Grotius*, London: The Society For the Promotion of Christian Knowledge, 1965.

Weisheipl, James A. *Friar Thomas de Aquino*. New York: Doubleday, 1974.